Bill "The Kid"

Peter Pan of the Old West

Aliases: William H. Bonney, Kid Antrim, Henry Antrim, Henry McCarty, The Kid, Billy, The Kid, and last, but not least, his real name...

William Henry McCarty

AND for the First Time:

The True Stories of Catherine & Michael McCarty

[1]

By: Red Johnson

[1] Printed with permission of Mr. Don Sweet, Billy The Kid Museum Fort Sumner, New Mexico. Owner of painting done by Rev. Bob Brittain

Catherine McCarty

Photo is an artistic rendering of Leon C. Metz's photograph.

Birth Place: Cork City, Cork County Ireland

Died: September 16, 1874 in Silver City, New Mexico

Cork City, Cork County, Ireland

(Source: Photographer unknown, Public domain photograph.)

(Thank you ***Thomas Bianchini of TBDesign*** *for your cover illustration and design.)*

RJE
Billy "The Kid"

RJE books are published by:
Red Johnson Enterprises
10845 Waterman Rd. Ione, CA 95640
The name Red Johnson is a federally registered Trademark. Co-Publisher: Aardvark Publishing Company

Table of Contents

Dedication/Author's Comments

This book is dedicated to the memory of my wonderful **Great Aunt Blossom Davies,** who told me the story of Will Davies her uncle and my great-great uncle. In doing so she broke the family oath to never speak his name. It had not been spoken in the family for fifty years.

Explanation:

She said to me:

"I know how much you love the old west, and you should know your great-great uncle Will was an outlaw all his life. He did not die by the gun as he had lived. He is buried in an outlaw grave in West Sacramento."

She went on to tell me how she learned of him:

"Uncle Will was a very good shot. I saw him shoot a can off a fence and hit it two more times before it hit the ground. I thought it a waste of ammunition."

"I said to him: 'Uncle Will why are you wasting ammunition?'"

"He turned, stared at me with the coldest set of blue-grey eyes you have ever seen. The kind that look straight through you, and replied, 'Blossom that is how I have stayed alive so long.'"

"I went to my father and asked what he meant by that statement."

"My father told me his brother (Uncle Will) was the most notorious outlaw in New Mexico of his time. 'What he said to you is true. That is how he has stayed alive.'"

I have researched and written non-fiction, historical novels, and fictional books about the west for 23 years. Each meticulously researched at the location of the events in those books. Never had I run into a notorious outlaw by the name of Will Davies anywhere, besides in the New Mexico Territory.

All I knew was that my great-grandmother was a Davies, and born during the California Gold Rush in San Francisco. Her parents worked on Indian Creek near Coloma, California, and they originated from Whales. They came west (most likely from Texas) to join the California Gold Rush.

My great-great grandfather owned and operated a saloon (1860 to 1880) in Gold Hill, Nevada (next to Virginia City). In 1875, my great-grandmother, Margaret Jane Davies, and great-grandfather Burtis H. Rumsey, who was a Virginia City miner after serving the entire Civil War in the Iowa Eleventh Voluntary Infantry under General William Tecumseh Sherman, were married in the Catholic Church in Virginia City. There they had a child, Burtis H. Rumsey Jr. (my grandfather). Then they headed to New Mexico Territory for the next great gold/silver rush. They had one child there, Harold Rumsey.

They were off again to the next silver rush in Butte, Montana. In 1904, Burtis H. Rumsey Jr. had a daughter born in Butte, Montana named Doris Margaret Rumsey. She is my mother.

By now you must be wondering what in the world does all this spurious genealogy that means little to you, have to do with William Henry McCarty alias Billy, The Kid. Well here it is:

One day I received a call from a much-respected historian of the United States Marshall Service, Mr. David Turk who simply asked:

"Red, do you have a Will Davies in your family?"
I replied: ***"Yes, I do."***

He said: ***"ok, before I tell you what I know about him, you tell me what you know of him."***

I agreed and related the above story to him including the part of never having found a notorious outlaw by the name of Will Davies in the old west. I was embarrassed by his response:

He said: ***"Red, have you ever heard of an alias? Have you heard of Jesse Evans?"***

I replied: ***"Yes, of course!"***

He said: ***"I believe your Will Davies used the alias of Jesse Evans and is the same Jesse Evans of the Lincoln County War fame. Your great-aunt was right, he was arguably the most notorious outlaw of New Mexico in his day."***

He asked me if I had any photographs.

I sent him two photographs of Will Davies aka Jesse Evans.

Author's Comments

Why another book on William Henry McCarty aka Billy, The Kid? For the same reason a new book on Abraham Lincoln was just released. Certain people's lives are important to the "character" of our national identity. **New information based on sound research is important to all of us when it involves such a historical character.**

Billy, The Kid is one of those characters. His life struck a chord with all Americans of every age group, demographic, and sociographic group.

Was he mischievous? Sure, but as a friend of mine once said: "What red blooded American boy hasn't been? The only difference between a juvenile delinquent and a 'normal' teenager is that the latter didn't get caught."

Somewhere along our early lives most of us decide to adhere to society's norms. The risk of punishment outweighs the benefits of serving a productive life. In doing so we discover how wonderful life can be and how much joy there is in serving our fellow man. It is because of this fact I have spent the time on chapters herein to disclose the "society" of the southwest Billy, The Kid came to adolescence in. Environment matters.

We seem not to get enough of every detail of his life. Of these special characters, I have read the same story a dozen times. People can look at the same facts and come to totally different conclusions. This book is my conclusion.

This book is as much, if not more, about Catherine (Antrim) McCarty. Many historians had her a prostitute, each son from a different man. That could not have been further from the truth. Although illiterate, she not only took care of her children after her husband's death, she helped found Wichita, Kansas, became a very successful business owner, real estate speculator, and land developer. She was an extra-ordinary person.

Preface

Billy, The Kid was the Peter Pan of the American "old west." He just never grew up, and lived during a time when it took tough, persistent, resilient adults to survive. He wasn't that, and didn't survive to real adulthood because of it.

Some may argue that he was 21-years-old when he died, therefore an adult. Not in my judgement, he still had peach fuzz for whiskers and a childlike personality and behavior.

Yes, he was intelligent, bright, and literate, but would rather "play" with his guns than mend a broken fence. As Frank Coe said: "He spent all his money on ammunition."

Some young people today, like Billy The Kid, try their hardest to do what is right, and/or at least right a wrong. But without good role models in their life they end up making the ends justify the means to do so. The Kid's "means" was his exceptional talent with horses and guns. The use of those talents, no matter how good their intentions, did not end well.

It doesn't take much to see ourselves in The Kid, in a perfectly free world without inhibitions or restraints of being civilized. He is the "survivor" in all of us. He is the ultimate in confidence held by an underdog, handicapped by nature at birth, and struck by the fickle finger of fate in living his life. He is the original story of fighting the bullies and succeeding. He is the spirit's desire to be free from any constraints.

The Kid gives us a strange sense of justice in an unjust world that we all can relate to. In a strange twisted way, we would all like to be The Kid, without his ending of course, or having committed all his killings. Just be him! The carefree spirit.

Many times, The Kid tried to live a "normal" life by having a "regular" job to earn a living. A few examples: after the horrible death of his mother (four months bedridden), and his stepfather off to prospect in Arizona, The Kid worked in Wright's butcher shop for his board and keep.

Fate stepped in with his poor judgement when he agreed to hide Sombrero Jack's stolen clothes from the laundry. The lady he was boarding with found the clothes, and turned him in to the Sheriff.

Sheriff Whitehill placed him in a cell trying a "scaring straight" tactic. Although he was 16-years-old, the Sheriff later said he thought him "10 or 12 at the time." It backfired as The Kid could not stand being penned up. He escaped.

Arriving in Arizona and being turned away by his stepfather, he convinced the Hooker Ranch foreman to hire him as a cowboy. He had learned riding at the Wright Ranch in Silver City, but little else of cowboying or cattle. He was hired, but The Kid's juvenile personality and lack of strength caused him to be fired. The foreman told Mr. Hooker: "I must let him go. He can't do a man's work."

There were many other examples, such as when he went to work for Frank Coe as a ranch hand. It was there that he befriended Fred Waite and the two planned on having their own ranch in Ruidoso Valley. Fate stepped in again with the Lincoln County War.

Good male role models did arrive in The Kid's life, such as Dick Brewer and John Tunstall, but did so in the middle of a war. The Kid's efforts for a "normal" life seemed to be doomed. All he had left was his talent with guns, love of song and dance, and a happy-go-lucky personality. All were hard to use to earn a living.

Billy, The Kid was deeply loved by family, friends, and sometimes complete strangers. He was admired by nearly every Mexican he met, and that was during a time when white men, in general, were not respected by Mexicans, or vice versa.

Mexicans made him one of their own, and admired him as a person, beyond his skill with guns. To them he was a Mexican that happened to be white. He loved them and their language.

To quote a man that listened to a lecture I gave on The Kid: ***"My God, nothing has really changed, has it?" I replied: "You're right sir, money, power, and politics still rule."*** That man clearly saw our own times in the times of **Billy, The Kid.** One might say: "Well, sure but we don't have the violence of the 'wild west' times." Actually, we have more violence. There are life lessons for us, and our children to learn in The Kid's story.

Having said all that, there was not a plan on my part to write another book on Billy, The Kid. I enjoy subjects like Henry

Plumer who was maligned, and his name misspelled for 153 years. I spent six years researching and writing *Hell Will Be to Pay, the True Story of Henry Plumer*, and enjoyed almost every minute of it. I knew I was making a major contribution to western history. I enjoyed the endeavor, even if decedents of the Vigilantes of Montana hated my probing for the truth.

I was prodded by friends and family, because I have a "dog-in-that-fight" of the Lincoln County War, to write a book on the Lincoln County War. I declined, as I was not able to see that I could contribute any more than many very good non-fiction writers had already accomplished. Billy, The Kid is a very well documented old west character.

There were men like Maurice Garland Fulton that dedicated their entire lives to researching and documenting New Mexico and the Lincoln County War. Last, but certainly not least, I promised myself not to write another non-fiction. I don't have enough life left to accomplish one the way I do them, *Murder in The Gold Country* took two-and-a-half-years of research for a 130-page, non-fiction book.

What changed my mind? I agreed to "look into" a "historical novel" on Billy, The Kid. I did an exploratory trip to New Mexico, and some preliminary research in Lincoln County. Collected and read books on The Kid. Then revisited the film library on The Kid. I came away with the conclusion there was a very real need for a historical novel on The Kid.

The Hollywood film and television studios made money on The Kid, but ignored his true-life story. In fact, they fictionalized his story so much the work products (films, screenwriter's products, etc.) have not even come close to the real story.

The television "History Detectives", "Decoders", and "Young Guns I and II" manipulated the facts to lead a viewer to believe Brushy Bill Roberts was Billy, The Kid. That certainly increased interest in their projects. Anyone objectively looking at the evidence knows he was not.

I will probably not thoroughly understand why Hollywood does what it does. I realize they see themselves as entertainers and not historians. Ironically, I think many historians will agree with me in saying that: **the true stories are just as entertaining, exciting, and in some cases**

more spectacular than what Hollywood screenwriters come up with.

Robert Utley's most current book on The Kid (he is one of the best biographers of The Kid) was published in 1989. It remains the gold standard for modern Kid writers. Another is Fredrick Nolan, who in my opinion, has the best researched book on Billy, The Kid.

I highly recommend reading Michael Wallis's "Billy The Kid, The Endless Ride." Mr. Wallis has new information on The Kid (which is hard to find). His writing style makes for a comfortable read.

I have read most of the contemporary books[2] and stand by my opinion that Robert Utley, Frederick Nolan, and Michael Wallis have the best historical books on Billy, The Kid on the market today.

If you're "visual" and are looking for dates, times, and places easily viewed, hands down Bob Boze Bell's "The Illustrated Life and Times of Billy, The Kid" should meet your reading pleasure.

As I said, Michael Wallis brings some new facts and knowledge to light i.e. The Kid was ambidextrous (which I suspected of The Kid, it takes one to know one), and the trip to Georgetown to visit the teacher he admired in Silver City, etc. Also, his discovery of the fact that the Georgetown mining camp had made Sombrero Jack their Justice of the Peace. Wow, talking about hiring a thief to catch a thief? Who left that out of our history books? Great job Mr. Wallis!

My great-grandparents Burtis H. Rumsey and Margaret Jane (Davies) Rumsey were in the gold camp of Liedendorf, New Mexico Territory during The Kid's time there. It was in the Liedendorf Mountains south of Lordsburg, New Mexico Territory. Through my great-grandmother (Margaret Jane Davies) I am related to Will Davies, aka Jesse Evans.

---

[2] I refuse to spend money on any books based on "interviews" with The Kid after his "supposed" death. Several books exist…they are all hoaxes designed to appeal to the "conspiracy theory" people in our communities, and of course to make money off The Kid's name. Those are the people that love to acquire any theory that goes against the norm. They love to be different and will never allow facts to stand in their way.

What I like about writing historical novels is if it walks like a duck, talks like a duck...it is a duck. They are far more interesting and emotionally appealing to a wider audience of readers. I firmly believe a reader may retain and learn more from a historical novel than any non-fiction.

I was able to solve some "mysteries" of The Kid's life myself, and therefore, I could contribute with a new historical novel.

This book goes far beyond the fact I have a "dog-in-the-fight" called the Lincoln County War: Will Davies, aka Jesse Evans my great-great-uncle. The family has not been, and is not, proud of him in any way, shape, or form. This book is about William Henry McCarty alias Billy, The Kid.

The intent of this book is to entertain, inform, and educate the reader as to who The Kid really was, what made him tick, and why has he struck a chord in the American psyche for so long, and will do so long after this writer is gone.

If fact, he will do so long after every writer alive to today is gone. Some 100 years from now a man or woman will pick up the pen and say:

"I think I will write about Billy, The Kid...I think I can contribute something to his sad story."

Acknowledgements and Recognition

David Turk, Official Historian for the United States Marshall Service for inspiring me to take another look at writing The Kid's story.

Brittany Klingsheim, Editor, holds a B.A. Degree in Communications from Sacramento State University. She has touched every page of this book, even the cover! Thank you Brittany!

MaeBeth Johnson, my wonderful wife who has put up with me for so many years. She has been drug all over the west, from Beecher's Island, Wray, Colorado to Coffeeville, Kansas, Deadwood, South Dakota, and from Springfield, Missouri to Fort Laramie, Wyoming, and all points in between. She sat in the car at Dodge City reading Danielle Steel while I did research. She never complained in Hayes City, Abilene, Wichita, or Caldwell Kansas. She relaxed in the hotel while in El Paso, Texas reading another Danielle Steel. I should add, once she did ask: "Can we leave Kansas now?" That is the only complaint I can remember. Sorry Kansas!

One place she really liked was Tombstone, Arizona. We vacationed there four times. She must hold some sort of suffering wife record for the following: She endured four years spending our first day and last day of every vacation in the Mojave Desert looking for Wyatt Earp's Happy Days Gold Mine...yes, we found it!

Or, the time I asked her to walk several blocks in Denver, Colorado to the Windsor Hotel, just so we could stand in the exact spot Wyatt Earp and Doc Holliday last saw and talked to each other. Arriving there she gave me that funny look that said: "Really...this is why we came all this way?" For me it was a western spiritual experience, but for her it was the lobby of a hotel we were not even staying at.

Thank you, thank you for living in the 19th century with me when you were always well grounded in the 20th and 21st centuries. I love you!

Sources

I have not the number of pages to acknowledge all the sources of this book. "Sources" are like mysteries continuum. One mystery solved gives a lead to another, and at some point one must use self-talk and say "***Stop!*** Write about what you have found!" Every historical writer will know exactly what I am talking about.

Having said that, there are some very special writers and researchers that deserve to receive acknowledgement for their contribution to the quality of this work product. They are:

Robert M. Utley, Western historian and author of: *High Noon in Lincoln: Violence on The Western Frontier* (1987), *Cavalier in Buckskin: George Armstrong Custer and the Western Military Frontier* (1988), ***Billy, The Kid, A Short and Violent Life*** **(1989).** His research was mostly done prior to the internet, and very detailed.

Frederick Nolan, Western historian and author of ***The West of Billy The Kid*** one of the best researched books on The Kid. A must read for a serious Kid enthusiast. Excellent details revealed in an understandable manner. Numerous photographs you'll find in few other sources, and no other sources in one book.

Michael Wallis, author of ***Billy, The Kid, The Endless Ride.*** Mr. Wallis brings some new facts to light: The Kid was ambidextrous, the trip to Georgetown to visit the teacher he admired in Silver City, etc. Also, the fact that Georgetown had made Sombrero Jack their Justice of the Peace. His discoveries reflect his dedication to independent research. Excellent book for The Kid enthusiast.

David L. Caffey, author of ***Chasing the Santa Fe Ring Power and Privilege in Territorial New Mexico.*** His book is a must read if one wants to know the early New Mexico Territory politics, policies, and the culture its residences lived in. A well-researched and documented book.

Bob Boze Bell's, author of ***The Illustrated Life and Times of Billy, The Kid.*** **Outstanding timeline and related illustrations.** If you're visual and looking for dates, times, and places easily viewed, hands down this is the best book on the market for you. We always enjoy his art too.

Charlie A. Siringo's author of ***History of Billy, The Kid.*** One needs almost to be an expert on The Kid to know what good information is in this book, and what Mr. Siringo believed from third parties to be true (i.e. Pat Garrett). In general, the written response he received from men like James East contains very valuable information. Mr. East articulates his involvement with the capture of The Kid at Stinking Springs with great detail and a good memory of the event. One also must note Charles A. Siringo in fact knew The Kid personally. When his employer was buying stolen property from The Kid he was a friend, but when The Kid stole from his employer he became The Kid's most dangerous enemy. Charlie was not one to cross.

Paul L. Tsompanas author or ***Juan Patrón a Fallen Star in the Days of Billy the Kid,*** **forward by Frederick Nolan.** Juan Patrón was born on November 20, 1852. He was educated in Bishop Lamy's "polite" educational system: Latin, art, music, and useful subjects (3 R's). Juan excelled and was given the opportunity to attend Notre Dame University. He declined it to help his father with his new business in Lincoln, Lincoln County, New Mexico Territory. At 18-years-old he was teaching in Lincoln (it's first school). At 19-years-old in November of 1871 he was elected Lincoln County Probate Clerk. After two terms he decided to run for higher office, and in November of 1877 he was elected to a seat as

Territorial Representative for Lincoln, Don Ana, and Grant counties. He was a witness, victim, and participant in the Lincoln County War.
The Horrell brothers killed his father Isidro Patrón. John Riley, partner in The House, shot him in the back intending to assassinate him, but he survived. He housed Billy, The Kid in Lincoln. This is an important book to understanding the bigger picture. Juan Patrón was an exceptional man of that place and time, and is rarely mentioned in any Kid books.

Bill Rakocy, author of ***The Kid Second Edition the Artist's and Writer's Saga*** 2000 Bravo Press, El Paso, Texas. Mr. Rakocy dedicated his book to the "artists and writers who have told the romantic story of the west and The Kid." He disclosed and features one of his main sources of information as coming from: **Walter and Nora Henn of Lincoln, New Mexico, 1982**. Mr. Rakocy describes them as "Kid experts" and "very good people."

The reason I found Mr. Rajoy's book a wealth of information is that he copied newspaper clippings, articles, letters, and interviews with first hand participants in the Lincoln County War. Also, stories told by individuals that had met "The Kid", i.e. **Singleton George Washington** of El Paso, Texas. He was 82-years-old on May 17, 1936 when he told the El Paso Herald (Page 9, column 2):

"We were driving a bunch of cattle up into New Mexico when The Kid joined us. There were 82 of us altogether. About five miles out of El Paso a band of Apaches attacked us, and I got to see The Kid's famous shooting. I didn't have time to count them, but when we got through there were dead Indians scattered all around us. Billy looked like he was only a boy. He was a nice fellow. He rode on to Las Cruces with us after the fight."

Mr. Rakocy's book is a difficult read as he lays everything out as an "artist" would, (the good, bad, ugly, misinformation, glory hunters, mythical, legendary, and factual) leaving conclusions to you.

Therefore, a serious researcher must spend weeks on his book to extract the "accurate, good stuff", but it is well worth the venture and time. His book has many hidden diamonds of information about William Henry McCarty alias Billy, The Kid.

Military Records: Reflected Marion County, Indiana laborer Michael McCarty volunteered and was enlisted into 5th Battalion of Artillery Volunteers, commanded by Captain Simanson at its original organization September 22nd, 1861 to serve in the Regiment for three years.
"Having served honestly and faithfully with the 5th Indiana Battalion to November 30, 1863 is now entitled to a discharge by reason of death in general field hospital at Chickamauga November 30th, 1863 of a gunshot wound received at the Battle of Chickamauga, Georgia." The surgeon's letter to his commanding officer was also referenced.

My research reflected only one other Michael McCarty enlisted at Indianapolis, Indiana, and he was from Gettysburg, Virginia and a deserter. His description, age, and home town eliminated him as The Kid's father. That left only the above referenced Michael McCarty killed at the Battle of Chickamauga, Georgia of the right age, description and place of enlistment.

This is how the military records describe Private Michael McCarty at his death: "**Age 27-years-old, 5' 6" tall, fair complexion, blue eyes, and brown, sandy hair.**" Nearly the exact description of William Henry McCarty, alias Billy, The Kid.

The Indianapolis, Indiana city directory for 1868 quotes Catherine McCarty, Henry's mother, as declaring her status as widow of Michael McCarty. If it walks like a duck, talks like a duck, it is a duck! William Henry McCarty's father was the above referenced Michael McCarty!

The Internet: All information received from the internet was only used when the evidence reflected an absolute conclusion of the facts.

The internet is a wonderful new tool for today's writers as long as it is carefully utilized. One of the most important pieces of information obtained was the confirmation of **70 Allen Street as the birth place of William Henry McCarty alias Billy, The Kid.** Reference: *The Street Book: An Encyclopedia of Manhattan, Street Names and Their Origins* by: Henry Moscow, Fordham University Press, 1990. The street was named after Captain William Henry Allen, a well-known War of 1812 sea captain hero.

Coincidence Catherine McCarty named her second son William Henry...possible, but unlikely for the times. The official street records reflect 70 Allen Street as the birth place of William Henry McCarty, Alias Billy, The Kid. The building was torn down in 1932 to widen the street from 50 feet to 138ft.

The information and history concerning Tammany Hall, the Bowery Boys, Dead Rat Gang, "Boss" Tweed and the politics and living conditions of the Lower East Side of Manhattan was all obtained in detail from the internet.

For a visual of how the neighborhood looked during the McCarty's residence there...rent the movie "Gangs of New York." It is <u>not</u> an exaggeration but a realistic representation of the Lower East Side and "Five Points" Manhattan, New York, New York from 1846 to 1868. The Kid was born there in November 1859.

It would not be until the mid-1990's that acceptable research quality information began to appear on the internet. Then it was still not reliable information. It would take the internet 20 years to become a great research tool, although one still needs to be very careful of the information. For example, Jesse Evans aka Will Davies has truth mixed with myths. Internet "contributors" used men whose actual names/pictures were Jesse Evans. Not too many outlaws used their real names. On the other hand, the internet documents the information of Jesse Evans's gang "The Boys" (another source) is accurate.

Other Sources: To quote Mr. Robert Utley: "Any modern student who follows Billy, The Kid quickly meets several indefatigable researchers who have scouted the trail in the past."

Writers and researchers are like builders of sky scrapers, a foundation is built and then each one adds on, and adds on, and adds on until a clear picture evolves of the character, and the times they lived in.

Some of these individuals and institutions are:

Lincoln State Monument, Lincoln New Mexico: Including the collections of Philip J. Rasch who worked independently and in collaboration with: **Robert N. Mullen whose collection is at Haley History Center in Midland, Texas. Also, there are the J. Evetts Haley interviews with Lincoln County War participants.**

Maurice Garland Fulton, English professor at New Mexico Military Institute in Roswell, New Mexico. Mr. Fulton dedicated most of his adult life to the study of, gathering of evidence of, and documenting the Pecos Valley, New Mexico, Santa Fe, New Mexico, the significant families living in those locations, The Lincoln County War, and Billy, The Kid. Also, the Military Court Records (i.e. Dudley Court of Inquiry, etc.). His collection is at the University of Arizona Library in Tucson, Arizona (MS057) Request information:

University of Arizona Library
Tucson, Arizona
P.O. Box 210055
Tucson, Arizona 85721-0055

This book you're reading now is the best researched biographical historical novel ever produced on William Henry McCarty, alias Billy, The Kid, until the next one...ha! The Kid would have loved that line!

Don and Tim Sweet's Billy The Kid Museum, Ft. Sumner New Mexico.

This museum is an absolute must see for any Billy The Kid enthusiast. Do not make the mistake I did the first time I visited the museum and budgeted one day. Book at least two days at the Valley View RV Park. My next trip I'm reserving three days. Up-date: I returned in 2016 and did spend three days at the Museum. Also, I was blessed with the honor of being pictured with Billy The Kid's 44-40 Winchester rifle.

I want to thank Don and Tim Sweet for all they had to do to affect that one photograph. Obviously, The Kid's artifacts owned by the museum are guarded like Fort Knox.

Mr. Don Sweet on left, Red Johnson, author, on right.

Above: Red Johnson holds Billy The Kid's Rifle

Don Sweet inherited the Museum from his father. Don at the time of this writing is 82-years-old. His father introduced him to Jesús Silva in 1940. Jesús personally knew all the major characters of the Lincoln County war. He managed a sheep operation for Pete Maxwell, but that was not what made him one of the most popular personalities of The Kid's time. He was the best cook on the plains and always had enough food for every drifter that visited his sheep camp. The Kid, Pat Garrett, etc. etc. The stories he told were precious. He built the casket The Kid was buried in, and was one of his pall-bearers.

Billy the Kid

Setting the Record Straight, The Kid Speaks for Himself[3]

I'd like to set the record straight on a few matters. Therefore, I have taken over Red's pen to do just that! Don't fret, I'll give it back to him to tell my story. I'll only interrupt when he gets something wrong, ha!

I'm sick and tired of all the lies, twists, wrong interpretations, for profit "public" investigations, and historians that wouldn't know one end of a horse from the other. All making money off my life story. I don't mind them making money, I've always been for that, but they should be a little more careful on getting their facts straight. So, I'll give some facts to you, straight-up:

First let me start with that Brushy Bill Roberts fellow...no he was not me! I saw those "decoders", screen writers, professors, and authors suck into his lies like flies to dung. Frankly, I found it comical. Just look at his ears. Mine are not that ugly!

It is true Pat Garrett put me in this spirit world. He did not shoot me in the back while lying in wait, as some of my overzealous supporters reported. No, he shot me right through the heart. It was totally my own fault, I hesitated, asking Pete who was sitting in the dark on the end of his bed. I didn't want

[3] This section is fictional...after living with The Kid for five years...oh! It is so him.

to shoot a friend. I had a lot of friends in Fort Sumner that could have been visiting Pete that night.

With those two strangers out front I should have shot first and identified the bodies later. As it turned out I'm the one they had to identify ha!

Yes sir, if Pat had given me one more second, he would not have made that shot! How about all those lies about Pat shooting me unarmed? Now, that is funny! I never went anywhere without my "little 41", no not even to the privy.

I heard a tale that I carried a British Bull Dog 41. Now that is a joke! How could anyone find me that stupid? You've heard that saying of "not being able to hit the broad side of a barn", the shooter had to be using a Bull Dog ha! No sir, my 41's are Colt long-barreled Thunders. That night, as I approached Pete Maxwell's house, I had a butcher knife in my left hand and one of my "little 41s" tucked in my waist.

I pulled it out before I entered Pete's bedroom. I suppose you heard about the "back shooting" because I backed into Pete's bedroom. I was keeping an eye on those two strangers I saw out front when I entered the gate to Pete's yard. One was sitting on the porch with his legs down on the step, the other leaning on the fence railing. I asked in Spanish:

"Quién eres?", "Quién eres?" "Quién eres?" which is in English: "Who are you?" "Who are you?" "Who are you?" First time to one man, then the other, and then to them both. I did so as I was backing into Pete's open door. The moon was almost full, and I could clearly see the men were strangers to Fort Sumner.

The one stranger answered: "Don't worry, we won't hurt you." As I backed into Pete's bedroom I turned and could clearly see Pete propped up on his headboard. I asked him in English: "Who are those fellows out there, Pete?"

Pete seemed startled and jumped up to a sitting position as he said: "It's him!" I saw a movement in the shadow at the end of Pete's bed, which was right in front of me. I jumped back and drew the bead of my "little 41"on the movement.

That is when I did that very stupid thing, I asked in Spanish: "Quién es ese? Quién es ese?" (Who is that? Who is that?). I not only said that, but I said it twice! I guess if you are going to do a dumb thing you might as well do it well, too! Ha!

That movement was Pat Garrett going for his Colt, which he didn't even have out. I had my bead on him before he even cleared leather, but I had my mouth going when I should have had my trigger finger moving...ha!

The fact is he shot me straight up because I didn't want to take a chance at shooting a friend in the dark. As I said, many good friends of mine could have been in Pete's room talking to him.

I usually think pretty fast on my feet, but all those odd things happening, even Pete saying, "It's him!" I thought he was talking to me about someone else, not telling Pat it was me! That crazy fickle finger of fate. Those guys outside? I asked several times in both English and Spanish who they were, and no one was telling me. All that confusion I should have shot first and asked the rest of the questions later.

Let me tell you why Jesse Evans lived to old age. He would have shot the two men out front, asked Pete the question of who they were from outside his door, and if he saw a movement in the dark room he would have fanned three rounds to the shadow, drawn his second gun and killed Pete Maxwell for not warning him. Even if he was sleeping with his sister.

It is not true that Pat Garrett and I were friends, or that he rode with The Regulators. I knew Pat when he tended bar at Beaver Smith's in Fort Sumner. We worked together a little while on Pete Maxwell's cattle company. He had told me he came to New Mexico from buffalo hunting on the plains. He said it was good money, but he got tired of the stench. Most likely he had another reason for why he picked coming to New Mexico. He was probably on the run. Most of the men drifting into Fort Sumner were on the run from somewhere.

I must say that even at that first meeting in Beaver Smith's Saloon I knew he was a man determined to be successful at something. Pat Garrett was a determined man.

Ironically, I did run into Pat one night not long before he killed me. It was pitch dark as the moon was just a sliver then. I could see Jesús Silva's camp fire from a good distance. I was hungry![4]

I could smell his cooking a mile off. He was the best camp cook in the Pecos Valley. As I got closer I could see he had Pat Garrett as a dinner guest. Pat was a tall and wiry guy and he sat staring into Jesús's camp fire. I could clearly recognize it was Pat a hundred yards away.

I knew he had a warrant for my re-arrest, but he had no intention of taking me to Lincoln alive again. I surely did kill his two deputies Jim Bell and Bob Ollinger. He was a new Sheriff and I made him look bad in doing so.

I did feel bad about having to kill Jim Bell, but not Bob Ollinger. He was a six foot two hundred pounds of muscle that he loved to push around smaller men with. If you look up the definition of "bully" in the dictionary you will find his name next to it. I enjoyed filling that barrel chest of his with 18 buck shots from his own shot gun! And it was from a 5'7", 135lbs kid that sent him to hell...it just doesn't get sweeter than that! Ha!

I heard that surely did anger Pat Garrett. His anger was expressed in enhanced determination to settle the score. I was told he wasn't emotional about it at all, just determined to bring me in slung over a saddle instead of straddling it.

That night I snuck up on Pat, I gave serious thought as to what Jesse Evans would do. He would put a bullet in the back of Pat's head, and then ask Jesús for a meal. Finishing his meal, he would order Jesús to bury the body where it could not be found by man or beast, and if it was found he would come back and personally dig a grave for Jesús.

I discovered that Pat had nerves of cast iron. He was still staring into the flame, which he knew was the wrong thing to be doing at that moment. I could not tell exactly when he knew I was there.

I came up behind him and this is how the conversation went: I said to Jesús Silva:

"Buenas noches, mi amigo." (Good evening, my friend).

He replied: "Y a ti amigo." (And to you my friend).

---

[4] This story is from Mr. Don Sweet, owner of the Billy The Kid Museum in Ft. Sumner, New Mexico (a must see for any Kid fanatic like me). His father introduced him to Jesús Silva in 1940. The story is very significant to the personality of Billy The Kid. Obviously, the conversations are hearsay.

I asked: "Quien es esta contigo?"(Who is this with you?).

He replied: "Conoce el bien Pat Garrett." (You know the good Pat Garrett).

I asked: "Tienes suficiente comida?" (You have enough food?).

He said: "Si, hay mucho para todos. Ven y siéntate aquí, mi campamento es tu campamento, mi amigo!" (Yes, there is much for all. Come and sit here, my camp is your camp my friend).

I said: "Gracias, mi amigo." (Thank you, my friend).

He replied: "De nada." (Of nothing).

I sat on the rock Jesús was pointing to when he asked me to sit down. It was situated between Pat and himself. Pat was to my left. I could cross draw my "little 41" with my right hand and my gun barrel would not have to move more than 3 or 4 inches to belly shoot him. One wrong move and he was dead!

I said: "Buenas noches Pat. How are you doing?" (Good evening Pat. How are you doing?).

He replied without hesitation or the slightest indication of being uncomfortable: "Jesús, as you know, is the best cook in the Pecos Valley. Kid, when I get hungry out here I find his camp, just as I see you do also."

He had arrived long before me and was finishing up his dinner. He calmly cleaned his dishes, thanked Jesús for the meal, mounted his horse and then said to me:

"You'll not have trouble from me tonight," and rode out of sight.

When he was out of ear shot Jesús asked me:

"Tuviste la oportunidad de matar a Pat, tu sabe que el esta hacia fuera a matar, por que no mataste lo primero?"

(You had the chance to kill Pat. You know he is out to kill you. Why did you not kill him first?).

I'm explaining this conversation in such detail because I assume you want to get to know who I really am. My answer will confuse historians and they will misinterpret this as it was because Pat was my friend. No, he was not, and I would have done the same for anyone else.

My answer was:

"Pat acaba de casar. Es un hombre de familia. No puedo disparsa un recién casados en la parte posterior."

(Pat just got married. He is now a family man. I can't just shoot a newlywed in the back.)

I finished eating and threw my bed roll out and away from the fire. Jesús smiled and repeated to me:

"Mi campamento es tu campamento, mi amigo." (My camp is your camp, my friend.)

I replied: "Gracias, mi amigo gracias." (Thank you my friend, thank you.)

He replied: "De nada." (Of nothing.)

I replied: "No, mi amigo, no de nada, pero una ayuda muy grande, mi amigo!" (No, my friend, not of nothing, but a very big help my friend.)

Twice I could have killed Pat Garrett before he killed me. Jesse Evans wouldn't have passed on either one of them.

You probably have read those stories I have killed as many men as I had years alive. For the record, that was twenty-one years. Well, that's not true either. Some historians say I killed eight men, that isn't true either. I can't imagine why the historians never count Apache Indians (historians know I hate Apaches, but that doesn't mean they don't count as men). They know I killed **five Apaches while in Arizona**. That wasn't all.

Once, I joined a cattle drive of a large herd from El Paso, Texas to the Mesilla Valley in New Mexico. When I joined them, we had eighty-two cowboys in all.

Not far out of El Paso we were attacked by a large band of Mescalero Apaches. They were intent on killing us all, and taking the whole herd. This wasn't a small band that wanted to cut out a few for food.

I stood ground and emptied one Indian pony after another. I emptied both my "little 41's." I believe I made a clean sweep of **one dead Apache for every bullet I fired, which was ten.**

I also killed **"The Indian" Manuel Segovia during The War (Lincoln County War)**. I did so because he killed Frank McNab shortly after he became the new leader of our Regulators.

Therefore, that makes **sixteen Indians I killed**. They were all fighting "men". Most were better warriors than many white men I knew. It is inexcusable for the historians not to count them. I realize they know of the derogatory remarks I made about Apaches in my travels. I didn't find one I liked. If they are going to count men I've killed, they should include the Apaches too. I do.

Now, as far as white men I killed, I divide them into two groups:

First, the ones I really enjoyed killing. When I say I enjoyed it, with each one I could have celebrated with a cold beer slushing down my throat. That is if I drank, which I did not. After killing those men, I got a "rush" like you cannot imagine. I know that sounds terrible to you church going folks, but it is the truth. You cannot know the high I got from killing an evil person, a bully, or one that just needed it! It equaled the pleasure of a hot-blooded senorita on a cold desert night...almost anyway! Ha!

Those white men were:

Francis P. "Windy" Cahill, blacksmith Camp Grant, Arizona Territory. Bully!

Joe Grant Texas braggart gunman, Fort Sumner, Bob Hargrove's Saloon. He told me: "I'll bet you $25 that I kill a man today before you do." He lost the bet! I killed him first ha!

Bob Ollinger, Deputy Sheriff Lincoln County. Fought for Jimmy Dolan during The War. Bully!

Billy Morton, One of three that killed John Tunstall. He most likely shot Tunstall's horse. He led the sub-posse ordered to kill Tunstall and any men with him.

Buckshot Roberts: John Middleton claimed this killing. His bullet went wide. I shoved the barrel of my rifle into his belly and pulled the trigger. He died of one gunshot to the belly. I killed him with pleasure. Fate was on my side that night. As I shot he had shoved his rifle barrel into my belly so hard he knocked me off the porch. His rifle was empty, or I would have died with him.

Robert Beckwith was killed when we escaped McSween's burning house. Shooting from a crouch while running is something I practiced almost as much as shooting from under my horse's neck. It was an easy shot for me and I would have taken great pleasure in killing old-man Beckwith's son too. I wish that was true, **but it is not**. One of the men with McSween killed him with a shot right through the eye. It was dark and several fired simultaneously, so no one knows for sure. If I were to guess I'd think it was Salazar. He was the best shooter in the group. Sheriff Brady and Jimmy Dolan could call on the Beckwith's outfit any time to do their killing. They hated the Regulators. Damn, I wish it was my bullet.

Second, are the ones I killed that needed to be killed and I was the right man to do the job. I must add, among these are men I truly regret having to kill. The killing was needed at the time, but I found no pleasure in doing so. They were:

Jim Bell, Deputy Sheriff Lincoln County. Nice fellow.

Jim Carlyle, Blacksmith from White Oaks was a member of the posse who intended on arresting us. He was foolish to give himself up as a hostage and then try to escape through a window. I did shoot him, but I blamed the posse, as they opened fire after I did. Jim had it coming, too. He was a close friend of mine, yet he led the posse right to us.

Frank Baker, he was the most difficult and the killing I regret the most. He helped me many times while riding with "The Boys." He was a great gunslinger and taught me a lot about guns. He taught me the hoot owl trail. Frank looked like a large ape, hair and all. He was deadly with fists, knives, and guns. He had a great personality too. It is a shame, but it had to be done.

I had to shoot Frank Baker out of the saddle to get a bead on Billy Morton when they attempted an escape. Many believed I killed Old Man McCloskey too. **That is not true**. The Old

Man rode his horse between Billy Morton and me. He knew I wanted to kill Billy Morton. He openly swore he would prevent me from doing the same. Billy Morton was a good friend of the Old Man.

I did taunt Billy Morton from the time we left the main trail, onto the Blackwater Creek trail, toward the Capitan Mountains. I told him he was yellow if he didn't try to run, and if he didn't escape, he wasn't going to arrive alive in Lincoln.

Billy Morton kept getting his horse closer and closer to the Old Man. I knew what he was up to, and it happened exactly as I thought it would. Billy leaned over to whisper something to the Old Man. He then yanked the Old Man's pistol from its holster. While leaning over he had accidently spurred his horse and it bolted sideways. The Old Man's horse reared up. Billy tried to shoot me and hit the Old Man as his horse came down.

I had to rein around the Old Man's horse as his body was falling to the ground. I wasn't in a hurry, Billy and Frank were on horses that couldn't out run a sick cow. They were foolish to try an escape on those plugs. Frank Baker had reined right behind Billy Morton while spurring those plugs as hard as they could.

I shot Frank with a single shot to the head. He slumped over his pommel and slid from the saddle. I then killed Billy Morton, and I already told you how good that felt!

Dick Brewer seemed upset. Actually, angry, but he couldn't determine exactly what he was angry about. He ordered every Regulator to put a bullet in all three bodies, and leave them lay. I only had to put one in the Old Man McCloskey. He was already dead when I did so. I did not have anything to do with his death.

Sheriff William Brady, I did put a bullet in him from an ambush (which is acceptable in a war). Although, five other men also put bullets in him at the same time. I was the only one charged with his murder. I'll count it, but it really was a shared killing. He formed the posse to kill John Tunstall. He hired known killers to do the job (Jesse Evans and his Boys).

He did the bidding of Jimmy Dolan and was a Civil War buddy of Lawrence Murphy.

So, if you're keeping count it is **sixteen Indians and nine white men for a total of twenty-five men**. And they all needed the killing.

Another thing to get straightened out: I must say first I did enjoy and express with outright laughter the high pedestal those newspaper men and dime novelist put me on. Heck, when I was under arrest in Las Vegas, some treated me like Lola Montez, and others like Boss Tweed's butcher. I loved the attention. That has always been a great weakness of mine. I must confess I enjoy getting attention more than anything else...ah...almost anything else.

Those newspaper folks claimed I was "the most notorious outlaw in New Mexico Territory". Now that is not true. That is funny and shows how little some of them know about their own territory. That title without doubt, or question, goes to Will Davies, aka Jesse Evans. I joined his gang called "The Boys" in September 1877. Many famous outlaws rode with and learned the hoot owl trail from Jesse Evans. For example:

William Bresnaham aka "Curly" Bill Brocius who became the leader of "The Cowboys" in Arizona. Yes, he got his training from Jesse Evans.

Charles "Pony" Diehl who went on to Tombstone to outlaw with The Cowboys.

Dick Lloyd, same as Charles Dielhl. Killed in Arizona.

Jack Long, same as Charles and Dick became Arizona "Cowboys".

John Slaughter, rode with Jesse Evans on Chisum's outfit. He was a rustler and a gun slinger before he went straight in Arizona. His first ranch on his own was near Seven Rivers, Pecos Valley New Mexico.

He killed a man on the Pecos who was hunting him down in revenge for the killing of a man in Texas. The William Slaughter Ranch in Texas was on Yellow House Creek, which is where he hailed from in Texas.

After that killing he drove a herd to Arizona and started over. The Apache called him the "Dirty Little Gringo." He warned them not to pass over his ranch. One band did, and he and his men killed all of them, warriors, women, and children. They never crossed his ranch again, nor stole his beef.

John went straight as an arrow and became Sheriff of Cochise County. He is the one that really cleaned out the outlaws in that county. He would tell a bad man to leave his county in 24 hours. If he didn't, John would be seen riding out of Tombstone the next morning alone. He would return and never make any kind of a report. The outlaw was gone. There was little doubt he had killed him, and buried him in the desert. They were never found, and dead men can't talk.

One married man lived in Contention told John it was not possible for him to take care of selling his house and moving his family that quickly. John said nothing, he just left and returned the next day. Some friends of the man had advised him to get out of the county, or John would bury him and his whole family in the desert. John returned, and the man and his family were gone, and never to be seen again in his county.

I could go on and on about all the outlaws Jesse Evans taught the hoot owl trail. When I rode with him The Boys could expand to any number he needed at the drop of a hat. If he told you to come, you better come. I was the only one I know of that left him without permission, and did not get his revenge. Not that he didn't attempt to kill me. The fickle finger of fate was on my side then.

Every member of Jesse's gang had to have two pistols, a lever action rifle, and cross bandoliers full of ammunition, a minimum of 100 rounds on you.

Everyone practiced, practiced, and practiced. I think he would have made a great military general. He was determined to never be outgunned in a fight. Jesse was always about the numbers. Twice he took a bullet, both times he broke his own rules.

One day the most powerful cattleman in the United States of American, John Simpson Chisum had had it with all the rustling of his cattle. He sent a message to Jimmy Dolan: "I will take every gun hand I have, come to Lincoln and kill you and all your hired guns (Jesse Evans Boys)."

Jesse Evans put together forty-gun slingers overnight. He told Jimmy Dolan not to worry as Chisum was smart enough not to attack him (Jesse). John Chisum was, and he didn't.

Another thing I need to get straight, I'm talking about John Chisum. Yes, he did owe me fighting wages from the Lincoln County War. He never paid the money he promised. Once John Tunstall was killed, he was the only one that could finance the Regulators. We were the only ones he had to fight Jesse Evans Boys under the direction of Jimmy Dolan. He agreed to $5/day while at war with Jimmy Dolan and Company. That was fair fighting wages at the time.

Now, it is not true that I threatened to kill one of his cowboys for every day he owed me. That was a complete fabrication from a newspaperman.

When the story broke Mr. Chisum wasn't sure if the story was true or not, so he sent me a messenger that he wanted to talk with me. I returned the messenger with a message for him: "The newspaper story is half false!" I figured he should know which half, ha!

I did get what he owed me with interest! I set a cow camp up at Portales, New Mexico just due north east of Chisum's north ranch near Fort Sumner. I took payment in cattle and interest in horses...ha!

Portales was perfect for me. I could drive the herd through the Brazos Valley on Yellow House Creek, or head north to the XIT Ranch on the Palo Duro Creek. I could get top dollar for cattle and horses up in Tascosa, Texas. No one paid any attention to brands, except a few of the old Goodnight Boys.

It was an easy drive north across the old Comanche Trail to the Santa Fe/Texas trail. There, you cross the Palo Duro Creek and head due north to Tascosa, Texas.

I liked Tascosa! My kind of town! It was there I met Dr. Henry Hoyt. We became very good friends. I sold him my all-time-favorite horse. He loved that animal and the only reason he got it was he had become a good friend. Later in Las Vegas, New Mexico it was Dr. Hoyt that introduced me to a fellow named Howard, whose real name was Jesse James.

I had read about Jesse and Frank James in the Police Gazette and dime novels since I was a small tot. Now, right there in Las Vegas was the country's most famous notorious outlaw, and the local papers didn't even know he was there...ha ha! We sat next to each other in the hot springs north of town.

I couldn't help but compare him to "my" Jesse...Jesse Evans. He was quiet...so was Evans. He was confident...so was Evans. He seemed very determined...as did Evans. The clincher, you knew if you crossed him he would kill you. It didn't matter how good I was with a gun...I would be dead!

Anyhow, that story is a true one. My being the most notorious outlaw in New Mexico Territory is not true. Will Davies, aka Jesse Evans of Texas fit that bill, except possibly when the other "Jesse" James was in our Territory...ha!

The last thing I want to straighten out is I did NOT kill a man in Silver City for insulting my mother. My Silver City days were some of the best days of my life. Except for watching my mother suffer so greatly, and take four months to die bed ridden with consumption. Those were the worse days of my life!

By-in-large, I got in very little trouble in Silver City, and had a lot of wholesome fun. I did get into some minor theft problems with Sombrero Jack.

His real name was George Schaefer and I have never met a man that loved to steal more than him. He literally shook with the thrill of getting away with stealing anything...anything! I have to admit I liked his free spirit and devil-may-care-attitude. It may have been contagious, I wore a sombrero every chance I had...some say I have a devil-may-care attitude too! Ha! I'll leave that judgment to you. I still can't believe they made him a Peace Officer in Georgetown Gold Camp.

ok, I am about to give the pen back to Red. You have gotten straight talk from the horse's mouth. Red got to know me and my life pretty good. No one knows anyone else perfectly, heck, one doesn't even know themselves that good. I do think it is ironic that Red got to know me so well, and he is a relative of Will Davies, aka Jesse Evans. Now that is funny! Ha ha!

Prologue

You may think this the longest prologue you have ever read. You'll be tempted to jump ahead to Chapter One, the beginning of Billy, The Kid's life story. Well, if that tickles your fancy, go right ahead.

If you really want to know and learn about how the New Mexico Territory that shaped his personality, learn how power corrupts (which applies to politics today too), and that the good guys don't always win (like in the movies), then I think you will enjoy reading the long prologue.

I emphatically believe one cannot truly know and understand the person and the life of William Henry McCarty without learning about the violent environment of the New Mexico Territory of the 1860, 70s, and 80s. They are intricate and inseparable.

Furthermore, who was in charge of "civilizing" The New Mexico Territory? Did those people want it "civilized" in the 1860s and 70s?

We will start our journey at the building of Fort Stanton in the spring of 1855. Its purpose and mission was to control the Mescalero Apache band living in the Sacramento Mountains. The Mescalero's were raiding immigrants taking the southern route (preferred in the winter time as it is now) to the California Gold fields. The immigrants followed the Overland Mail Route which was still very much in use.

The industrial revolution was gaining steam in the east. Industrial Titans were in charge of private and public enterprises, but still small in scale. Textile businesses in Boston and New York and the first railroad between Boston and Long Island were built. Cornelius Vanderbilt's new steam boats dominated the freighting in New York Harbor. That was after he had hired Daniel Webster to argue before the Supreme Court for his employer at the time, Thomas Gibbons. He managed Gibbons' steam boats and his own at the same time. Gibbons taught him how to manage large operations. He won the case for Gibbons, which greatly enriched him too.

Government entities could no longer create

private monopolies through contract letting. The states could no longer interfere with private enterprises.

John Peirpont Morgan, better known as J.P. Morgan, was born in 1837. Andrew Carnegie was born in 1835 and John D. Rockefeller was born in 1839. They defined titans of power, wealth, and monopolies. Arguably, they built America! They were the role models of those desiring wealth and power. They were also ruthless men!

Daniel Webster's Supreme Court case basically said: "**free enterprise rules, not government entities**." These titans of business and finance were felt in every state and territory of the United States of America. Indescribable wealth in raw resources lay out in the west. It would take trains to transport it east and people west to settle the wilderness.

Gold and silver in vast quantities were being discovered in what is now California, Nevada, Colorado, Idaho, Montana, South Dakota's Black Hills, and New Mexico. The Indian problem had to be solved once and for all.

Then there was the Civil War right in the middle of this great expansion and accumulation of wealth. Western resources had to be diverted to fight the war, and only skeleton troops, mostly volunteers, were left out west to continue the Indian fighting and "civilizing" of the west.

Confederate States of American President Jefferson Davis wanted the territories of New Mexico, Arizona and southern California to be CSA territories. He placed Brigadier General Sibley in charge of the task.

General Sibley was a former Fort Union, New Mexico Territory Commander in the U.S. Army before the Civil War. He intimately knew of the great quantities of gold and silver in New Mexico and southern Colorado. The South needed that gold and silver. It did not have the resources the north had.

Furthermore, the master plan was for Sibley to march north to Cheyenne and effectively cut all freight and communications of the Union from the east and west coasts. Then he was to move on and take California for the south.

Next I'll discuss the post-Civil War New Mexico Territory. How one Confederate and one Union Officer partner to become game changers in that territory.

Then, The Kid's life story.

Fort Stanton New Mexico Territory[5]

Spring, 1855 South Central New Mexico Territory

The 1st Dragoon Cavalry, and 3rd and 8th Infantry of the United States Army marched in to a small Mexican village on the Rio Bonito River

The captain signaled to halt and ordered:

"Sergeant, find out the name of this village," he said in his naturally commanding, but not offensive voice.

"Yes sir," the sergeant, who spoke Spanish like a native, replied respectfully. He knew the village, but would seek a local to introduce to the captain.

He was able to quickly find a local farmer. The farmer expressed how happy the town was to see them arrive. The Mescalero Apaches had been raiding on a regular basis, and they were living in fear.

The sergeant reported back to his captain and introduced the local farmer to him.

"Sir, he said this village is La Placita del Rio Bonito,

---

[5] Built in 1855, this fort has served our country and people in many ways to this very moment. Many original building (built of local stones) still stand. First, it was important in protecting settlers and travelers from Mescalero Apache raids. During the Civil War, General Sibley's Confederate Brigade occupied it for one month. Kit Carson reoccupied it in 1862 for the US. The great California Column, led by one of the U S. Army's best ever Generals, General James Henry Carleton retook the New Mexico Territory for the Union. That caused the Confederates to retreat and pull all their resources back to Texas. Fort Stanton was rebuilt after the war. Three times the troops had to be used to prevent the killing of innocent civilians in range wars, the most famous of which was the Lincoln County War, and incarceration of William H. Bonney (Billy, The Kid) for his own protection as a witness against Jesse Evans and Co. Buffalo Soldiers pursued Apache leaders Victorio and Geronimo from the fort in the 1880s, also in the '80s John J. "Blackjack" Pershing did two tours of duty at the fort. He received his nickname from leading "Black Buffalo Soldiers" at Fort Stanton. He trained a young Lt. George S. Patton, who said Pershing was the greatest military man he knew. After the Army the fort served as a Merchant Marine TB Hospital, in WWII it served as a German Internee camp, after that war it was a training school for the mentally disabled. Most recently it served as a low security women's prison, and offered juvenile, drug and alcohol rehabilitation programs. Today it is a state Monument and museum.

sir...and they are very happy to see us here as the Mescalero's have them living in fear sir," the sergeant explained.

"Sergeant, explain to him we are going to build a fort here to control the Mescalero Apaches," the captain declared.

The sergeant explained the same to the farmer, who immediately responded:

"Aqui?!" He pointed to the ground under his feet, which was in the middle of the village. The captain did not need a translation.

"No, sergeant, not right here! I want to know if the gentleman knows of good, level ground near the river, that won't interfere with anyone's farming land," the captain asked, and the sergeant translated to the farmer.

"Si, una hora norte es buena hierba y ano redondo agua," the farmer said, pleased they were not considering their village or farming land.

The sergeant translated: "Sir, he said: 'one hour north of here there is good grass and year-round water.' I know the place he speaks of, it would be a good place for a fort."

The captain looked at the farmer and said: "Gracias señor," as he tipped the front of his hat.

"De nada, el capitan," the farmer replied with a smile.

"Well, Sergeant let us find where we are going to build our new home," the captain declared as his hand signaled a forward march.

Nine miles north of the village the captain pulled up. "Yes sir, this is it," the sergeant declared.

There was at least 1200 acres of prime grass and more than thirty acres that were exceptionally level, and adjacent to the river.

Construction began in earnest immediately after setting up a camp site. Horses were picketed with hobbles, long tie lines, in high grass, and guards were placed every thirty feet. Horses were very valuable. Cattlemen would pay $100 for a good horse. Indians would risk their life for a "soldier pony". The infantrymen were assigned to building and protecting the fort.

The cavalry preformed the main mission of patrolling and controlling the Mescalero Apaches. Without horses the fort could not perform their mission, hence they were guarded tightly and with instructions to shoot first and ask questions later if any intruders went near the horses.

Each cavalry soldier would be responsible to walk their horse to water twice a day.

The captain shared his plans with all the men. He had been selected for this mission due to his engineering skills. One look at the area and he knew stone would be the best building material.

He arranged for well-guarded, wood wagons to venture into the forests south of the fort location. The mountains north bore few trees. The ones south had good trees, but a whole lot of apache Indians in them too.

He planned every move to minimize any casualties. He sent out patrols toward the valley's basin and around the base of the mountains to the west. That drew the warriors away from the wood trains. He would do the same around the eastern side of the Sacramento Mountains. The Mescalero Apache thought their main camp was going to be under attack and would recall all their warriors to defend the band's camp.

The masons cut and hauled stone from sunrise to sun set. Buildings started to take form. It took only six months to complete a fort that was built to stand for centuries.

Captain Henry W. Stanton was out on a routine patrol and was attacked with an overwhelming force of Apaches. He was killed instantly.

The captain completed the fort and received word his recommendation for naming the fort was approved. It would be named Fort Stanton in honor of Captain Stanton.

Fort Stanton served the people of the United States and the local communities very well over the next six years.

In 1860 the winds of the Civil War were blowing. Most of the forts in the west were equipped to provide protection for mail routes and main arterials for travel east and west. First it was the California Gold Rush, then the land speculators and prospectors. Then cattle barons of Texas were eying the great grass lands for open grazing to build large herds. Lucrative government contracts for beef would be awarded at great profits to the industrious cattlemen. Although, it was a high risk high reward venture.

Then suddenly the fort quartermasters in the west couldn't buy beef out of Texas (even at 8 cents a pound using Army drafts). They had to pay in gold, and not many had gold!

December 20, 1860 South Carolina seceded from the Union. January 9, 1861 Mississippi seceded, January 10, 1861 Florida seceded, January 11, 1861 Alabama seceded, Georgia eight days later on the 19 of January 1861. January 26, 1861 Louisiana seceded from the Union, and February 1st, 1861 Texas seceded from the United States of America. Seven states in little over a month seceded from the Union. Virginia April 17, 1861, Arkansas May 6, 1861, North Carolina May 20, 1861, and last was Tennessee June 8, 1861. Eleven states made up the Confederate States of America (CSA).

The CSA had ordered Sibley's Brigade of Texas Mounted Volunteers to advance a column into Mesilla, New Mexico Territory, under the command of Colonel Baylor. At first in the form of spies, sympathizers, and agitators. They would decide who friends were and who were not.

They found a great ally in "Old Man" Hugh M. Beckwith, whose ranch was located at Seven Rivers in the Pecos Valley. He would play an important role in the coming battles.

Worse for the US still, was the fact that most of the Union forts could not withstand an artillery attack. They were built to protect against Indian attacks, not attacks from a trained and equipped professional army.

Civil War
New Mexico Territory
(Southern half of which The Confederate States of America would call this Arizona Territory)

A letter from Captain A.M. Jackson, Secretary of State, New Mexico addressed to Honorable Jefferson Davis and was Titled:

"A Confederate Assessment of New Mexico in 1861"

Note: The Pike's Peaker's are all northerners.[6]

---

[6] It is assumed he is referring to southern Colorado and the northern section of New Mexico: Taos, Santa Fe, Albuquerque, and Las Vegas New Mexico. The gold and

Protected by Indians[7] its (New Mexico) stock raising capacity is unsurpassed on the face of the earth. From fifty miles south of the city[8] the Valley of the Rio Grande is the paradise of the vine.

[If] New Mexico is to be acquired for the south, it must be done by the south[9].

Your Obedient Servant
Captain A.M. Jackson

The plan was approved by Jefferson Davis and General Sibley's 5th Regiment of Texas Mounted Volunteers was assigned the mission. His subordinate, Colonel Baylor, had been working through his subordinate, Captain Philips, prior to the formal approval. As early as January 19, 1861[10] Col. Baylor ordered Captain Philips to hang Crittenden Marshall as a Union spy among his insurgents in Mesilla, N.M. He did so immediately, which shook up the people of Mesilla and Las Cruces, New Mexico.

July 14, 1861 Major R. S. Canby (full name was Edward Richard Sprigg Canby), Commanding 10th Infantry, Headquarters Department of New Mexico at Fort Defiance orders withdrawal of all "interior posts".

July 24, 1861 the invasion of New Mexico by Colonel Baylor was in full force. He set up his personal headquarters in Mesilla, New Mexico Territory, which he promptly renamed The Confederate Arizona Territory. His map for the "acquired" Territory is the lower half of the Union's New Mexico Territory, and the lower half of the Union's Arizona Territory.

July 25, 1861 1st Lt. Brooks, U.S. Army attempts to withdraw from Mesilla, New Mexico Territory as ordered. He is confronted by Col. Baylor's advance troops. A skirmish ensues, three enlisted men are killed, Lt. Brooks himself and one Charlie

---

silver rushes of Colorado brought Northeastern capitalists and prospectors into northern New Mexico Territory. He is stating Northern New Mexico would be far more difficult to take by force as they are "all northerners" (assume Union supporters).

7 He is referring to the southern half of New Mexico.

8 Presumably he is referring to Albuquerque or Santa Fe.

9 Southern route from West Texas via El Paso up the Rio Grande to Mesilla, N.M.

10 Ten days before Texas seceded from the US (February 1, 1861 and two and a half months before the attack on Fort Sumter).

McNally are wounded. Five horses are killed. They are able to escape before a total loss of the company. They head north to Fort Craig.

On August 9, 1861 Colonel Baylor identifies the local Catholic priest as a Union spy. He orders him to be hung immediately. This alienates the local Mexican population (Mesilla is 90% Mexican).

Colonel Baylor orders the seizure of Fort Stanton, which he discovers has been abandoned. He holds it for one month and orders the troops back to Mesilla for "larger fish to fry". He lays the plans to march north to Santa Fe.

Union forces maintained control of Northern New Mexico Territory. Drawing a straight line across New Mexico from Fort Craig to Bosque Redondo (which remained in Union control) all land north of it was in Union control and all land south of it was in Confederate control, for the moment.

December, 1861 General Joseph "Jo" Sibley and his Brigade of Texas Mounted Volunteers arrive in New Mexico. He is 3,500 men strong and marches up the Rio Grande Valley north. His mission is to first, take all of New Mexico and then, the gold and silver mines of Colorado. He was going to by-pass Fort Craig where newly promoted Brigadier General Canby has 4,000 troops.

February 21, 1862 Brigadier General R. S. Canby goes on the offensive and meets General Sibley in the field. He is decisively defeated at the **Battle of Valverde on the Rio Grande** by Confederate Brigadier General Jo Sibley's forces.

Brigadier General Sibley marches north taking Albuquerque and Santa Fe. The latter is the New Mexico Territory capital. He then turns his sights on Fort Union, the last Union fort between him and the gold and silver mines in Colorado.

Unknown to him, Colorado has raised 1,000 volunteers. They marched through a blizzard to reinforce the 700 Union soldiers at Fort Union.

Brigadier General Sibley ordered Captain Hunter to march to Tucson, Arizona. Successful there, re-enforcements would join him to march on to the Pacific Ocean in Southern California. That was Jefferson Davis's dream plan. Word of all this reached Abraham Lincoln in Washington D. C.

Abraham Lincoln, President of the United States of America, orders the formation the **"California Column".**

Its mission was to put down insurgents and declared rebels in California to take Arizona and New Mexico back for the Union. Hold all of this for the duration of the war. That was his directive.

General Wright was Commander of the District of Southern California reporting to **Brigadier General Edwin Vose Sumner[11] who was Commander of The Department of The Pacific. As a Lt. Colonel he was the Military Governor of the New Mexico Territory from 1851 to 1853.**

In 1855 he was promoted to Colonel and assigned the leadership of the new U.S. 1st Cavalry at Fort Leavenworth, Kansas. There he saw field action against hostile Cheyenne Indians.

In 1858 Colonel Sumner became the leader of the Department of the West.

March 16, 1861 he was promoted to **Brigadier General Sumner** and relieved Brigadier General Albert S. Johnson as **Commander of the Department of the Pacific.**

General Wright, Commander of the District of Southern California, drowned in a tragic boating trip on the Columbia River, Oregon Territory.

Brigadier General Sumner recommended the promotion of Colonel James Henry Carleton to replace General Wright as Commander of the District of Southern California and **to form and lead the California Column**.

Abraham Lincoln and the War Department approved of the promotion. Colonel Carleton's name and achievements were well known in Washington D. C. His reputation was that of an experienced Indian fighter and a very capable officer.

In recent history, Colonel Carleton, as a Brevet Major, leading Company K of the 1st Dragoons at Fort Tejon, California

---

[11] Later, then Brigadier General Carleton, Commander of the Department of New Mexico, would name Bosque Redondo new Indian Reservation Fort Sumner in honor of Major General Edwin Vose Sumner, who had become a true Civil War hero. He died of a heart attack on leave from total exhaustion at his daughter's home March 21, 1863. He was the oldest active General in the U.S. Army at 66-years-old.

was given an important assignment. He was to investigate the **Mountain Meadow Massacre** in southern Utah Territory that occurred in September of 1857.

May of 1859 Major Carleton arrived at Mountain Meadows. Captain Ruben Campbell and Surgeon Charles Brewer had buried, in four mass graves, the remains of 73 people. The remains had been scattered over the plain for twenty months.

After an investigation Major Carleton wrote a report to Major W.W. Mackall, Assistant Adjutant-General US Army San Francisco, California:

"Mormons, some dressed as Indians, had murdered and plundered the possessions of 120 men, women, and children of a California bound emigrant train with the assistance of Paiute Tribesmen."

In 1860, a year later, Major Carleton attacked the suspected Paiute raiders, with re-enforcements of the 1st Dragoon, Company K.

Washington had made the right choice in an officer to create and lead the new California Column.

October 1861 San Francisco, California Colonel Carleton creates the new fighting Regiment called the **1st California Volunteer Infantry Regiment** as ordered by President Abraham Lincoln.

At its formation one of his Captains is **Captain Emil Fritz, 1st California Cavalry Company B.**[12] The U. S. Congressman from the San Francisco District at this time is **Samuel B. Axtell.**[13]

In addition to the above, he forms four more companies of the 1st California Cavalry totaling five companies of cavalry.

---

[12] Emil Fritz is destined to play a major role in what would be called the Lincoln County War of New Mexico.

[13] Samuel B. Axtell is destined to play a major role as Governor of New Mexico Territory (1875 to 1878) during the Lincoln County War. He would pour fuel on the fires of the Lincoln County War and be declared, in an official Federal Agent Frank Angel report to the Interior Secretary Carl Schurz: "that his administration as having more corruption, fraud, mismanagement, plots, murder than any other Governor in the history of the United States of America." Secretary Schurz suspends him as Governor and Rutherford B. Hayes appoints the famous Civil War General Lew Wallace to fix New Mexico's problems.

Then he added ten companies of the 1st California Infantry, and a 2nd Regiment of California Volunteers Calvary and light Battery A of the 3rd U.S. Artillery which had 1,500 well trained and disciplined fighting men.

Later he would add Lt. Colonel George Bowie's 5th California Infantry.[14] That brought his total to 2,350 fighting men.

Colonel Carleton was exactly the right man at the right time for the Union. He marched 2,350 men across many deserts in the summer time with minimal casualties (losing only six soldiers). **The march its self was the longest across-desert in the history of the United States Army.** From California to Texas he had fighting skirmishes with confederate forces led by Captain Sherod Hunter, serious fights with Apache Indians (including the famous Apache leaders Cochise and Mangas Coloradas).

His planning and strategies were brilliant. For example, advanced companies would find water and then dig out the hole larger for the following companies. If a water hole was dried up they were to march north to the Gila River, load and transport water back for the following column. Supplies were planned far in advance being transported up the Gulf of Mexico to Yuma, Arizona. The units were separated enough to allow water to build up in springs, and yet close enough to allow a unit to act as reinforcement in a fight.

April 15, 1862 Colonel Carleton's first battle was at Picacho Pass, Arizona. There the Confederate Arizona Pickets attempted to cut his supplies by burning hay stacks at the remount station built by the Butterfield Overland Stage Company before the war.

Lt. James Barrett led an advanced company with orders **not to engage** with the enemy until re-enforcements from the

---

[14] George Washington Bowie was the Attorney General for the State of California and former Governor of California (1858). He had earned a brevetted rank of Major during the Mexican American War. He stayed with the California Column through completion of its duties in New Mexico and mustered out with his unit as a Brevet Brigadier General November 1864. Died August 11, 1901 in Martinez, Contra Costa County, California. He served his country well and one of the few having a western fort named after him while still alive and active.

column could arrive. He disobeyed those orders when he ran into Confederate Sergeant Henry Holms Pickets.

The ensuing fight lasted for hours resulting in the death of Lt. Barrett, and two of his soldiers, and the wounding of three more. His men were able to capture three Confederate soldiers. Worse than anything, Lt. Barrett's actions sent a wounded Sgt. Holms back to Tucson to sound the alarm of the approaching California Column. Colonel Carleton no longer had the element of surprise on his side in Tucson.

Confederate Captain Sherod Hunter declared Tucson was the Confederates Capital of the Western District of the Confederate Arizona Territory, and Colonel Carleton had every reason to believe it would now be a fierce fight to take it.

He sent two companies into Tucson (one from the north and one from the south). **Captain Emil Fritz[15] led the charge into Tucson** to discover that Confederate Captain Sherod Hunter had fled the town of 8,400 people (70% Hispanic) and was on his way back to Texas.

On **March 26th – 28, 1862,** unknown to Brigadier General Carleton, his colleague **Brigadier General R. S. Canby**, Commander of the Department of New Mexico and his troops at Fort Union, reinforced by the 1,000 Colorado volunteers had decisively defeated his nemesis Confederate General Jo Sibley at the **Battle of Glorieta Pass in the Sangre de Cristo Mountains, New Mexico (near Santa Fe)**. Later that battle would be called the **"Gettysburg of the West".**

Confederate General Sibley's supplies were exhausted. He had no choice but to return to Texas. He had received word from Captain Sherod Hunter about the size of the advancing California Column. Also, that it was being led by a pre-war old acquaintance of his: Brigadier General Henry Carleton. Sibley knew him as an Indian fighter, but respected him as determined

[15] In 1866 Colonel Emil Fritz and his subordinate Major Lawrence G. Murphy formed a partnership in a general mercantile sutler store located at Fort Stanton, New Mexico Territory. When they were forced to evacuate the Fort, the USA bought their building for $8000. They went Lincoln and built the two story building that would become to be known as "The House." It had eighteen rooms and included a bank, store, saloon, and boarding rooms. The House had an iron fisted monopoly on all business in Lincoln County, New Mexico Territory.

man. Low on supplies and with a poor likelihood of a reinforcement of troops or supplies, Sibley's Confederates left New Mexico Territory, and would never return.

April 28, 1862 in route from California to Yuma, Arizona Colonel Carleton was promoted to **Brigadier General Henry Carleton.**[16]

Having received the information that Brigadier General Canby had had a decisive victory over Confederate General Jo Sibley at the Battle of Glorieta Pass, and the latter General was on his way back to Texas, Brigadier General Carleton was able to send several advance units out quickly. The first unit to arrive in Mesilla, New Mexico and declare it the 1st California Volunteer Column headquarters on July 4, 1862!

On July 15, 1862 another unit commanded by Captain Thomas Roberts Company E of the 5th California Infantry was brought under ambush attack in Apache Pass only a few hundred yards from a much-needed Apache spring.

The attackers included none other than the Apache leaders Mangas Coloradas and Cochise. They had 500 warriors and Captain Roberts had only 116 Infantry and 22 Cavalrymen. He did have two 12-pound artillery Howitzers. It was a decisive win for the U.S. soldiers.

Captain Thomas Roberts had lost two men and three were wounded. Mangas and Cochise lost 66, had undisclosed wounded, and escaped in the darkness of night. They said later that they would have done well if it was not for the "wagons". That is what they called the Howitzers as they were mounted in wagons.

In Captain Roberts report he included that he found nine civilians on the other side of the pass. They had been killed by the Apaches before the Battle of Apache Pass.

General Carleton ordered the 5th Cavalry Infantry to build a fort to guard the springs and pass for military and civilian travelers. They were to name it Fort Bowie in honor of their leader Lt. Colonel George Bowie.

---

[16] Later promoted to Brevet Major General (two star).

Brigadier General James Henry Carleton's Mission is Changed

August of 1862 Brigadier Generals Carleton and Canby link up in New Mexico. Brigadier General Canby was ordered to return to the east. Brigadier General Carleton was assigned the District of Arizona (which included The Department of New Mexico).

His orders and new mission was to now solve the "Indian depredations" in New Mexico and The Arizona Territories. His efforts were now to be focused on the Navajo, Apache, Kiowa, and Comanche hostiles. He is also to protect the re-opened Overland Mail routes.

He must bring the Indians "under control and submission" of the United States Army. He is to do so with the California Column of Volunteers and the New Mexico Volunteers. Most of the regular U.S. Army personnel were to be sent to the east in support of the Union's Civil War effort there.

Washington wanted him to relinquish direct command of the California Column and command the District of Arizona (which included The Department of New Mexico). He requested and was granted to remain the Commander of the California Column. He agreed to have reporting to himself and in charge of the Arizona District Colonel Joseph R. West and headquarter him in Mesilla, New Mexico. Brigadier General Carleton would be headquartered in Santa Fe, New Mexico.

Brigadier General Carleton met with his commanders, which included the famous explorer, scout, Indian fighter Colonel Christopher "Kit" Carson.

The General developed a plan that would quell the Navajo problem forever, he at least thought at the time. They would burn the crops of the Navajo, kill any that resisted (except women and children), and drive them to the Bosque Redondo in the middle of the Pecos Valley. They would build a fort there. It could guard the Overland mail route from Texas and across the middle of the New Mexico Territory. A fort in southwest Texas would guard the southern Overland Mail Route.

First he assigned Colonel Kit Carson to rebuild and reopen Fort Stanton. Then a new fort was to be built at Bosque Redondo. It was to be named Fort Sumner in honor of Brigadier General Sumner who recommended him to lead the California Column.

Colonel Kit Carson's first mission was to capture and drive the Mescalero Apaches to Bosque Redondo Indian reservation in the Pecos Valley. He was to be the Commander of Fort Stanton and make it his headquarters.

His next mission was to defeat the Navajo and drive them to Bosque Redondo. This would be a hard, six-month campaign and would not be completed until January of 1864 when he entered Canyon de Chelly, on the northern border of New Mexico and Arizona. Nine-thousand Navajo surrendered and began the "Long Walk" to Bosque Redondo, Pecos Valley New Mexico.

Colonel Kit Carson accomplished all his ordered tasks. Although, as he confessed later, he did not have faith in Brig. General Carleton's plan in the long term. He thought it would not be possible to "convert" Navajo and Apache Indians to be farmers and herders. Also, most importantly, those tribes were traditional enemies. The Mescalero Apache were terribly outnumbered at Bosque Redondo (approximately 5,000 Navajo and 900 Mescalero Apache).

He was proven to be correct and the Mescalero Apache simply walked off the Bosque Redondo and headed back to the Sacramento Mountains, their traditional home in southern central New Mexico Territory. The government placed Fort Stanton in charge of guarding a new Mescalero Indian reservation.

Brigadier General Carleton executed his global plan of reopening almost all the military posts and forts in New Mexico and Arizona, rebuilding damaged forts, and building new ones where needed to achieve his mission.

He had the man power until at least November of 1864 when the California Column's enlistment expired. He requested, and it was approved to have new companies in California raised and sent as replacements for those mustering out.

Over the next few years all the forts reported dozens of major fights with all the bands of Indians. Many individuals began to rise in the ranks as outstanding Indian fighters. One was **Captain Emil Fritz. He is regarded highly by all officers and soldiers as an outstanding Indian fighter**. Just one example of many:

July 22, 1863 Captain Emil Fritz, 1st California Cavalry, with a detachment of California and New Mexico Cavalry, left Fort Stanton for the Rio Pecos to chastise (in revenge) a band of 200 Indians who had attacked Lt. Marques of the 1st New Mexico Infantry. After following the Indians for 45 miles Captain Fritz came upon their camp. He captured two horses, six mules, and all the plunder in their camp, the Indians made their escape.[17]

Another name that rose as a great Indian fighter was **Captain E. D. Shirland, Company C 1st California Cavalry** who captured Mangas Coloradas, Apache Chief and brought him into Fort McLean.

Another great **1st California Cavalry Indian fighter and leader was Major William McCleave.** He put in a report once: **"The Superiority of the Californians over the Apaches, at their own style of fighting, was evident".** He went on to give an example of Corporal Ellis, of Company A, who crawled to a rock with an Indian hiding behind it. Ellis gave a short cough, and when the Indian raised his head to discover his location, a bullet from Ellis' rifle dashed through his brain.

Another **great Indian fighter of the California Column was Captain James H. Whitlock, 5th Infantry, California Volunteers.**

April 7, 1864, Captain Whitlock commanded 26 enlisted men of company F and 20 enlisted men of Company I, under Lt. Barkell, and 10 enlisted men of Company C, First Cavalry, California Volunteers, and with them attacked 250 Indians close to Mount Grey, or also known as Sierra Bonita, Arizona. The fight lasted over an hour. The Indians were routed with 21 killed, a large number wounded, and the recovery of 40 horses and mules.

---

[17] Reference the California State Military Museum.

There are literally hundreds of examples of how bravely the members of the California Column and the New Mexico Volunteers preformed missions. Mostly under harsh conditions and almost universally won the skirmishes and full fledge battles with Indians of all bands. Report after report has them covering 700, 600, and 400 miles in single pursuit of Indians.

One incident in October of 1862 left a black mark on Colonel Kit Carson's career, although he had no direct involvement, it happened under his command of Fort Stanton.

One of his officers, Captain Craydon, of the New Mexico Volunteers ran into an old Mescalero Chief Manuelito with a small band (16) heading for Santa Fe to talk with Brig. General Carleton.

Captain Craydon "lured" the band into his camp at Gallinas Springs just north of Fort Stanton. He got them drunk, and had his men shoot them down in cold blood. He took their 17 horses back with them to Fort Stanton.

A good friend of Colonel Kit Carson was a doctor in Albuquerque by the name of John Marmaduke Witlock, M.D. He sent a letter to the Santa Fe Gazette "denouncing the act as barbaric treachery".

Captain Craydon reported to Colonel Kit Carson that he had refused to give whiskey to the Indians, and the old Chief decided to fight for the whiskey. He killed them in self-defense.

It seems impossible that an Indian expert, as Colonel Carson was, would have bought that story, but it was probably impractical to launch an investigation as there were no Indian witnesses that survived.

Dr. Witlock came to Fort Stanton to visit his old friend Colonel Kit Carson. He was engaged in a card game in the Sutler's store when Captain Craydon's name came up. There were "serious criticisms about the Captain's killing of sixteen Indians". One player left the tent to inform Captain Craydon.

He returned with a note from the Captain to Dr. Witlock. Dr. Witlock read it and signed at the bottom "accepted" sending it back to its author.

Dr. Witlock declared to the card players:

"That's a challenge. I'll have to fight."

They tried to talk him out of doing the same, to no avail.

The doctor picked up a colt from the table, and checked it over closely. He opened the flap of the tent and Captain Craydon was already there and armed.

Dr. Witlock fired first and Captain Craydon immediately returned fire. Both missed their targets and ducked for cover. The captain behind a wagon and the doctor crouched behind a Sibley tent. More shots were exchanged.

Captain Craydon grabbed his chest and yelled out: "The son of a bitch has killed me."

Doctor Witlock is wounded in the side and right hand.

Lt. Morris, of Captain Craydon's company, rushed to the site with 75 soldiers. They pursued and gun down Doctor Witlock. His body is thrown in a ditch and the soldiers kept firing round after round in to the lifeless body. Later it was estimated 130 bullets had been fired into the Doctor's body.

Colonel Kit Carson goes into a "towering rage". He had the entire company disarmed, and everyone believes with the intent of having them all shot! He investigated and placed the four "ringleaders" under arrest and held for civil authorities.

The four were: Lt. Phillip Morris, Private John Murray, Private Albert Oveall, and Private Estevan Aquilar.

The four were sent to be jailed in Santa Fe, New Mexico. On January 1, 1863 three of the prisoners escaped (Morris, Oveall, and Aquilar). Oveall is captured the next morning. The remaining two, Morris and Aquilar, are captured January 18, 1863 by Brigadier General Carleton personally.

The California Column performed their mission admirably and as agreed were mustered out August 31, 1864

Two new companies were organized from a few of the men whose terms had not expired. The new enlistments made up Company B and C. Two new companies of volunteers arrived from California to make Company A and E, and were assigned to Arizona.

A snap shot of leaders in Fort Stanton and Fort Sumner in 1865:

Fort Stanton –

Captain William Brady, Fort Commander and leader of 1st New Mexico Cavalry, Co. A[18]
Lt. Edwin J. Edgar, 1st New Mexico Cavalry, Co. A

Fort Sumner –
Captain Emil Fritz, 1st California Cavalry, Co. B[19]
Captain Lawrence G. Murphy, 1st N.M. Cavalry Co. G[20]
Captain Henry B. Bristol, 5th U.S. Cavalry Company D
Captain Samuel Gorham, 1st California Cavalry, Co. G
Lt. Robert Edmister, 1st California Cavalry, Co. A
Lt. Charles Speed, 5th U.S. Cavalry Company I

Las Cruces -
Captain James Whitlock, 1st California Cavalry, Co C
Lt. John E. Oliphant, 1st California Cavalry, Co M

Captain Brady, Colonel Fritz, and Major Murphy muster out of service in 1866.

Emil Fritz and Lawrence Murphy form a partnership and open a sutler store on Fort Stanton in an abandoned, adobe building. They were able to obtain a title to the adobe building. A young, eighteen-year-old Irish drummer boy mustered out and went to work as a bookkeeper for Murphy and Fritz in the sutler store. His name was James Dolan[21] and went by "Jimmy".

---

[18] William Brady became Sheriff of Lincoln County, a puppet lawman of Lawrence G. Murphy. It is for his murder that William H. Bonney alias Billy, The Kid is sentenced to hang in Lincoln, Lincoln County.

[19] Emil Fritz became a full partner with Lawrence G. Murphy in the Sutler Store at Fort Stanton. His life insurance policy triggers the Lincoln County War.

[20] Some historians report that Captain Lawrence G. Murphy also acted as Quartermaster reporting to Colonel Christopher "Kit" Carson. Col. Carson was the only commissioned officer in the history of the United States that was illiterate. He could not read nor write. That meant one of the biggest crooks of that era was his buyer of goods and services. It does give light to how and why he could start a Sutler Store at Fort Stanton. He also became friends with Thomas Benton Catron of Mesilla, New Mexico (later Santa Fe) who became the most powerful and wealthiest man in New Mexico. He was king of the Santa Fe Ring. Murphy was born in Wexford, Ireland in 1831. Died 7 am October 20, 1878 (47yrs old). He died in St. Vincent Hospital, Santa Fe, New. Mexico. In 1927, Frank Coe said: "The sisters cut him off his whiskey and he died shortly after that. And everyone rejoiced in it," (in Lincoln County). His estate was able to sell his Bar W Ranch for $225,000. Clearing a lot of his debt to Thomas Catron.

[21] James Dolan was born in Laughrea, County Galway, Ireland May 2, 1848 died February 6, 1898 on his ranch The Flying H Ranch, formerly John Tunstall's Felix

Colonel Emil Fritz - Jimmy Dolan and Lawrence Murphy - Captain William Brady

Two Men from Missouri Became Good Friends Missouri, 1860 - 1863

Thomas B. Catron and Stephen E. Elkins became good friends while attending Masonic College in Lexington, Missouri. They both went on to attend and graduate from the University of Missouri in Columbus, Missouri. Thomas received a degree in Law and Stephen a Business Administration Bachelor Degree in 1860.[22]

The storms of the Civil War were blowing strong. Stephen took a teaching job in Cass County, Missouri. One of his students was a young man named Thomas Coleman Younger, who went by Cole Younger. Their paths were to cross

---

River Ranch. Sometimes bad men win in the end. He is buried on Spring Ranch below Fritz Cemetery near Rio Bonito, New Mexico. As an accounting clerk for Lawrence G. Murphy he lost his temper and shot at Captain James Randlett at Ft. Stanton, resulting in L. G. Murphy and Co. being evicted from the base. After the death of Murphy's partner Emil Fritz and Murphy succumbing to sever alcoholism, he took over their company and changed the name to J. Dolan and Co. He ruled it with an iron fist. He took care of his friend and partner Murphy until Murphy's death. On May 9th, 1877 Jimmy Dolan killed Hilario Jaramillo personally, claiming self-defense. He was acquitted. After that he hired Will Davies aka Jesse Evans to do his killing. Evans and Company killed John Tunstall on Dolan's orders, igniting the Lincoln County War.

[22] He would go on to achieve a MBA Degree in 1868 from the same university. He did so while serving as U.S. Attorney for New Mexico.

several times in the near future.[23] The same would also have an effect on New Mexico.

When the Civil War started Thomas Catron joined the Confederate States of America and was commissioned an officer in the Confederate Army. His close friend Stephen Elkins joined the Union Army of the United States of America on a one year enlistment, and was commissioned a Captain of militia 77th Missouri Infantry serving under Colonel Kersey Coates.

Stephen's father and brother joined the Confederate Army. The Elkins family was divided father against son, and brother against brother.

After joining the Union Army Stephen not once, but twice, found himself surrounded by Confederate Captain William Quantrill's guerilla band, and both times he was alone. Both times there was a call for his immediate execution, and both times his former student, Cole Younger, was able to convince Quantrill to let him go in honor of his father and brother. Stephen got a strong sense there would not be a third time if caught again in the uniform of the Union Army.

The 77th Missouri Infantry was ordered to root out the Confederate guerillas recruiting in the Lone Jack area.

The small community of Lone Jack, Missouri had suffered border wars since 1854, seven years before the Civil War, and they continued long after the Civil War ended.

Neighbor against neighbor, all spying on each other, informing roving bands of guerillas who they "thought" were not loyal to their cause, resulting in innocent families being raided and killed.

Although Lone Jack was not right on the border roving bands of guerillas rode deep across both sides of the border with Kansas. Union renegade soldiers did the same. They crossed the border from Kansas and raided, killed, plumaged, looted, and stole slaves to free across the border.

Hatred was the flag banner on both sides of the Kansas Missouri border. Some raided and murdered for profit.

---

[23] Stephen Elkins would testify for Cole Younger in his request for a pardon after being sent to prison for the bank robbery attempt by the James-Younger gang in Northfield, Minnesota.

William Quantrill started his raiding career on the Union side under Captain Lane. That was until Captain Lane caught him stealing loot and killing his own men to eliminate witnesses. Quantrill switched sides and joined the Confederate cause.

The routing of rebels at Lone Jack turned into a full-fledged battle to be known as the Battle of Lone Jack. It was a fierce fight that lasted two days.

Captain Stephen Elkins looked across the battlefield and saw a young 18-year-old brave Confederate soldier riding up and down the front line helping supply troops with whatever they needed, including a great example of courage. It was Cole Younger! He then saw Younger disappear and reappear with Captain Foster a wounded Union officer. Later he would find out that Cole Younger had saved the Captain from being executed in a cabin.[24]

Stephen was sure Younger had seen him on the battle field.

Stephen's one-year enlistment was up. He felt his luck was running out in Missouri. He couldn't go home as his father and brother were still fighting for the Confederate cause. He was sure Cole Younger and other Quantrill men had seen him on the battle field. He would not survive another encounter with them, in or out of uniform.

He heard that the California Column of the Union had a strong hold on the New Mexico Territory and was headquartered in Mesilla, New Mexico. That was far enough away from Missouri to be comfortable, and get a fresh start without having to look over his back all the time. It was decided, he would move to Mesilla, New Mexico immediately.

[24] Captain Foster would also testify for Cole Younger in his request for a pardon after being sent to prison for the bank robbery attempt by the James-Younger gang in Northfield, Minnesota.

Stephen B. Elkins and Thomas B. Catron Change Everything for The New Mexico Territory

Thomas Catron

Stephen Elkins[25]

Stephen Elkins arrived in New Mexico at exactly the right time. The CSA had pulled out of their "Arizona Territory of the CSA", which included the New Mexico Territory. Brigadier General Canby had decisively beaten Confederate Brigadier General Sibley at the battle of Glorieta, New Mexico.[26]

General Sibley knew the California Column was about to reach New Mexico and he did not have the supplies to fight another battle against 2,300 well supplied and trained fighting men commanded by Brigadier General Carleton of whom he knew well. He knew he had no other choice but to pull back to Texas, and hope for another day to take New Mexico and Arizona (that day never came).

Brigadier General Carleton's California Column arrived in New Mexico. Brigadier General Canby was transferred back to

---

[25] Wikipedia photographs Source Palace of Governors New Mexico

[26] More accurately, 1,000 Colorado Volunteers and 700 regular Union soldiers at Fort Union won the battle for the Union. They did report to Brig. General Canby. Ironically, Fort Union was Sibley's last command as a Union officer before resigning to join the CSA army. Another irony was that all the Union troops were sleeping in "Sibley Tents" designed by Sibley while in the Union Army.

the war effort in the east.[27] Brig. General Carleton's orders were to focus on *"solving the depredations of the hostile Indians in New Mexico and Arizona Territories."* He re-occupied the abandon forts and began to do just that. He had a combined force of New Mexico Volunteers under Colonel Christopher Carson (Kit Carson), and the California Volunteers of the California Column.

Stephen Elkins noticed upon his arrival in Mesilla that there were very few attorneys in Mesilla and Los Cruces, New Mexico. He immediately opened a law office, was admitted to the Territorial Bar, and began practicing law. He practiced law for a year and was elected to the Territorial Legislature in 1864.

Many of the California Column soldier's enlistments were up in 1864 and chose to be discharged and stayed in New Mexico. Two new companies of soldiers arrived from California to replace them. Stephen's law practice was growing very well, as was his influence in the Republican Party of New Mexico.

Stephen Elkins spoke and wrote Spanish fluently. Most of Mesilla and Los Cruces were Hispanics. In fact, most of New Mexico was Hispanic. They flocked to him for all their legal work.

In 1865 the Civil War was over and many more decided to be discharged and settle in New Mexico. His friend Thomas B. Catron had been discharged from the CSA Army and returned home to discover his home and farm destroyed. He had nothing of value left.

Thomas received a message from his old college friend to join him in New Mexico. He had an idea that would (not could) make them both wealthy men. Thomas had everything to gain and nothing to lose, he headed for New Mexico. He arrived in 1866 after settling what affairs he could in Missouri.

Thomas Catron joined his friend's law firm as a full partner and went to work on the law offices back log of legal work. Stephen Elkins had been appointed to Territorial District Attorney and had been in that position a year upon Thomas's

---

[27] He distinguished himself, by taking the blame several times for General McClellan's short comings in battle strategies. He was the oldest general in the Union Army. He died while on leave to visit his daughter.

arrival in New Mexico. Thomas decided to settle in Las Cruces, a "new" town a few miles from the "old" town of Mesilla.[28]

Stephen shared his master plan with Thomas. He had made important connections with the Republican Party in Washington D.C. Ulysses S. Grant, the President of the United States, was going to appoint him United States Attorney for the New Mexico Territory. As such he would represent the United States in all legal matters in New Mexico.[29]

Elkins was also founding a bank named Santa Fe National Bank, and would also be its President. He had finagled himself into being President of the Maxwell Land Company after representing them in a Spanish grant dispute. His goal was to control the company and make him the largest land owner in New Mexico. That is where Thomas came in. He had the legal mind to pull off the largest land fraud scheme in American history.

The scheme was simple: the Maxwell Land Company would file law suits to evict "squatters" on its Spanish Grant (who were actually the legitimate heirs to the grant). Stephen had powerful connections in his position of U.S. Attorney, such as, U.S. Surveyor General, Territorial Judges, and Congressmen. He used these connections to patent Spanish and Mexican land grants in his name as a legitimate heir to the grant. This was in direct violation to the Treaty of Guadalupe Hidalgo of 1848 that ended the Mexican American War. Stephen and Thomas weren't going to let a treaty stand in the way of their becoming wealthy.

Their law firm being the only "experts" on land grants and the fact Stephen spoke fluent Spanish ended up representing <u>both</u> sides of the inevitable disputes from

---

[28] Mesilla was founded in 1851 and was part of "No-man's land", also referred to as the "New Mexico Badlands", which were the area bordering El Paso up to and including the Mesilla Valley along the Rio Grande River. It was claimed by both the U.S. and Mexico until the final border agreement of 1853. For a long time after the settlement of the borders it earned its reputation of "Badlands." The area was a rough and violent area to live in. Politics were sometimes settled by gunfights in the Mesilla Plaza. An honest governor of New Mexico in 1875 said he did not have the resources to solve the violence of Southern New Mexico.

[29] Stephen Elkins held that position from 1867 to 1870.

legitimate land grant heirs. They were not going to let a small thing like legal ethics stand in their way of becoming wealthy.

Stephen Elkins and Thomas Catron pulled it off and ended up owning, in their name, approximately thirty-four grants totaling almost three million acres. This made them the largest land owners in the United States, and the most powerful men in New Mexico.[30]

Quickly the Santa Fe National Bank was also in the railroad business, real estate financing, and mining interests. Stephen and Thomas were the center piece of what people were openly calling “”The Santa Fe Ring”. In general, it was a ruthless group of businessmen scattered all over the New Mexico Territory. If you wanted to buy real estate, they probably owned it. If you wanted to finance the construction of a building, they had the money. The Republican Party ran the politics of the territory, so if you wanted to run for office you would need their nod of approval.

Thomas Catron purchased a full city block in down town Santa Fe, the political capital of the territory. He decided to move there. He had married Stephen’s sister and wanted to pursue his own professional goals in politics. They remained partners in the powerful law firm.

Stephen Elkins remained in Mesilla and continued to accumulate extra ordinary wealth and political power at the national level.

As Stephen moved up the ladder of important positions he recommended Thomas to fill the position he was abandoning. First, Territorial District Attorney (1867 – 70). During this time, he was also granted a Master in Business Administration (MBA) from the University of Missouri in 1868. He was elected

---

[30]By 1875 the Santa Fe National bank was investing in railways, mining, and ranching interests. That year Stephen Elkins met and married his second wife Hallie Davis, which would have a major impact on his personal, professional, and financial future. In 1890 he would move to West Virginia to join his father-in-law in the family business The Davis Coal and Coke Company. In 1892 he was made a full partner and his father-in law Henry G. Davis represented West Virginia as a Senator in the U.S. Senate. The Davis Coal Company became the largest coal company in the world. Stephen was appointed Secretary of War from Dec. 17, 1891 to March 5, 1893. He ran in in 1895 to replace his retiring father-in-law in the Senate and won the election. He was re-elected twice and died in office in 1911.

Territorial Delegate to Congress of the U.S. in 1872 and re-elected in 1874 where he served until 1877. He met and married his second wife Hallie Davis in 1875. That was the year he formed the Santa Fe Nation Bank.

The Indian "Depredations" Under Control Who's Got the Beef?

Brigadier General Carleton was doing an excellent job of taking care of the Indian "Depredation" problem. Before eastern capital would invest large amounts in the west the Indian problem had to be solved. The general was being very aggressive in doing just that.

He ordered his right-hand man Colonel Christopher (Kit) Carson[31] to re-build Fort Stanton as a base of operations for rounding up the Mescalero Apache. Once rounded up drive them to Bosque Redondo. When completed he was to round up the Navajo tribe and drive them to Bosque Redondo. He was also to complete Fort Sumner to provide adequate accommodations for all personnel involved in controlling, clothing and feeding both tribes.

Colonel Carson was successful in completing his mission. One consistent problem was having enough beef to feed not only the approximately 5000 Navajo Indians and, 900 Mescalero Apache, but also all the soldiers at Fort Sumner and Fort Stanton.

Cattlemen Charles Goodnight and Oliver Loving had pioneered a trail up the Pecos River and camped at what they called "Camp Bosque Grande" just south of Fort Sumner. Unfortunately for Fort Sumner, his 2,000 head of cattle were heading for the high prices paid in Denver Colorado.

He had purchased that herd from a large cattle rancher John Simpson Chisum on his Concho River Range in Texas.

---

[31] Kit Carson was already a household name in the east as an explorer, scout for Fremont Expeditions, and a dime novel hero. Most importantly to Brig. General Carleton he was, in fact the most knowledgeable

Goodnight ordered a second herd from John Chisum for Chisum to drive up the Pecos Valley and on to Bosque Grande.

He informed Chisum he was going to abandon Bosque Grande Camp. John Chisum (starting with 900 head from the Concho River Range) arrived in Bosque Grande with about 2,500 head of cattle. He picked up every stray cow and unbranded calf, along the trail and placed his brand on them.

If the legitimate owner made claim he would fight to keep all cows with his brand on them (no matter how they were obtained) in his possession. That was his "policy".

To enforce this policy, he always had tough Texas gunmen receiving fighting wages to protect and execute his "policy". The result was that all the small cattlemen along the border and up the Pecos (such as, the Seven Rivers Ranch of "Old Man" Hugh Beckwith) hated John Chisum with a passion. Chisum acquired some powerful enemies in New Mexico.

Chisum saw the potential in the Pecos Valley to build a huge herd to be delivered a short distance to Las Vegas, New Mexico. It was only a matter of time until the railroad would follow the Santa Fe Trail to Santa Fe and it would go right through Las Vegas, New Mexico.

The Pecos Valley had tall grass and year-round water. Chisum's herd grew fast. The herd was scattered from Bosque Grande south to the Hondo River inlet, to the Pecos River.

He had two serious obstacles in building his herd. Mescalero Apaches were now raiding his remuda de caballos. He didn't mind them taking a cow every once in a while to feed a family, but to raid his remuda and steal his most valuable asset...his horses! That had to stop! A good horse could cost $100 and that was big money. If they stole a mare it was as good as taking two horses. All his mares were breeding mares.

His second serious obstacle was Lawrence G. Murphy and Company. Murphy put the word out that he would pay $5 a head for any cattle brought to his ranch with no regard to brand. He had the contract to supply the military base in the area and the allotment given to the Mescalero Apaches. He had the contract but few cattle.

Two rustlers could cut out 15 head of cattle, spend three days driving them to White Oak, and make a month wages each. That infuriated John Chisum to no end.

One day in 1872 a young Texas gunman arrived at Bosque Grande. Chisum hired him after a recommendation from his foreman, and gave him the following orders: "When the next Apaches raid my remuda, you get my horses back and punish the offending Apaches. Kill the offenders and shoot up their camp, but return safely with my horses," or words to that to that extent.

Chisum believed it would only take one or two times and they would stop raiding his remuda. He thought wrong.

The young gunman went by the alias name of Jesse Evans.[32] The reports to Chisum reflected the young gun was doing his job very effectively, but the Apaches kept up their raiding.

Every time they raided a remuda Jesse Evans hand-picked some Texas hard cases and returned with the horses after punishing the offending band of Mescalero Apaches. He killed many Apaches on each recovery. It went on for nearly three years before the Apaches stopped raiding Chisum's remuda.

Evans' reputation was well established as a cold-blooded killer. He did not play with his pistols or rifle like Frank Baker and others, spinning them, pulling them in and out of their holsters, practicing a fast draw. No, when Evans pulled a gun, someone died.

Those that rode with him said they always warned a new rider to not argue with Evans, or go against his instruction in the slightest way. If they did not listen he would shoot the cowboy between the eyes, and it would be reported the cowboy was killed in action with Apaches. Jesse Evans had a zero-tolerance policy when it came to his orders.

John Chisum suspected Evans was rustling for extra income, even when he was paying him top fighting wages. He had no proof as no one would "witness" or "testify" against Evans.

In the **fall of 1874** Jesse Evans packed his bed role, saddled up, and rode west to the Mesilla Valley across the Rio Grande. There he met John Kinney[33], who had started a ranch

---

[32] Real name was William "Will" Davies, the author's great-great uncle.

[33] U.S. Army Cavalryman, 1867 -1873. Born August 31, 1847 Died August 25, 1919 in Prescott, Arizona. He was known in New Mexico as the "King of the Rustlers". He was once found guilty of murdering Frank Emmons, sentenced to 7 years, but

in the Mesilla Valley not far from Los Cruces, New Mexico. He had been discharged from Fort Selden.

In a short time, John Kinney had gathered together what a local newspaper man described as every scoundrel, rustler, and killer in southern New Mexico as his "ranch hands". They were rustling and robbing all over southern New Mexico. They killed anyone that got in their way.

John Kinney and Jesse Evans became good friends. Kinney declared Jesse as his second in command. Whatever orders Jesse gave, his gang was to consider it from him.

Evans continued to build Kinney's gang to a solid twenty men and could double that number if needed. They entered into a mutual relationship with other gangs in what was being described as "chain gangs". These gangs were as far away as the Clanton's in Arizona to The Seven River Warriors ("Old Man" Hugh Beckwith) at Seven Rivers on the lower Pecos River Valley.

One gang would rustle Mexican cattle and sell to another gang who would sell to another gang so that the "chain" of ownership and original offending rustlers could not be discovered easily. The same went for cattle rustled from Chisum. Ownership went through a couple "outfits" before arriving at Murphy's Ranch near White Oaks, New Mexico.

The Horrell Brothers Escape the Hangman's Noose in Texas, and Arrive in The Ruidoso Valley, New Mexico.

Mart, Tom, Merritt, Ben and Sam Horrell were the bad boys of Lampasas, Texas. They pretty much did whatever they wanted to do, when they wanted to do it. They expected absolute loyalty from their ranch hands, and in turn gave it.

---

served only 3 years. He was hired as a "gunman" by Lawrence G. Murphy, and later by James (Jimmy) Dolan of Lincoln County. His only known close friend was Jesse Evans an alias for William "Will" Davies of Texas.

January 1873 Lampasas County Sheriff Shadrick T. Denson arrived at the Horrell ranch to arrest Wash and Mark Short. The Horrell brothers defended their friends. A gun fight broke out resulting in the sheriff's death.

February 10, 1873 seven state police officers under the command of Captain Thomas Williams arrived in Lampasas, Texas to arrest the Horrell brothers for the murder of Sheriff Denson.

March 14, 1873 State Police Officers Andrew Melville, Wesley Cherry, and Jim Daniels arrested Bill Bowen who was married to the Horrell brother's sister.

The officers brought Bowen to Jerry Scott's Saloon where the Horrell brothers were having a few drinks. It can be surmised that the officers interrogated Bowen as to where their prime targets for arrest were, and he accommodated them.

An "unfriendly" conversation took place for a few minutes, when all hell broke loose in a gun fight. The result of which killed all four state police officers, including their commander Captain Williams. Before succumbing to his wounds, Captain Williams severely wounded Mart and Tom Horrell.

The Horrell brothers knew their time was up in Lampasas, Texas. Their time was up in Texas period. The Governor would next send a company of Texas Rangers and they would not survive a fight with them. The Texas Rangers were given unlimited ammunition and expected to practice shooting every day they were not on an assignment. To quote a Texas Ranger of the Frontier Battalion when asked by his grandson Chester Locklear[34]:

"How did you get so good with a gun?"

He answered: "Not by saving ammunition."

He then shot a can off a fence post, hit it two more times in the air, and re-holstered his pistol before it hit the ground. Young Chester smiled ear to ear and hoped someday he could be that good.

---

[34] Chester Locklear was a very good friend of the authors. His father had a ranch on the Texas-New Mexico border north east of Fort Sumner. His grandfather was one of the first Texas Rangers in the Frontier Battalion. He spent most of his service time in West and Southwest Texas.

Mart Horrell needed to heal up from his severe wound. He was the oldest and leader of the brothers. He sent his brother Ben and some hands to investigate settling in the Ruidoso Valley of New Mexico. Lawmen hesitated chasing anyone into the "Badlands" of New Mexico, and the Texas Rangers had no jurisdiction in New Mexico.

Ben arrived in the Ruidoso Valley, Lincoln County New Mexico Territory. He immediately befriended the newly elected Sheriff of Lincoln County Jack Gylam. The Horrells had a way of taking someone they liked in like family. If they liked you they would lay their own life on the line for you.

Sheriff Gylam and Ben Horrell became blood brothers. Where ever you saw one the other was sure to be around. The remainder of the Horrell family arrived from Texas driving every head of cow they had in Lampasas. Mart was left behind still recovering from his wound.

Texas State Police found Mart Horrell with some friends and arrested them all. They placed them in the Georgetown, Texas jail. Thirty of Mart Horrells friends stormed the jail and broke him out a free man. He immediately headed for Ruidoso Valley, New Mexico Territory.

The sleepy little village of La Placita Del Rio Bonito had been renamed when the county was named "Lincoln County" in honor of Abraham Lincoln. The Territory of New Mexico was solidly a Republican Territory. It was now the town of Lincoln, Lincoln County New Mexico Territory. It had grown to be a real township and center of all commerce in Lincoln County.

Lawrence G. Murphy had been forced to move his sutler store off the Fort Stanton base. His bookkeeper, Jimmy Dolan, had lost his temper one day and shot at Captain James Randlett. That was the straw that broke the camel's back.

It turned out to be a blessing in disguise. The U.S. Army paid L. G. Murphy and Company $8000 for the dilapidated adobe building on the base.

Murphy moved into temporary quarters in Lincoln while building his "house" across the street. A large two-story building that greatly expanded his capacity to store and present hard and soft goods.[35] It, and all the men in it, became to be known as "The House."

He built "The House" with forced labor of Mexicans, local Anglo farmers, and ranchers. They owed substantial amounts in building their own ranches to L. G. Murphy and Co. It was the only source of supplies without traveling all the way to Mesilla, Las Cruces, or Santa Fe.

Murphy forced them to work it off constructing the new two-story store, or face foreclosure on their ranches, or worse. He had hired some rough characters to execute his will on them.

The Horrell brothers were introduced to the Mexican dances in Lincoln. They enjoyed the dances and senoritas, but not the Mexicans in general. They were strongly prejudiced against Mexicans.

December 1, 1873 Sheriff Jack Gylam and Ben Horrell got drunk and were shooting in the streets of Lincoln. Lincoln Constable Juan Martinez was able to disarm them, but made no arrests. The two acquired two more pistols and this time were shooting up the inside of a Lincoln brothel.

Constable Martinez attempts to arrest them, but is shot dead by Gylam and Ben Horrell. The two try tried to escape from Lincoln but were killed by deputies before being able to.

Mart Horrell was furious and had nothing less than serious retaliation is on his mind. The brothers kill two prominent Mexican ranchers.

Newly elected Sheriff Alexander Hamilton Mills forms a posse and a short distance from town are confronted by the Horrell brothers and their ranch hands. The stand-off is intense. The posse backs down and retreats to Lincoln.

December 20, 1873 Mart Horrell, his brothers, and ranch hands storm a Hispanic celebration in Lincoln. They kill four men and wound one woman. Shortly after Edward "Little" Hart, a Horrell hand, kills Deputy Sheriff Joseph Hakins for marrying a Hispanic woman.

Just after Christmas around **December 27, 1873** the Horrell brothers stop a freight wagon near Roswell, New Mexico

---

[35] "The House" still stands to this date. It also served as Lincoln County seat, Lincoln County Court House, and as J. Dolan and Co. store after he took over Murphy's business.

Territory on the Hondo River road. They kill all five Hispanic men with the freight wagon.

The new Territorial Governor put a $500 per head reward for the "cowboys" that killed the Hispanics in Lincoln, New Mexico. Finally, the horrific Horrell brothers leave New Mexico and head back to Lampasas, Texas.

The official records state they killed twelve men during their killing spree in New Mexico. The Hispanic community disagreed with that number. They said before they left the Horrell brothers and their ranch hands rode up and down the Ruidoso Valley, the Bonito River, and the Hondo and killed forty Hispanics in that last killing spree alone.

The new Sheriff of Lincoln County requested help from Fort Stanton, but by the time the soldiers arrived in the Ruidoso Valley the Horrells were long gone with all their cattle and horses. [36]

---

[36] Extracted and updated from Wikipedia whom sourced public no-fee internet site on July 18, 2013. A list of sources for this document can be found at the end: "**February, 1874**, the Horrell brothers had returned to Lampasas, Texas but found they were not given a warm welcome. They were still wanted for the killing the Sheriff. The brothers were arrested for the murders of the lawmen in Lampasas, but due to a local jury hearing the case, they were acquitted. Shortly after their acquittal, John "Pink" Higgins accused the Horrell brothers of cattle rustling. The brothers were arrested, but again due mostly to a local jury hearing the case, they were acquitted. Although things were tense between the two families, no actions were taken by either side until **January 22, 1877**. On that day, while in the *Wiley and Toland's Gem Saloon* in Lampasas, John Higgins shot and killed Merritt Horrell in a gunfight.

The three remaining Horrell brothers vowed they would take revenge against John Higgins. His brother-in-law Bob Mitchell, and friend Bill Wren, voiced this publicly on several occasions. On **March 26, 1877**, Tom and Mart Horrell were shot and wounded during an ambush, but both survived. John Higgins and Bob Mitchell were being sought for the Merritt Horrell gunfight, and both surrendered shortly after the ambush to Texas Ranger Captain John Sparks, best known for his earlier 1876 capture of gunman Billy Thompson. Both men posted a $10,000 bond and were released. The local courthouse was burglarized shortly thereafter, with several records stolen including their bonds. The shooting of Merritt Horrell was later ruled self-defense, and the charges dropped.

Lampasas Square Shoot Out

On **June 7, 1877**, John Higgins', brother-in-law Bob Mitchell, Bob's brother Frank, Bill Wren, and another brother-in-law, Ben Terry, rode into Lampasas. The Horrell brothers and several friends were already in town that day, and gathered at the square. It is unknown who fired first, but it is believed that someone within the Horrell faction opened fire on the Higgins faction. When it was over, Bill Wren had been wounded, Frank Mitchell had been killed, and Horrell faction members Buck Waltrup and Carson Graham were killed.

Texas Rangers descended on the town only days later. All three Horrell brothers were arrested, and Texas Ranger Major John B. Jones acted as a mediator between the two sides to calm matters. Less than one year later, Mart and Tom Horrell were arrested in Meridian, Texas for armed robbery and murder. While confined to the local jail, vigilantes broke in and shot them both, killing them. Although never proven, it was speculated that John Higgins instigated the murders. Sam Horrell was now the only remaining Horrell brother. He moved his family to Oregon in 1882, then later to California. He died there in 1936. John Higgins was viewed as a hero locally, and is often credited with bringing down the Horrell Brothers. He later worked as a range detective, and developed a considerable reputation as a gunman, and in September, 1877, Higgins killed cowboy Ike Lantier, whom he caught stealing cattle, after Lantier drew on him. That shooting was also ruled self-defense. On October 4, 1903, he killed gunman and former lawman Bill Standifer in a gunfight, after Standifer had threatened Higgins son Cullin, a local district attorney. Higgins died on December 18, 1914. At the time of his death, Higgins is believed to have killed fourteen men in gunfights." Sources: https://en.wikipedia.org/wiki/Horrell_Brothers, https://web.archive.org/web/20121023063041/http://www.tshaonline.org/handbook/online/articles/jch03, and https://www.legendsofamerica.com/tx-horrellbrothers.html, http://www.waymarking.com/waymarks/WM11X0.

Governor Marsh Giddings, An Honest Governor for The New Mexico Territory, is Replaced by

A Dishonest Governor: Samuel Beach Axtell

January 1874 the first day the new Territorial Governor of New Mexico, Marsh Giddings, took office he quickly discovered what he had taken on. Also, possibly why Washington D. C.'s first choice turned the job down. A summary of critical "problems" was on his desk that morning:

Mesilla, New Mexico had a riot in the square with politicians from both parties shooting it out across the square.

The Horrell brothers and the elected Lincoln County sheriff were shooting up the town of Lincoln together.

Cimarron was a hot bed of lawlessness; Colfax County War was simmering. The Santa Fe Ring wanted the "trouble-makers" eliminated.

Fort Sumner was a magnet for wanted men from everywhere: Texas, Kansas, Colorado, Arizona, and New Mexico. Southern New Mexico had roving gangs of gunmen led by John Kinney that pretty much did and took whatever they wanted.

He immediately requested troops to assist him in controlling all the violence across the Territory of New Mexico, especially in the southern region. He was told in clear terms that no help would be coming forth unless requested by the U. S. Marshall and then only in the most extreme circumstances.

The governor couldn't imagine anything more extreme than what he was facing. The good Governor Giddings, an honest man, died of a heart attack in office June 3, 1875 not realizing his mission to civilize the New Mexico Territory.

Ulysses S. Grant, President of the United States, would then make one of the worst appointments of his career, he appointed Samuel Beach Axtell as the new Territorial Governor of New Mexico. Honesty is certainly a word not used to describe Governor Axtell. He was described by one federal employee as: "having more corruption, fraud, mismanagement, plots and murder than any other Governor in the history of the United States."[37]

Now New Mexico had a corrupt Governor, corrupt financial institutions, corrupt judicial, and bought and paid for law enforcement. The bad guys were in charge! When all else failed, they murdered their opponents without hesitation. One example of this was how Governor Axtell responded to a request by "leading citizens" of Cimarron to meet with them concerning the merging of Colfax County to Taos County. One of the Santa Fe Ring members in Las Vegas, Ben Stevens, was to "arrange" the meeting in Cimarron. The Governor sent the following letter to Ben Stevens:

> *"Dear Ben,*
> *I do not think your definite business is suspected... Hatch [Col. Edward Hatch Commander of the Military Department] says their opinion is that you weakened, and did not want to arrest the man. Have your men placed to arrest him and to kill all the men who resist you or stand with those who do [no]) resist you. Our*

---

[37] Frank Angel report to the Treasury Department and the Department of the Interior.

man signed the invitation with others who were at that meeting for me to visit Colfax... Porter, Morley, Springer, et al....do not hesitate at extreme measures. Your honor is at stake now, and a failure is fatal. Yours, etc., S.B. Axtell[38]

Read again the Governor's first sentence: **"I do not think your definite business is suspected."** His business was to kill Robert Clay Allison and all the other leaders of Colfax County that thought they were going to meet with the Governor. His last sentence: **"Your honor is at stake now, and a failure is fatal."** One possible interpretation of this simple instruction...get it done or you will be the next target of The Ring. Kill Allison or die yourself.

What did Clay Allison do to bring the wrath of the Santa Fe Ring down on him? Answer: he switched sides. He was a Judas to them. He was their man in Cimarron and Colfax County. The problem was he discovered the status quo leaders in New Mexico were the bad guys. They were crooks and could not be trusted. The merger of the two counties was to dilute the influence of Cimarron's leading citizens. Clay Allison was the leader of the Cimarron citizens. He decided not to do their bidding. That was a terminal offense to Catron and Elkins. The Ring made a deal with an accused murderer, he goes free, but must assassinate Clay Allison. The assassin was too slow, and Allison shot him dead in a Cimarron hotel saloon.

Clay Allison decided to go back to Texas and leave New Mexico with all its corruption. The Governor was probably fortunate that Clay Allison did not know of that letter at the time. He may have well walked into Governor Axtell's office in Santa Fe and shot him, and then left New Mexico. Allison was not a man to take threats lightly. He did know the Governor broke his word and no-showed their "arranged" meeting. That

---

[38] Sharon Cunningham article Wild West Magazine October 2013 issue pages 40-45. Miss Cunningham has researched and studied The Colfax War and Robert Clay Allison's involvement in it. She retired as editor of Pioneer Press and the National Muzzle Loading Rifle Association's Muzzle Blasts magazine. She changed this author's opinion of Robert Clay Allison.

spoke volumes as to what the Governor, and the Santa Fe Ring, thought of Cimarron Citizens.

The fact was New Mexico was "owned" by the Santa Fe Ring and if you were a friend of theirs you could commit murder in broad daylight and nothing would be done about it. But if you were an enemy, you could count the days you had left on this earth, because they were numbered.

Politically, all The Ring members were powerful men in the Republican Party. Steve Elkins, and eventually Thomas Catron, were also well connected in Washington D.C. in the Republican Party. All the stars were lined up for Catron and Elkins. By 1875 they were the largest land owners in the United States, and the wealthiest in the New Mexico Territory. Anybody or anything that stood in their way would be crushed.

Lawrence G. Murphy was their man in Lincoln County. Thomas Catron financed "The House" and held a first trust deed on it and Murphy's ranch. Ironically, Murphy was a kingpin Democrat. The Santa Fe Ring didn't care much about local politics, only that you did their bidding and didn't go against them in any way, shape, or form. Another example of that was their attempted assassination of Juan Patrón. He was in their party! A Republican! Santa Fe Ring Rule #1: They are in charge of everything! Rule#2: If in doubt read rule # 1. The bad guys are in charge! Of everything!

New York City, Lower East Side - mid 1800s
Source: Digital Collections.archives.nysed.gov

Chapter One

New York City
Lower East-side
November, 1859

Mother Nature seemed to skip over fall and go directly into winter this year. The temperature was almost a record low. It snowed at night and melted into slush the next morning.

Wood and coal were being sold at ridiculously high prices. The northern wind off the Hudson River could chill you to the bone.

A small, six-year-old girl was on Bowery Street begging

for coins to help feed her mother and herself. The wind was blowing, and she began to shiver from the cold. Her cotton dress and shawl were not enough against the elements.

Her mother had given up and returned to their basement apartment they shared with twenty-five other people. Her daughter insisted on staying longer on the street in hopes of collecting enough for food. She was very hungry; her stomach was aching.

One man, a ruffian living in the basement, had assigned himself as the landlord and collected from everyone to pay the actual owner of the building. He was taking a cut for his "services" to the owner.

The little girl's mother had agreed to allow her daughter, at enormous risk, to stay begging as she had not paid her share of the rent that week. Those that did not pay on time would be thrown out in the cold, or worse.

The little girl gave up begging on the street having been defeated by the cold wind cutting through her flimsy clothes, freezing her to the bone. She had a blue look about her as she snuggled up next to her mother in the basement.

Her mother wrapped her thin arms around her and pulled her closer to give whatever little warmth that she had left in her own body.

"How much did you get?" The ruffian's asked as he stood over her and her mother.

"Nothing!" The little girl answered.

"You're a damn liar," the ruffian replied, as he hit the little girl and her mother across both of their faces with the back of his large hand.

A couple of brave souls began to get up to come to their rescue. The ruffian roared like a lion fending off competition:

"I will kill the first man that defends this little thief."

The ruffian then turned his attention back to the little girl, who was now crying uncontrollably.

"Now, I'll ask you one more time... How much did you get?"

As he said the words he could see the little girl had a coin in her tiny fist. The edge was showing between her finger and thumb as she clenched her fist.

"Nothing!" She repeated.

The ruffian pulled a large knife from its sheath and raised his left hand as though he was going to hit the girl and her mother again.

The two, mother and daughter, covered their face in a defensive move.

The ruffian lunged his knife through the little girl, into her midsection below the sternum. Hideously he moved the big knife left and right, almost cutting the little girl in half.[39]

The little girl's mother let out a blood-curdling scream. The ruffian back handed the mother as she reached for her dying little girl and bellowed:

"You don't touch her!" as he swung around to find the entire room in shock. He yelled at them:

"That goes for all of you too!"

He then pried open the little girl's death grip on the coin in her fist. He pulled out the coin, it was a penny! The little girl had given her life for one penny! He stuck the penny in his pocket, and turned to the basement inhabitants:

"Anyone touches her, I'll kill them next. She is to remind all of you not to lie to me! Never, never lie to me!" He barked out like the animal he was.

Three days went by before the little girl's mother convinced the ruffian to allow her to bury her daughter. He finally agreed, but she had to do so in the corner of the basement. He wanted all living in the basement to see the grave as a reminder of what he would do to them.

It was very hard to dig in the near frozen dirt of the basement floor. She dug a shallow grave, and placed her beloved daughter into it. There was some comfort knowing she wasn't going to have to suffer any more. She missed her little angel so much she cried most of the time. She cried until there were no more tears to cry with.[40]

On the fourth morning since her little girl was killed, the mother awoke because several people were standing around her

---

[39] This is a true story, only the conversations are fictional.

[40] This a true story that happened during the stated period of time. All after this footnote is fictional writing. The newspaper reports of this little girl being killed did not state anyone being arrested or revenged for it. As I'm sure there was no arrest I have written the latter to calm my own soul, and the reader's as well.

in a half circle. For a moment she was frightened, and then the group of people peeled back leaving her line of sight open.

As they separated, they pointed towards the opposite wall. There was the ruffian, propped up against the wall with his throat cut ear to ear! The mother's tears began to fall, this time they were tears of happiness. A man in his mid-forties stepped up and handed her a sheathed butcher knife. He said:

"You keep this ma'am...it is yours," he said softly.

She looked into his soft eyes and knew he had used this knife to end the ruffian's life. She replied:

"No, but thank you so very much! I would cut myself with it." She gave a smile, the first she had smiled in very long time"

"Alright, here...I want you to be able to protect yourself in the future," he said as he handed her a small dagger in a leather sheath.

"Thank you," she replied as she placed the sheath in her calf-length boot. "I can handle this one," she smiled again.

The man turned and ordered two men to carry the ruffian's body out to the street.

"If there are no police in sight...take the body to the end of the block and place him in the drain trough. Then go find a policeman and tell him you found him there, and he is to get the body out of the area."

The men had the body down the street and in the drain trough in a minute. There wasn't a policeman in sight. There never is when you really need one. This time it worked to their advantage.

The man then turned to the mother and said: "We will find a cemetery and your little girl will get a Christian burial."

She replied: "Thank you...thank you," as tears rolled down her face.

"I promise you had I known what he was up to I would have killed him that night. It happened too fast and then I had to wait for the right moment. I'm sure you didn't know, but he slept with one eye open for three days. When he shut both, I took him out! You are safe now, ma'am."

The American Dream was not very good for the Irish living in New York City.

It was one thing to have to survive with the Dead Rats Gang and the Bowery Boys Gang fighting in the streets, back alleys, or where ever they ran into each other, and quite another to have a murder-a-night on just one street in the Lower East-side of New York City.[41] Law enforcement did not investigate any of them. Human life was worthless with so many ruffians running wild and ruling the streets.

The Irish arrived in the Lower East-Side of New York City at 30,000 people a year since the Potato Famine in Ireland had begun in September 1845 and ended in 1852. Ireland lost between 1-to-1.5 million people to the famine.

They pushed the Blacks out of half the lower-east-side. The middle class had exited decades before when the water supply became so contaminated that diseases ran rampant.

The Irish took over Tammany Hall, the political center of the lower east side. Next, they took over the politics citywide and eventually took over top political positions in New York State.

Nothing happened in New York without a cut to "Boss" Tweed. He ruled New York City with an iron fist, and William "Bill the Butcher" Poole, the leader of the Bowery Boys, was his enforcer.

The good people of lower-east-side really thought the worst was over when a man named Baker shot and killed William Poole, aka "The Butcher."[42] They thought wrong! "Boss" Tweed just put another ruffian in charge and carried on, business as usual.

---

[41] This is a real statistic for this period of time. On one street there was a murder recorded on average every single night for several years. Source is New York Historical Street Archives.

[42] Reported by The Brooklyn Eagle 3-10-1855. The Butcher was killed (died from his wounds received February 24, 1855) 3-8-1855 "Baker fired the shot that killed the elite rum shop rowdy, forgoing, biting, brutal savage whose end is quite in accordance to his past life residing in the 9 ward. He died at 33 years and 8 months of age."

William "The Butcher" Poole

The Irish political machine was all about power and money. The good Irish people who sought a better life in America were living like slaves to their own kind, Irishmen that drank the devil's wine and ate the devil's food.

"Boss" Tweed didn't care much about city services like law enforcement, sewer systems, clean water, or better schools. The Irish on the lower east-side were to provide cheap labor, pay for protection, and donate to his reelection. God needed to help the man who was caught voting against him, or even speaking out against him.

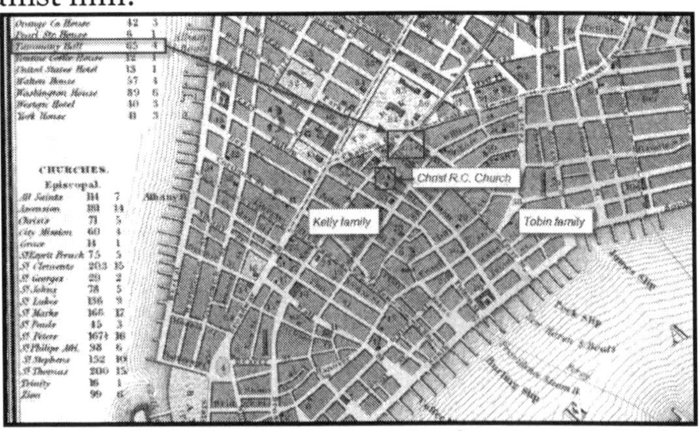

New York City 1850 Arrow pointed to Tammany Hall
Digital Collection.archives.nysed.gov

Source: New York Historical Society, New York city 1860 Photographs

Chapter Two

Michael and Catherine McCarty
New York City
Lower East-Side
April, 1859[43]

Michael and Catherine arrived from Cork, Cork County Ireland with their minds and hearts full of the "American

---

[43] The following chapter stories are fictional. William Henry McCarty was born at 70 Allen Street November 23, 1859. The author was able to confirm this through the street archives of New York City. In 1932 the city was widening Allen Street from 32 feet wide to 138feet wide. They noted it was a shame they had to tear down 70 Allen Street where Billy, The Kid was born.

Dream". They had heard fantastic stories of success in America. Young men had become millionaires overnight.

Anyone that worked hard, had initiative, and determination could be very successful. They were both intelligent and Michael had a grade-school level education obtained from Cork. The University of Cork had just opened its doors to qualified students when they had the opportunity to go to America. It was an easy choice, America for the McCarty family.

Being intelligent as they were, they saw the "big picture" arriving at the docks in Lower East-Side, New York City. The dock workers were all Irish and had serious looks on their faces. One asked Michael:

"Protestant or Catholic?" he asked, as though it really mattered.

"Protestant. Is that important here in America?" Michael asked sincerely.

"Yes, it is. Young man, make sure you do not travel across the Catholic streets at night," the husky redhead warned Michael.

"How can I tell? I don't know any of the streets here." Michael was very concerned for his family.

"Take that pretty wife and your boy up to Allen Street. The further away from the docks and five corners the better" the redhead answered with good advice.

They were interrupted by the redhead's boss:

"If catch you lollygagging and talking one more time, you will be making your living cleaning spittoons, and living in a Bowery basement with fifty others like you. Get to work!" The man threatened.

"Stay away from Bowery Street! My name is James McClung," he said to Michael just before barking back at his boss:

"The day you fire me you'll inherit a brand-new pig sticker," James bellowed authoritatively back at his boss.

His boss stopped in his tracks, turned around, and stared at James. The two men stared down for a full minute. It seemed like ten minutes to Michael, as he directed his wife and son to move on.

James's boss broke the stare down by firmly saying: "James that would be a fool's errand. Now get to work!"

James knew he had pushed his boss to the edge, so he walked past him toward the unloading ship, and began working twice as hard as anyone else on the crew.

He knew that was the real reason he could get away with snapping back at the boss. He would have to hire two to replace him. Pushed too far though, he would do just that, but not this time.

Carriages were driving up and leaving every few seconds. After listening to James McClung, he decided to use part of his savings to hitch a ride to this "Allen Street" James was talking about.

"Hail, here sir!" Michael called out to the carriage driver.

"Where to young man?" the driver asked as he pulled up and Michael was helping Catherine into the carriage.

"Allen Street sir," Michael replied.

"Allen Street is a long street sir, what address?" the driver inquired.

"We don't know yet, sir. A Mr. McClung told us it would be best for us," Michael answered.

"You must be Protestant?" the driver asked.

"Yes sir, and that seems to be a big thing in America. I thought this was the land of freedom of religion and freedom of speech?" Michael replied puzzled.

The carriage driver gave out a loud, belly laugh as he pulled his carriage onto the muddy road.

"Yes, that it is laddy! You are also free to get yourself killed in the wrong neighborhood. Five Corners is survival of the fittest. Nature's law rules in New York City. If your Protestant you best stay away from Bowery Street and your Mr. McClung guided you correctly...Allen Street would be good for you. Say, did he tell you how it got its name?" the driver asked like an anxious story teller hoping McClung had not.

"No sir, just to find living quarters there," Michael replied.

"Well, it was named after Captain William Henry Allen. He is a great American hero of the War of 1812! He sailed to the English Channel and sunk 8 Brit's ships before they got him! He was the Brits worst nightmare. How could one American ship sail into their harbor and sink eight ships? They are still asking themselves that question...ha!" he laughed with that bellowing laugh again and continued saying:

"You know, I know of an apartment that is available. I don't know how much it is, but I'll take you there. You are lucky you got me as your driver, but you wouldn't know that. You are a green horn, and as green as they get," the driver stated matter-of-factly.

"I don't understand sir," Michael honestly responded.

"Well, first a lot of those carriages are carrying green horns like you to Dead Rats and Bowery Boys alleys to get rolled of every cent they have! It is pay up or die, right there, right then!" he replied.

Catherine could not hold herself back: "That is disgraceful, ungodly, immoral, and just plain mean!"

"Yes, ma'am, that it is...all that and more! Don't get angry with me I'm not on any gang's payroll. You are lucky you got me as your carriage driver, that you are, ma'am!" The driver concluded. He pulled up Allen Street and continued five blocks to a two-story brick building on the right. It was 70 Allen Street and looked much better than any of the other buildings they had passed.

"Here you are sir. I didn't catch your name?" the driver asked politely.

"Michael McCarty, sir. I do know how lucky we were to get you as our driver. Thank you very much!" He paid the driver one British pound.

"No, sir that is not right. That is way too much! Two bits. If you need change I have it. Also, don't show pound notes around town. They are valuable on the black market. Please understand for your family's sake, these streets are very dangerous." He advised Michael as he gave him change. The driver helped Michael with his two large trunks. Everything they had in the world was in those trunks.

Michael was able to negotiate a fair rental for their new apartment, and they got settled in quickly. Catherine seemed pleased with the apartment. She broke the news to Michael that she was pregnant again.

"I must find a job, now!" Michael's immediate reaction to the news was an extreme sense of responsibility and urgency.

Joseph was four-years-old, and he had learned a lot about fatherhood with him, but another baby at this time. Whew! That was a lot for Michael to comprehend at this moment.

"Don't worry Michael, I have decided to take in cleaning for extra money. We will do just fine!" the always optimistic, jolly, Irish lady Catherine came out in full bloom. She knew how worried her husband was, so she waited until they found a house they could call home before telling him she was pregnant.

70 Allen St. Lower East-Side New York City Map 1860
Source: David Rumsey Historical Map collection

Chapter Three

William Henry McCarty Born New York City Lower East-side November 23, 1859

November was one of the coldest on record in New York City. Michael worked hard labor at the docks. Catherine took in laundry to supplement Michael's meager wages.

Michael was very apprehensive, he had to inform Catherine that the warehouse owner he worked for was buying more slaves.

The practice was frowned upon in New York, but it was happening more and more, and every time an Irishman lost a job. The owners claimed they needed to stay competitive.

The only reason they were not operating with all slaves was the Irish made it clear if they did, so they would burn everything the man owned. Therefore, they would buy a slave every once in a while, but not enough to start a riot.

The Irish didn't mind the paid blacks in the factories. They were not real competitors, but slaves were!

It was near dark when Michael arrived home from work. He entered their apartment, kissed Catherine and said:

"Dear, we are moving soon to Indianapolis, Indiana," he said apprehensively. He had no idea how she would take this information nine months pregnant with their second child.

"ok, how soon is soon?" Catherine replied in a very agreeable manner.

"When you're well enough to travel," he answered authoritatively. Then he realized she had agreed! He softened his tone and said:

"I will go ahead and get a job and a place for us to live before I send for you."

"ok! Now can you see if Miss Aednat is available...the baby is coming right now!" she said through a labor pain as she found their bed.

Michael went into a panic mode: "OK! My God...ok, ok...I'll get her now...stay right there!" he said under duress.

"Of course, dear, where would I go?" Catherine replied with a chuckle covering another labor pain. She smiled at her husband and said:

"Now dear...go now!" she said with emphasis on "now"!

"Yes, yes...I'm going...now!" he replied as he ran out the door to find Miss Aednat. She lived in the same building and was the midwife for the entire block.

Miss Aednat arrived in time. She boiled water on the wood stove and went to work plying her trade.

The baby came soon after she completed her preparations. It was a blue eyed, light haired boy with a great set of lungs!

"It's a boy Catherine!" Aednat declared with enthusiasm. She truly loved her job and continued: "Ten toes, ten fingers, and the spitting image of his father."

Catherine smiled her contagious Irish grin and softly said: "His name is William Henry McCarty, and he will be famous someday like William Henry Allen."[44]

Michael nodded his approval. Although he wished he could have named him Joseph Michael the third, but he had learned in such matters to yield to his wife. Plus, how confusing would it be to have three Joseph's in the house! She wanted a good omen name that their child could carry all his life, and Michael did like the association with such a great American hero.

The very next day, still weak from labor, Catherine was cleaning clothes and standing over a ten-pound cast iron, ironing. She was a stubborn Irish woman.

Michael tried to get her to rest a couple days to get her strength back. She pointed out that a baby and a five-year-old wouldn't let her rest anyway, so she might as well earn some money to save for the move.

Joseph was a quiet, and a very helpful five-year-old boy. His disposition was more like his father's. People always complimented his parents as to how well behaved he was. However, he still had to be supervised.

"I have thought about it a lot, my dear. I will start looking for a job in Indianapolis in the spring." Michael informed Catherine.

"ok, dear...you know best. I just don't want our boys growing up to join the Dead Rats or Bowery Boys. We came to America to give them a better life, not have them running the streets like street Arabs.[45] This is no place to bring up our boys!" Catherine said with a bit of disparity in her voice.

"I agree! I will have our family out of here before summer next year. I promise," Michael committed to Catherine.

Baby Billy sure seemed determined to prove just how good his lungs were. One day the usually quiet and nice neighbor Mr. O'Connell, was at their door.

---

[44] The Irish believed it a good omen to name a child after a famous person. No one knows for sure if Catherine named him after William Henry Allen, but it is highly probable. This chapter is fiction.

[45] Street Arabs was a common term used to describe kids playing, gaming and being mischievous on the streets of any town.

“Please put something in that baby’s mouth. I’m sorry to complain, but I’m working 12-hour shifts. I can’t afford to lose sleep or work,” Mr. O’Connell requested sincerely. He seemed to be such a nice man and a good neighbor. Catherine liked him instantly.

“I’m so very sorry, Mr. O’Connell. Joseph was such a quiet baby I don’t know what to do,” Catherine replied. He interrupted as he ran back to his apartment, “Wait here, I’ve got something that will work.”

Returning he had an odd-shaped leather object. It looked like a leather covered miniature mallet.

Mr. O’Connell declared: “Babies love the taste of leather and this is shaped so your boy can’t swallow it. I think it will work, for both of us!” Mr. O’Connell said as he placed it in Catherine’s hands.

“I will certainly try it! Thank you Mr. O’Connell. Do you have any clothes to wash...? No charge today for you,” Catherine asked with her wonderfully contagious Irish smile.

“Sure, I’ll drop some over a bit later,” Mr. O’Connell replied as he exited through the door.

Catherine stared for a moment at the odd shaped device. There were no nail heads or anything that could harm little Billy. She didn’t want to look a gift horse in the mouth at the door, but now she would make sure it was safe for her little Billy. Mr. O’Connell was right, it was too large to pass even in an adult’s throat.

She had no more finished looking at the device when little Billy tested his lungs again:

“Here you go!” Catherine said as she placed the little device in his mouth. It worked immediately! Little Billy was as content as a horse in a green pasture. “Problem solved!” Catherine thought to herself.

Time would soon disclose a new problem with little Billy and his new device... getting a leather pacifier away from him. He would let loose with a holler that you could hear down the block.

Chapter Four

Storms of Civil War Brewing New York City Lower East-side and Indianapolis, Indiana 1860

The winter of 1859-60 was one of the coldest on record. Four inches of snow had fallen October 26, 1859 to kick off a long cold winter. January, 1860 was a record cold since records were kept.

Finally, the cold gave way to spring, which was Catherine's favorite time of year. Spring was full of life! Catherine loved life of all forms.

Michael was off to Indianapolis, where a new life for his little family had great promise.

He found work immediately. Unlike New York, jobs were plentiful. There were many manufacturing facilities producing products for the great migration west: carriages, wagons, heavy tack, and tool making.

Also, the storms of a Civil War were brewing. Back in New York all the talk was about Abraham Lincoln coming to town to give a speech.[46] The city was pretty much divided 50-50.

In Indianapolis it was also 50-50, 50% of the population was for Abraham Lincoln and the other 50% for Douglas. The

---

[46] Abraham Lincoln delivered his speech as a presidential candidate at Cooper Union Hall. A New York newspaperman said, "No man ever made such an impression on a New York audience." Lincoln said, "There is no middle ground between right and wrong." Stephen Douglas ran on a "states' rights" platform. He had defeated Lincoln after the famous Lincoln-Douglas debates for Illinois State Senator. The debates were centered on the slavery issue and picked up tremendous national press coverage. That loss was the best thing that happened to Abraham Lincoln. The Republican Party put him up as their candidate for the Presidency. November 6, 1860 Abraham Lincoln was elected President of the United States. The final vote count was Lincoln 1,866,452 and Stephen A. Douglas 1,376,957. Lincoln carried all the northern states, California, and Oregon.

debates were raging on in every saloon, hotel lobby, and at the dinner table in every home.

The southern states wanted no interference on how they conducted business. They stood for "state's rights" and nothing else. No one could tell them how to run their states.

The Southern interpretation of the Constitution was that the federal government should not dictate anything to the states. That the federal government's job was to tax and defend the country in time of war...period.

If they wanted to be "slave states", they could be. New states entering the Union could choose to be "slave" or "non-slave" states. Stephen A. Douglas stood for all of that.

Abraham Lincoln promoted all new states to be "free states". The North found slavery not only immoral, but they knew their manufactures could not compete with southern factories that used slave labor.

The north was very industrious and growing at a rapid rate in the new industrial revolution. It was only a matter of time that industry would expand in the south and use 100% slave labor to produce products that the north could not compete with. That was unacceptable to the northern states.

Abraham Lincoln, a Republican (formerly a Whig, as was Douglas who was now a Democrat) simply stated: "There is no middle ground between right and wrong." Several southern states threaten to secede from the United States of America (the Union) if Lincoln was elected. Industrialist in the north began preliminary preparation for a possible civil war. Which they believed, if it did happen, would be very short...maybe only a few months long.

Strategically, Indianapolis was a perfect place to begin preparations. It was growing rapidly, supplying the prospectors of the great gold and silver rushes out west. There were eight railroad lines now going to Indianapolis.

Politics were an important part of every adult man's life. The 1860 presidential election turn-out was 84%. Virtually, everyone, except those that were bed-ridden or injured participated. It was considered un-manly not to get involved and participate in politics. This held true for people from all walks of life from laborer to executive, farmer to doctor, everyone participated in politics.

Chapter Five

A Post from Michael
New York City
April, 1860

Catherine faithfully checked the local post office in the corner grocery and dry goods store for a post from Michael. He promised to post her as soon as he arrived.

Her frame of mind only knew the lower east-side of New York City. A wife did not know if her husband would make it home from work, due to the violence on the streets. It may be the same where Michael had gone.

To her Indianapolis, Indiana was a mysterious place far away, a place that could be worse than New York. How could she know differently?

This day she walked into O'Brien's store and he had a grin on his face, ear-to-ear. She nearly ran to him. Mr. O'Brien held out his hand, it was a post from Michael. She held it tightly all the way home. She would open it in front of Joseph and little Billy. Miss Aednat was watching them for her.

She made it home, gathered Joseph and Billy together. Little Billy was too young to understand, and seemed to be just trying to figure out his mother's emotions, as to whether they were good or bad ones.

"I've received a post from Michael."[47] She was so excited she nearly tore it opening it. Mr. O'Connell happened to be there to pick up some clothes she had cleaned for him.

"It's from Michael, Mr. O'Connell! It's from your Daddy!" Catherine repeated herself in her excitement, as she informed Joseph and Billy. Joseph was very excited now too. He missed his father a lot.

---

[47] This letter and the following stories are fictional. Michael was educated and would have posted Catherine in those times. No actual letters have ever been found.

Mr. O'Connell replied: "Go ahead now, hand it here and let me read it to you," as he patted the five-month-old Billy on the head. Joseph was all ears!

Catherine looked it over and then handed it to Mr. O'Connell, so he could read it aloud to her:

"My Dearest Wife,

I pray all is well with you, Joseph, and Billy. I love and miss you all very much!

Indianapolis is a wonderful place to live. You will love it. They have formed a city government and have even established a school system. That alone should take a big burden from you.

The city is growing so fast. Eight rail lines now come and go from here. New manufactures are appearing all the time and need workers. Stores of all kinds have opened: dry goods, groceries, hardware, earthenware, and even a book store!

I applied for jobs at Osgood y Smith's Peg and Glass Factory, Geisedorff's Woolen Mill, Drew's Carriage, Shellenbarger's Planning Mill, and Macy's Pork House. I did so my first free day after finding housing.

All of them except Macy's made me an offer for employment! Can you imagine that? All of them needed help. I took employment with Drew's Carriage builder. I have a job!

Please give a hug to Joseph and little Billy. I bet he is growing like a weed. I know I have only been gone two weeks, but it seems like a year!

My dear, I promise to save all I can to transport you here as expeditiously as possible. It is terrible to be away from you, Joseph, and little Billy.

Your loving husband,

Michael

P.S. They don't ask whether you are Protestant or Catholic Irish. This is a completely different country. Post me general delivery Indianapolis, Indiana.

Mr. O'Connell was moved by his letter. This was such a fine, young family. A fine, young, Irish family. It was terrible they had been stuck so long in New York City.

Catherine immediately gave the promised hugs to Joseph and little Billy.

Catherine looked at the letter a dozen times over the next few days. It seemed almost too good to be true. Unknown to Michael she was also saving money for the trip. She was now the most popular laundry lady on the block. She was paying rent, feeding the family, and saving $2 a week.

His post came at exactly the right time. She was getting discouraged as to how long it would take her to save the money for the trip to Indianapolis. Now, it would not be long at all!

Joseph must have asked her every hour:

"When are we going to see Daddy?" he would ask in perfect New England English. Most of the time they spoke Gaelic.

"As soon as you stop bothering me about it, so I can get my work done," she would politely respond.

Catherine thought of how lucky they were to have a new place so good to go to.

She and Michael had learned British English in Cork, Ireland, but spoke their native tongue of Gaelic. Joseph was young when they arrived here in America, so he learned New England English from his friends, and some lady teaching preschool children for free on their block.

Billy was only five-months-old, and she could tell he was trying to communicate in Gaelic already. Not succeeding, but still trying. She found it amazing. Little Billy was grasping the concept of speaking and communicating. Catherine noticed he also held the leather pacifier with one hand and then the other.

"My little Billy, I think you are ambidextrous. That is a very good omen! I will help you by training both of your little hands to do everything! Ambidextrous people do very well in life my little Billy," Catherine said as she smiled her contagious smile. Little Billy smiled right back at her as though he understood every word!

Chapter Six

Mr. O'Donnell's Troubles
New York City
April, 1860

Mr. O'Donnell, Catherine's neighbor, had brought over his laundry for the week, and it was ready to pick up. He was always very efficient and would arrive at her apartment just as she completed it. She had joked with him as to how he always knew when she had finished ironing his clothes. A couple hours went by, so she decided to take it to him.

Catherine knocked at his door with Billy strapped to her chest, and Joseph in tow with part of Mr. O'Connell's laundry. She carried the shirts herself.

There was no answer and she was about to return to her apartment when she thought she heard something. She placed her ear against the door, and sure enough there was a moaning sound coming from his apartment. She decided to enter without permission.

"Oh my God!" Catherine yelled out as she ran to Mr. O'Connell's side. He was laid out on a cold floor with no covers.

She could see he was bruised badly, and had dried blood crusted all over his face. He had been beaten and stabbed in his side also.

"Joseph! You're the man in the family now, right?" Catherine asked urgently.

"Yes Mom, that is what Dad said," Joseph replied.

Catherine closed the front door to Mr. O'Connell's apartment. As she gave instructions to Joseph, she converted the chest harness she had made for little Billy around to be a backpack with him facing outwards.

"You stay here with Mr. O'Connell, close the door behind me, and lock it! Do not open it for anyone but me, no matter what they say to you...do you understand young man?" Catherine asked firmly.

"Yes Mom. I understand," Joseph replied solemnly.

Little Billy loved the back pack, as he was facing outward, his curious mind took everything in. She left and ran to the midwife's door knocking a bit too much which startled Miss Aednat.

"It is me Aednat...Catherine McCarty," she declared and then the door opened.

"Please come with me and look after Mr. O'Connell...he is injured very badly. If you could watch Joseph and Billy I'll run for a doctor...ok?" Catherine pleaded, almost begging.

"Of course, I will," Miss Aednat replied quickly.

Catherine recalled what she had told Joseph and thought now would be a good time to test how well he followed instructions.

Arriving at Mr. O'Connell's apartment Catherine had Aednat knock and ask to come in to help Mr. O'Connell. There was no answer. Catherine then told Joseph it was her too and it was ok to unlock the door. Still no answer.

"Joseph, this is your mother unlock this door now!" Catherine said authoritatively. Joseph unlocked and opened the door.

"You did very well Joseph, I am proud of you!" She said to him, and he grinned from ear-to-ear.

Aednat went right to Mr. O'Connell's side.

"Catherine, before you leave could you help me get him off the floor, and on his bed." Aednat asked in her professional manner. It was phrased as a question, but was actually an instruction. She knew what she was doing.

"Of course!" Catherine replied. They inched him to the edge of the bed. It took both strong women to first get his upper torso on the bed and then his legs.

Catherine closed the door behind her as she was off running at full pace to the only real doctor in the area about two blocks north on Allen Street. He was a regular customer of hers.

Arriving at his office she went directly into his inner office.

"I'm so sorry Doctor, but this is an emergency," Catherine blared out as the doctor was examining a male patient.

"Oh! Oh! I am so dreadfully sorry sir!" She said as she

just noticed the nude man. She placed both hands over her face and turned her head.

"Is it Joseph or Little Billy?" Dr. O'Hara asked. He was a blazing redhead with large muscles that gave him tremendous upper body strength. Yet his voice was low and soft as the educated man he was. Nothing seemed to excite him. He was the kind one would trust to be in charge in battle.

"No, no sir. It is my neighbor Mr. O'Connell. I fear he may not live if you don't come immediately," Catherine said in her excited Irish accent.

"Alright, I will come immediately," Dr. O'Hara replied calmly.

"May I pack my medical bag? It contains instruments I may need," He said a bit sarcastically. His male patient was already about fully dressed.

"Oh, yes, of course doctor. I'm sorry if I'm a bit excited. He is a very good man, and I just don't want him to die," Catherine said a little more calmly.

The doctor turned his attention to his male patient as he loaded his medical bag, or better stated "Possibles bag":

"You are doing very well, Mr. Hopkins. Take one teaspoon of laudanum at night before sleep. No more than that Mr. Hopkins. That stuff can kill you in greater quantity." He said in his soft mild manner.

"Will do Doc," Mr. Hopkins replied.

Doctor O'Hara took off running toward 70 Allen Street. He was so fast Catherine could hardly keep up. If it wasn't for the crowded boardwalk that slowed him down, she would not have been close to staying up with him.

They arrived at Mr. O'Connell's apartment. Dr. O'Hara went right to work examining and treating his multiple, serious wounds. Joseph had stayed by Mr. O'Connell's side comforting him the best he could for a five-year-old. Aednat had boiled water, cleaned the wounds, and stuffed the open cuts with a clean cloth to stop the bleeding.

"What is your name lassie?" the good doctor asked in his own Irish accent, directing the question to Aednat.

"Aednat, sir!" she replied.

"Ah, that is Gaelic for 'Little Fire'. Do you live up to your wonderful name?" Dr. O'Hara asked Aednat.

"Yes sir, I do," she replied matter-of-factly.

"Well, Little Fire you have saved this man's life. Your first aid to him was very good. He may have bled out from this wound had you not stuffed so well.

"Yes sir," the doctor directed to Mr. O'Connell: "These two women saved your life today!"

The doctor began sewing up the multiple knife wounds. There were so many the attackers had thought they left him dead. He had done his best to pretend to be dead, which saved his life at the time of the attack.

"Do you have any whiskey?" the doctor asked.

"I do!" Aednat replied and ran to her apartment retrieving some 100-proof Irish whiskey. In the south they called this whiskey "moonshine".

"You drink this?" Dr. O'Hara asked Aednat.

Aednat laughed and said: "Only when I get cases like this and you're not around!"

She chuckled again and followed up: "This is for my patients, but I have been known to nip a bit on a hard case!"

Aednat was 35-years-old, and very attractive. She was single because she said she had never met a man that understood that her first love would always be being a midwife. She loved that more than life itself.

"Alright, Mr. O'Connell, take a good swallow of this and you must hold very still. If I don't close this wound correctly it will become infected and all our beautiful work here would be wasted, not to mention you will die, too. So, please do hold still." The doctor said in an authoritative tone.

He began sewing all the large, open wounds created by a very large knife. It took an hour of sewing by a very efficient doctor. Completing the job, he wrapped Mr. O'Connell's mid-section tight enough to hold the stiches, but loose enough to allow healing.

"With rest, he should recover as good as new" the good doctor declared, and turned to speak directly with Aednat:

"Aednat, please up-date me on his condition at my office, if you would ma'am? I know he is in good hands with you here," he said to her as one medical professional to another. In no way was he ever condescending to Aednat. He had a lot of respect for those that dedicate their lives to medicine no matter what capacity they do so.

"Absolutely Doctor O'Hara," Aednat replied.

"Mr. O'Connell, I think you're well enough on that 100-proof to tell me what happened here," the good doctor asked point blank.

"Well Doc, I took a short cut home and went through a Catholic neighborhood. Some Catholic Dead Rats recognized me from work and caught me. I was surrounded with no way out. I think that was their excuse for wanting to rob me. We just got paid and they knew I had a week's worth of earnings on me. A very kind Catholic woman ordered them off me and helped me to my feet. They left with one of them saying: 'Won't do any good, he is finished," to the lady.' I don't even know or remember how I made it here. That is the all of it, Doc."

"There will be no charge for today. I insist! If you promise me never to take that short cut or one like it again?" the good doctor required for his withholding of fee. "Also, do you know why this attack was so vicious? You were very lucky...a couple of these cuts a few inches over would have bled you out before you reached home."

"Thank you, Doctor. I promise I will never return to that street. I am not one to seek revenge. Those things never end well. I don't know why they wanted to kill me. I've only seen a couple of them from work, and had no trouble with any of them." Mr. O'Connell promised and explained.

The Doctor replied with an old Irish quote:

"Like the warmth of the sun and the light of the day, may the luck of the Irish shine bright on your way" he added: "It certainly has today!"

"You have a very good wife here," the doctor said, referring to Aednat

"Oh! No sir, she is our midwife, but she is not married to my knowledge." Mr. O'Connell stated factually.

"Enough about me Mr. O'Connell if you want me a changing those bandages?" She said in her Gaelic accent.

The doctor was pleasantly surprised. From the time he arrived he thought them to be man and wife.

Catherine stated her own Irish saying to the good doctor:

"Thank you, doctor, and may God grant you many years to live, for sure he must be knowing the earth has angels all too few, and heaven is overflowing." Then she continued: "You are one of his angels!" Catherine said with conviction.

The doctor tipped his hat to Mr. O'Connell and then to the ladies present. The hat of which had never left his head, as it covered up a bald top. He picked up his doctor's valise and left.

Catherine placed Mr. O'Connell's ironed clothes away and stacked the other clothes where they belonged.

"You may pay me later Mr. O'Connell," Catherine said and left him in the capable hands of Aednat.

Catherine was feeding little Billy when Aednat arrived the next day with Mr. O'Connell's money.

"Oh no! That is way too much! I cannot accept it! A hundred dollars! That is a year's worth of wages for some people!" Catherine refused to take the money and attempted to give it back.

Aednat spoke softly and matter-of-factly: "His instructions were if you refused it, I am to burn the money."

"What? You wouldn't do that!" Miss Aednat shifted her head is such a manner and with an expression in her face that said she would certainly do as he instructed.

"Sorry, Catherine, Mr. O'Connell gave me an equal amount to care for him and to follow his instructions explicitly!" she said, determined honor his request.

"Alright, I wouldn't want it burnt. Please give him my deepest gratitude and affection. I now have more than enough to join my husband in Indianapolis. Unfortunately, you both will be losing your laundry lady!" Catherine said with a smile.

"I will find both of us another, though not as good as you! That is impossible! He said you would be traveling soon, and was happy to be putting the McCarty family back together again." Aednat informed Catherine.

"Please tell him I will be down to see him tomorrow. I have much planning on my mind right now. I need to make all my deliveries before dark," she asked of Aednat.

Aednat took Joseph while Catherine carried little Billy on her back to make the deliveries. Billy seemed to relish the time spent exploring from his mother's back during her travels delivering clothes.

Chapter Seven

McCarty's Irish Roots
New York City
May, 1860

Mr. O'Connell spent a good three weeks healing up from his beating. The two women took good care of him.

In most of Aednat's free time she was as a nursemaid to him. Catherine checked in on him periodically. As with most people who met Catherine McCarty, he became a good friend besides a customer.

Catherine invited Aednat and Mr. O'Connell to an Irish stew dinner. They quickly accepted and arrived early.

Mr. O'Connell sat across from Aednat and looking right at her said:

"Oh, tis nothing like an Irish stew to fill a man, leaving his heart vulnerable to an Irish lassie like you."

"Now you're a poet, Mr. O'Connell. Keep your eye on this rascal, Aednat. He'll steal your heart away before the devil knows he's tried," Catherine said with her contagious smile.

Aednat had not had such romantic attention in a long time. She wasn't sure how to respond, so she did her usual and was bluntly honest:

"Now don't go saying such things leading a lassie on, Mr. O'Connell," she said with sincerity.

"Who said I'm leading you on? Tell me you can make stew like this and we are getting hitched in the morning!" He replied with sincerity.

He then turned his attention to Catherine: "What part of Ireland are you and Michael from, if I may ask?"

"Mr. O'Connell, you are a friend and I don't mind you asking any questions of our family. We come from Cork, in Cork County." She replied with pride in her voice. Cork was one of the most progressive Counties in all of Ireland.

"Well, I be!" Mr. O'Connell reacted with and continued:

"I too hail from Cork. I filled the gas lights for five years, and worked part time at the Cork Constitution."

"That was Michael and my favorite newspaper," Catherine volunteered.

"I also worked on the construction of Cork University. That seems a wee bit strange to me. There I was working to build a university while people were starving in the countryside. I figured it was just a matter of time the starving would reach me. Hence, I passaged to America," Mr. O'Connell explained.

Catherine explained: "As we did too! Michael had a good job, but it couldn't last. So, we saved for our passage, and his family helped us a lot. He sends money on nearly every ship back to Ireland. He said we cannot be free here until they are paid in full, with interest," Catherine informed.

"I knew I was right in liking that husband of yours. Good lad he is!" Mr. O'Connell declared and continued:

"Makes sense...he is of great heritage."

"What do you mean great heritage?" Catherine asked sincerely.

"These boys you have here...have it too!" Mr. O'Connell added.

"It... being what?" Catherine asked a little frustrated.

"McCarty is one of the oldest family lineages of the Provence of Munster. Some say all the way back to Oilioll Olum, 300A.D. during King Munster's reign. I do know for sure it came from Carthach, Lord of Eoghannacht. He died in 1045 A.D.," Mr. O'Connell was obviously educated on such matters.

Surprising everyone, young Joseph spoke up: "Tell me more, Mr. O'Connell," Joseph asked with sincere curiosity in his voice.

Catherine directed her son to be politer, excuse himself and then say please to any such request. She was a stickler on manners. Joseph corrected his behavior immediately:

"I'm sorry Mr. O'Connell. I was just so excited to hear you talk about Ireland. Please tell us more about Ireland." Joseph spoke very well for a five-year-old.

Mr. O'Connell looked at Catherine for approval. She nodded her approval, so he continued:

"Well, young Joseph, your most famous relative was Fineeu MacCarthy Reagh, Chief of Blarney of Carbery in West Cork 1512. He resided in the Blarney Castle."

Catherine interrupted: "Oh My! How many times I have told Michael he had kissed the Blarney too many times!" She broke out in laughter. Catherine's tickle box was tipped!

Catherine then got serious: "Are you saying my Michael, Joseph, and Billy descend from Fineeu MacCarthy Reagh, Chief of Blarney?" She asked sincerely.

"Most likely, yes" Mr. O'Connell replied and then continued: "The spelling has changed many times and several branches exist to this day: MacCarthy, McCarthy, MacCarty, and McCarty. They all stem from the Gaelic MacCarthaigh," Mr. O'Connell concluded.

"'Son of Loving'," Catherine said to Joseph. "That is what your last name means...'Son of Loving'," she repeated softly, but Joseph was too young to understand Gaelic translations...he just liked what he was hearing.

Catherine then held little Billy up and told him: "Billy, you have the blood of an Irish King in your veins." He smiled not knowing a word she was saying, but it too sounded good to him.

Catherine became more serious:

"Mr. O'Connell, you are a walking book of knowledge on Cork County. Some of that university you were building must have rubbed off on you." Catherine smiled and continued:

"Why do our people treat each other so badly here in America. They would not think to do these things in Ireland?"

"I can only speak for New York City, Catherine. Too many people of different up-bringing crammed into too small a space. Survival, yes...that is your answer, survival like the animals. That is not a good excuse, but that is what is happening here. Survival of the fittest." He continued:

"It is sad, Irishman against Irishman. It has brought out the Celtic warrior in many Irishman in America. They kill with passion and firmly believe they are right in doing so. The Bowery Boys, Roach Guards, and the Dead Rats, all Celtic warriors killing each other, and for what? No good reasons. They should be fighting for clean water, good schools for their children, trained policemen. And what do we have here in New

York City? A murder every single night on one street for fifteen years…that is since the famine drove us here. Every single night! There is no excuse for such killings. It is good that Michael is finding a place far away from here as your new home. Oh! I am sorry to have spoiled such a good dinner with my talk of this city."

"No, no Mr. O'Connell remember I asked you? Thank you very much for all this information, and I want to thank you again for the money. I have a customer that has volunteered to freight all our household goods to the train station. I am so excited we will be seeing Michael soon. I also am sad to leave you two. Both of you must come visit at least…ok?" Catherine begged.

"I can't promise anything, but if it is possible we will come to visit. I can promise you one thing though…you are looking at Mrs. O'Connell right here," he said as he pointed to Aednat. She blushed and nodded in agreement.

"That is wonderful! I will not worry about either of you now. Well, maybe a little…ha!" Catherine said with glee.

They ended the evening singing some Irish songs. Catherine had a very good singing voice. Aednat also could sing. Mr. O'Connell could not but did not let lack of talent stop him from having a good time singing.

Chapter Eight

The Long Train Ride to Indianapolis, Indiana May, 1860

All packed and ready to depart for the train station, Catherine said her good-byes to Aednat and Mr. O'Connell, who saw her off. Saying good-bye to these two close friends was not easy. She would love to take both of them with her, but the rest of the block they lived on would not be too happy about that. Aednat was midwife and nurse to many.

Arriving at the train station it appeared the whole city was leaving. Now she was concerned her trunks and one chest drawer (her favorite piece of furniture), would make it on the same train.

Her fears were warranted. The station master said her bags and goods would be on a dedicated freight train that would follow her passenger train. He assured her all would arrive safe and sound in Indianapolis.

She boarded the passenger train with Joseph and little Billy. With the extra money she was able to purchase three seats, which would allow her to rest her shoulders on the long trip.

As the train pulled out of New York City, it reminded her of taking the train from Cork to Dublin. Again, she was excited to go to a better place, and sad to leave her friends in the old place of residence.

Catherine had the shawl that one of her customers knitted for her thrown over her right side, covering Billy as she breast fed him. Staring out the window, the entire world flew by and changed quickly. Brick and stone to a beautiful country side. In less than an hour she could not see a remnant of a city.

"Joseph! See out there? That looks much like Ireland!" Catherine said with excitement in her voice.

Joseph thought it a beautiful land and sincerely asked his mother:

"Mom, why did you leave such a beautiful place for New York?" The inquisitive five-year-old asked. Joseph was at the stage of asking many questions...he had questions about everything! This one seemed important to him.

"Although Ireland is very beautiful, she did not have enough food to feed all her people. Your father and I had heard America was bountiful and beautiful. Looking out there I can see why your father wanted to move west." Catherine said with a look of satisfaction, she loved the countryside.

The train ride to Indianapolis was much longer than Catherine had expected. The train seemed to stop at every town along the way. Somehow, she had missed the information that Indianapolis was only 100 miles short of being 1000 miles from New York City. She imagined Indianapolis was a few hundred miles west in the next state.

Catherine was so busy in New York she did not give much thought to the train trip. She knew she did not want to raise her boys in the living hell of the lower-east-side of New York City. Ironically, she was actually on the train before she learned how far they were traveling. Her first thought was: "That is good, the further away from New York the better."

Catherine wasn't interested in politics, but the subject could not be avoided on the long train ride. She was surrounded by political conversations. The talk was centered on Abraham Lincoln becoming the next President of the United States.

"The south will secede from the Union if Lincoln is elected. My parents in Richmond said orders are huge for cotton clothes and ammunition. One gun manufacture is openly copying Yankee guns, and manufacturing them right now in large quantities. That tells me they believe Lincoln will win the election," a southern gentleman said to his Yankee friend sitting next to him.

"Copies are rarely as good as the original," his Yankee friend replied with a chuckle and continued: "I agree, that they must think war is imminent. What will you do my southern friend?"

"I would have to go home to Richmond. I must stand with my family, and I do believe strongly in state's rights. What about you my friend?" he returned the question.

"Well, as you know I'm just now showing a profit in my business. If I left it I might as well close shop. I'm confident that there will be an increase in demand for carriages and wagons. Possibly a demand for all kinds of wagons I could build and supply in quantities. As much as I detest war it would boost my business, and I'm sure the government would want me doing my business instead of being a foot soldier who can't hit the broad side of a barn with a scatter gun...Ha!" the Yankee concluded.

Another man tuned into their conversation jumped in: "There will be war! Secession cannot be tolerated, or we will have no Union at all. Any time the people of a state did not like a tax or treaty they could just secede and avoid paying, or adhering to it." The man said with conviction.

Another passenger joined in: "The North is afraid of competition with slave labor, it cannot afford to allow slavery to continue. Personally, I abhor the practice of slavery. How can we say, 'all men are created equal', except the ones we own? Nah, slavery is just plain wrong." The man said with conviction.

A southern gentleman spoke up:

"I will tell you of my own experience, my family's slaves would not last a month on their own. They are very well taken care of and never mistreated. They have learned several trades and I'll tell you something else. If you told them they are free and can do whatever they want, go wherever they want to...I would bet our farm not one would want to leave our family. We treat them like family. If they get sick we have a doctor at their side immediately. No, sir, not one would leave," the southern gentleman concluded.

Another man joined the conversation. He sat directly across from the southern gentleman: (The train's seats were grouped in fours on one side of the isle and two seats facing each other on the other side of the isle).

"That sounds so very cozy. I'm ready to join your slaves." He said in a sarcastic manner, and continued: "Do you send them to school, educate them, inform them how much money they could make selling their trade skill services? No need to answer, I know you don't. If you did they would leave you in a heartbeat, and you know it, sir" the strongly opinionated Yankee declared.

The southern gentleman kept his composure and simply said: "With all due respect, you do not know what I would or not do."

Catherine listened intently as she knew she was hearing firsthand the issues of the North-South conflict. She also knew her beliefs were strongly on the side of the North. She found slavery a horrible state for human beings to be in. If she could, she would free them all!

Growing up in Ireland she read and heard of the "slave trade" ships traveling to Africa and shipping hundreds of Africans to the Americas to be sold. It was so far away then, but now it was right here next to her. She wanted to say something, but the Northern gentleman had expressed well all she thought of it.

It also seemed inevitable that the conflict may affect her young family. She wondered what Michael would do if war broke out. She hoped he too would have important work to allow him not to have to fight.

"Next stop Indianapolis, Indiana!" the conductor announced.

Chapter Nine

The McCarty Family's New Home
385 N. New Jersey
May 1860
Indianapolis, Indiana

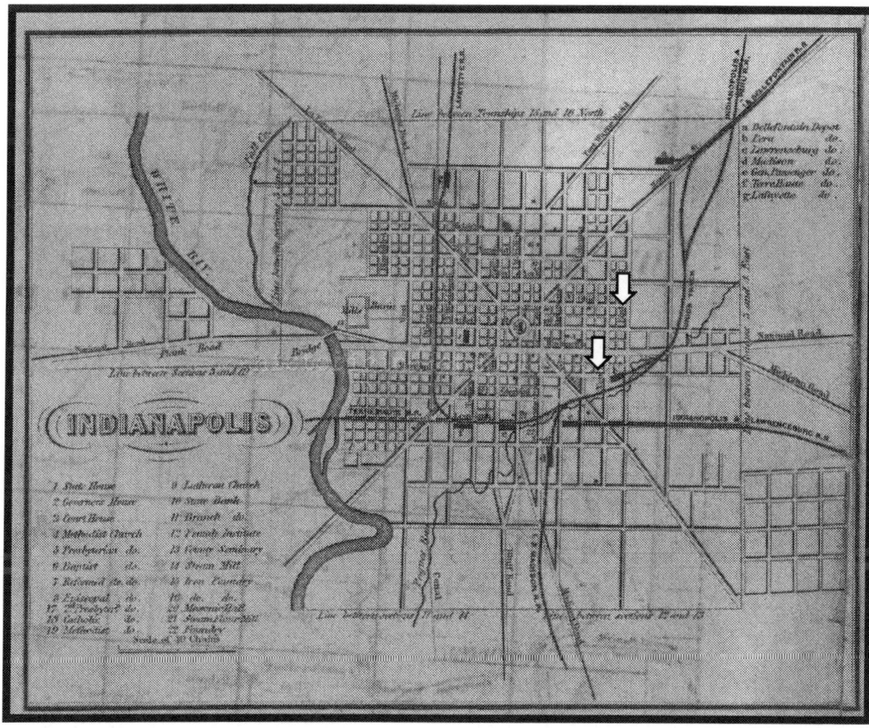

Indianapolis, Indiana 1852: Top Arrow is 199 North East Street Bottom Arrow is 385 N. New Jersey Street. Library of Congress.

Catherine examined her new town out the window as the train came to a halt. She could see it truly was a boom town. Wagons were loaded with building materials, hard goods, soft goods, and furniture. Several were loaded with milled lumber. The street past the train station was crowded with people, animals, and wagons galore traveling all different directions.

Disembarking the train, Catherine had her carry-on carpet bag in grip with one hand as she tried waving down a taxi carriage with the other.

Little Billy was a curious six-month-old baby in her front harness and taking in all the sights and sounds. Joseph was a more reserved unhappy five-year-old still thinking of all the friends he left behind in New York.

"Mother, there is not anyone my age here," Joseph whined, very concerned.

"Dear they are all in their homes and apartments, not at the train station. Look over there! That boy is waiting with his mother just as you are," Catherine placated.

"That is one boy!" Joseph replied.

"I promise you will meet new friends and will grow to like this town a lot," she assured Joseph.

She had learned on the train that the train with her household goods was delayed and would not arrive until tomorrow. That actually worked out better to give her time to arrange for freighting them to their new house.

Finally, a carriage pulled over and the driver hopped out to assist her and her boys. She handed the driver a written note that had Michael's posting address on it.

"Ma'am, this is a mercantile store location for general delivery," the driver explained.

"Yes, I know. I'm figuring he will check for a post after work, and he'll discover his whole family has posted," she answered with a loud chuckle.

"It will certainly be a surprise!" replied the driver.

"That is my intent. He doesn't know we are coming," she responded in her Irish accent and contagious smile.

Arriving at the mercantile business the driver unloaded her carpet bag.

"I will be stopping back later to check on you. No need to say it is not necessary, I will do it anyway," the driver said firmly.

"Well, thank you very much sir. I do appreciate your kindness." Catherine replied.

Inside the store was a small area set aside for a post office. Catherine waited in line and when it was her turn she asked the postal clerk:

"Do you know one Michael McCarty?

The clerk thought for only a couple second and replied:

"Yes, yes I do, ma'am. A fine looking young man, sandy hair, five foot six or seven, and blue eyes that pop out at you. I could not forget those eyes," he said as he looked down at Billy and continued: "Eyes just like your son there. I know where he got those from."

"Oh, that is very good sir. Do you know when he usually comes in to check for posts? I am Catherine McCarty, his wife. This is Joseph and Billy, his two boys." Catherine asked.

"No, ma'am, I do not know for sure," the clerk replied.

Catherine's heart sunk to her stomach. She may have made a big mistake wanting to surprise Michael.

"I remember seeing his name this morning. Let me check....Yes, here it is! Your husband moved from here," the postal clerk said matter-of-factly.

Now fear overcame Catherine, and now the driver's promise when he left her seemed very comforting.

"Catherine!" a calm, but emotionally filled voice came from behind her. She quickly turned toward the voice.

"Michael!" she declared and jumped into his arms almost crushing Little Billy between them. "You are a sight for sore eyes! I thought..."

Michael interrupted: "I just came here to see if you had posted me. Well, you sure did!" He replied as he hugged Joseph and tapped Little Billy on the head.

"All our goods are arriving tomorrow. Don't worry about the money. Everything is paid for! Do you remember Mr. O'Connell?" Catherine asked Michael in an excitedly.

"Of course I do, why?" Michael replied becoming more curious about her statement not to worry about the money.

Catherine explained: "He was nearly killed by a street gang. I ran for a doctor and Aednat nursed him. He gave both of us $100 for saving his life. I refused it, but he said he would burn the money up, and I believed he would do just that! Therefore, I accepted it. He said he was very happy to put the McCarty family back together," she concluded.

"We need to repay him!" Michael said.

"I'm telling you he will not take it," Catherine said just as firmly.

"That is up to him. We will repay him Catherine," Michael said as he waved a taxi carriage over to them.

It was a pleasant drive to the newest section of town. Arriving out front of their new home/apartment building. Catherine liked what she saw.

The next day Catherine and Michael left the boys with their new neighbor to retrieve their household goods. Asking around, they decided on and hired a freighting company. The owner introduced them to their driver as Jack Magee.

"Jack, is fine sir, and ma'am!" the young man volunteered. Jack was an 18-year-old that had dreams of owning his own freighting company someday. He was strong, polite, and a hard worker.

"Young man, we named our son after William Henry Allen, the famous naval sea captain of the War of 1812. My son was born on Allen Street in New York City. Were you named after the famous fighter Jack Magee?" Michael asked with curiosity.

"I don't know, sir. Maybe. My mother always did talk about her fighter friend. They have never said how they decided on my name. Left me to figure it out I guess," Jack answered with a chuckle.

Jack seemed to have a steady look about him that gave the impression he was more mature than his chronological age would dictate. Michael was twenty-five-years-old. Catherine was thirty-one-years-old, six years older than Michael.

Although thirty-one, Catherine's demeanor, attractive face, bright gleaming blue eyes, and bubbling outgoing personality made her appear equal to Michael's age. Not one person they ever met thought she was older than Michael, quite the opposite!

Jack Magee demonstrated he was a hard worker. Michael and he had the goods loaded in the wagon in short order. Jack slapped the four team reins and made that clicking sound out of the corner of his mouth that cued the large draft horses to move on

Catherine was excited to think she was about to see their new home. She knew anything would be better than their living environment in New York City, but her imagination glittered with expectations.

The wagon was built for passengers having an extra bench seat behind the driver. Michael and Jack sat up front.

Michael said: "385 N. New Jersey, Jack."

"Yes sir," Jack replied. It took but ten minutes to arrive at their new home.

Catherine was very pleased. One could smell the new lumber it was constructed with.

Michael and Jack had all their goods unloaded and placed exactly where Catherine wanted them to be in short order.

"Please come and share our first dinner in our new home tonight." Catherine said with that Irish way one knows she is not going to accept no for an answer.

Bill felt as though he would be intruding on the family's first dinner in their new home and began to politely decline.

"I will not take no for an answer...see you here at 7 tonight Mr. Magee," this time using her motherly commanding voice.

"Yes, do join us Jack," Michael confirming the invitation.

"I would be honored to join you in dinner tonight," Jack responded.

Michael ran all over town finding all the ingredients Catherine wanted for dinner. This dinner was far beyond the fact they were having a guest over. It was much more than that. The Irish strongly believe in omens. The first dinner would have to be very special, as a good omen for all the ones to come. Besides, they could afford it at this time.

That evening Jack Magee arrived in a borrowed carriage. His boss loaned him the same if he promised to complete a list of things after its use: oil and polish the wood, rub down the horse, comb out its mane and tail, feed and grain the horse. He agreed, and it was worth all of that to see the McCarty family's look when he pulled up in front of their new home at 7 pm sharp. All the McCarty's had come out on the front porch to see his carriage.

"I'm impressed!" Michael said as Jack stepped from the carriage.

"It's borrowed." Jack quickly replied. "My boss loaned this to me. Someday I will own one of these myself."

"We are new, and all our neighbors now believe we know someone important. That is a dandy of a carriage Mr. Magee, a dandy it is!" Michael said as he admired the rich hard wood that had to have been sealed, stained, and polished a half dozen times to leave such a rich, deep finish.

"It was made right here in Indianapolis. My boss is friends with the factory owner and really went all out on the construction of this carriage. I was fortunate to have him loan it to me." Jack concluded and they all followed the stream of wonderful food smells that permeated the night air from the open door of the house.

The dinner was a good omen, and very exceptional! It had been a long time since Michael had home cooking. He was not a good cook himself.

Jack was from Anderson, Indiana and did go home for some home cooking every once and awhile. His mother too was a good Irish cook. What made this dinner so special was the McCarty's did treat him like a special guest. Most of the time he had beef jerky for breakfast, lunch and dinner. This dinner he would never forget.

After dinner the men retired to the living room and discussed what all the men in Indianapolis were talking about, politics and the lurking civil war.

Jack was a wealth of information as in his business he hears a lot from wealthy and influential patrons.

Catherine wanted to ask Jack a question: "Is it true the militia have already organized here?" Michael was surprised by her question. "I overheard men talking on the train ride out here," she explained how she had acquired the local information.

Michael and Jack answered in unison: "Yes!" Jack yielded to his host.

"Five companies of militia have organized and are training in military matters right now!" Michael said with emphasis on now.

Catherine observed Michael's expressions and body language as he talked about the forming of the militia. She instantly became concerned, as he spoke as though he fully intended on joining a militia. He never outright said anything, but Catherine's woman's intuition knew he meant to do exactly that.

"Michael, you're not thinking of joining a militia, are you?" Catherine asked point blank.

"I already have Catherine. We came to this country and it has kept all its promises to us. Look around this town...here is where we belong. Our boys are going to have a school to attend. There are plenty of well-paying jobs. This is a boom town because this is America!"

"Now the American Union is threatened. My father once told me every man must pay his dues to his country one way or another. I have joined a militia that has some of the finest men I have ever met in it. When the war starts, and it will, we will be fighting to protect this country.

Catherine knew it would be useless to try and talk him out of it. He gleamed with pride just talking about his militia unit.

"How long do you think this war will last? Catherine asked sincerely, but her tone gave her true feelings away.

"A few months, maybe a year at the most" Michael answered with authority.

"Have you joined a militia, Jack?" Michael then asked.

"No, sir, I have not. My boss said freighters are going to be needed a lot in the war effort if it does come about. He said I will be exempt from the subscription orders and he needed me to fill the army's orders." Jack replied hoping Michael would understand, and read his true feelings.

Jack was not interested in fighting a war he did not understand. If those states, which did not include his state, wanted to go their own way...let them go! Why would he want to die to keep someone who didn't want to stay? To Jack it was like having a girlfriend that wanted to break up with you and you said: "stay with me or I'm going to shoot myself in the head." Who suffers? Not the girl, she got what she wanted.

"Your boss is right Jack. Wagon-masters will be in high demand. Although, I did not know anyone was going to be exempt from the draft if war breaks out. Actually, it is not a law yet, but if war comes it will be passed into law fast." Michael informed Jack.

Michael turned his attention back to Catherine. She was not happy with all the talk about war.

“Catherine, Abraham Lincoln, President of the United states is coming to Indianapolis! The President is coming here!” Michael said with great emotion.

Catherine smiled and replied: “I guess if Indianapolis is good enough for Abraham Lincoln its good enough for me” she ended with her wonderful Irish chuckle.

“Yes, ma’am, the president himself and I know the date!” Jack bragged a little.

“Really, when?” Michael asked directly.

“February 12, year of our Lord 1861. Guess what carriage company has been hired to take him all over the town? Jack smugly asked as his chest puffed up with pride.

“You are going to drive the President?” Catherine asked amazed.

“Well, no, my boss is though, I’ll prepare his rig” Jack said proudly.

“He is here to inspect the militia, and meet with businessmen. They are preparing for war” Michael informed Catherine.

“I don’t want you to go to war...period!” Catherine’s face turned flush from her temper about to explode, she went on to say: “Michael you have two boys you could leave fatherless. People get killed in wars!” Catherine insisted.

“Not your decision, it is mine. This is truly a free country and I want my boys to grow up in a free country! If people or states are allowed to break the constitution of the United States, it won’t be free long. Sometimes fighting is necessary and this is one of those times.” Michael informed what he was going to do.

“Men! You are all crazy! Michael, you listened to that Celtic warrior stuff too much back home. I want a live husband not a dead Celtic warrior hero!” Catherine took one more swing.

“Enough, no more talk on the subject. When it happens, it will not last very long and it is the right thing to do. No more discussion on the matter.” Michael said in no uncertain terms...the discussion was closed.

Jack said his good nights and thanked Catherine for the wonderful dinner and Michael for his company.

“This was the best evening I’ve had since Christmas at home. Thank you both so much for inviting me to dinner.” Jack said as he climbed into his borrowed horse and buggy.

Chapter Ten

Civil War Declared

February 1861 Indianapolis, Indiana. Time seemed to fly by! Indianapolis did get their new school system organized. Catherine's Little Billy being only 1 year and a little over one month old was obviously too young. Joseph, now being nick-named Josie, was six-years-old could enroll in first grade. He looked forward to it to finding new friends.

The boy's father Michael was extremely busy. He held down two jobs and all his free time was spent with the militia. He was being trained in light artillery. Catherine joked with him in her half Irish truth way: "We certainly won't have any more children...you haven't the time to produce another"...and she let go her great Irish laugh. Michael looked around to see if the boys could hear her.

"They are with the neighbor as I'm making some deliveries this afternoon" Catherine informed her anxious husband.

Michael approached her and pushed the hair back from her face in a very gentle manner. So gentle it wouldn't have shooed a fly. He slowly lowered his head at the appropriate angle and gently kissed Catherine as he had the very first kiss...their lips gently touching with pure love.

"I take it all back" Catherine whispered in Michael's ear. He smiled and pulled her to his chest, not too hard, just enough she could feel his heart beating as he wrapped his arms completely around her. They retired to their bedroom.

They exited the room just in time for their neighbor to arrive with the boys. Timing is everything.

"Thank you! Mrs. Cole" Catherine said sincerely.

"No trouble at all. You have very good boys. Just as you said I put that miniature leathern in Little Billy's mouth and he settled right down. He is a very curious baby. His eyes and mind are going lick-a-tee split all the time." Mrs. Cole volunteered.

"You are right, and I think he is picking up things faster than we even imagine he is" Michael contributed to the subject.

"February 12 is day after tomorrow." Michael reminded Catherine.

"President Lincoln will be arriving here...what does that really mean to us, Michael?" Catherine asked with anxiety in her voice.

"Preparation for war, Catherine. In December last South Carolina seceded from the Union, in January Mississippi, Florida, Alabama, Georgia, Louisiana and the beginning of this month Texas seceded" Michael responded. He kept up with all the news. Michael could read and write. Catherine still signed with her mark. That is why she was so determined her boys would read and write.

The President did arrive and was very through with inspecting all the militia companies formed. He also met behind closed doors with selected businessmen. It was apparent he did not trust all those people, military included, that he had met with on his trip. He was very careful in selecting known pro-Union businessmen.

When the President left rumors flew all over town that there were southern sympathizers among the general population and the militia. It was everyone's duty to report whomever they discover meeting that description.

April 12, 1861 Fort Sumter Attacked

Newspapers headlines all over the country rang out with these words of war! General P.G.T. Beauregard, Commander of Confederate Forces of Charleston Harbor opened fire on the Union Garrison at Fort Sumter. At 2:30 pm April 13, 1861 Major Robert Anderson, Union Garrison Commander, surrender the fort and all Union forces evacuated the same. The Civil war between the Confederate States of America and the United States of America had started.

A post card of Military Park, Indianapolis. It was in this park that Michael McCarty enlisted for 3 years. Source: Indianapolis History Society Digital Image Collection.

Michael McCarty Feels Obligated To Join the Union Army.

Michael enlisted with a three-year enlistment in the 5th Battalion of Artillery Volunteers of the State of Indiana on September 22, 1861. Ironically, he did not join the militia Volunteers that made up the Voluntary Infantry Regiment.[48]

Just as everyone had rumored Lt. Francis A. Sharp, another militia Volunteer leader, switched sides and became a Confederate Officer.[49]

Jack had not stopped by in some time. Michael wanted to know if he had enlisted. Contacting his employer, he found out that Jack had returned to his family in Anderson, Indiana.

"I find it strange that he did not say anything to us" Catherine observed.

"It was probably a serious personal matter at home."[50]

---

48 One of the militia leaders was 1st Lt. Frederick Knifler who would rise to the rank of Brigadier General during the war. He would be the highest ranking Jewish Union officer in the Civil War.

49 Francis A. Sharp also became a Brigadier General in the Confederate Army.

50 William Henry Antrim was in a legal battle over whether the government could "draft" him against his will. The case would go to the Supreme Court and pretty much muted by the "Subscription Law" that was passed by congress. He would enlist in June of 1863 and be mustered out the following September, 1863 under the

Michael surmised.

"Honey, I heard today that Governor Oliver Morton[51]has raised 130 companies, that is two times what President Lincoln asked of him...two times! One of his political friends Lew Wallace[52] was given the credit for his success. He put him in charge of the 11th Regiment. Actually, there are only six Regiments recruited...there is no 1st through 5th I guess, well anyway it is confusing to me[53] so I'm sure I'm boring you"

---

minimum enlistment period of 90 days. He spent his time as a guard at Fort Morton on the outskirts of Indianapolis, Indiana.

[51] Governor Morton was the first "Hoosier" born Governor of Indiana, and the man Fort Morton was named after. Fort Morton was first a training camp and then converted to also be a prisoner of war camp.

[52] Lew Wallace misread orders from General Ulysses S. Grant at the Battle of Shiloh in Tennessee (He said, others say he simply got lost) Doing so caused him to arrive at the battle field when it was over. Grant was furious. Wallace said the written order had been given to Frederick Knifler and had in-turn had lost it on the road. General Grant was having none of that excuse and relieved Lew Wallace of his command. Wallace would never see field command again. He remained a Brigadier General in supportive missions. General Grant would eventually also be criticized for his lack of preparation at Shiloh. He was caught by a surprise attack. Actually, he didn't realize the attack was on until his own aide was shot and killed in front of him. He yelled out "They're attacking!" General Grant believed the Confederate Army of Johnston was still at Corinth re-supplying. The Heroes of Shiloh were those who fought at "The Hornet's Nest", General WHL Wallace killed in action (no relative of Lew Wallace) and General Prentiss who survived and gave equal credit in his report to his colleague General WHL Wallace. The second hero was Confederate General Johnston (notably the best fighting general of the Confederacy) had the mind to get himself killed early in the morning of April 7th, 1862. Experts all agree had he lived the Confederates would have won the Battle of Shiloh. One more attack that afternoon and the Union army would have collapsed, and with them Generals Ulysses S. Grant and General Sherman.

Author's comment: I have some bias as my Great Grandfather Burtis H. Rumsey was with the Iowa 11th Infantry Volunteers Company H which fought under the command of Colonel William Hall at Shiloh, which was in Crocker's Brigade and General McClenard's Division of the Army of Tennessee commanded by General Ulysses S. Grant. After General Grant's promotion he fought under General William Tecumseh Sherman until the Regiment's mustering out July 15, 1865. During which time he fought also in the Battles of Shiloh, Corinth, Port Gibson, Raymond, Champion Hill, Big Black River, Siege of Vicksburg, Atlanta, and the March to the Sea.

[53] At enlistment his company was in the 9th Brigade 3rd Division Army of the Ohio. November of 1862 it was re-assigned to 3rd Brigade 2nd Division Right Wing of XIV Corps, Army of the Cumberland until January, 1863 when it was re-assigned to artillery 2nd Division, XX Corps, Army of the Cumberland until October, 1863 when

Michael continued..."You remember Frederick Knifler...he is close friends with Lew Wallace and was promoted to Colonel in command of the 79 Indiana Infantry.

Catherine smiled and replied: "You are never boring to me." Obviously leaving out that she was very bored with the military organizational stuff. She memorized Michaels outfit for posting purposes. The rest would go in one ear and out the other.

"When will you be leaving, dear?" Catherine as usual had her feet planted square on the ground.

"We muster in November 22nd. I suppose they are putting together all the clothes and equipment we need. I plan on reading the newspaper every day. The reporters know what is happening before our own company commander." Michael replied.

"Who is your company commander?" Catherine inquired.

"A fine gentleman with the rank of Captain...Captain Peter Simonson. He is well liked by all those I spoke with. They are already calling us "Simonson's Battery."

November 22, 1861

Catherine fought off her terrible premonition that that morning was going to be the last time she ever saw Michael. It obsessed her from the time she woke up and prepared breakfast. She told herself it was a fear driven emotion and nothing else. God willing, nothing would happen to her husband. She gave herself harsh "self-thought talks" of "Stop the bad thoughts...leave your husband with good feelings...say nothing of this premonition", etc.

"Are you well, Catherine? You have a strange look about you this morning" Michael inquired.

"I'm fine...just missing you already dear" she quickly replied.

"I will keep you posted and tell you as much as I can. They said in most cases I'll be able to say where we have been, but not where we would be going, or anything like that. Don't worry this war will be over soon enough. I do want you to know, should anything happen...not that it will...I want you to find a

---

re-assigned to Artillery, 1st Division, IV Corps, Army of the Cumberland to July 1864 when again re-assigned Artillery Brigade, IV Corps, army of the Cumberland.

good man for these boys and yourself. I want both of them to read and write, even if you have to hire a private tutor. Promise me that, okay?" Michael struggled to give words of his desire beyond his own death.

"Nothing will happen, dear. If it did you know I want the same as you do. I was never given time enough to learn to read or write even when I went to school. We were so hungry in my family that is what we always thought of...how to get food. Our boys will not go hungry and they will go to school." Catherine ended firmly looking Josie in the eye. Josie seemed to fight schooling all the way. He saw no use in it at all.

Michael knelt and looked his oldest boy square in the eyes and said: "You're the man in the house while I'm gone. Do whatever your mother wants, and you will learn to read and write...right?" he asked softly, but firmly.

"Yes, father, I will. Please come home soon!" Josie pleaded and then added: "How can I be a man...I'm 5-years-old?" he said in an innocent and sincere manner.

"A man does not have an age to it...don't ever believe that, son. A man does what he has to do whether he likes it or not. Do you understand?" Michael smiled and hugged his son as he replied that he did understand.

Catherine was standing there enjoying every second of this conversation and thinking of how smart Josie was to have asked that question. She was proud of him.

Michael gave Catherine a last hug and kiss, picked up his gear...then put it back down and picked Little Billy up over his head. Billy smiled ear to ear. He was far too young to understand anything that was happening, only that it was exciting to have his father put him in the air over his head. He felt like he was flying.

"Billy, your mother named you after a famous man...you will be famous someday!" Michael drew him to his chest and then let him down to the ground.

Josie spoke up: "Will I be famous someday, father?"
"If you take schooling serious" he replied as he hugged Josie one more time.

Picking up his gear he left to muster into his company.

Indiana State Fair 1867 was held in Camp Morton. *This camp was formed to train new recruits at the beginning of the Civil War. Later it served as a prisoner of war camp. It was located on outskirts of Indianapolis, Indiana.* ***Michael McCarty trained here. Bill Antrim served here his short enlistment as a guard at POW Camp Morton.*** *Source: Indiana State Library*

Chapter Eleven

Pvt. Michael McCarty, 5th Battalion of The Artillery Volunteers of Indiana November 22, 1861 Indianapolis, Indiana

Captain Simonson watched as his new recruits fell into company formation. They showed promise, but only that at this time. In front of the men were six pieces of artillery.

"Stand at ease" Captain Simonson said in a firm voice.

"Can any of you tell me what kind of artillery you have here in front of your company?" He asked in the same monotone voice. His voice clearly stated he was an educated, confident, military man.

"Yes, sir I can" Michael replied just as confidently.

"They are?" the captain inquired.

"You have two, three-inch Parrott rifles and four, 12-pounder 1857 Napoleons, sir" Michael replied

"Very good. Your name is Private?" the captain asked.

"Michael McCarty sir" Michael replied in a respectful military manner.

"Private Michael McCarty, have you been in the service before?" the captain inquired.

"Sort of, sir. I was in a local militia and trained with those very same pieces of artillery, sir" Michael explained.

"Very good Private McCarty. You will be on a 12-pounder squad. Any of the rest of you been trained in the militia?" Captain Simonson inquired of the company.

A dozen hands went up. He was obviously pleased, so many had at least some basic training. He assigned all the artillery squad teams, and then gave the bad news:

"I must apologize for the United States Army, we usually do not do business this way. Normally, you would receive much training before being ordered to march into war. This war dictates other methods of training. Why? You ask. Because we leave tomorrow morning for Louisville, Kentucky. This will be the last time I ever disclose where we are going... Frankly, whatever I disclose will find its way to the enemy. "

"No sir!" a loud voice came from the ranks. "No spy in this company, and if there is we will hang-um high...quick!"

Captain Simonson knew this was a learning opportunity for his new company.

"Soldier! Step out here in front" the captain ordered the man that had spoken out.

"Are you going to speak out every time you hear me, or any other officer say something you don't like?" the captain said with a firm voice.

"What if you're speaking out gives our position away to the enemy, you do have a very loud voice? My point is soldier, no matter your good intentions you keep such opinions quiet and all decisions to your company commander. Do you understand?" the Captain finished his dressing down of the loud mouth soldier.

"Yes sir, I understand!" the soldier responded politely.

The Captain added: "All of you must remember my job is to get every one of you back to your families alive and well! Of course, we also have a war to win! Right?" he asked with a louder emphasis on the "right."

"Yes sir!" The entire company said in unison.

"Your training will be done on the fly. Each of the squads has a trained man on it. Listen to that person no matter their rank. Treat every word they say as though it is coming from me, your lives will depend on it. Do you all understand this order?" The captain asked firmly.

"Yes, sir!" Again, the entire company said in unison.

Captain Simonson really liked what he saw in these men. They were going to get the job done.

Simonson's Battery was part of the 3rd Division, 9th Brigade, I Corps of the Army of the Ohio, which was commanded by Major General Don Carlos Buell.

Major General Buell made the 3 Division a "special" Division in his Army of the Ohio. The 3rd was like his Commando Division that went where he wanted to strike first and hard, or cover his back door from enemy attack and/or possible retreat. He first ordered them to Kentucky as that states neutrality had been broken. That meant the CSA would certainly try to take Louisville, Kentucky. They could control the whole Ohio Valley from there and cut the Union in two. Not to mention the main railroads supplying the entire Department of the West which included Ulysses S. Grant's Army of the Tennessee, and the Army of the Cumberland in east Tennessee.

Chapter Twelve

Pvt. Michael McCarty, 3rd Division, 9th Brigade Army of the Ohio November 27, 1861 to April 14, 1862

Pvt. Michael McCarty now with the 3rd Division left for Louisville, Kentucky November 27, 1861. They stayed there until December 20th, 1861. Then on to Bacon Creek, Kentucky.[54]

Pvt. Michael McCarty and his outfit stayed at Bacon Creek almost two months until February, 1862. They were then ordered to occupy Bowling Green, Kentucky, which was/is located further south on the L and N Railroad line. On February 15, 1862 the 3rd Division occupied Bowling Green.

Major General Ulysses S. Grant took Fort Henry and Donelson for the 1st major victory for the Union in the war. He captured 14000 Confederate soldiers. His boss Lt. General Henry Halleck[55] gave him a promotion and took full credit for the victory asked Washington to promote himself to solely in command of the Department of the West, which he then shared with Lt. General Don Carlos Buell Commander of the Army of

---

[54] This town had two significant events recently. First, it was where the first Kentuckian blood was shed in the Civil War (on October of 1861).

The CSA had attacked Columbus, Kentucky breaking the "neutrality" of Kentucky.[54] The second significant event was that the nucleus of what would become the Army of the Cumberland was formed near Bacon Creek, Kentucky.

Bacon Creek was located on the main tracks of the L and N (Louisville – Nashville) Railroad, and critical militarily to protect transportation to middle Tennessee. Eastern Tennessee was Pro-Union, Middle Tennessee split, and western Tennessee was pro-Confederate.

[55] Lt. General Halleck was a very difficult man to work for. He was a "headquarters general" never in the field of action. Yet, his strength of organizing, administrating, coordinating, and planning military campaigns was at the genius level. He is considered one of the fathers of modern warfare. General Grant said: "He is one of the greatest men of our age", Major General William T. Sherman said he is a "directing genius."

the Ohio. His request was denied. Using rumors of alcoholism, he relieved Grant of his command.

While Michael McCarty's outfit occupied Bowling Green, Kentucky a short distance south Major General Grant was meeting with General Buell in Nashville, Tennessee.

Abraham Lincoln himself put pressure on Lt. General Henry Halleck to reinstate Major General Grant's command. It did matter to Lincoln that Halleck was considered America's first professional military scholar, or the fact he had lectured at Lowell Institute in Boston on the "Elements of Military Art and Science," and later published the same. Also, that his nickname was "Old Brains."[56]

Yes, that mattered, but his egotistical display of power, overt reflection of glory to himself, and relief of command of a winning general, that was unacceptable. In no uncertain terms Lt. General Halleck was informed of President's Lincoln's displeasure with **his** decision.

Major General Grant's command was reinstated, and he was told by Lt. General Halleck that he was "righting a wrong." Major General Grant wrote him and said: *"I did not know I have an enemy between you and me."* General Halleck replied: *"You have no enemy between you and me."* Major General Grant was not one to hold a grudge in such matters and Lt. General Halleck remained in his high regard militarily.[57] Politically, he would become far more aware in those matters.

Abraham Lincoln needed fighters in the west. He was aware that his Army was about to engage one on one with a man both sides considered the best fighting field general of either

[56] At the time the term was a compliment, later it became derogatory. Halleck had also studied in 1844 in Europe on European Fortifications, and Henri Jomini's "Vie politique et militaire de Napoleon."

[57] When promoted to General of the Army Ulysses S. Grant made General Halleck (whom he replaced and was his old political enemy) his Chief of Staff and relied on "Old Brains's" consultation a lot. He knew Halleck was the most brilliant and scholarly military man in America at the time. Halleck strongly endorsed General Sherman's March to the Sea and General Sheridan's March through Shenandoah Valley which broke the back of the South and by-in-large won the Civil War for the North. After those two battles it was just a matter of time for the South to run out of bullets and bread.

side: Confederate General Albert Sidney Johnston.[58] He knew General Grant was a fighter. When told through the chain of command of Grant's heavy drinking (originated by Halleck) Abraham Lincoln replied: *"Find out what he is drinking and send it to all my generals,"* or words to that effect.

General Grant requested, and it was approved to have The Army of the Ohio provide reinforcement to his Army of Tennessee and the newly formed Army of the Mississippi at the upcoming battle that would occur somewhere between Corinth, Mississippi and Pittsburg Landing in Tennessee.

Corinth had four railroad lines merging to it. It was a true hub for rail transportation in the south. General Grant needed to take it and hold it. Major General Don Carlos Buell ordered the Army of the Ohio to meet General Grants Army at Pittsburg Landing. Except his 3rd Division! The division that Michael McCarty belonged to.

Major General Buell was going to cut the south in half. He ordered Michael McCarty's 3 Division to march to Murfreesboro, Tennessee for three days doing reconnaissance on Shelbyville, Tullahoma, and McMinnville. Then advanced to Fayetteville and captured Huntsville, Alabama April 14, 1862.

Major General Buell and the rest of his army marched to arrive just in time to save General Grant's Army of the Tennessee at Shiloh (Hebrew for "Place of Peace," there would be no peace at Shiloh April 6, and 7th, 1862).

General Grant had gotten extremely lucky on the 6th of April 1862. He was caught with his whole army unprepared to fight. He thought General Johnston was recruiting, supplying, and planning in Corinth. The old man out foxed Major General Grant and snuck his entire army up from Corinth (24 miles) at night and bivouacking only two miles from Union forces. None were detected until 5:15 a.m. by a reconnaissance patrol from Major General Prentiss' 1st Brigade, commanded by Colonel Everett Peabody. The spirited exchange of gun fire with a Confederate outpost helped a little to position some Union

[58] General Johnston had fought with three armies, US Army 1826 – 1834, 1846 , and 1849 to 1861, Republic of Texas as a brevet Brigadier General 1836 to 1840, and then the Confederate Army 1861 to April 6, 1862 (Killed in action).

soldiers. By-in-large the full attack at 6 am was a total surprise attack to Major General Grant at Shiloh.

Major General Grant did not realize the attack until his own aid was shot and killed in front of him. He then declared very loud: "They are attacking!"

His luck came when Confederate General Johnston was shot and killed that morning. Confederate General P.G. R. Beauregard took command of all Confederate troops at Shiloh. He received word that General Buell was at Pittsburg Landing, and would be arriving anytime for a counter attack. General Grant's 11th Iowa Volunteer Infantry[59] were pushed back but held their line preventing Confederate General Bragg from penetrating the Union's left flank. General Benjamin M. Prentiss formed what would become to be known as the "Hornets' Nest," and repelled wave after wave of attacking Confederates from Confederate Generals Bragg, Polk and Breckinridge.

Major General Sherman almost lost the Union right flank. He had left Major General Lew Wallace (of Lincoln County fame when Territorial Governor of New Mexico) as a reserve at Crumps Landing at a place called Stoney Lonesome. He sent an urgent message for him to rush as fast as he could to Pittsburg Landing.

Major General Wallace got confused and ended up marching in a large circle landing right back at Crumps Landing. After he got his directions correct he marched the river road to Pittsburg Landing arriving about 7 at night of April 7, 1862. The Battle of Shiloh was over.

Major General Sherman and Major General Grant were not happy with Major General Lew Wallace. Major General Sherman had miraculously held the right flank (crediting a lot to the 11th Iowa Volunteer Infantry and others) and wanted nothing more to do with a general that shows up late to a battle.

Major General Lew Wallace was able to convince Major General Grant enough of his innocence to allow him to stay in

[59] The 11th as a large monument erected at Shiloh in honor of their holding the line. Also, I must declare my Great Grandfather Burtis H. Rumsey was in the Iowa 11th Volunteer Infantry and survived Shiloh and the rest of the battles he fought under General Sherman to the end of the war.

the army. He participated in the Siege of Corinth as commander of the 3rd Division of the Army of the Tennessee.[60]

What Confederate General P.G. R. Beauregard did not realize, none of Major General Grant's army could have withstood one more attack when he ordered the retreat of all Confederate forces to Corinth, Mississippi? Luck was on General Grant's side at the Battle of Shiloh.[61]

---

[60]Wallace also was at the Protection of Cincinnati. His last battle was another disgrace for him: the Battle of Monocacy near Frederick, Maryland on July 9, 1864.

Major General Lew Wallace had 5800 soldiers and Confederate Lt. General Jubal A. Early had 14,000 soldiers. It was a decisive victory for the Confederate General. General Wallace got lucky when it was considered a "strategic victory" for the Union. That was his last battle field command.

[61] Had General Johnston lived his colleagues (and some Union generals alike) agreed he would have known he had the momentum, and without any hesitation kept attacking and won the Battle of Shiloh.

General Don Carlos Buell was a cautious man and would have thought twice of attacking Johnston when he was one full division short in the Army of the Ohio. Leaving him with no reinforcements himself. The 3rd Division was too far away to serve in that capacity. It is speculation, but had General Beauregard continue with his attack (which he had the momentum and soldiers to accomplish the same with) he may have won the entire Department of the West from the Union.

General P.G. R. Beauregard would live the rest of his life with that decision and subsequent criticisms. He held strong that he did not have the supplies to continue the fight. He could resupply at Corinth.

Confederate General Gibson, his worse critic, publically stated after the Civil War ended:

"General Johnston's death was a tremendous catastrophe. There are no words adequate to express my own conception of the immensity to the loss of our country. Sometimes the hopes of millions of people depend upon one head and one arm. The West perished with Albert Sidney Johnston and the Southern Country followed."

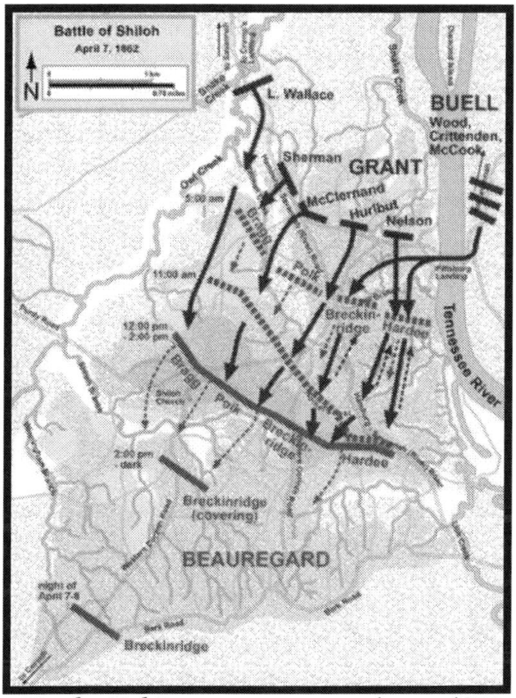

Map by Hal Jespersen, www.posix.com/CW

Chapter Thirteen

Pvt. Michael McCarty,
3 Division, 9th Brigade
Army of the Ohio
April 14, 1862 to January 2, 1863

Michael's outfit was ordered to capture Decatur, Alabama on the Tennessee River. They captured Decatur on April 14, 1862.

Next they were ordered to take Bridgeport, Alabama. From there they were to detach all along the Nashville and Chattanooga Railroad and protect the same for the North.

Michael McCarty's outfit was critical to Major General Grant's plan to use the Tennessee River and the railroads to defeat the Confederate Army of Tennessee. Virtually, they were the "commando" Division to capture all of Tennessee.

The 3rd Division was ordered next to Stevenson, Alabama, where that summer the Union Fort Harker was built. It was an earthen redoubt 150-foot square with walls 14 feet high, and an 8-foot-deep dry mote around it. Also having a draw bridge and an eight-sided wooden block house in the middle, it gave the appearance of a miniature medieval castle.

It contained seven cannon platforms that had easy firing range on the railroad at the small town of Stevenson. This little town was the junction of the Charleston – Memphis and Nashville – Chattanooga Railroads. It was small but militarily critical to control the middle Tennessee and to supply armies in Eastern Tennessee.

It was then that Major General Don Carlos Buell learned that Confederate General Braxton Bragg (the same general that had almost broken the right flank of Major General Grant and Major General Sherman at Shiloh) had "end-run" him and was marching his Army of the Mississippi north to Louisville, Kentucky.

The 3rd Division was ordered to march to Nashville, Tennessee and on to Louisville, Kentucky to pursue and defeat of General Braxton Bragg.

Michael McCarty and his fellow soldiers didn't know what was up, but they knew it had to be important to have left Stevenson in such a hurry. Where ever they were going it was going to be a big battle. They were very correct in that assumption.

It took almost a month (August 31 to September 26, 1862) for them to arrive in Louisville Kentucky. They had beaten Braxton to Louisville, but not by much. His forces were advancing toward the small town of Perryville, Kentucky with the intent of marching into Louisville from there.

Major General Don Carlos Buell pushed his entire army 55,000 men strong south the 75 miles to Perryville. The two forces met each other at Perryville and the battle began in full October 8, 1862.

Michael McCarty's 5th Independent Battery, Indiana Light Artillery were some of the heroes for the Union in this important battle. They secured the high ground for their artillery and held it.

Major General Buell's Infantry was not as successful, and the two sides pushed each other back and forth, again and again.[62] The battle ended with a Confederate tactical victory, but unquestionably a strategic victory for the Union.

Although General Braxton Bragg knew he had won the Battle of Perryville he had exhausted all his supplies in doing so, with no replacements of supplies or troops available. He had no choice but to retreat. He retreated all the way to Tennessee to never to enter Kentucky again.[63]

Major General Don Carlos Buell had made a serious military error that could not be overlooked by his superiors. He had positioned his headquarters 2 miles from his nearest soldiers, and much further from Major General Alexander McCrook's I Corps. The I Corp was hit the hardest and had to fall back with major casualties. Only his Artillery groups were holding the high ground.

Major General Buell was too far away to know what was happening in the field and by the time he discovered I Corps needed reinforcements the battle was over. He had to pull all his army back to regroup. Of his 55,000-man army only 22,000 were engaged, therefore, he had plenty of reserves to win the battle overwhelming General Braxton who had only 16,000 total troops engaged. Major General Buell lost the battle with twice the resources because he waited too long to use them.

Major General Buell was relieved of his command by Lt General Ulysses S. Grant now in charge of all forces in the West. He was replaced by Major General William S. Rosecrans (nick named "Old Rosy") who had just won his 2nd battle with a Confederate Army, which was the 2nd Battle of Corinth, Mississippi. Confederate Major General Earl Van Dorn had

---

[62] The Battle of Perry became the bloodiest battle of the civil war to that date, in terms of total casualties to total soldiers involved. Historians have also said it was one of the most important battles of the Civil War.

[63] Ironically, Bragg won the battle. Had he planned better he could have controlled the Ohio Valley, Ohio River, and halted the Union supplies to the Department of the West. That would have been a deathly blow to the Union. Would ah,-could ha, and should ah.

tried to retake Corinth with his 22,000-manned army. It was a decisive win tactically and strategically for the Union.

Major General Rosecrans at the direction of Lt. General Grant merged his Army of the Mississippi with the Army of the Ohio and named the "new" the Army of the Cumberland.[64]

In the reorganization Michael McCarty's unit became part of the 2nd Division, 3rd Brigade, Right Wing of XIV Corps, and Army of the Cumberland. It remained with that Corps until January of 1863 when it became part of the Artillery of the 2nd Division of the XX corps, Army of the Cumberland.

The Army of the Cumberland's mission: Pursue and Defeat Confederate General Braxton Bragg.

The pursuit began immediately after the reorganization. The individual field units pretty much remained intact, therefore, leadership at the field level was consistent.

Michael McCarty and the Army of the Cumberland marched south all the way through Kentucky without a sign of resistance. Confederate General Bragg had retreated all the way to Murfreesboro, Tennessee. There he planned to recruit, train and resupply before another major battle.

The Army of the Cumberland marched to Nashville, Tennessee. General Bragg's Army of Tennessee was a short 34 miles south and slightly east of Nashville. It was critical to the control of Middle Tennessee as two railroads merge there and a major river named Stones River flowed north and south of Middle Tennessee.

December 26, 1862 Michael McCarty and his Battery left Nashville and on December 31, 1862 found themselves facing 35,000 determined Confederate soldiers at Murfreesboro, Tennessee. Determined to remove the Union Army from Middle Tennessee.

Both commanders had decided to attack on the right flank first. Unfortunately for the Union, Confederate General

---

[64] Major General Rosecrans had a future President of the United States on his staff: Brigadier General James A. Garfield.

Bragg beat Major General Rosecrans to the punch! He struck first and hard.

December 31, 1862 Confederate Major General William J. Hardee (of the Shiloh fame) attacked the Union's right flank first...then right behind him came Major General Leonidas Polk for another attack on the right flank (and was another Shiloh Confederate General).

Union Brigadier General Phillip Sheridan saved the Union from complete collapse. He held the Center against Confederate General Polk's determined attack. This gave Major General Rosecrans the time to reinforce his right flank. It had backed up almost to the railroad tracks. He also sent his Artillery units, including Michael McCarty, to cross the Stones River and occupy the high ground overlooking the entire battle field, railroad tracks, and Stones River. He also sent more soldiers to defend the Nashville road and his soon to be needed supplies and reinforcements.

Brigadier General Sheridan held the line at a tremendous cost. In the fighting he had been literally surrounded on three sides. His position would become to be known as "The Slaughter Pen." All three of his Brigade Commanders were killed that first day. One third of all his soldiers were casualties in four hours of the first day. Yet, he held!

Colonel William B. Hazen's Brigade held a rocky four-acre wooded area known as Round Forest. Brigadier General Milo S. Hascall sent Hazen the 3rd Kentucky as re-enforcements. He ordered Colonel Hazen *"It had to be held even if it cost the last man he had."* Col. Hazen's brigade was the only one that held its original position through-out the battle. The locals from then on called Round Forest *"Hell's half Acre."*

Overall by 10 a.m. General Bragg had captured 28 guns and 3000 Union soldiers. He had driven left, right, and center back to almost the railroad track. He had the momentum without question, then a few things went very wrong for him.

His first mistake was depending on his General Beckenridge to follow his order of crossing back across the river to reinforce the left flank. His general refused saying he should attack Union Major General Crittenden position first.

General Bragg allowed him to his hunch. General Beckenridge was said to be embarrassed to find no Union

General Crittenden or any of his troops at all. Union General Crittenden had pulled back early in the morning.

His second mistake was believing a false report that Major General Rosecrans had a strong reinforcement moving up the road from Nashville. His scout had mistaken the heavy guards as there to protect large amounts of troops and supplies.

During the evening of January 2nd, 1863 General Bragg decided to retreat and resupply his battered army. He felt he had won a victory, but was mistaken about that also. He had just pushed the Union army back into a tighter more defendable position and let its Artillery units win the battle.

Michael McCarty was one of the heroes of the Battle of Stones River (the Confederate's called it the battle of Murfreesboro). Their artillery position was never taken out of action and delivered the final blow to the Confederates.

General Bragg soon realized he was up against just as a determined a General as himself. General Rosecrans had committed 41,400 troops, and had proven to be a strong leader, and he would not make the same mistake General Buell had at Perryville. He also had supply lines and reserve troops in Nashville. The Nashville road was very well guarded and heavy escorts were attached to each supply train. His Counsel of War had rallied his generals to hold at all cost and win! Which they did!

The heavy fighting at Stones River made it the costliest battle for both sides in the Civil War to that date.

	Union	Confederate
Total engaged:	41,400	35,000
Total casualties:	12,906	11,739
Killed:	1,677	1,294
Wounded:	7,543	7,945
Captured/Missing:	3,686	2,500

Confederate General Braxton Bragg's total retreat from the battle field made it a decisive victory for the Union.

It rejuvenated the morale of the entire Union army when they heard of the victory at Stones River.

The Union soldier's morale was low after the Union loss at Fredericksburg, Virginia by Union General Ambrose Burnside against Confederate General Robert E. Lee December 11 to December 15, 1862.

General Lee had beat General Burnside with 35,000 less troops engaged. General Burnside had suffered 12,650 casualties to General Lee's 5377. General Burnside had disengaged and retreated, a decisive victory for the Confederates. The loss had been demoralizing to the entire Union Army.

The Union victory at the Battle of Stones River restored the morale of the entire Union Army. President Abraham Lincoln sent a message for The Army of the Cumberland:

"You gave us a hard-earned victory, which there being defeat instead, the nation could scarcely have lived over."

Chapter Fourteen

Pvt. Michael McCarty, 3 Division, 9th Brigade Army of the Cumberland January 3, 1863 to July 3, 1863

Kentucky and Middle Tennessee had been won by the Union. Most importantly was Nashville, Tennessee. It was a major supply base for the rest of the war. Railroads ran north, south, west, and east from Nashville.

Having said that Michael McCarty and his outfit's job was not completed. General Braxton Bragg was alive and well in Tullahoma, Tennessee.

Major General William S. Rosecrans understood how close the last battle with General Braxton Bragg was. Again, General Bragg had disengaged and retreated when he really had the momentum. Had General Breckenridge followed his orders and reinforced the left flank, and have stayed engaged a couple more hours, he quite well might have won that battle.

Now General Braxton Bragg was in friendlier territory recruiting. The further east and south in Tennessee the higher the Southern sympathy.

Major General Rosecrans began a major recruiting and supplying, and tactical field training effort before chasing General Bragg any further. He stayed at Murfreesboro until June of 1863.

To the west on May 18th, 1863 his boss Lt. General Ulysses S. Grant had attacked Confederate General John C. Pemberton at Vicksburg, Mississippi. Unable to take the well-fortified city of Vicksburg after a couple serious tries with high casualties, he did what all good generals do in such times. A well-fortified city is also one very hard to resupply under a siege. General Grant put a siege on the entire city from land and water approaches. General Pemberton held out for forty days before surrendering. He became a Prisoner of War of Lt. General Ulysses S. Grant on July 4, 1863.

Major General Rosecrans had spent five months training his Army of the Cumberland for the next battle with General Bragg. He had repeated requested cavalry units and had been repeatedly turned down by Washington. Finally, he received permission to mount some of his infantry. He had to obtain horses, mules, and tack from the locals.

He ordered Colonel John T. Wilder's Brigade of Reynolds division (1500 men of the 17th and 72nd Indiana Regiments and the 98th and 123rd Illinois Regiment) to create a cavalry unit. The new cavalry brigade would be led by Colonel Mitchell.

They scrubbed the countryside mounting and arming themselves. They all had hatches for close hand to hand combat and their fellow soldiers initially nicknamed them the "Hatchet Brigade." That nick name was about to change. Major General Rosecrans was very pleased and issued every cavalry man with a brand-new Spencer seven-shot repeating rifle.

This battle was very well planned out by Major General Rosecrans. He would give General Bragg a feint by sending his cavalry unit in advance making General Bragg believe the main attack would come from his left flank. It wasn't until after this movement Major General Rosecrans met with his Corps commanders to give them the details of the battle plan.

June 23, 1863 Colonel Wilder's cavalry brigade struck Hoover's Gap like a bolt of lightning and captured the critical spot on the first day. From then on his unit would be called the Lightning Brigade. Confederate Brigadier General William B. Bate reinforced by Brigadier General Bushrod Johnson assaulted Wilder's position several times and were each time driven back by those Spencer rifles.

Union Major general George Thomas, arrived with his XIV corps and shook Colonel Wilder's hand and said: *"You have saved the lives of a thousand men by your gallant conduct today. I didn't expect to get to this gap for three days."*

Technically called a "campaign," the Campaign of Tullahoma went on to July 3, 1863. Major General Rosecrans' panning paid off in a big way. He had 50 to 60 thousand soldiers engaged on and off and suffered only a total of 569 casualties:

The Campaign of Tullahoma

	Union	Confederate
Total engaged:	50 – 60,000	45,000
Total casualties:	564	Unknown
Killed:	83	Unknown
Wounded:	473	Unknown
Captured/Missing:	13	1,634

Some historians have stated Major General Rosecrans performance was the best of the Civil War on either side. He planned and executed his plan like a Swiss watch. It may very well have been on paper the best performance, but he failed in one major aspect, General Braxton Bragg was still alive as was his Army of the Tennessee. The Confederate general was good at "high-tailing" to fight again later.

Another problem that Major General Rosecrans had was that two other major victories (Gettysburg July 3, 1863 and Vicksburg July 4, 1863) were getting all the attention from the press and Washington. Major General Ulysses S. Grant, his boss, wanted him to eliminate the Confederate Army of Tennessee. Although his progress was good, and he controlled all the Middle Tennessee, it did not meet Major General Grant's expectation. He was ordered to pursue General Bragg immediately, and he did so.

Major General Rosecrans

General Braxton Bragg

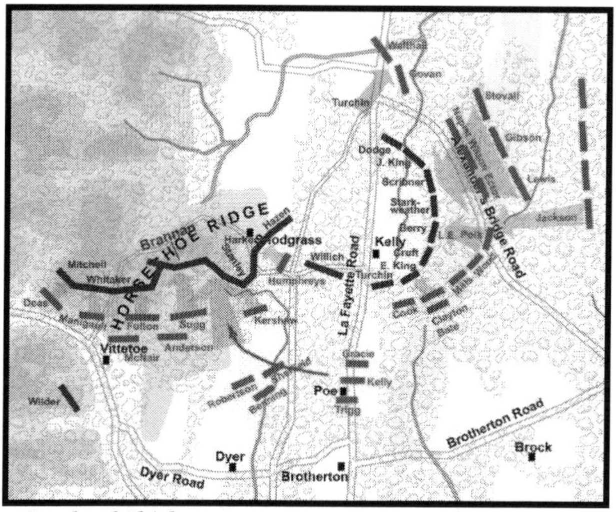

Battle of Chickamauga, Georgia September 20, 1863
Source: Hal Jespersen www.posix.com/CWmaps/

Chapter Fifteen

Pvt. Michael McCarty, 3 Division, 9th Brigade Army of the Cumberland August 16, 1863-November 30, 1863

The Union Army of Tennessee chased the Confederate Army of Tennessee out of Tennessee into Georgia (considered then and now as the "Deep South"). Major General Rosecrans passed through Cumberland Mountains, across the Tennessee River and faced Confederate General Braxton Bragg at **Chickamauga, Georgia.**

General Braxton Bragg was determined to defeat Major General Rosecrans and re-occupy Chattanooga, Tennessee. His retreating was over. He felt he had set the right trap and was about to spring it on Major General Rosecrans.

Major General Rosecrans proved himself not to be a good planner on the fly (shooting from the hip in the field as the old

saying goes). His communication fell apart. He made one drastic error at the Battle of Chickamauga:
September 19, 1863 General Bragg made a strong assault to break the Union line. He continued all day with relentless assault after assault.

Battle of Chickamauga started here at Lee & Gordon's Mill, West Chickamauga Creek September 19 and 20 1863.[65]
Source: National Archives & Records Administration

September 20, 1863 General Bragg began assaulting Major General Rosecrans line again. Then the latter made a huge error in judgment, he did not confirm with his field commanders' intelligence he received that there was a "gap in his line." He ordered units to reposition to fill the supposed gap. He had no gap, and the units he sent to fill it did create a big gap in his line. Yes, he had created his own gap in his defensive line.

That gap opened right in front of Confederate Lt General James Longstreet who immediately attacked with eight brigades' right through the gap.

Major General Rosecrans and one third of his entire army had to flee the battlefield or be wiped out.
Major General George H. Thomas assumed overall command of all Union forces that remained in the field.

---

[65] "Landscapes of The Civil War" edited by Constance Sullivan, published by Alfred A. Knopf, New York 1995 Pg. 88

Although wave after wave of Confederate attacks inflicted casualties, Major General Thomas held their positions until dark. They would not be able to retreat until darkness; a day light retreat would have resulted in complete annihilation. They had to hold at all host until the cover of darkness.

This also meant the wounded would not receive proper attention until they could retreat to Chattanooga, as the field surgeons were forced to leave the field with Major General Rosecrans.

Major General Thomas had every able-bodied soldier on the line fighting for their very survival. It would be called the **Defensive of Horseshoe Ridge**. It can be assumed they knew they were holding to allow thousands of their fellow soldiers could escape back to Chattanooga. They were surrounded on three sides in short order.

One of the heroes of Stones River, Michael McCarty, received a musket bullet to his knee at the Defense of Horseshoe Ridge at the Battle of Chickamauga. It was not a fatal wound. He needed a field surgeon that would cut the leg above the knee, cauterize it, sterilize it, and he would be sent home (in this case Indianapolis, Indiana) to live a long life with one wooden leg representing a "red badge of courage."

Michael McCarty was carried out after dark and brought back to the field surgeon at Chattanooga, Tennessee. He held to life with all he had in him to do so. He survived some of the bloodiest battles of the Civil War.

Chattanooga represented another problem for the Army of the Cumberland. They were under siege. Confederate General Bragg had Missionary Ridge and Lookout Mountain. He had stationed troops in the valley and along the Tennessee River. He had placed a tight siege grip of the entire city. Nothing and nobody could move in or out of Chattanooga. He would starve them out.

Hours after Major General Rosecrans reported the loss of the Battle of Chickamauga Secretary of War Edwin W. Stanton ordered Major General Joseph Hooker to Chattanooga with 15,000 troops consisting of 2 full Corps of the Army of the Potomac. He also ordered Major General Ulysses S. Grant to send 20,000 troops under Major General William T. Sherman from Vicksburg, Tennessee to Chattanooga immediately. He also ordered Major General Grant to go to Chattanooga himself as Commander of the Military Division of Mississippi from there.

The new responsibility would put all Union forces from the Appalachian Mountains to the Mississippi River under Major General Grant.

Grant immediately put Major General George Thomas in command of the Army of the Cumberland. His telegram said: *"Hold Chattanooga at all hazards. I will be there soon as possible."* Major General George Thomas replied: *"We will hold the town till we starve."*

Major General Grant traveled over a treacherous mountain road with terrible weather conditions and arrived in Chattanooga on October 23, 1863.

Brigadier General William F. "Baldy" Smith was Chief of Engineers for the Army of the Cumberland. He presented an idea of how to get supplies into Chattanooga. Major General Grant was ecstatic and approved of it immediately. It would be named the "The Cracker Line".

October 27, 1863 Major General Hazen's men floated down river at night right pass the Confederates guarding Brown's Ferry.[66] Major General Turchin followed Hazen. Major General Hooker amazingly marched his column through Lookout Valley and linked with Hazen and Turchin on October 28, 1863.

Confederate General Bragg was getting confusing reports and in some cases as with General Longstreet no report of any Union movements. Bragg ordered Longstreet on two separate occasion where Longstreet chose to ignore the order and do what he thought best at the moment.

Major General William T. Sherman brought his last three Divisions across the Tennessee River on November 23, 1863. He dug in at "Billy Goat Hill."

---

[66] Confederate General Bragg had serious personnel problems. A number of his direct report Generals had petitioned President Jefferson Davis to have him relieved of command. President Davis actually came to the Chattanooga Siege and met with General Bragg. He decided to keep Bragg in charge, most likely an error in judgment that would cost him Tennessee, and much more!

Major General Grant ordered Major General Thomas to test the center line of the Confederate position on Lookout Mountain. If he received fire to retreat. The general must have not paid much attention to the latter part of that order. He arrived at the base of the mountain and received some heavy fire from higher ground. They charged up the mountain and sent the Confederate Army of Tennessee on the run. They had broken the center line and General Bragg had to retreat or be destroyed.

General Bragg retreated to Dalton, Georgia never to return to Tennessee. He had sent General Longstreet on a mission to lay siege on Major General Burnside at Knoxville, Tennessee and Longstreet did follow that order.

President Abraham Lincoln sent a telegraph to Major General Grant:

"Well done. Many thanks to all. Remember Burnside."

Short but said it all. Major General Grant sent General William T. Sherman with 25,000 men to relieve the siege of Knoxville. General Longstreet abandoned the siege and "went to his winter quarters and reported to Virginia in the spring of 1884."

November 30, 1863 Michael McCarty lost his fight to live. He lived long enough to see the Army of the Cumberland win Kentucky and all of Tennessee for the Union. The actual cause of death was more than likely an infection, in-that to have survived from September 20, 1863 to November 30, 1863 his initial wound had been given attention.

Infection and disease killed almost as many soldiers as bullets and cannon balls in the Civil War.

John Ross House, Rossville, Georgia was the Union's "blood-soaked field hospital" for the wounded of the Battle of Chickamauga, Georgia. Pvt. Michael McCarty, 5th Indiana Battery wounded September 20, 1863 clung to life until he lost the battle for it November 30, 1863. He died in this house.
Source: National Archives & Records Administration

Letter from Captain A. Morrison:[67]

"I certify, on honour, that Michael McCarty, a private of Captain Simonson's 5th Battery of Artillery Volunteers, of the State of Indiana, born in Cork County of Ireland, aged of 27 years, 5 feet 6 inches tall, fair complexion, blue eyes, brown hair, and by occupation a labourer, having joined the company on its original organization in Indianapolis, Indiana on the 22nd day of September 1861, to serve in the Regiment for the term of three years and having served honestly and faithfully with the 5th Ind. Battery to Nov. 30, 1863, is now entitled to a discharge by reason of death in General Field Hospital at Chickamauga Nov. 30th 1863 of gunshot wound received at Battle of Chickamauga, Georgia.

The said Private Michael McCarty was last paid by Paymaster Fullerton to include the 30th day of June, 1863, and has pay due him from that time to the 30th day of Nov. 1863, he

---

[67] The letter from Captain Morrison and the letter from the surgeon appear exactly as they were written, including misspelled words. If it seems strange that army officers would misspell or use poor grammar, keep in mind that Christopher "Kit" Carson was a regular officer in the United States Army and was illiterate…he could not read nor write.

is entitled to pay and subsistence for travelling to place of enrolment and whatever other allowances are authorized to volunteer soldiers, or militia, so discharged. He has received twenty ($20.94) dollars, advanced by the United States on account of clothing.
Signed,
A. Morrison, Captain, Commanding Company ***September 28, 1864***[68] *Chattanooga, Tennessee*

Letter from the Surgeon in charge to the Senior Artillery Officer, 5th Battery General Field Hospital, Chattanooga, Tennessee:

December 1st, 1863:
"Sir, it becomes my duty to inform you that Michael McCarty, of the 5th Ind. Battery, died in this hospital Nov. 30th, 1863, from a gunshot wound of the knee joint. His effects are one pocket wallet containing fifty cents in money and one three-cent postage stamp.[69] *One hat, one blouse, one pair pants and one pipe."*

Catherine McCarty is now a widow with two children, William Henry McCarty (who had just turned 4-years-old) and Joseph McCarty (who was nine-years-old). Of course, she has not yet been made aware of her new "widow" status.

---

68 This date is almost a year after his actual date of death. Possibly Captain A. Morrison was making an audit of the original three-year enlistments that expired in September, 1864. He may have discovered a letter had not been written after his death at Chattanooga, Tennessee. The city was under siege and nothing came in or out of it for a long time, and when the siege was lifted with Major General Grant's arrival all focus was on organizing for the push into Georgia, and the saving of Major General Burnside trapped in a siege of Knoxville. This author is sure that Michael McCarty's death was one of many that went unrecorded during the Siege of Chattanooga. Even the burial was not standard procedure. When ask how the officer in charge wanted them buried…by states? His reply was: "No, mix them up. I've had my fill of state's rights" or words to that effect.

69 Having a postage stamp on him at death meant he was posting to Catherine. This is significant as it appears she was not notified of his death before the September 28, 1864 accounting by Captain Morrison. Therefore, from her perspective he was posting and suddenly stopped for many months. That had to drive Catherine near crazy. She did not know if he was alive or dead.

Chapter Sixteen

Widow Catherine McCarty 199 North East Street Indianapolis, Indiana October, 1863 to October, 1864

Catherine received posts from Michael periodically. There would be sometimes months between the posts and then she would receive several at one time. Now, she had not received a post for six months. That made her very anxious.

She started cleaning clothes for a living soon after Michael joined the army, as Michael's military pay sent home was not enough to pay the bills, besides sustain her and the boys.

It was spring, May 1864, when Catherine had a strong intuition that Michael was not coming home. She was confused why if something happened to him, the Army would not inform her. Many of her customers had received notice that their loved one was killed in action or even injured. She heard nothing.

The work was hard and the hours long, but she was not complaining. Her Joseph was attending school, and little Billy loved to see what his older brother was learning. He had a bright and curious mind.

Catherine had to move from 385 N. New Jersey because her business out grew their original little townhouse. The new location gave her more room to dry clothes, and a lot more of them.

She internalized her fears and had accepted that she may never see Michael again. She loved him very much, but held an ill feeling, very close to a resentment, for his insistence on joining the army when he had a wife and two young children.

She couldn't write, but she had one of her customers post the new address to Michael. The lady was so elegant and stylish. She brought clothes to her every week. Catherine knew every one of her dresses. One week she noticed the lady had dropped off a dress that she had cleaned the week before. It was also obvious it had not been worn. When the lady came to pick it up she gave it back with no charge.

The lady said:

"Catherine you forgot to charge me for this one," she declared in a very polite manner.

"No ma'am, I didn't clean it this week...I cleaned it last week and it's not been worn." Catherine replied honestly.

"Oh no...your wrong...I'm sure I wore that one," the nice lady replied with surprise.

"Ma'am, believe me, I know your clothes very well. Anyway, I cannot charge you for work I did not do," Catherine said firmly.

"okay, but please keep it here and clean it again," she asked very politely.

"Alright, I'll do it, but I'm sure it doesn't need it. This will be the cleanest dress you have ever worn," Catherine said with her wonderful jolly Irish laughter and continued with:

"Oh, you know if you're doing this to help me out, I accept tips!" Catherine said hoping she was not offending her wonderful customer.

"Oh...yes....okay I'll take the dress." She realized she was creating more work for Catherine. She replied with a big smile. The lady's smile was beautiful and gave happiness in its happening.

She pulled out a $20 gold piece from her purse (those were very rare during the war).

"Wow...that is way too much ma'am," Catherine complained.

"No...it is not. Please take this and it will make me feel good. Kind of... like I have done something for the war effort in my own way...Please take it for me?" the lady asked in such a manner Catherine couldn't say no without feeling like a heel herself.

"Mrs. Reilly, thank you very much," Catherine said as she looked down at the twenty-dollar gold piece.

"Have you heard from your Michael?" The kind Mrs. Reilly asked.

"No...I haven't. He usually posted once a month, but I haven't heard anything for six months. I am worried." Catherine said in a sad manner, her voice falling off to almost a whisper at the end.

"Six months! That is unacceptable! My husband is Colonel James William Reilly.[70] He is a Brigade Commander in the Army of the Ohio. I will find out what is going on. What outfit is Michael in?" The mild mannered polite lady turned into a she-lion. She would get to the bottom of why Catherine hadn't received posts.

"He too was in the Army of the Ohio, but last post from him said he was then in the Army of the Cumberland. That was confusing to me. How do they change armies? I thought there was only one army. Oh! Yes, I do know he was with Simonson's Battery. At least that is what they called it. I'm sorry ma'am, I can't write this down...I cannot write.[71]" Catherine sadly informed Mrs. Reilly. Her voice fell off again, so low at the end Mrs. Reilly barely understood her.

"No problem, Catherine. Some of my best friends cannot read nor write. Here, I have paper and pen with me." Mrs. Reilly spoke not in a condescending manner, but attempting to put Catherine at ease.

She pulled out a miniature ink well and quill pen, and proceeded to take down all the information Catherine gave her about Michael and what she knew of the outfits he was serving in.

"I will let you know as soon as I hear anything about your husband." Mrs. Reilly stated with confidence. Catherine already

---

[70] Colonel James William Reilly was with the 104 Ohio Infantry. He was assigned to Major General Burnside when he took over the Army of the Ohio after having had a disastrous loss to General Robert E. Lee at Fredericksburg. Abraham Lincoln obviously likes Burnside as he did not relieve him of combat command, but put him under Major General Ulysses S. Grant.

Colonel Reilly would go on to distinguish himself at the Siege of Knoxville, under Major General Sherman in the Atlanta Campaign, he was promoted to Brigadier General of Volunteers commanding 3rd Division XXIII Corps and assigned to Major General Schofield (a Medal of Honor recipient) during the Carolina Campaign, He resigned his commission and returned home honorably discharged April 20, 1865.

[71] Historical evidence exists that Catherine McCarty was illiterate. Subsequent to this event, in her land transactions she utilized her "mark" to execute signatures on the same.

felt much better. It is so difficult when one is illiterate to obtain information.

"Catherine, I cannot imagine how you are holding yourself together so well. Last year I rushed to the telegraph office to send my husband a telegraph. I had not heard from him in two months."

"My mouth fell open when the agent told me there was no communications in or out of Knoxville, Tennessee. I'm afraid I yelled: 'Why?' at him pretty harshly.

"'It is classified ma'am. I cannot say any more about the situation, other-than to try back again tomorrow,' the young telegraph agent had said.

'Tomorrow! Tomorrow!' I had yelled at the young man and blared back at him: 'I must wait until tomorrow to find out if my husband is alive or dead?'

"Catherine, I am afraid I did so in a too overbearing and aggressive manner."

He replied: 'Yes, ma'am. I am sorry, check with me tomorrow. Hopefully, all is well when your telegraph arrives.' Again, he replied in a professional manner. I was the rude one. I turned on my heels and marched out of his office."

"I was upset at a one-day delay...you haven't heard from your husband in six months! That is very unacceptable on several levels. I feel so sorry for you Catherine, but I will get to the bottom of why that has happened. I promise you that!" Mrs. Reilly concluded as she walked out toward her carriage.

"Thank you so very much for everything, Mrs. Reilly," Catherine overcome with emotion.

Mrs. Reilly stepped through the mud that reached the top of her new shoes without awareness of the same. Her mind was fixed on getting the information she needed for Catherine. She was carrying her dresses in one hand and waved with her free hand a good-bye.

Mrs. Reilly dropped clothes off each week and gave Catherine an up-date. Her husband had not learned of Michael's whereabouts yet, but was giving it all his attention within the confines of military procedures. He had to be discrete as northern officers inquiring too much about other military units would be suspected as a southern spy.

It was the end of July 1864 when Mrs. Reilly was able to give Catherine some concrete information as to why she had not received any posts. It turned out that his 5th Indiana Volunteer Artillery unit had been transferred several times in a short period of time. For fear of enemy intervention all posts are halted when new assignments occurred.

Her husband found out that a totally new artillery outfit had just been formed, the Artillery Brigade, IV Corps army of the Cumberland, and Michael's artillery unit was again transferred to it.

"Mrs. Reilly, I remember clearly that Michael said he had a three-year enlistment, which would be up this November. Will the army keep its promise, do you know that for a fact? Will we be through with this war then?" Catherine asked politely, but obviously hoping it would be true.

"Yes, Catherine, they do keep their promises. They always ask them to re-enlist because they become valuable as a veteran fighter, but never insist on it. It is their decision. My husband told me that and he never tells the slightest fib." Mrs. Reilly explained the best she could.

October arrived but it seemed to Catherine it was a year since July. That was the longest two months and still no word.

There was a knock on her door. Catherine anticipated it to be a customer picking up their laundry. It was not! It was an Army Captain. She knew immediately, she could not control herself. Both her hands rose immediately to her face and she began to cry out loud! She buckled over with one hand grabbing her stomach.

The Captain immediately said: "I am very sorry to inform you that your husband Michael McCarty was killed in action and died a true hero. Many soldiers lived because of his sacrifice. His artillery unit was the last to leave the Battle of Chickamauga where he sustained a serous wound. He held to life for the next two months, but died from his wounds November 30, 1863."

Catherine had not heard much of what the captain said. She was filled with enormous grief, but when he said the date of death her grief turned to anger.

"Did you say November 1863?" she blared the question at the Captain.

“Yes, ma’am, I did say November 30, 1863, ma’am. I am deeply sorry for your loss, and sincerely apologize for the army’s gross error in not informing you sooner. There is no good excuse for that negligence. I do have some information for you, would you like me to return at a more convenient date or time?” The Captain was exactly the right man for the job he was doing, but as he said to a fellow officer: “I would rather be facing a battalion of Rebs alone than these widows.”

Catherine had sat, better stated, had fallen into her one large chair. Hearing the captain through her tears and grief she pointed to him to sit in the small couch next to her.

Joseph (nine-years-old) and Little Billy (had just turned 5-years-old) had overheard the whole conversation. Their reactions were quite different. Joseph stomped out of the house. Little Billy was not upset by the news, as he had only faint memories of his father, but very much so by his crying mother. He ran to her side putting his little arms around her.

She didn’t bother removing Billy from the room when she answered the captain:

“No, sir, please sit and tell me what you need to, so I can get on with my life. I told Michael it was a stupid idea to join in that stupid war, and now these kids have not father! I told him that! I told him his kids were going to end up with no father! I cannot forgive him for that.”

“Captain, I had a strong premonition the day he left to muster in, that I would never see him again. My premonition was right! No, I never told him of it. I blamed it on my imagination. Tell me what you have to say.” Catherine had calmed down substantially.

Although she had suspected this news was coming, even to the point of mentally accepting it as a reality. Yet, when it actually became a reality, her grief was so great. Almost like it was a pent-up emotion that just exploded.

Once she had let the captain know her premonition when Michael mustered in, well, it brought her back to her senses. Little Billy calmed down too, but stayed by his mother’s side.

“Ma’am, these are the items Michael had at the time of his death.” The captain handed her a small bundle wrapped with leather strips and neatly tied off.

"Also, ma'am, here is his pay owed him at the time of his death, minus $20.94 for clothing advanced to him." He said in a soft low tone reflecting great respect.

"Did I hear you correctly...you deducted $20.94 for clothing...are you talking about his uniform?" Catherine asked in a business-like manner with a sharp edge of disgust in her tone.

"Yes, ma'am, I did. All the soldiers proudly pay for their uniforms, ma'am, as I have this uniform I am wearing." The captain replied with pride in his voice.

"I would think if he gave his life they would pay for the uniform he is buried in. Where is he buried sir? Where is my husband buried?" Catherine insisted.

"He was buried in Chattanooga, Tennessee with the entire soldier that died in the Chickamauga and Chattanooga campaigns, ma'am."

Catherine spoke her thoughts out loud not directing them to the Captain, but to Little Billy:

"I will have a wake right here, with or without his body. That is our Irish tradition. We must have a wake." She just knew it was the right thing to do.

"Is there any way I can be of assistance, ma'am?" The good Captain asked.

"Get me a uniform exactly like the one he was wearing at his death. Could you do that?" Catherine said with her beautiful blue eyes locked on the Captains eyes.

"I will do that...consider it done. Well, please do give me until tomorrow." The captain said his good-byes and left the house.

The Captain had only been gone a few minutes and Mrs. Reilly arrived to confirm she had received the information. It was her husband who insisted on a commissioned officer delivering the information. Usually just a letter would be sent, and in the cases of recognized heroes a Non-Commissioned officer would deliver the information.

"Oh, Mrs. Reilly! Thank you for coming!" Catherine said almost gleefully, which took Mrs. Reilly aback. She expected the grieving widow, not a jolly Irishwoman.

"Were you delivered the information about Michael?" she asked assuming she had not received the information.

"Oh, yes. A very nice Captain just left. Oh! You must think badly of me the way I'm acting. I got that all out of my system when the poor Captain was here. Now, I want to plan a wake for Michael!" Catherine explained.

"Oh! I see...yes I would love to help...just tell me what you want me to do? Ah...Michael's body won't be here...right?" Mrs. Reilly asked.

"No, but I want to do a wake for him anyway...as though he was here. You know our traditions, can you find a clay pipe, tobacco and snuff?" Catherine asked.

"Absolutely Catherine, all are right in my house! My husband uses both. Do you need a white linen?" Mrs. Reilly asked.

"No ma'am, a customer moved away and left all their linen with me. I guess to compensate me for what they owed me. So, I have plenty of linen." Catherine confessed and chuckled.

Chapter Seventeen

October, 1864
The Wake at
199 North East Street
Indianapolis, Indiana

Catherine spread the word among her customers that she was going to have a full wake for her husband Michael. Dozens informed her they would like to attend and help in any way they could. She told them all to bring food and drink and whatever they wanted for a merrymaking, but to not forget the tobacco and snuff.

Catherine and Mrs. Reilly cleared the large kitchen table and prepared it as though Michael's body was actually there. The white linen was decorated with black ribbons around the entire circumference of the table linen cloth. Black was for commoners and white for "high society."

"I see you have your Widow's Weeds on? That says you're a lady...you should have white ribbons!" Mrs. Reilly declared.

"No ma'am, no offense, I'm no lady like you, and I'm proud of my black Widow's Weeds." Catherine said with pride in her voice.

"Well, I think you're a lady and you won't change my mind. I can be as stubborn as you, Mrs. McCarty." Mrs. Reilly said with a chuckle in her voice.

"Thank you ma'am." Catherine replied with her big jolly Irish face gleaming.

"Did you here that Queen Victoria[72] put them on with the death Prince Albert four years ago, and had not taken them off. She declared she would have them on the rest of her life," Mrs. Reilly volunteered.

---

[72] Queen Victoria of England wore her husband's ("Prince Albert" of Saxe-Coburg and Gotha) Widow's Weeds" until her death January 22, 1901. His death was December 14, 1861. That fact got worldwide news.

"Yes, I have heard that. I can state that will not happen to me. One year is our Irish tradition, and that is what I will do," Catherine replied matter-of-factly. Mrs. Reilly decided not to probe any further.

"Ma'am, can you greet the ones that come to show their respect at the door?" Catherine asked.

"Yes, of course. I will make sure all the men take a puff of the pipe tobacco to keep the evil spirits away," Mrs. Reilly volunteered.

"Oh, yes, and I'll make sure no women do any keening, not a whimper will be allowed until you state everything is proper and it is time to start the keening,[73]" Mrs. Reilly assured Catherine.

"That is perfect. I hope enough men attend to give a good smoke," Catherine stated.

"I have it on the sly...there will be plenty of men here. My husband will inform some of the soldiers and the word will spread that there is an Irish wake on...that means plenty of liquor," Mrs. Reilly chuckled.

"Perfect, again, Mrs. Reilly," Catherine replied.

Catherine decided that the boys would not attend the wake, and a friend of hers would take care of them that entire day. She felt uncomfortable doing a wake for her husband who was not there in front of her children. Adults would clearly understand and have a good time at the merrymaking. Which was definitely not a place for youngsters.

"I'll tell a few cute stories about Michael and then say: Cheers to Michael...Lord you have got a good man...of course, you knew that! That will signal the start of merrymaking, ok?" Catherine rhetorically asked Mrs. Reilly.

"I think that is perfect," Mrs. Reilly replied and continued with: "I have a beautiful prayer book, would you like me to bring it? Oh, yes, I will do the reading from it." Mrs. Reilly said almost forgetting Catherine was unable to read anything.

---

[73] Keening is when the lead keener, the Caointhe, would be first to lament the deceased and would recite poetry lamenting the loss of the loved one. Then all the women join in crying and wailing and do so upon the arrival of each new caller arriving to pay their respects. After a determined period of time the Merrymaking begins, food, tobacco, snuff, and lots of liquor in the case of an Irish wake.

"If you do the reading...that would be very special...thank you!"[74]Catherine said with much appreciation.

Everything was ready in two days. Catherine had black ribbons sewn to all her dresses. She carefully sewed each one on with reverence to Michael.

The dress she would wear at the wake also had a white handkerchief laced with black ribbons sewn on it as an arm band around one sleeve. This signifies that she will be in mourning for one year and not available to be pursued.

The wake was very well attended and went off like clockwork. Mrs. Reilly was amazing! She was really in charge. Catherine just had to stay quiet, mourn, and greet the people that showed their respects. More than one needed to be told why there was no body.

Many soldiers from the 5th Independent Volunteer Artillery who knew Michael were in attendance. Their enlistment had expired, and they came home just in time to hear about the wake for Pvt. Michael McCarty. Several had stated directly to Catherine that her husband had saved their lives at the Horseshoe Defense at Chickamauga. That made Catherine feel very good about having a wake with no body. Had she not done that, she would not have met any of his fellow soldiers, and had only resentment for his service. Now she felt pride in his service, something she had not ever felt before the wake.

It was a very good wake!

---

[74] It was special in-that only the wealthy had prayer books and bibles at that time.

J. Michael McCarty's Final Resting Place. He Died a Hero.
27-years-old, 5' 6" tall, fair complexion, blue eyes, and brown hair. He was survived by his wife Catherine McCarty and two sons: Joseph McCarty and William Henry of Indianapolis, Indiana.

Chapter Eighteen

Catherine's Laundry Service
199 North East Street
Indianapolis, Indiana
October, 1864 – April, 1865

It was a sad day when Mrs. Reilly informed Catherine her husband and she were moving back to his home town in Ohio. He had a successful legal practice there and would most likely return to be a politician too.

"Oh, I almost forgot to brag a bit to you my friend Catherine...my husband James was promoted to Brigadier General!! I told him I will never call him "General"! Both Catherine and Mrs. Reilly chuckled at that.

"No, ma'am, I told him in our family I am the only general!" Mrs. Reilly declared, and Catherine gave a great belly rolling jolly Irish laugh at that.

"Seriously, Catherine, I have a good friend that is going to bring and read to you my posts. She said she will always bring pen and ink to take your response. Please keep it the response short, as she is an impatient woman." Mrs. Reilly requested with a chuckle.

"I will respond," Catherine said and continued with: "Thank you so much for your deep friendship...I will treasure your friendship forever," Catherine said as she gave Mrs. Reilly a big Irish hug. When Catherine stood back she saw tears running down Mrs. Reilly's face.

"Now, now, save some of those for later," Catherine repeated an old Irish saying.

"Catherine, you are the strongest woman I know. You have no idea how often you helped me in my near maniacal depressions. All I had to do is think of how you are caring for those two children and yourself, alone! How hard you work. You have been my strength and you never knew that, huh?" Mrs. Reilly said with tears still running down her cheek.

"You have been my strength too," Catherine said with emotion in her voice.

"Don't you worry I won't become a "grass widow"[75] for any reason. You can bet on that."

"I have both boys in school now, and I've had Joseph schooling little Billy at home the past year. So, Billy is way ahead of his class now."

"No, ma'am, this family will do just fine. God speed be with you, and may you get to heaven before the devil knows you left." Catherine said as her good friend and customer got in her carriage.

"How old is Little Billy?" Mrs. Reilly asked

---

[75] A term used to describe widows that were discarded mistresses, or turned to prostitution to make ends meet. Indianapolis had many due to the civil war.

Catherine answered: "He looks younger than he is. I had a heck-of-a-time getting the teacher to believe he will be six this November. She only agreed when Billy read a sentence to her, and added and subtracted some numbers for her. She said then she didn't care how old he was, she would enroll him for the fall session. I guess I never did get her to believe his actual age." Catherine explained knowing that was why her friend had asked. Billy could barely pass for four-years-old to a stranger.

"He is a smart kid. I knew that the first time I met him. His blue eyes are going to give a lot of girls' broken hearts," Mrs. Reilly chuckled.

"He has his father's eyes. I fell head over heels for him the first time I looked into those baby blues. I miss him...now I'm not saying I'm still not mad as a hatter he got himself killed...I am!" Catherine's a bit of Irish temper showing.

"Good-bye my friend. God bless you and the boys," Mrs. Reilly said as her carriage pulled away.

Catherine waved until she could not see Mrs. Reilly in the carriage any more. She knew the best friend she had in Indianapolis was riding far away. More than likely she would never see her again. They lived in two different worlds, but that did not matter to either of these strong women. They would never forget each other. They would be sisters forever.

Catherine was busy getting her customer pick-ups ready when Joseph came in from school. Billy had met him down the street talked a mile a minute all the way back home. Joseph just listened, but was obviously not interested in what Billy had to say. They both arrived home Billy still talking away.

"What is that you have in your hands, Billy?" Catherine asked.

"It is the Police Gazette, Mom," Billy answered and continued with: "These are true police stories from all over the country," Billy excitedly told his mother.

Catherine if it from the police it had to be good information, so she approved and went on with her work. Billy ran outside with the Police Gazette. Joseph stayed behind. He wanted to tell his mother something very important to him.

"Mom!" Joseph said to get her attention.

"Yes, Josie, what is it?" Catherine answered.

"You have to shut Billy up...he is driving me crazy...please!" Joseph asked with firmness.

Catherine turned to her older son and said: "We all have our crosses to bear...I suppose Billy is yours. I will never stop him from being excited about reading...never son, and you know why," Catherine informed Joseph just as firmly.

"I understand, but I'm not his father, and I don't have all the answers to his questions," Joseph responded with irritation in his voice.

"No, you don't have to know all the answers...just be honest and tell him you don't know the answer. He can ask me. If I don't have the answer I'll get it somewhere. If I didn't have to work so many hours I would go to school myself, but somebody needs to put food on the table and a roof over our heads." Catherine concluded with a bit of frustration in her own voice.

"Look, Joseph, I'll talk to Billy, ok?" Catherine said in a softer tone of voice, as though she understood Joseph's problem. He is five-years-older, has a whole group of friends his own age, and Billy tags along and becomes a royal pain to his older brother. He would continue to ask questions and he was embarrassed in front of his friends when he couldn't answer, and one of his friends would jump in and answer the question. It made Joseph feel like a dummy. That part he left out telling his mother.

"Go outside and tell Billy I want to talk to him," Catherine instructed Joseph.

"You think he is out in front, or even in our yard, don't you Mom?" Joseph asked in an "I know something you don't" attitude.

Catherine stopped working immediately and replied:

"Joseph, where is he?" she said sharply.

"Don't worry Mom. He has a couple places he goes to read his Police Gazette. Quite places where he won't be disturbed. One is three blocks from here in the fruit trees. There is an old log there and he never strays from there. I always keep an eye out for him." Joseph tried to assure his mother of Billy's safety. It didn't work.

"You go find him right now, and tell him he has two minutes to be in front of me!" Catherine barked and pointed to the door.

Joseph always knew when he was in as much trouble as Billy. This was one of those times. He supposed he should have told his mother about Billy's ventures in the neighborhood. He didn't want to squeal on his little brother. Besides, in Joseph's mind Billy was never in any danger. Truth be known Billy had already talked himself out of a couple scary situations.

It was only the previous week that he was surrounded by some street Arabs twice his age. They discussed, or better put, argued among themselves as to where they would put his body after killing him. At first he thought they were just trying to scare him. Then one of them said: "I want to be first. I want to find out what it is like to stick my knife in his belly. I deserve to be first," the street Arab said with such emotion Billy now knew he wasn't kidding around. He was going to kill him for no apparent reason other than to see what it was like to do so.

Billy pointed to the corner of the orchard where a man was walking toward them and said:

"He is the owner of these trees!" he said and the six boys all looks toward the man. As they did Billy escaped with a left flank end run, and took off lickety-split toward his house, which was the other direction. He did so in less than two seconds Billy was out of the circle of street Arabs. He was at full run within five seconds.

Not one of the older boys saw him until he had a good head start. Then they did not even try to catch him, they could clearly see how fast he was. Although, Billy did look faster than he actually was. Oh, he was very fast for his age, but his small frame body had his arms and legs churning so fast his legs were almost a blur. The street Arabs were lazy, they liked easy targets and were off to find one.

It was late afternoon when a man walked by his favorite reading spot. He crumpled up the newspaper and threw it into the orchard right next to Billy. As he noticed Billy he yelled at him: "Like hell it is over!" The man stomped off very upset.

Billy was still struggling with words he considered "large", but he knew enough to fill in the blanks and figure out what an article was about, or a story was conveying in print. His creative mind was enhanced substantially by his early attempts to read. He had not seriously tried reading a newspaper yet. A few times he glanced at it, but it was all jumble to him. The Police Gazette had sketch drawings, and simple words. He sometimes was stopped on a story and just didn't understand it, but usually he could struggle through.

Billy curiosity over rode his fear of reading a newspaper by the man's obvious emotional out-break of what that newspaper had to say.

Billy unraveled it and the heading said: "Indianapolis News," and under it in very large fonts was:

"WAR IS OVER!"

Lee Surrenders to Grant at Appomattox

The Army of Northern Virginia surrendered to The Army of the Potomac after a long and costly battle. Lee's lines were spread so thin for so long he could not supply his troops or provide reinforcements at key battles. Grant charged through his weakest portion of the line, Lee knew it was over. So goes Lee, so goes the Confederacy."

The front page declared.[76]

Billy could not make out much of what all that meant. An older gentleman was walking by when he noticed the five-year-old struggling with the paper. The boy looked three, no more than four-years-old. His first thought was what is he doing out in an orchard all alone at that age. He approached the boy.

---

[76] Lee surrendered to Grant at the McLean's House April 9, 1865 and was followed by General Richard Lidell's troops at 6 pm the same day. Mosby's Raiders disbanded April 21, 1865. The last "super" General the south had General Joseph E. Johnston surrendered all his various armies under his command April 26, 1865. The Confederate Department of the Gulf commanded by Major General Dabney Herndon Maury surrendered May 5, 1865. Jefferson Davis, President of the Confederate States of America was captured May 10, 1865 at Irwinville, Georgia. He was held as a prisoner of war for two years at Fort Monroe. Major General Samuel Jones, commander of the Department of Florida and South Georgia surrendered May 10, 1865 and Thompson' Brigade May 11, 1865. President Andrew Johnson declared the end of the Civil War August 20, 1866.

"Son, what are you doing out here? Where is your home?" the kindly gentleman asked politely not to frighten the boy.

Billy looked up and down this stranger. He figured he could certainly out run him, but the man could easily overpower him if he gets his hands on him.

The older gentleman saw the young boy would bolt if he got too close. He then noticed the headline on the newspaper.

"Oh, I see. You were reading the news about the war being over?" the gentleman asked rhetorically.

"Yes, yes I was!" Billy replied after the man stopped advancing toward him.

"Where did you learn how to read at such a young age? How old are you, son?" the gentleman asked.

"I'm almost six-years-old, and I first learned from my brother. Now, I am going to school, but I'm way ahead of the other kids. I can write my whole name too...no one else in my class can do that. I few of them can write their first and last name, but not their whole name." Billy said with great pride in his voice.

"I believe you!" the gentleman said sarcastically. He found it amazing that even a six-year-old was really trying to read the newspaper. Especially the Indianapolis News, their writers' noses were in the air as wrote their articles. Each one seeing how they could out write their colleagues. They put words in that it took a Master's Degree in English to understand.

The gentleman kindly asked: "I am old, and you are young, do you think I could sit on the log and you could stand away for a while?" asking politely.

In the blink of an eye Billy jumped up like a cat leaping away from a pouncing dog.

"Thank you, son!" the gentleman said as he sat down.

"Why do you call me your son, when I'm not your son?" Billy asked sincerely, but with an edge on his voice.

"That is a good question. I have done that all my life with boys I don't know the name of...what is your name?" the gentleman replied

"Billy Henry McCarty, and what do they call you?" Billy asked point blank without adding "sir" on the end.

"Sam, and didn't your father teach you to say yes sir and yes ma'am to your elders?" Sam asked directly.

"I have no father...no one has taught me that. Why would I say that?" Billy asked the embarrassed gentleman named Sam.

"I am sorry you lost your father," Sam said very sincerely and continued with: "Sir shows respect for a man and ma'am, shows respect for a woman."

"I never knew my father. He was killed in the war. Show me what this says... please...sir," Billy pointed to the printing below the head line "WAR OVER!"

Sam read it very slow, stopping on several words to explain their meaning to Billy. Billy studied each word and could remember a word with only a couple readings of it.

Billy thanked Sam and took off at a full run toward his approaching brother two blocks away. Sam was surprised by his quickness and barely had a chance to say good-bye. Billy was yelling out to his brother and anyone else that was listening: "The War is Over!! The War is Over!"

"You have to do better than that with Mom. She is furious you left the yard," Joseph informed Billy.

"And you told her where I was, didn't you?" Billy replied.

"I had no choice. She sent me to call you into the house, of which, you could not have heard my call and come in in time. No choice, I told her. I also told her she did not have to worry, you know a safe place to practice your reading." Joseph told the truth.

Billy just glanced at him and took off for home. Joseph was not in the mood to race his little brother. Billy was angry with his brother, but he would get him back. Even the thought of it made him feel a little better. He also figured Joseph was wrong...the newspaper would divert mother's anger quickly.

"Mom, Mom! Look...the war is over. Please let me read this to you and then you can whip my tail," Billy begged his mother as he ran in the house sliding to a halt in front of his mother.

Catherine wasn't buying the diversion. She just stared down at her little boy who at the moment looked really good to her. Anything could have happened to him, even an accident, and there was nothing on him to identify him, or where he lived.

"You are never to leave this property without permission again...have I made myself clear, young man?"
Catherine withheld her Irish temper that so much wanted to explode and spank him to an inch of his life.

"Yes, ma'am. I promise," he said with his fingers crossed behind his back.

"ok, read me your newspaper," Catherine agreed to stop work and listen.

Although he stumbled on many of the fancy words the columnist had used. Catherine was very pleased with her son's ability to read as he did. He was getting the essence of what was being communicated. She was also pleased the war was over. No more young men like her husband Michael would be killed.

"That is wonderful news, Billy. Now you need to do your chores," Catherine said matter-of-factly.

"Oh, ok ma'am," Billy went to work completing his chores.

Catherine though to herself: "Ma'am...wow...where did he get that from?"

Chapter Nineteen

Catherine's Laundry Service 199 North East Street Indianapolis, Indiana April, 1865 to October, 1865

Catherine's Laundry Service business was growing very fast. She thought it would fall off after the war ended, but instead it was growing even faster.

Little Billy no longer wanted anyone to call him "Little" again. Joseph would still do it any time he wanted to get revenge for something. Billy was more cognizant of his relative size to his actual age. All the kids his age were larger than him, with a few exceptions and they were probably lying about their age.

Billy worked hard at his reading practice. He still snuck off but became much smarter at it. He could now just about catch Joseph in a fair race.

Just as Billy had snuck out the front door to find his favorite reading spot, up the walk comes this young man arms full of dirty laundry.

"Boy, is this Catherine's Laundry Service?" the man asked point blank while looking at the address on a piece of paper. He had expected a store font business not a house.

"Are you referring to me, sir?" Billy said in a most sarcastic way. Showing off a few large words he had learned.

The young man was taken aback with the sophisticated language coming out of what he believed to be a four-year-old

.

"Excuse me I didn't know a grown man had jumped into that small body of yours," the young man responded with a chuckle.

Billy had to laugh at that response. He instantly liked this guy with the quick wit about him.

"Shucks, no sir, nothing like that, I just learned those words. You were the first one I could use them on...ha" Billy responded and continued with: "Yes this here is my mother's laundry. I'll go get her," Billy said, turned on his heels, and was gone like a cat.

Catherine came out front and immediately said: "I am sorry...my son should have invited you in the house," she said as she glanced at Billy with frown.

"Good afternoon ma'am, my name is Bill Antrim, Catherine I presume?" he asked as his eye caught the black ribbon on her dress. He immediately said: "I am sorry for your loss ma'am," his voice dropping.

"Thank you, sir. Please come in." She turned and guided the young man to her living room converted to her office area.

She had two fifty-gallon flower barrels and two 12 x 12 planks laying across them for a desk. The planks were six feet long to accomoodate for dirty laundry to be tagged.

Catherine had a simple system using numbered tags. One customer had one number assigned for all their clothes and was placed in an apple crate or basket. So, all the clothes of that customer would be done at the same time and it minimized "lost" clothes.

Mr. Antrim sat on the turned over milk can and placed his dirty clothes on the planks. Catherine counted out the clothes and declared: "sir, this will be five cents for the bunch."

"That sounds fine to me," and reached in his pocket to find a nickel.

"No sir, you pay when you pick them up. If you don't pick them up I will sell them to retrieve my money," Catherine said in a polite but professional manner.

"I understand. You are a good businessman...ah...woman," Bill agreed and complimented her.

"Thank you." Catherine replied just as Joseph came running in.

"Mom...Mom! Some friends of mine are going on a camping trip. Their fathers are going too, so you don't have to worry," Joseph blurted out with no regard to the customer sitting there.

"Mr. Antrim, this is my rude son Joseph," Catherine said in an apologetic manner.

"Oh, sorry!" Joseph said an immediately followed with: "Can I go...please Mom?"

"When and where is this camping trip? Catherine asked Joseph wanting to approve but very apprehensive. Many thoughts went through her mind. If she doesn't approve, at his age, many young men run away from home, or disappear for a while. That would be much more dangerous.

"It is for three days down river. We will hunt and fish for our food. We leave day after tomorrow. Mom, please say yes!" Joseph was now begging. That was uncharacteristic of him.

"I want to go too!" Billy cut in. "I'm old enough now and I have studied very hard...I should go too," Billy concluded.

"No...you can't go! This is for older boys only," Joseph made his position on that matter very clear.

Bill Antrim saw the strain Catherine was going through. She had never had these boys out of her sight for so long. Many times she worried even when she knew Joseph was in school. Three days would be an eternity to her.

"Ma'am, I know we just met, but I can give you references." Bill volunteered, and Catherine interrupted:

"References, what for? I don't require references. I've got your clothes for collateral," she informed Bill

"No ma'am. I meant to say I would be more than happy to guide the boys on the trip. That way Billy could go, and Joseph can still do what the big kids were doing. Of course, I would keep an eye on both of them for you. I have nothing better to do those days. I start work at a freighting company in a week," Bill volunteered.

Billy jumped in: "Mom, pleeease! You know I have always wanted to see the country I read about." It was the only thing Billy could think of. He knew how sensitive his mother was about reading.

Joseph jumped in next: "Mom I promise you I will get all my chores done on time for the rest of my life! I will stop giving Billy a bad time...for a week!" He had to chuckle at that.

"Yea sure you would! If I could get you to do all your chores for one month, it may be worth the risk." Catherine said sarcastically with a smile on her face. That was a good sign to Joseph, who knew his mother very well.

"I would need those references Mr. Antrim," Catherine asked of Bill Antrim.

"Do you have pen and Ink?" he asked Catherine.

"I do!" Billy interrupted saving his mother's embarrassment of having to say she couldn't read or write. He brought paper, ink bottle and quill to Mr. Antrim.

Bill wrote down his birthplace, parent's farm near Anderson, Indiana, his first job as a miner in Indiana, his freighting experience in Philadelphia, PA, and his discharge from the Union army September of 1863. Then he added that he was going to work for a freighter here in Indianapolis.

Catherine looked it over and unable to read what he had written, she simply asked:

"How old are you, Mr. Antrim, if you don't mind me asking?" Catherine liked this straight forward young man.

"I am twenty-three in December, ma'am," Bill replied.

Catherine thought to herself that in any event there would be the fathers of the other boys there. She needed to know them a bit too.

"I can't believe I am going to say yes, you two can go on this trip, but you better mind your p's and q's and do whatever Mr. Antrim says without any sass or argument of any kind. Do you understand?" Catherine said forcefully to both her sons.

"And I must be there when all of you leave. That is a must. I want to meet the other parents, too," Catherine insisted.

"Ma'am, young men, I must go now. I'll see you all early day after tomorrow," Bill Antrim said as he was leaving. He then stopped and said: "I'll bring the camping equipment. I'll have all of it for everyone. You can't believe how much stuff people don't pick up in the freighting business." He concluded and left the house.

"Whew! I hadn't even thought of that!" she declared to her two boys.

"You better be nice to him. He just saved your camping trip. I couldn't afford all that camping equipment right now. Yes, boys you better be thankful to Mr. Antrim," Catherine said sincerely.

Somehow she really trusted Mr. Antrim. Even a couple months ago she would not have agreed under any circumstances. She was very insecure about her children's security.

Every day there were reports of young street Arabs causing havoc all over town, teenage bullies harming young children, and young people running away from home to "head west" to find gold or silver at the Comstock? These were very dangerous times for a young person to be growing up in. Like all mothers Catherine was over protective with her boys.

Now, for some strange reason she really did have confidence in a young man she had just met. In any event she would also meet and check out the other parents that would be going on this camping trip.

Chapter Twenty

A Camp-Out to Remember
Indianapolis, Indiana
October, 1865

It was a cool fall morning when the small group of adults and children gathered to begin their camping trip down river. It had not rained in a month, but this time of year any kind of weather may arrive while you're camping.

Bill Antrim was very early and noticed many of the other men were not experienced in packing their animals. He had learned from an old packer in the freighting business. How you pack is very important. Most of the other men had heavy loads on one side of their animal, and light easy to retrieve items on the other side.

Catherine arrived with Billy and Joseph just as Bill was showing the other men the proper way to distribute the weight on the animals back.

"Too much weight on one side will sore your animal's back quickly, and you will be carrying the load or leaving it behind," Bill said as he untied the load, distributed the weight evenly and retied the pack saddle. He also placed folded over blankets where the "A" frame of the pack saddle rubbed against the animal's skin.

Catherine observed Bill really did know what he was talking about. That made her even more comfortable about him chaperoning her boys on this trip.

Billy and Joseph stood staring at Bill's work. As young as they were they too saw and admired the way Bill handled the ropes. The same rope looks totally different in an experienced man's hands. The rope seems to slide through the hand graceful as a handkerchief, or a scarf in a woman's hand does.

She met several of the other mothers there to see their children off. They were all just as apprehensive as she was, That was with their own husbands going along. She understood now that her feelings were definitely a "mother" thing.

A small petite woman named Betty said to Catherine:

"Your boys are awful quiet. How did you learn them that?" She said in her broken English.

"Ma'am, I have never seen them that quiet in a long time. They are studying Mr. Antrim's work on that mule. I wish I could get them to do that kind of studying in their school work. "Catherine replied with her great Irish smile.

She thought to herself: "I feel good about this camp-out now." The boys were learning something from a man that she could not teach them. Even more so, their obvious interest reflected they need a male influence in their lives.

The boys were clothed well, but what few knew they were leave behind clothes from her laundry. She had not purchased clothing since opening her laundry. When the boys or her had a need, someone would leave their clothes unpaid and somehow it exactly fit their needs. She figures it is a guardian angel watching out for her.

Finishing with the other pack animal Bill brought the two boys over to his own pack animal. Catherine was watching as he explained a couple things to the boys. First he winked at Catherine to alleviate any concerns she may have of what he was about to say:

"Boys, I am going to point out where everything is packed, so if I do something stupid and get myself killed, you'll know where everything is to get you back home safe and comfortable." Bill Antrim said in a monotone, matter of fact manner.

"Please don't do anything stupid Mr. Antrim," young Billy volunteered.

"I don't plan on it, but my point is any time you take a trip, or even a camp-out like this, you must think long in the planning. Anything could happen."

"See this, I have a back pack on both sides of this animal hanging from the pack saddle tree. If this animal breaks his leg, eats bad grass, shakes his hobbles and runs off. Whatever might happen to him, we can load our supplies on two back packs and make it home safe and sound. Those folks have not one back pack among them. Don't say anything to them, it won't matter if you did, so don't waste your words." Bill informed and instructed the two boys glued to his every word.

"Well, we are ready so say your good-byes to your mother and we'll get on our way," Bill told the boys.

They both gave their mother a big hug and thanked her again for letting them go on this trip. She reminded them to mind Mr. Antrim, to the letter! They agreed and were off on the camping trip.

Those were the longest three days of Catherine's life. She had never been a whole day from her boys. Three days! Whew, she could not sleep a wink the first night, and only fell asleep the second night from total exhaustion. The third night she was wide awake again. She was able to put a closed sign out early in the morning and caught two hours sleep, again from exhaustion.

Finally, it was time to meet the boys where they had left for the trip. She was there an hour before any other parent showed up. They all discussed how hard the three days was on all of them.

They heard The Kids before they could see them. Out through the brush they all ran toward their parents. They were jabbering like a bunch of chickens fighting over food.

"Wow, we all saw a deer, a bear, and an Indian!! A real Indian!!" Billy said excitedly to his mother. All the other boys were saying the same, and similar things to their mothers.

"Indians! I had not thought about that!" Catherine said aloud.

"He was a friendly Indian and talked with all the boys. He had learned broken English with a trader, and got some schooling at a mission where he worked. "Bill Antrim explained and continued with: "He certainly was the highlight of the camp-out. We couldn't even get the boys to fish that day. They wanted to talk all day with the Indian." Bill said with a chuckle in his voice.

"Well, thank you so very much, Mr. Antrim. I see by the light in their eyes they had a great time, and learned a lot from you," Catherine said with the deepest sincerity.

"Mom, we...Billy and I...asked Mr. Antrim over for one of your fantastic Irish dinners...you can't say no, Mom...you can't because it was how Billy and I wanted to say thank you to Mr. Antrim." Joseph said with a big emphasis on "you can't say no."

“Ma’am, I had nothing to do with this...you have no obligation at all to me. I enjoyed this camp-out as much as they did!” Bill Antrim volunteered.

“If my sons promised you a dinner...next time you will ask me first (she said with a frown to her two boys)...a dinner it will be, sir. Please allow me the pleasure of your company at dinner two days from today?” Catherine asked of Bill Antrim. No one could turn down Catherine with those big blue eyes begging for anything...not that Bill wanted to. He accepted immediately!

Catherine heard twenty stories the boys had from the camping trip in the next two days...a couple times over! She now realized just how important such things are to growing young men. It would have been the very last thing she would have thought of...in fact camping out would never have come to her mind.

Over the two days Bill thought a lot about the boys on the camping trip and how well they had bonded.

He kept catching himself having more than platonic feelings toward Catherine. As soon as they snuck into his brain he would give himself a self-talk: “Stop it! She is in mourning...one, and much older...two, and it just isn’t right...three...so stop those thoughts!” Then he would divert his mind to other things like the time Billy took off up river on his own.

Bill Antrim thought: “Wow, Catherine will have her hands full with Billy. If my parents thought I was independent...Billy is ten times me at that age. He demands to know everything there is about everything around him.

Bill thought about when they were around the camp fire that first night he noticed Billy’s eyes were moving all the time. Not in a suspicious way, but in a curious way. It seems he was studying everybody there and everything said and done. Later he decided to see if he was right he brought an extra blanket to Billy at bed-down time and asked: “Billy, what was Martin Brown wearing? Was it a vest or coat with a high collar?”

Billy looked at him strangely...not that he didn’t have the answer, but why was he asking this question? He responded: “It was a Confederate coat with a high collar, five buttons with the CS on each button. He had an inside left pocket with a pocket pistol in it. His hat was a Union officer's hat. I figure he didn't want to upset either side too much," Billy said with a chuckle.

Bill Antrim was amazed that this six-year-old kid had observed more than he did! He had gotten the three pieces of clothing, but not the pocket pistol. Billy was very smart and very observant. "Nothing was going to get past him in life," Bill Antrim thought aloud just before arriving at the McCarty home for dinner. He really liked Joseph's ability to handle Billy's outgoing personality when his was just the opposite.

One found it hard to believe the two boys had the same mother and father. Of course, it was possible they didn't, but that question would never to be asked. He would assume they did unless Catherine volunteered to say differently, which was highly unlikely to happen even if they have different fathers. That just wasn't talked about.

Bill was just looking at their personalities, but then he remembered how different he and his sibling were...who knows? Approaching the front door, it opened just as he was going to knock.

"Surprise!" Billy said as he had timed Bill's arrival perfectly. More accurately had timed his knock on the door accurately. Billy saw him approaching through their front window and counted to himself what he thought would be the perfect time to leave Bill's hand dangling with no door to knock. He got it perfect!

"Mind reading through doors now Billy?" Bill asked with a smile.

"Hmm...was that mind reading?" Billy asked himself. "Nope! Just good timing," he answered his own question.

Joseph was standing over at the family table waiting for Billy to finish his little game to allow his turn to invite Bill to the dinner table.

"Over here Uncle Bill!" Joseph said. Bill thought "Joseph doesn't talk much but when he does he sure says a lot."

"Mom said we can call you Uncle Bill because of there being two Bill around when you're here," Joseph explained.

"I hope you don't mind Bill?" Catherine asked from the kitchen.

"No, not at all. Uncle Bill is just fine," Bill Antrim agreed. "It makes me feel I'm part of the family...and that feels good to me."

They had a wonderful Irish dinner.

"Well, Uncle Bill, if you would teach these boys a few things men teach their boys, I will have a dinner like this for you any day that you do so!" Catherine surprised Bill Antrim with her offer. He never expected anything like that. His face gave the wrong impression and Catherine started back peddling:

"I am sorry. I should not have been..." Catherine started to say when Bill interrupted her:

"No, I'm the one sorry...I was just surprised and...and I would love to take you up on that offer. As long as you don't have me cook," he laughed a loud!

Billy spoke up: "That is for sure, Mom. He burnt everything on the camp-out! Ha," Billy laughed loud.

"Say, you weren't supposed to tell your mother that...remember?" Bill Antrim asked directed to Billy.

Joseph interrupted: "You can't trust Billy...believe me you cannot trust Billy with any promise. Billy looks after Billy...period!" Joseph said meaning every word of it.

Billy smiled and replied to Bill Antrim: "Josie is right...you can't trust me. That is the truth," Billy said with pride.

Catherine now got involved: "Billy, you must grow up to be a man of your word," she directed sternly to Billy.

"Mom, I had my figured crossed behind my back when I promised Uncle Bill not to tell...I did! I did! Josie you tell him...you saw my figures crossed," Billy insisted.

"Yes, he did have his figures crossed," Joseph told his mother and Bill Antrim.

Catherine remained having a frowned expression toward Billy:

"I don't care. Don't lie to any adult, Billy...unless your life depends on it...I guess anyone would then...right Uncle Bill?" She asked Bill at the end.

"Yes, ma'am you're absolutely right at that." Bill answered.

"Bill, if you're Uncle Bill, please just call me Catherine," Catherine requested.

“Yes, ma’am...ah...Catherine.” Bill agreed. His heart to a skip at calling her Catherine. There was no question he had a crush on this wonderful Irish woman. He dared not express his feelings. She still wore that black ribbon...wait a minute...he looked over, and for the first time all night noticed she did not have it on. He thought back and there was no question she had it on when he arrived for dinner. Yet, at dinner he does not remember her having it on then. She purposely took it off while cooking.

Bill pointed to where the ribbon was missing off her shoulder.

“Oh, yes, it has been one year now, and it would not be appropriate to have you for dinner while still wearing the ribbon. Frankly, I forgot I had it on until I started serving dinner. Then I took it off,” Catherine explained to Bill Antrim.

Bill was pleased to hear the explanation.

They said their good-nights and Bill headed home a very happy man. He had enjoyed the entire evening.

Chapter Twenty-One

Four Long Years In Indianapolis, Indiana November, 1865 December, 1869

Ulysses S. Grant takes office As President March 4, 1869 Newspaper Headlines in May, 1869 were: "Pacific Railroad[77] is Complete Omaha, Nebraska to Sacramento, California"

March 4, 1869: Ulysses S. Grant was sworn in as President of the United States, Schulyler Colfax was Vice President.[78]

May 10, 1869: The last spike was driven at Promontory Summit, Utah. This reignited the excitement of settling the west. Young men could now travel in days that which took a month to do. The west was open...the ball has started rolling. Land, land, and land!

---

[77] It would later be called the Transcontinental Railroad and still later as the "Overland Route" it consisted of 1,907 miles of track constructed continuously from 1863 to 1869. It was built by the Central Pacific Railroad Company of California (Sacramento to Promontaory), Western Pacific Railroad Company (Oakland to Sacramento), and from the east it was the Union Pacific Railroad.

[78] President Grant will have a profound impact on the "settlement" of the west. The military had shifted emphasis from just guarding the pioneer travel route and railroad construction crews to taking care of the "Indian depredation." He will continue his predecessor's policy in that regard aggressively. The military will not interfere with civilian authorizes, or matters, unless directed to do so by the War Department, Department of Interior, or himself.

Over the past three and a half years Bill Antrim's crush on Catherine grew to full fledge passionate love. Catherine knew it but never said a word or would do anything to "lead him on." She seemed to discourage his affection, and always made it clear he was there to have a male adult influence on her two boys. He significantly filled that desire of Catherine, and more. The boys learned about freighting, knot tying, tack, horses, mules, and hauling with wagons.

Bill Antrim and Josie built a tool shed in Catherine's back yard. Josie learned the basics of constructing a building from Uncle Bill on that project.

Josie was now fifteen-years-old and strong for his size. Outwardly he didn't appear strong, but he surely was. He and Uncle Bill built that shed it short order. It was sorely needed as most of his tools were left out under the eve of the house.

The economy had taken a turn for the worst and those tools had a sign on them "Any desperate person...come and get me...my owner doesn't care about me." Catherine finally agreed to split the cost with Bill, as she said: "after all they are your tools," then she would give that wonderful Irish chuckle, and flash her bright blue eyes, which meant: "You know I'm going to win on this issue...right?" Of course, Bill would cave in and do whatever she wanted. This time he left scratching his head as to why he had to pay half of her shed.

Josie was working so good with him they decided to build a buggy cover next to the shed. Bill chipped into finish it. He then told Catherine the buggy shed was his and he would rent it out to her if she ever needed a buggy shed. She replied: "How much will you rent it to me for?" Bill scratched his head and replied: "Well...I figure $2.00 a month would be a fair price for such a handsome buggy cover."

"That sounds fine to me...I think it a very fair price. How long did it take you to build that with Josie's help?" her tone dropped at the end of her sentence.

"Ah...three days for both projects...so probably one day on the buggy shed." Bill Antrim concluded and followed up with a question of his own: "Why do you ask? We did an excellent job and there was no horsing around on the job," Bill declared and asked respectfully.

"Well, Mr. Antrim (anytime Mr. Antrim was his name he knew trouble was brewing) I would not want to charge you land rent for the three days you were building the shed and buggy cover. That would not be appropriate. Your rent will be $4/month and the cost of labor for my child's work is a dollar a day. Therefore, you owe me now $3 plus the first months' rent of $4 for a total of $7." Catherine said as she held her palm up hand out. She kept him on the hook a minute or two and then let him off the hook by saying: "I'll not charge you if you don't charge me," She asked in a business-like manner.

"Oh, Catherine, you are way too good a businesswoman for the likes of this teamster. You got me again. You know I wasn't really going to charge you anything...right?" Bill said in consolatory manner.

Catherine broke out in a great laugh: "Yes, Bill, I knew that," she replied.

Bill Antrim had spent most of his life in the Anderson and Indianapolis, Indiana area. The short time he was in Philadelphia he learned a lot about freighting but returned to Indianapolis again not liking the big city.

Now he was really getting the itch to travel and find new horizons...new opportunities. Besides, Indianapolis was becoming a big city too. Before and during the Civil war it exploded in growth, but since the wars ending, the economy was on a down slope.

Jobs were harder to find, and more men were willing to work for small wages to get a job. His boss had flatly told him he would have to take a pay cut or he would have to replace him. His boss was not able to charge the public the same amount and keep the business. He had to lower his prices for the freighting. Bill understood and took the cut.

He remembered when Billy had run into the house (he was always running...he could not remember a time he wasn't running) and was yelling the newspaper headlines out to the family:

"Pacific Railroad Is Done!" Mom look here...the railroad to the Pacific Ocean is done...when can we go?" Billy seriously asked his mother.

"Never! Never! Those Californians are crazy...gold...gold...gold! Billy, you know how many spent their entire life saving to go to California to find gold and found their ruin! Most of those boys were ruined. It's a devil may care place...no we will not go to California." Catherine had said that with such passion it was obvious she had at some time given it thought.

"Mom, the gold rush has been over a long time...now it's just like any other place, but far from here," Billy replied sincerely.

Billy was going to be 10-years-old in November. He had four years of schooling, but his education was expanded greatly by his love of reading. Not a week went by he did not read a newspaper, not a week went by he did not read in his Police Gazette, or a dime novel. He had convinced his mother it was school work to read those. She doubted that but went along with it. She figured any reading was better than no reading.

Besides, Billy had a true love of those Police Gazette stories. He felt so grown up when he was the one to bring the latest big story in the headlines home. Josie never thought to do that. To him that was adult's business. Billy loved the news too. He was learning more in his reading than he ever did in school.

In school the teacher he had made a big difference in his formal schooling. His first-grade teacher was excellent! He really liked her, and was glued to every word she would say.

She talked about Europe, the original American colonies, the revolutionary war with England, the east coast as the cultural center of America, and the expansion west.

She had a large hand drawn map of the whole United States and all the Territories. As she talked her pointer would take The Kids to that place. Then she would describe the area.

Billy always had a story from the Police Gazette or a Dime Novel location he would ask her to point out. She always did so. One day he slipped and told her why he asked. That was the last time she did so. After class she asked if his mother knew he was reading those stories about Wild Bill Hickok in the dime novels. Billy answered honestly that she did know and liked him reading everything. He also told her he was learning to read the newspapers (He had just started on the newspapers then). He thought her answer was strange: "Billy that is almost as bad as the dime novels." His first-grade teacher was not a fan of newspapers being read by kids. Billy left out that his mother could not read nor write.

Next came the writing drills for what seemed like hours on end! That was the only boring part to Billy. Yet, he believed her when she said that reading and writing was the mark of a person's success in society. Of course, he hadn't figured out what "society" was yet, but it must be important if she said so.

Second grade was not as good to Billy. He had a teacher that was a tough disciplinarian. His knuckles got whacked more than once. Billy was out-going and laughing all the time with his friends. They passed notes about what they were going to do after school and before going home.

Simple notes coded like: "your house," really meant: "at the mill," "my house," really meant: "at the orchard," etc. Billy had started the code system from a story he read in the Police Gazette.

One day the teacher intercepted the note. She knew it was a code and demanded to know what it really meant (obviously, one of his fellow students snitched to impress the teacher). Billy held to: "it means what it says." She whacked his knuckled good and said: "This is for lying to me."

Another time she sent him to the corner nose and toes to the wall. That was for talking while she was talking. Billy started talking to the wall. The teacher told him to be quiet and he started to laugh so hard he almost wet his pants. She sat him in a broom closet and closed the door. Billy hated that dark, crowded closet.

He discovered that day nothing frightened him more than a dark, enclosed, small room. He wasn't afraid of the dark in any other setting. He had taken off in the middle of the night while on a camping trip, he did the same at home a couple times exploring the neighborhood. But that day in the closet got him suspended from her class for two days for kicking the closed door so hard it could be heard a half block away. She let him out but sent him home with a note for his mother. The note never made it! Nor did Billy, until the regular time he would have arrived from school.

Second grade was a hard one. Third grade he got his first-grade teacher back and he progressed very well in her class.

He never made a disturbance, talked when she did, or passed notes except at break-time.

She liked Billy too. She thought him far ahead of any of her students, which he was. She once said to him he was exceptional, and he replied: "I may agree with you ma'am, once you tell me what exceptional means." She broke out into a full laugh and had to excuse herself.

Billy was a bit upset at her laughing at him and said nothing when she came back in the room. She asked him to step outside and explained to him what exceptional meant and why he had "tickled her tickle box" with his answer. His answer was so very exceptional for a boy his age.

Billy said: "I know that tickle box thing. Sometimes you do that to me too," he laughed with her this time.

He did manage to get into some serious trouble with her. He snuck in a lizard and placed in in the seat of the prettiest girl in the class. Her screech was so loud it even shocked him.

Billy had to write an apology note to the girl twenty times!! That wasn't worth the prank, but even more so his teacher took him to the side and just said: "I'm disappointed in you," and walked away. That affected Billy more than all the knuckle busting of the other teacher.

He never wanted to disappoint her, he was just having fun. Then those few words made it clear to him it was her class he was disturbing for his own satisfaction. He never pulled another stunt like that.

He couldn't stop talking, that would be the same as to stop breathing, but he made sure he wasn't disrupting her teaching. His friends were always interested in the Dime Novel stories, and Billy loved telling them.

One day after school three of them were at the orchard sitting on the old log when several eleven-year-old boys approached. They were one year ahead of Billy and his friends. One of them was a known bully. He was tall for eleven and demanded that Billy give him his Dime Novel about Wild Bill Hickok he and his friends were looking at.

Billy replied: "Sure after we have all read it five times and only then if you're still standing right here," Billy's friends laughed. One of them was very concerned because that bully had beat him up once before.

The bully reached down to grab it from Billy with the attitude it would be like taking candy from a baby. Billy moved so quickly he was just a blur to the bully. Positioning himself to the side of the bully, he placed one leg through the bully's two legs (He had practiced this many times with his older brother Josie). Using two closed fists held together he slammed the lower back of the bully thrusting him forward and over the log. All that happened in a split second.

Billy jumped over the log like a cat and had his shin bone straddling the back of the bully's neck, with his face pushed into the ground. The bully pushed up and threw Billy off him. Billy was on his feet before the bully. He knew his arms may not be strong enough to have any effect on the bully, so he kicked him as hard as he could and caught the bully right on the chin. The bully's body flopped to the ground, he was knocked out cold as a cucumber.

Billy quickly turned his attention to the other two eleven-year-old boys and they waved him off wanting nothing to do with their friend's troubles. Truth be told they didn't like his bully tactics either, they certainly were not going to get involved with his attempt to steal a magazine. They walked away leaving their former friend in the dirt.

Billy learned a lot about himself that day. At no time was he afraid, or even had the slightest doubt how things would turn out. He knew he could move faster, think faster and was willing to do whatever was necessary to protect himself and his friends. Also, there was a real advantage of having an older brother that was very strong for his age of fifteen-years-old to wrestle with.

One of his friends said to another: "He may look younger than ten, but he can fight like a teenager." The other replied: "Yes he can and I'm glad he is our friend. That bully banged me up the other day and he won't forget I was with Billy. I don't think he will mess with me anymore." His friend replied: "I think his bullying days are over. He'll think twice before he bullies anyone." They all took off for their respective homes.

Billy arrived home and Uncle Bill Antrim was there. He quietly asked if he could talk to him outside. Bill agreed shrugging his shoulders to Catherine.

Outside Billy told Uncle Bill the whole story of the bully. He wanted to tell his mother, but she wouldn't understand and make a big thing out of it.

Uncle Bill said to Billy: "You did the right thing. Most bullies back down when they are challenged. Keep an eye out on your back side for a while. He may try to jump you from the rear. He won't do it with the same friends, but others he may recruit. More than likely he will do nothing but keep his distance from you." Billy thanks Uncle Bill and they went back into the house.

There stood Catherine with hands on her hips.

"I don't like secrets...you two know that," Catherine calmly explained.

"No secrets Catherine...just a man to man discussion," Uncle Bill replied.

"You're sure?" Catherine lowered her tone when asking.

"Yes, Mom...man to man," Billy replied with pride in his voice.

"Alright," Catherine reluctantly agreed.

Chapter Twenty-Two

Call of the West 1870

The Homestead Act signed by Abraham Lincoln had been around since May of 1862. It was designed to populate the west, and many took advantage of it. Although, most who would have done so, did not. Why? The west was still a dangerous place to live. Free land was not worth having your scalp hanging from a tepee, or warrior's war shirt.

By 1870 much had changed, and many young men were looking to take advantage of the free 160 acres on government land.

Red Cloud had signed a treaty. Only the most northern Teton Lakota Indian bands of hostiles were left to harass settlers. Few wanted to settle that far north. President Grant had his two favorite Civil War generals General Sherman and General Sheridan assigned to take care of the problems with the Plains and northern Indian tribes once and for all.

Brigadier General Carleton had made great progress in handling the Navaho, Mescalero, and Apache tribes. In Indian Country (oklahoma today) the tribes bragged at being "civilized." The Pawnee were helping the U.S. Cavalry through-out the plains. In New Mexico the U. S. Cavalry drove the "wild" Comanche back into Texas. There they faced a determined Texas Ranger organization. Determined to civilize them or exterminate them.

Most significantly the railroads provided safe travel to the "civilized" towns that sprang up across the rail lines. The railroads were branching out to southern communities in the plains, too.

Excitement was in the air. Bill Antrim was inhaling it. He really wanted to make a move. He truly felt the McCartys and himself would do much better in the west.

He read of the longhorn cattle being driven up the Jesse Chisholm trail (a half-breed Wichita Indian trader) through Indian country to Kansas.

The last April, 1869 Ulysses S. Grant signed the Osage Indian Trust Land to open up for settlement the Kansas-Indian Country border by October 22, 1870. [79]

Bill read about a small plains community that had sprung up at the convergence of the Little and Big Arkansas Rivers in Kansas. It was serving the Texas outfits driving the wild longhorn cattle up from Texas. They named it after the local Wichita Indian tribe. The railroad had committed to bring a line of tracks to the new town. It would be sometime before they did so, but that was perfect for land speculation purchases now. Certainly. last but not least, it was part of the Osage Indian Trust Land Act signed by the President of the United States.

Now he only had Catherine McCarty to convince. He figured that was not going to be easy. She had a successful business, and had just recently picked up a contract for hospital linen washing. She was looking for a store front as she had completely outgrown her house. Worst of all, she was finally making very good money.

Uncle Bill arrived early for dinner at the McCarty's house. Billy greeted him and invited him in the house. Josie was not there, but due any minute.

Bill navigated around all the clothes waiting to be ironed or folded. Baskets on top of baskets with numbered tags in each one. He pulled up his usual chair at the table.

Billy stated: "I think Mom's laundry invited itself to dinner," ending with a chuckle.

"That is all right young man...that laundry is buying your food, clothes, and books for that school of yours." Catherine declared from the kitchen.

Uncle Bill leaned over to Billy and asked Billy in almost a whisper: "Billy, the books at school are free. I know because I deliver them. What books are your mother talking about?"

Billy put his index finger to his mouth: "Shew...I told her the Dime Novels are required reading," Billy answered and continued with: "Please don't tell her."

---

[79] Frederick Nolan: The West of Billy, The Kid Pg. 8

Uncle Bill did not answer. Billy figured he was busted. He thought to himself: "Well, I made it four years...that pretty good."

"What are you two cooking up while I'm slaving over this stove? I heard you whispering...what's up Billy, Uncle Bill?" Catherine said in her most demanding tone of voice.

Uncle Bill responded quickly as Billy figured he was a goner: "I asked Billy why he wasn't earning extra money to pay for his own school expenses," Uncle Bill said not finding it in him to lie. Well, it may still be classified as a white lie, but not an out-right lie.

"That is a good idea!" Catherine declared: "Billy you are old enough to do some work for money," Catherine added.

"Yes, Mom! Bill and you are right. How much would you pay me to deliver laundry?" Billy asked his mother.

"No, I would worry too much while you ran all over town. I'm thinking working the wash board out back," Catherine volunteered.

"How much could I earn, Mom?" Billy asked

"I figure two hours a day could make you 4 cents, if all the clothes are clean. For every dirty clothes I subtract half a cent until the 4 cents is gone. So, you must clean them very well!" Catherine offered and qualified what she would pay for.

Billy did the math in his head, every five days he would have enough for a dime novel. Newspapers he was getting free. He agreed: "Thanks Mom...I'll start tomorrow."

Then he leaned over to Uncle Bill just as Josie came in for dinner and said: "Thanks, Uncle Bill." Catherine came in the dining room just in time to over hear him say that. She found it strange that he was thanking Uncle Bill for having to work for his books rather than get them free. She just curled her eyebrow a bit, but decided to let it be.

"Just in time Josie!" "One more minute..." Josie interrupted his mother "But Mom...it wasn't one more minute," Josie declared. Billy's tickle box flipped over and he couldn't control himself. Josie just looked at him like he thought his little brother was surely crazy and said: "It wasn't that funny."

They all sat down and enjoyed a wonderful Irish dinner.

Catherine was so tired she could hardly stand up to clear the table.

Uncle Bill said: "You sit right here Catherine. Boys you clear the table. Josie, you clean the dishes and Billy you dry for your mother. She works too hard all day to be cleaning too. Now get to it!" He directed the boys. They took to it immediately. They never heard Uncle Bill so autocratic.

Catherine sank in her seat in a sigh of relief. Those words were music to her ears! She thought to herself just how much she really liked this young man. He was always helping out and she had grown to wonder what she would do if she didn't have him. He had really filled the void left by Michael's death with both boys...and herself.

Today Bill seemed a little different somehow.

"Are you ok?" Catherine asked point blank.

"Oh, yes, just have had something on my mind," Bill replied.

Catherine was older and wiser than Bill she asked:

"Can you share it with me, are you leaving here?" She took a stab at woman's intuition.

Bill was surprised at her accuracy. He had never mentioned a word before now. He also came to the point:

"I think we both should leave Indianapolis and homestead at Wichita, Kansas. We could get 160 acres next to each other. With 320 acres we could raise a lot of beef cattle, cow calf, or even dairy cows."

"That is enough land to do whatever we wanted to do. I read that right now there are quarter sections near town still available. Of course, they may be saying that just to get people to make the trip and then find out it isn't true."

"Bill you have been thinking about this for some time, haven't you?" Catherine was surprised by the amount of detail he had discovered.

"Yes, I have. Also, Wichita will need a 'City Laundry'. It is the perfect time to get a fresh start in a growing western town," Bill volunteered.

"I have heard from a customer that a railroad was going to Wichita to pick up the Texas Longhorn cattle. How could we compete against Texas cattle?" Catherine inquired.

Bill knew she had an interest or wouldn't have discussed anything about it. Knowing Catherine, she would have simply said no.

"I thought of that, too. We could raise much better beef cattle than those scrawny, tough-meated Texas longhorns. Also, again, we do whatever the need and demand is for, maybe a calf cow or dairy. With 320 acres we could do both. A new community must have dozens of opportunities for people like us. It would take a lot of work, but we could do it! What do you say, Catherine?" Bill asked with butter flies in his stomach. He knew Catherine was the type to decide on the spot and follow through on it.

Catherine thought on it a couple minutes. It felt like an eternity to Bill.

"The boys have received a good education here, enough to carry them through their lives very well. City Laundry, that sounds really good! We'll do it!"

Bill had to confess something: "There isn't a city yet, or even much of a town, just a few buildings. There will be, and we will be ready!"

Joseph and Billy came into the room just as Catherine made her declaration. Joseph was not happy! This is the second time they were moving away from where he had friends. Billy was excited!

"Where in the west are we going?" Billy asked enthusiastically.

"Wichita, Kansas! Billy." Does that fit your approval?" Catherine said.

"Well, I haven't read anything about it. I know about Springfield, Missouri, Kansas City, and Fort Hayes. I just don't know about Wichita, Kansas. Where is it Uncle Bill?" Billy asked sincerely.

Uncle Bill knew exactly what to say to Billy to spark his interest.

"Billy, it is due west of Springfield, Missouri and north a little from Indian Country. Civilized Indians of course, Catherine." He directed to her then went back to Billy with:

"Heck, Billy, you might even meet some of these western men you have read about. In fact, I'm absolutely sure of it," Uncle Bill concluded.

"Let's go Mom! Right now, I'm ready!" Billy declared.

Joseph was silent. Catherine asked him:

"Joseph, I know how hard it is to leave your friends. Remember when we moved here you made new friends quickly. It should be the same out west. What do you say?" Catherine asked her oldest boy.

"I won't leave you, mom." Joseph answered honestly.

"Alright, it's final...We're going west!" Catherine declared again and then added: "Only one thing left to do before we start planning and packing," Catherine said to her small group of family.

"What Mom?" Billy quickly replied and asked.

We must say a prayer to Saint Christopher, the saint for travelers. We will need him on this venture west. That little family matter taken care of they began their planning.

Catherine's customers were not happy to hear she was leaving. Many tried to talk her out of it, including the hospital she was working for recently. She wouldn't miss them as they had the worst cleaning job she had ever attempted. She felt as though the linens were contagious, and she was exposed to all of it.

Above: ***The original survey team of Sedgwick County, ca 1867*** *Source: Wichita State University Library Department of Special Collections wsu_ms91-3.10.5*

Left: ***James R. Mead ca 1878*** *Born 5-3-1836 New Haven Vermont. Arrived in Kansas Territory in 1859. Plainsman, Kansas Pioneer, and one of the founders of Wichita, Kansas. Wichita had 123 men and one-woman founder: Catherine McCarty who owned the City Laundry.*
In 1871 Mr. Mead began his campaign to raise a $200,000 bond to construct the Wichita & Southwestern Railroad. It arrived May 16, 1872 and changed Wichita forever. Source: Wichita Sedgwick County Historical Museum, wsch_Meads, James.R

Indian camp a few miles south of Wichita, Kansas *on the Big Arkansas River. Photograph by Roger's studio 1879.*

Texas Cattle crossing the Arkansas River at Wichita ca 1869: *Wichita State University Library Department of Special Collections.*

Chapter Twenty-Three

Trip to Wichita
Spring 1870

The McCarty/Antrim party took the train to St. Louis, Missouri. There they had to change trains to reach Kansas City, Kansas. It was a total of 680 miles and took four days. Only a few years earlier it would have taken a month of rough travel across dangerous country to make that same trip.

In Kansas City Bill took the boys shopping. They purchased a good freight wagon. He knew wagons and turned down a dozen for sale before he selected the one they bought. The boys were learning a lot. In the final purchase he let them believe they were making the purchase. The owner of the wagon looked down at Billy and said:

"You drive a hard bargain, young man!" the man said sincerely.

"You have a very fine wagon, sir. It was worth the haggle. Thank you!" Billy replied.

The owner chuckled out loud and told Bill Antrim: "Next time leave these two behind, so I can see a profit, huh?" The man requested with a wink of his eye.

"Oh, I couldn't do that...they know their stuff when it comes to wagons." Bill responded with a smile.

It was a very good wagon. Well made with thick springs that could handle twice the weight of the average wagon. Bill had asked around and found the trip to Wichita would be 200 rough miles across mostly open country. It would take 10 good days without any troubles along the way.

Most people said they could plan on some kind of delay, and to make sure they should grease good and take an extra axle, spokes, and tack if they can afford it.

Catherine found a Dutch oven she liked, one large and two small cast iron frying pans. She had a large flower barrel and a smaller sugar barrel. The builder had built boxes on both sides of the wagon to carry everything from utensils to spices.

Next they went a mercantile business to load up on all the needed supplies. While there the clerk suggested:

"I highly recommend you purchase a couple Colt pistols and a Henry repeating rifle. You will most likely run into renegade Indians on the plains."

"I have my Springfield and a Remington revolver." Bill informed him.

"Those savages can throw five arrows at you before you can reload that Springfield. If they have a Henry...you're done! You better listen to me on this," the clerk said as Catherine was over-hearing the whole conversation she intervened with:

"Go ahead and buy what he suggests we do," Catherine directed to Bill and then turned to the clerk and asked:

"And with the Henry how many arrows will they throw?" Catherine said with emotion.

"Ma'am, they see that Henry and they high-tail their horses immediately. They go look for someone that didn't listen to me." The clerk said with conviction.

"Fine, we will see their high tails," Catherine said with a chuckle.

"Ma'am, one other thing, Kansas and Missouri have been at war since 1855. Don't trust any marauding young men."

Bill found a pair of young oxen he could buy very reasonable, because they were still green. A risk, but well worth it to him. He had broken many oxen in Philadelphia and knew they were the best for hauling across the plains. They were young but calm in disposition. Perfect for their use.

They were ready to pull out when the clerk came running out:

"Wait, wait!" He yelled as loud as he could. "Here you go!" he handed Bill several claim stakes with a smile and said, "These are on me...you'll need them out there."

"Thank you, very much for all your help!" And they were off for the adventure of their lives.

ON THE TRAIL TO WICHITA

The trail road seemed to have been well worn which made them feel a lot better. Many others had taken this same trail. According to the ruts a lot of people had come this way.

They found some comfort knowing they were traveling a well-travelled route.

For Josie and Henry, it was similar to the camp out they had been on in Indianapolis, but much longer. It would take almost two weeks to make the 200 miles with oxen. Oxen are strong but slow.

Only one time on the whole trip did they see any Indians, and they were "friendlies." That is what they call the Indians not out to kill you. Then they still kept their guard up as a scout had told them to trust no one. That included Americans.

It was a small band and had crossed the trail several hundred yards ahead. Bill pulled up and let them complete their crossing. The only Indians that even looked at them were the children. They were looking as curious about them as Josie and Henry were at the strange sight they saw.

Oh, they had seen pictures of wild Indians, but this was different. These were real! And didn't look anything like the photographs they had seen in newspaper etchings or dime novels.

They had reached the half way point to Wichita on the trail when Billy pointed out a fast approaching freight wagon that would soon pass them. Bill pulled his oxen over to the side of the trail.

"Our oxen may get too excited and bolt," Bill explained.

A hundred yards behind them the fast-moving freight wagon slowed to a near walk.

"Now that is a gentleman. He knows I have green oxen and is demonstrating his manners quite well," Catherin said to her boys as a lesson for them to remember.

Josie and Billy were staring at the approaching wagon with the intent of a guard dog. Suddenly, Billy bolted to the wagon and his possibles carpet bag. He pulled out a dime novel and placed it in his mother's lap for her to grab. She looked down and then back to the wagon as Billy was pointing to the man riding shot gun in it.

"I'll be darn...maybe," She said just as the wagon passed them. She decided to try something. She hollered out when the wagon was about a hundred feet beyond them:

"Mr. Hickok, is that you?"[80] Catherin's authoritarian voice could travel a half mile, and that is what she used.

The stranger's wagon pulled up to a stop to allow Bill to catch up to them. Bill then reined up while stating:

"I hope my wife's hollering has not caused you any inconvenience?" he said matter-of-factly, as though he had no control over her, which was quite true. It was also true they were not married. It was strange to Josie and Billy that their "Uncle Bill" was playing their father. Billy had to speak out when he knew well he should not.

"Is this you?" Billy said holding up the dime novel so the man riding shot-gun could see its cover.

"It is supposed to be me, but son don't believe all those stories you read in those dime novels. Heck, I've told those news people more lies than Carter has liver pills, and they print them and exaggerate on the lie I thought no one could beat."

All got a laugh on that. Of course, Billy was disappointed as Wild Bill Hickok was absolutely his hero! He had read every story ever written on him in the novels and the Police Gazette.

"I apologize for my rudeness, ma'am. This here is Colorado, my partner in our freighting business." Colorado tipped his hat. Both men were dressed in buckskins head to toe.

"How do you do, Mr. Colorado," Catherine politely asked as Bill Antrim tipped his hat to him.

"Ma'am, I'm doing just fine," Colorado replied and continued with: "Are you folks heading for Wichita?"

"Yes, we are, sir. Our intentions are to settle there. We have heard there are great opportunities in that community." Bill Antrim answered, as is the custom with such personal questions.

Mr. Hickok volunteered: "That very well could be. It is a bit primitive at the moment though. My partner and I estimate there will be 10,000 head of cattle coming through Wichita every week very soon."[81]

---

[80] Wild Bill Hickok and Colorado Charlie had a freighting business between Kansas City and Wichita Kansas. Circa 1870. It is quite likely they met most of the travelers on that trail including Bill Antrim and the McCarty's. The meeting written herein is fictional with the historical purpose of reflecting what The Kid would think had he met one of his "western frontier" heros in the dime novels he furiously read.

[81] By 1871 there was 15 to 20 thousand cattle passing through Wichita every week.

Colorado Charlie added: "That means 100 Texian cowboys a week! There is only one sheriff in town. He is a good one and does a heck of a job, but he is stretched pretty thin. I suggest you keep those boys off the street at night. If not, they will pick up a stray bullet sooner or later. Just my advice, not trying to mind your business," Colorado concluded.

"No offense taken, quite the opposite. Thank you very much for your advice and information," Catherine replied with sincerity.

They all said their good-byes. Colorado and Hickok were out of their site with those big mules pulling even a heavier wagon, in no time at all.

Wichita in 1870, as it looked at their arrival. *Source: Wichita State University Library Department of Special Collections wsu_ms91-3.9.14.1*

Chapter Twenty-Four

Arrived! Wichita, Kansas Spring, 1870

Coming over a small rise they could all see their destination ahead.[82] The sight was better than they had expected. Bill had told Catherine there would only be a few buildings, well there were more than a few, but they were scattered around.

---

[82] J.P. Allen, owner of Wichita Drug Store, said: "the town looked like a group of buildings in a sea of grass, creating a vivid mental image of civilization amid wilderness." Circa 1870.

There was a semblance of a main street where several buildings were in a row. It ran north and south up from the river.

To their right they saw a mixture of people crossing the Arkansas River on a make-shift ferry. An unusual sight was a squaw with two small children in a buffalo hide tub boat tied to the ferry. Obviously, she was getting a free ride.

The old Jesse Chisholm trading post was at the convergence of two rivers.[83]

The town was situated in a sea of grass. The only few trees standing were further south along the river. None in or around the small town. Before the civil war there were only a few camp sites along the river.

As their small party approached main street Billy's excitement ran wild. It was exactly how the writers described western towns. There were buffalo hunters, freighters, plainsmen, townspeople, wagons and buggies going every direction imaginable. Almost every man he saw had a pistol and a bowie knife.

Bill Antrim pulled their wagon in front of the Empire House Hotel where they would stay until they found other accommodations. He left Catherine and the boys in the wagon until he had checked into the hotel.

The normally talkative Billy wasn't saying a word. His eyes kept jumping from one sight to another. Many he had seen in the dime novels and Police Gazette he read constantly, but they were pencil or ink drawings.

Across the wide road (at least a 100 feet) were Indians gathered around a wagon full of furs. The hides were a mixture of buffalo, bear, wolf, and even antelope.

A bullwhacker pushed the two Indians getting too close to a buffalo hide they seemed to be liking a bit too much.

---

[83] Jesse Chisolm lived with the Wichita Indian tribe which were Union sympathizers during the civil war. They had moved to the convergence of the two rivers to avoid confederate Indian sympathizers in Indian Country. Jesse opened a trading post and the entire cattle trail from Texas to Wichita was called the Chisolm Trail. Jesse had never traveled the entire trail. He and William Greiffenstein (whom laid out the city and later became a Senator from Kansas) passed over Indian Country together and marked out what would become the Chisolm Trail.

It appeared the Indians were going to remove it from the pile and claim possession rights on it. The bullwhacker was having none of that. The Indians moved on.

Soldiers arrived well mounted on choice horses. Each branded with the "US", the Army brand. In unison the soldiers dismounted in front of the mercantile store.

One man was dressed the same as Colorado Charlie and Wild Bill were on the trail. Billy knew he had to be the scout for that Cavalry outfit. He was looking at a real U.S. Cavalry scout.

For Billy the pages of his favorite books were coming alive right in front of him. He was 10-years-old, or as he would emphasize: "10 and a half." He didn't look a day over 7-years-old. He hated that fact. Few children wanted to grow up faster than William Henry McCarty. He wanted to be a teenager in the worst way. Then maybe they would stop thinking he was a "child." Especially, when he was better read and more knowledgeable than most kids older than him.

Five men rode pass their wagon. Two of them stared at his mother like they had never seen a woman. The fact was they hadn't seen a white woman in months.

Billy knew they were "hard cases," or maybe even "man-killers." In any event they had an air of recklessness about them. A devil may care attitude. They pulled up in front of a corner saloon a hundred yards up and across the road from the hotel. It had a hand painted sign "Keno Corner."

Just then Bill Antrim arrived and ignored the riders. He did comment to the family:

"They are why we are here," Bill Antrim stated matter-of-factly.

Billy replied:

"What do you mean Uncle Bill?"

Bill Antrim replied:

"Those men are drovers, they call them cowboys now. They have driven a herd of cattle all the way from Texas and across Indian country. They'll rest their herds here and then continue up the trail to Abilene. The railroad arrived there in 67'." Bill Antrim answered.

Billy could understand why they called them cowboys, some didn't look much older than himself.

Bill Antrim continued:

"Following them will be hundreds of thousands of cattle and their Texas cowboys. After delivering their cattle most of them will come right back through here to return to Texas and bring another heard up to Abilene."

"Billy, our new home is really a boom town. We have a lot of work to do, but you boys can grow up here to be whatever you want to be." Bill said directing his last comment to Joseph and Billy.

After the riders that had passed them dismounted in front of Keno Corner, they made it clear to the young cowboy he was not to go into the establishment.

"You stay with the horses! Don't leave them...got it kid?" the older cowboy barked at the young lad.

"Why can't I go in?" the young cowboy barked back.

"A couple more drives and you will go where ever you want. I promised your dad I would look after you, and you will do exactly what I say. Do you understand? Stay with the horses!" The man became more forceful with his order.

"Yes, sir!" the lad responded disappointedly.

Now, Billy wanted in the worst way to see what was inside that building too. He had a higher than average curiosity. He imagined jumping down out of the wagon, run behind the building to find a way inside, without being detected of course. It would have to wait, but there and then he decided he would do it.

Bill Antrim and Catherine entered the hotel, while directing the boys to stay put in the wagon.

Inside they were introduced to a man that owned several lots and buildings in town. He had heard of the opportunities from the founder of Wichita William Greiffenstein himself, buying as many lots as he could afford. He built several buildings using lots for trade of labor and materials.

The man asked Bill Antrim what he was looking for. He found the answer unusual for the times.

"I'm going to homestead out of town, but Mrs. Catherine McCarty, my friend, does have an interest in finding a place for her business." Antrim replied.

"I assumed you two were married," Bob replied politely.

"We are not, just good friends," Catherine replied and continued with: "I want to start a laundry business here. I have done that business for some years in Indianapolis. I know the business well, and assume Wichita has a need?" Catherine spoke in a business-like manner to Bob.

"Yes ma'am, we certainly do need a laundry here. One whiff of the nose around these parts will prove that quickly enough to any able-bodied," Bob declared with a chuckle.

"Fine, do you have a suitable building for my business?" Catherine came to the point demonstrating her business acumen.

"I think I do, ma'am. Yes, I think I do. Let us step out on the board walk." Bob politely replied.

Outside Bob pointed to a newly constructed two-story building on the north side of Main Street. It was only a few buildings down from the corner of Main and Douglas, the location of the rowdiest business in town, Keno Corner!

Of course, Catherine had no knowledge of that fact and Bob wasn't going to point that small blemish to his property's location to her.

Bob said: "Mrs. McCarty, you can locate your business down stairs and live in the upstairs. I designed the building to allow for that. It may not be the comforts of Indianapolis, but certainly is first class for Wichita, Kansas." He declared with sincerity in his salesman's heart. He conveniently left out that when business was a bit slow for Keno Corner the owner hired a brass band to play out front of it until the wee hours of the evening, trying to literally "drum up business" from as far as possible.

Catherine and Bill Antrim climbed into their wagon as Bob walked across and up the road to the building. They directed the boys to be polite and commit no acts of mischief around Bob. Their thinking was one wrong move on their part and Bob may back out of the deal.

Of course, it was highly unlikely Bob would back out. He had tried to rent the buildings to locals and no one wanted to be that close to Keno Corner. A couple rowdy kids was the least of Wichita's problems.

Although a simple design the building fit Catherine's needs perfectly. The upstairs wasn't large enough to accommodate having Bill Antrim live there too. Furthermore,

Catherine was sensitive to how it may look to have them living in the same house anyway. It just wouldn't be appropriate.

Bill had waited the appropriate year of mourning her dead husband Michael, before asking her to be his wife. She said she wasn't ready for that and wanted to remain close friends. Bill Antrim agreed, after all it was the next best thing to marrying the woman he loved and admired so greatly.

Bill spoke up first:

"Catherine, this looks perfect for you and the boys. I'm going to file on a homestead in the country side not too far from town. I'm sure Bob can find a room for me at less than hotel rates?" he concluded with both he and Catherine staring at Bob awaiting an answer.

"Oh! Of course! I have a bunk house you can use. You might have to put up with some Texans as rowdy roommates Mr. Antrim. Is that alright sir?" Bob inquired.

"Yes, that will do for now. You must have a good source of lumber to have built so many buildings? I'll pay market price for enough to build a house on my new homestead. Also, I'm agreeable to trade for freighting or carpenter work." Bill declared.

"I'll get all you need, sir. I saw your wagon. You bought it with freighting in mind, did you not?" Bob replied and asked.

"Yes, I did. It is a good wagon, sir," Bill answered.

"I will take you up on that freighting offer. I'm happy with the man I've hired except he can't carry as much as you. All you guys also charge by the trip. You will hear from me soon, Mr. Antrim," Bob concluded.

"A laundry needs a lot of water, Mr. Bob," Catherine said rhetorically. Bob had not volunteered his last name and it would be rude to ask.

"Yes, ma'am. Out back you will find the best well in town. Also, in the back of the lot on the down slope a fine outhouse." Bob answered with pride.

"Fine, we will take it, with the first month at no cost. I'll need the extra cash to set up the business," Catherine said assuming Bob would agree.

"Sorry, no ma'am. I must have a month in advance. I advise you to buy up as many lots as you can when this business gets going. Real estate here is a great investment, and there is always a good buyer waiting for you." Bob went on to say: "Ma'am you are tough businesswoman. We need you in our community," Bob declared.

"No need to patronize me, Bob. I understand." She said as she pulled out $50 in gold. I'll pay $25 a month, not a penny more. This is two months in advance. Do we have a deal?" She said in a businesslike manner.

"Lordy be, Mrs. McCarty! This is a two-story building and just the bottom story will rent for that." Bob complained.

"That is what I can afford," Catherine said firmly.

"Well, alright, as long as you promise not to tell anyone what you're paying?" Bob asked sincerely.

"That is our business, no one else's." Catherine agreed.

Bob took the $50 in gold and left feeling he had just met the toughest business person in Wichita.

Looking northwest at first block of north Main Street.
Wichita mid- 1870s Source: Wichita-Sedgwick County Historical Museum

Chapter Twenty-Five

Setting Up Shop and A Good sign

The boys looked like they were ready to adventure out and check out the town, then rest up. Catherine was having none of that:

"Ok, boys! Unload that wagon and get busy setting up our laundry business." Catherine declared and went on to instruct Billy: "Billy, you run after Mr. Bob and tell him I need a painter with white paint right now!" She said excitedly.

Billy took off like a bullet! Almost a half hour went buy. Catherine was beginning to become concerned when Billy arrived back with the painter in tow.

Billy declared:

"I had to wait for him to finish a job he was on. I told him I couldn't come back without him, mom," Billy said with a grin.

"Thank you very much for coming right over. What is your name?" She asked politely.

"It's O'Reilly, ma'am. Patrick O'Reilly at your service. What can I paint for you?"

"A business sign, sir. The best business sign you have ever painted. My name is Catherine McCarty of Cork 'County Ireland." Catherine said matter-of-factly, but also appealing to their shared Irish heritage.

"What is the name of your business?" Pat asked directly.

"The City Laundry, sir," Catherine replied.

"How big, and where would you like me to place the sign?" Pat followed up with.

"A sign one can see at least a block away. The slap boards on the front of this building should work fine, don't you think?" Catherine inquired.

"Yes, ma'am. I would recommend a black background with large white lettering. White gives the feeling of clean. Do you like that idea, ma'am?" Pat asked.

"You're the expert. You do what you think will bring in the most customers. How much for your service, sir?" Catherine became the business woman she was.

Pat knew he wasn't dealing with a business novice. He decided to be conservative in his quote.

"Well ma'am, I think if I use the existing building for a backboard of the sign, I'll still paint a boarder frame to give it an independent sign look," Pat said as his mind was calculating his cost, with a small pause he continued with:

"$5.00 ma'am." Pat declared

Catherine stared at the young man for a minute, or at least it seemed like a minute to him. She was reading him and knew he was giving a good price for a large sign. If a small sign, it was far too much to pay.

"Mr. O'Reilly, will the sign cover at least 3/4 of the front of the building?" Catherine inquired.

"Yes, ma'am. I was thinking a bit larger than that. You will be pleased." Pat replied addressing her concern.

Catherine reached into her purse and handed Pat a $5.00 gold coin.

"If I'm not pleased you'll give that back to me?" Catherine inquired.

"No, ma'am, but I will keep painting until you are happy," Pat replied honestly.

"Good answer, Mr. O'Reilly, good answer." Catherine was impressed with his honesty, and continued with: "When can you start?" she said with a touch of anxiety in her voice.

"Your timing is perfect. I can start right now. I will have it outlined by noon tomorrow, and painted by dark of the day after." Pat committed. He knew he should finish sooner than that, but it is better to figure on the unexpected happening. Also, he had a lot of satisfied customers by building under time and budget.

"Very good, oh, I will expect your laundry business. Actually, yours and all your friends." Catherine said with her great Irish smile no one could argue with.

"Yes, ma'am, you will get mine for sure!" Pat replied and then followed up with: "That is if you call me Pat?"

Catherine lit up the room with that Irish smile again, and sparkling blue eyes, she replied:

"Yes Pat, I will do just that, and you can call me Catherine." She said as she shook Pat's hand.

It was amazing how Catherine could switch from a shrewd business person to a jolly go lucky Irish lassie in a heartbeat.

Everyone who met Catherine loved her. She was talkative, knowledgeable, and smiled as much with her eyes as her face. She was quick of mind and read people very well. She held all the acumen of a very good business person, and a very good person.

She pointed and introduced the boys in her life to Patrick:

"Carrying that tub in is my good friend Bill Antrim. He has been a God sent since the loss of my husband. His helper is my son Joseph, and this toe head listening to every word we have said is my son Billy," She said

The boys had brought all her tubs in the building. Next she asked them to build a dividing wall so that customers would not see all the tubs at work, or clothes hanging inside.

In a half hour more, Bill Antrim had the materials being unloaded from the wagon with Joseph's help. Joseph was 15-years-old and followed directions very well. He wasn't one to take the lead, but if given directions he did his best to follow them closely. He was the opposite of his little brother Billy, Joseph was quiet, reserved, and rarely shared his view about anything.

Billy was 10-years-old going-on-35 in attitude, but looked 7-or-8-years-old. He was outgoing, quick of mind and opinions. He rarely asked for nor needed directions to do most any task asked of him. If he didn't actually know how to do a task he would figure it out, or find somebody that did know.

Billy was a student of his environment, and his mind stored the information for possible future use. He demonstrated those traits from his first steps. Generally, strangers were virtually in shock when they conversed with Billy.

First, most strangers thought him to be about 7-years-old and then he would speak like an adult. That was enough of a shock. Soon they knew he had to be well read and certainly was opinionated. He had an excellent command of the English language.

Billy had a baby face with twinkling blue eyes that were always observing everything around him. Any stranger had an instant positive impression. Most adults first question to him was: "How old are you?" He always told the truth in response.

Wichita 'Frontier Fire Company' 1872. *No doubt many of these men knew Catherine McCarty as she had the only City Laundry in town.*

Wichita's First Church ca.1873 built in 1870 *Protestant Episcopal Church.*
Source: Wichita State University Library Department of Special Collections
wsu_ms96-4.2.6.2

Chapter Twenty-Six

Henry Gets an Assignment! His First Job!

"Billy!" Catherine called out for assistance. Both "Bills" showed up quickly. She stared and thought a minute. This was happening far too often. Both waited patiently to see which "Bill" she wanted and to do what.

"I have a decision that affects both of you. Billy, I will address you by your middle name from now on. It is a good name that belonged to a hero of the War of 1812. He was a sea captain, adventurist, and American hero. You can wear it proudly. Besides, I'm sure all three of us are tired of both of you coming each time I call...ha. Is that alright with you son?" Catherine gave him an opportunity to appeal her decision.

"That is ok Mom. I like "Henry" too. It's my name too...I know that. It might take a little getting used to..." he chuckled in a mischievous manner.

"Henry, I won't accept that excuse," Catherine said firmly and added:

"I have a very important job for you," Catherine saw he was excited to contribute. Uncle Bill never invited him to do any physical work which he thought he could do. He always called on his brother Joseph.

"I want you to visit every business in every building on every street (which was only two at the time) and let the owners know 'The City Laundry' will be open for business tomorrow morning."

"Remember, you must be back here before sundown. I mean before the sun starts down. Do you understand that, son?" She asked firmly.

"Yes, mother," Henry responded and ran out the front door.

Henry's curiosity had been high from the first moment they had arrived in town that morning. The pages of his books had come alive in front of his eyes.

Catherine yelled out to him as he was exiting: "Don't forget to mention North Main Street."

"I will mother!" Henry yelled back.

Catherine then felt a little silly in-that this town was so small it would be hard for anyone to miss her new sign. She knew Henry was chewing at the bit to see the town. Then a little fear slipped into her mind. Was it safe for him to enter every business? She shook the thought. Henry was very smart and knew how to avoid trouble. She trusted him.

Bill Antrim's hammer was pounding nails, Joseph was holding the boards perfectly straight as he did so.

In about twenty minutes Bob stopped by to see how things were progressing for the newest business in town.

"Wow! I can hardly believe my eyes!" Bob declared to Catherine. "You will be ready for business tomorrow!"

"I assume my son visited your business?" Catherine inquired.

"Yes, he did!" He said you will be open for business tomorrow. Now I believe it! Good work Catherine! Here is my bundle of laundry. I wanted to be your first customer. Did I make it in time?" he said with a chuckle.

"Yes, you did. Thank you Bob," Catherine replied sincerely.

"I see you hired Patrick. He is a good painter. He is already outlining the sign out front. It looks like the wall in here is almost done, and you haven't reached your first sundown in Wichita." He chuckled at his own observation.

"You don't mind the wall, do you?" Catherine had forgotten to get the owner's permission.

"No, that is fine. You do whatever you need to run your business efficiently."

"I'm getting out of here. All I'm doing now is slowing you down," he smiled and started to exit. He stopped, turned around.

"Give me three days on your laundry," Catherine volunteered anticipating his question.

"That will be fine, ma'am," Bob responded with as he left the building.

Catherine McCarty's City Laundry was located on Main Street in the group of buildings across the street from the last large building you can see on the left side of Douglas Blvd. *Wichita State University Libraries' Department of Special Collections Douglas Blvd. looking west to Arkansas River (treeline). Wichita-Sedgwich County Historical Museum*

Chapter Twenty-Seven

Henry Explores Wichita

Henry ran from business to business relating the message his mother instructed him to deliver. Wichita was a boom town, most of the business owners were quite busy with their day to day business. It was not always easy for Henry to get their attention about anything.

Catherine felt Henry would be street gamin' in Wichita, as he did in Indianapolis. So, she would give him a job to do at the same time. She hoped it would keep him out of trouble.

Catherine had no family or friends in Wichita to be a day care help as she worked to support the family. She did what she could to keep her children busy and out of trouble.

Josie was sixteen-years-old and working full time with Bill Antrim. He was out of town most of the day helping Bill build his homestead house, learning carpentry as he did.

Bill did work part time in town. Josie then helped his mother with the laundry business.

It was her wide eyed energetic ten-year-old she had to watch closely, and she knew it. Henry's extraordinary curiosity, like the cat, could get him killed in Wichita.

Over the next two weeks Henry was successful, talking with every business owner in Wichita about their laundry.

Catherine introduced a special "Business" program of a pick-up and delivery as an introduction to The City Laundry service. Henry was to make sure they knew it could not last forever.

Henry was able to even penetrate the security of the Keno Corner. That was an amazing accomplishment, but it back fired with his mother.

His bragging about that feat got his mother thinking if she had done the right thing. Keno Corner was the wildest, toughest, most dangerous saloon in town.

She knew it well, as it was right down the street from her business. She heard the hurrahing late at night when the family was trying to get to sleep. She heard gun shots almost every week. Never knowing if a drover's hurray shot in the air, would fall on someone she knew, or worst her own family. Keno Corner was not a place her sons should know for any reason.

"Henry, please do not enter that business again. I will let them know I will service them personally, or Uncle Bill will honor your offer. That is not a business a young lad should be going into, do you understand?" Catherine said firmly.

"Yes, mom. I went through the back door. I didn't see much of the saloon," Henry explained.

"I don't want you to go through any door of Keno Corner," Catherine emphasized.

"Yes, Mom. I won't," Henry agreed.

Henry left quickly to watch a large herd of long horns being driven down Main Street. He watched with the heart of a young man that began to dream about what he wanted to do when he grew up.

A drover pulled over and reined up in front of Henry. He noticed the sparkling blue eyes of a toe headed kid staring at him.

"What you staring at, boy," the man said from atop a red sorrel, white faced stallion. Its mane was long and beautiful. The cowboy had tapaderos on a high-backed Spanish style saddle. He rode tall in the saddle.

"You sir. I want to be a cowboy," Henry answered bluntly.

"I can't imagine why. I just spent two months of eating dirt, crossing raging rivers with the dumbest animal on earth, fighting Indians, and sleeping on the ground. I have another month of this," the cowboy informed the lad.

"I wish I could do all of that right now," Henry replied sincerely. Henry had a strong desire for adventure, to do what he wanted when he wanted to.

The cowboy spurred his stallion and continued down the street. He just shook his head in a true sense of mystery. He was going to cowboy long enough to buy his own ranch, and raise his own cattle. He couldn't understand why so many young boys wanted to be cowboys.

Of course, that cowboy wasn't reading the dime novels romanticizing the American cowboy, or making him out to be the ultimate rebel.

Henry, like many young lads in America, saw the cowboy as the symbol of freedom, adventure, independence, strength, and his word as good as his bond. He carried a six gun on his side, open for all to see. It said: "Don't mess with me. Leave me alone, or pay a dear price. Watch what you call me, or you will be called out."

One cowboy after another passed in front of Henry. He studied their clothes, their guns, their saddles and their horses.

He tried to guess their personalities at first glance, i.e. light hearted, hard core, man killer, serious, vaquero or el patron.

Henry noticed the man riding drag. He was a large man that seemed to demand authority without opening his mouth. He looked like a man right out of Henry's dime novels. The man's body stood still in the saddle, but his eyes seemed to be looking everywhere.

Henry thought to himself: "That is the man I want to be when I grow up. That man demands respect. Nothing was going to get by his eyes, drover or citizen."

The back of the herd had scattered a bit more. The man he was watching swung to his right flank and placed himself between the toe headed boy and the herd. He stayed there until the entire herd had passed.

Henry wanted to talk to him so badly, but knew the man was busy at his work, his inquiry would fall on deaf ears. The man continued up the street keeping himself soundly on the right side between his herd and the citizens.

Henry and a half-dozen other boys ran along following the herd. In front of The Keno Corner a drunk cowboy came onto the street and drew his pistol, but before he could discharge it the tall man hit him over the head with the butt of his pistol. Henry concluded it wasn't by accident he was at the right spot at the right time.

The cowboy leader then yelled to the drunk's friends watching in shock:

"Tell him when he wakes up: had he shot that pistol to stampede my herd for his entertainment, I would have killed him." The tall man continued down the street without any more interference.

The foolish man's friends picked him up out of the dirt. They knew that patron meant exactly what he said. Their friend had come close to losing his life.

Henry wasn't twenty-five feet away from the whole event. He learned a lesson of his own, firm assertiveness, got results. He would never be bullied again, as had happened in Indianapolis. No matter who an opponent might be, larger, stronger, older, whatever or whoever threatened him would know his temper, and pay a price.

Henry worked and played hard in Wichita. His mother grew more and more concerned about the almost daily violence on the streets, and in the saloons.

Chapter Twenty-Eight

Wichita Street Gunfight

On February 28, 1871 a gun fight took place on the street a short distance from her laundry. The first thing she noticed was Henry running outside to see what was happening. She yelled at him to get back inside and he did.

Later it was Henry that brought the whole story of "Handsome Jack" Ledford being shot and killed in the street. Catherine and her whole family knew the man. He owned the Harrison House Hotel and was a client of her laundry. That shooting somehow was personal, and the fact Henry was the one who obtained the gruesome details disturbed Catherine even more.

Henry told her that Mr. Ledford was killed by U.S. Cavalry Scout Lee Stewart. The scout had shot him in the back as he was in a straight up street gun fight with U.S. deputy Marshall Jack Bridges.

Also, in January Mr. Ledford had beaten Jack Bridges badly in a fist fight and thrown him out of his hotel saloon. Bridges had sworn revenge and would kill him.

Jack Bridges got his opportunity, it came with a warrant for past crimes committed by Ledford. This time he wouldn't arrest him alone. Signed warrant in hand he got Lt. Edward L. Randall, 5th Cavalry officer, twenty-five Cavalry soldiers, along with Cavalry Scout Lee Stewart to escort him to serve the warrant on his personal enemy Jack Ledford.

"Handsome" Jack Ledford knew Bridges would never take him in alive, so he started the ball blasting away with both pistols. Before getting shot in the back he was able to severely wound Bridges in an arm.

Catherine had had enough. She decided to build and move into a cabin on her hundred and sixty acres she bought abutting Bill Antrim's homestead.

Henry was now eleven-years-old, and although not physically robust he was a strong wiry boy. As such he could help in its construction. She decided that Josie and Henry would stay with Bill Antrim until its completion.

She needed to present her idea to Bill. Doing so did not go quite as she expected. Bill pretty much went along with every idea she had presented him and vise a versa. Not this time.

"Catherine, Henry can't do a man's work. I would spend half my time baby-sitting him." Bill spoke honestly.

"Bill, he is stronger than he looks. If you give him a task he will complete it, I know that because I've done that myself," Catherine defended her decision.

"I know Henry too. He will spend too much time goofing around. He is a fun-loving boy and there is nothing wrong with that. It just doesn't fit with building a cabin, digging a well, fencing the property." Bill pleaded to her sensibility.

"I'm very concerned with him running the streets of Wichita at this time," Catherine wasn't giving up easily.

"I'll bring him out here a couple days a week. I wouldn't be concerned with his street gamin', Catherine. He is very street smart. More so than a kid five-years older. He is very smart and keeps himself out of trouble. You still look at him like your baby boy. He isn't. He is street smart and takes care of himself very well." He went on:

"Honestly, Catherine, I doubt Henry will be influenced any more than he already is," Bill spoke sincerely. Catherine let him complete what he wanted to say. This was the most he had ever shared with her about her boys.

"What do you mean by "he already is?" Catherine asked pointedly.

Bill thought before answering: "The Police Gazette, dime novels, and newspaper stories he reads ferociously. He has his heroes already and they do not include a carpenter, mason, bull whacker, or freighter." Bill informed Catherine confessing his inability to influence Henry.

"I stand behind my decision to allow him to read all those because he loves reading them. I will do anything to get him to read. I firmly believe reading, writing, and arithmetic are needed for any boys future. That is all I could afford in Indianapolis as a widow. He learns fast and seemed to enjoy reading. I thank you for the couple days a week. That will help." Catherine concluded the discussion.

Chapter Twenty-Nine

A Wichita Plainsman, a Pilgrim, and a Drummer Boy

The old plainsman had his chair cocked back against the wall of one of the only two saddlery and harness shops in Wichita. He worked for Henry Tinsdale Southern Kansas Stage Company.[84] His name was Bucky Bearskin Bob but all who knew him just called him Buck.

Buck found this time so relaxing. He was actually "working" at supervising the repairing of one harness and replacement of another for his six-horse team. It might take all day and he was up for that. It recharges his energy better than a Pawnee squaw back scratch. He was doing "productive" work without hardly moving a muscle.

In reply to Buck's inquiry, a rich man described how it felt to be rich. He said: "First you know you're rich when you're making a grand living while you're asleep, and second your mind has no worries when you're awake." Well, he was half asleep, and didn't have a worry in this world. He thought to himself as he gently rocked his chair: "I think I am a rich man."

Today Buck's job was to supervise the proper fixing of a harness, which needed little of the same, supervision that is.

Most of his days were spent being slammed around on the driver seat bench of the stagecoach. His mind focused on the six horses, two green, two high energy and trained, and two old professionals at the lead.

His eyes constantly scanned the surrounding area for the surprise attack, which was happening too regularly lately. It was constant physical and mental labor.

At this moment, he did nothing but people watch and animal watch too. He loved a good animal. He could spot one a half mile away. This was his vacation.

Another leatherman's customer sat down next to him.

---

[84] Wichita had two stage companies at this time: Terry and Company Kansas Stage Company and Henry Tinsdale Southern Kansas Stage Company.

"My name is David Turner, and yours sir?" the gentleman volunteered politely.

"Bucky Bearskin Bob at your acquaintance pilgrim," Buck replied just as politely.

The man grinned and replied:

"How do you know if I'm a pilgrim sir?"

Buck rubbed his chin with his fist in contemplation. "Was this young man worth the time of explaining that which was so clearly the case?" He thought to himself.

"Well, I have the time, so'es I'll explain what is obvious to a plainsman. Mr. Turner you didn't come here by stagecoach, cause' I would know that. You didn't come by horseback, on account of the clothes you're wearing. Last but not least, it's ok to give your name to a stranger, but out west never ask him to do the same to you. That is not polite out here. He will give his name if he feels to do the same. Your own words make you a pilgrim," Buck said matter-of-factly.

David had to grin in an agreeable manner. Everything made perfect sense to even a pilgrim.

"I guess your right Mr. Bob. I'm sure enough a pilgrim. I'm a land speculator, I buy and sell land..."

Buck interrupted: "There you go again. I know what a land speculator does. Pilgrims always assume plainspeople are stupid. Therefore, they need to have everything explained to them. Why is that pilgrim?" Buck asked sincerely.

"That is a good question. Probably because we're not as smart as we think we are." David replied without hesitation.

"Well, Mr. David Turner, you can call me Buck, if 'in you have a mind to." Buck passed the open palm of his right hand in David's direction. He liked this honest young man.

David clinched Bucks hand and said:

"I do have a mind to, that I do. Thank you, I'm thinking I now have a friend that can shed me of this pilgrim cloak."

Buck pointed across the 90' wide dung covered dirt road of Main Street. Thousands of cattle traveled Main Street almost every day now. Clouds of swarming flies hung in the air over the road. One's nostrils were filled with a putrid smell day and night. Local settlers had gotten so used to it, they rarely complained. It came with the territory.

"See that boy across the road? The toe-headed skinny lad?" Buck asked David.

"Yes, I do. Is he a street Arab?" David asked.

"No, but a street gamin' lad for sure. He'll be by here soon drumming up business for his Ma. She owns the City Laundry over there," Buck pointed to a one and a half story building half way between 1st and 2nd Streets, on the west side of north Main Street.

David could read the sign clearly a half block away. The leather and saddle shop was half a country block on the east side of Main Street from The City Laundry.

Buck volunteered: "She is one to know, a window by the name of Mrs. Catherine McCarty, and one of the founders of Wichita."

"Really! A widowed woman one of the founders! Very interesting." David sincerely declared. He had never heard of such a thing.

Buck went on to explain: "She knows her business. The kid's a hustler. I mean drummer, he has earned that title."

Just then the toe-headed boy arrived in front of them. David noticed he ran like cat, his feet seemed to glide effortlessly dodging the fresh dung on the road. Although thin and very youthful looking, one knew immediately he was athletic. Physically he made a great street gamer. Not many would catch him if he didn't want them to. As soon as he spoke one knew he was also intelligent, far beyond his years.

"Hi Buck! Can I check with Mr. Williams?" the lad asked politely as his light blue eyes sparkled. David noticed the lad's eyes immediately. The black pupil seemed to capture your attention. The lad didn't hold his eyes fixed in one place very long. They seemed to be everywhere and back in an instant. "Not the eyes of one holding a secret," David thought to himself, "No, more like they wanted to know everything going on around him." The lad smiled at David. His front two teeth were prominent, but not bucked. He had a pleasant smile that was almost contagious. You wanted to smile with him and didn't even know why. David extended his hand out and said:

"My name is David Turner," with a smile of course.

Buck thought to himself: "Good, the pilgrim learns fast, he didn't ask the boy's name."

"My name's Henry, Henry McCarty, sir. Nice to meet ya."

Buck spoke to David:

"Smart lad here. He knows Mr. Williams will leave working on my harness to take care of his business."

The lad grinned ear-to-ear, his flashing blue eyes dancing from Buck to David, through the door to Mr. Williams, and back again. Those eyes could speak loudly.

"Yes, go ahead Drummer Boy. Now I know your real name: Henry. I've called you Drummer Bill McCarty." Buck said with curiosity in his voice.

"I am Bill...Henry McCarty, sir!" the lad replied with a stutter.

"I didn't know you have a split tongue to go along with those shifting eyes?" Buck grinned. He knew the lad's eyes were not evil but just very observant and curious.

"Oh, I'm sorry Buck. You see, my mother changed my name. Well not exactly changed. I have been called Billy until Uncle Bill came here with us. Mom got tired of calling out "Bill" and both of us coming to her...ha. So, she said she will call me Henry, and I would have to get used to it. Henry is my middle name. I told her she can call me anything as long as she calls me for supper...ha. She asked where I got that from and, yes, I told her I got that from you, Buck," the laddy chuckled.

"Now that we got that straightened out...go ahead and drum up some business, Drummer Boy!" Buck instructed.

The lad now known as Henry went into the shop and came out with a potato sack full of rags and clothes. He tipped his head in a gesture of "good-day" and took off running across the street toward his mother's laundry.

David turned to Buck and commented:

"That's a hell-uh-va idea. Widow McCarty picks up and delivers!" he was thinking out loud as he continued to watch the lad dodge the fresh dung piles like a cat dodging biting dogs.

"It was a great idea to start her business, but it won't last long. She is so busy now, her walk-in business keeps her working long hours. I don't know how she does it. She told me she is keeping a few people like Mr. Williams because they helped her so much when she first started."

"They seem to be a very good family, but I can't figure out that "Uncle Bill" fellow. I've heard he is a good carpenter and has a part time freighting business." Buck informed David.

"What bothers you?" David asked point blank.

"I don't think he is an Uncle. I think she is calling him that for the boy's sake. Although, they don't live together, and he does seem to be part of the family." Buck concluded.

"I think that is honorable of her." David declared.

"Oh, I forgot to mention something, she is in your business too, and very good at it I'm told!" Buck chuckled as he gave a gentle warning to his new friend.

"Are you kidding me, Buck?" David responded with emphasis on "kidding."

Buck gave him a look like it may not be healthy for him to repeat that statement.

"I don't kid around!" Buck said firmly.

"Sorry, no offense meant." David corrected his slip of the tongue. He only wondered how much more he had to learn about "westerners."

Buck went on to explain his statement:

"Catherine McCarty purchased her first city lot a short time after they started the business. I'll bet she owns three or four lots now. She told me she filed on a quarter section homestead east of here. It boarders "Uncle Bill's" quarter section. Her homestead is in the next county."

David had a strange look on his face as he said:

"Buck, you fool a lot of people wearing those buckskins and pretending your only job is a teamster. What is your real job?" the more than curious David probed.

"There you go again, pilgrim! Asking question that could get you in a lot of trouble!" Buck declared and went on to teach this green horn a little more about the west.

"Look out there!" pointing to the heavy traffic of people and animals up and down the street.

"Gun runners, Indian fighters, mule skinners, man-killers, gamblers, drovers, spoiled doves, merchants, and buffalo hunters, you can smell them a country mile away."

"All of those people come from somewhere. Many are on the lamb from something or somebody. Some have sheep's skins on them and will kill any man with a badge that is foolish enough to try and take them. A few are just looking for a better life."

"All are looking for an opportunity to start over. Some really bad guys will never break the law again for that chance. Some have such evil hearts the change won't help them."

"David, the one thing they all have in common is they don't want to talk about their past. So, pilgrim, let me be the last one you make that mistake with," Buck finished firmly.

The only reason Buck tried so hard to help this young man is that he liked him, and knew his heart was not bad, just his western manners.

"Sorry I asked. I meant no offense. You just seem to be far too intelligent to be a teamster... No, I'm not asking now, just observing." David tried to explain.

"I hope you get to a point you no longer have to tell anyone: "no offense meant." I will share a bit more about me, if you will refrain from asking someone else as you may get your head blown off...ok?" Buck asked.

"I understand, Buck. You need not if you wish not to," David replied.

"After the war of the rebellion I came home to find everything I had gone. My ranch house and barn I built with these two hands, burnt to the ground. My father and two brothers killed in the war. My mother moved to town and took in laundry. She got sick and died of pneumonia. Every time I even think of Mrs. McCarty I think of my mother. I guess that is why I wanted to know her a bit better than most I meet. She told me her husband was killed in the war. I told her I was too."

"She knew exactly what I meant. The man I was before the war was dead. I don't even know him myself. I have some memories, but that is all. I came home a different person than the one that felt obligated to join the cause."

"Do you see now pilgrim? Many of those people out there," Buck pointed to the street again, "They have similar stories."

Chapter Thirty

Buck and Cole Younger and a Toe-Headed Drummer Boy

"You were right that I was very privileged to have had a good education. My mother had attended a good catholic school and I paid attention to her teachings." My father broke his back with my older brothers on our farm to send me to the University of Missouri. In the second year I befriended a young man named Cole Younger from Lee's Summit, Missouri."

David had to interrupt: "The same Cole Young of the James – Younger gang?" he asked in surprise.

"Yes, inquisitive one, the same fellow. To continue, Cole was the best recruiter the CSA ever had! He is a great orator. I listened to his reasons for quitting school and join the Confederate cause right then. Not to do so would be sinful, besides missing out on the glory, because it would be over soon."

"I fell for it hook line and sinker. He and I were commissioned Captains in the CSA immediately. I served with him before he left our outfit to join William Clarke Quantrill. I will tell you now, no braver man have I met. Once, at the only battle we had in Missouri, Captain Younger rode his horse back and forth in in front of our line. Union balls whizzed all around him. He never blinked but just yelled out how brave his men were and how they will have victory! Then the strangest thing happened." Buck stopped to gather his thoughts. It was obviously still strange to him.

"What was that Buck...what was it?" an excited David exclaimed.

"He stopped when he saw another Captain placing a captured Union officer against the wall of a small barn. He galloped his horse over to the barn, dismounted even before the horse had stopped, rushed to the man and yelled:

"Stop that now! What God gave you the right to execute this man in front of his men across there?" He pointed to the Union lines. "If you are that stupid you might as well go over and fight for them. You're doing more harm to us over here than if you were with them," Captain Cole demanded.

"What the hell are you talking about?" the young Captain blurted.

"You shoot that officer and his men have just been motivated to kill you and all the rest of us. Right now they are afraid. You kill him, and they have no more fear, just revenge! Do you understand that now, Captain?" Captain Cole dressed the young man down good!"

"The Union officer was taken as a POW, his life saved by my friend Captain Cole Younger."

"Our outfit was ordered south to Arkansas, and we all felt a loss when Cole decided to stay in Missouri and join Quantrill. He wanted me to join him. I knew Quantrill was a deserter. I believed he was forming his own "army" for his own reasons. I declined to go with Cole, and stayed with our outfit for the remainder of the war."

"When it was over, I had nothing...absolutely nothing! A man was going to Springfield, and offered me a job driving stagecoaches from there through Kansas to Fort Dodge. He had the mail contract and the pay was good. He neglected to mention the Southern Cheyenne, Arapahoe, Comanche, and Kiowa were on the war path in southern Kansas. Not to mention the "friendly" Pawnee. "Friendly" when the US Cavalry are around. Anyway, I have been driving for that man for five years, and he never asked me about my education. Is that enough information for you my young friend?" Buck factiously stated.

"Yes it is! Wow! Quite a story. I'm glad I risked my life to ask," David said with a chuckle, and Buck joined him.

"David, that young lad that was here, he is getting a life time of education with his experience on these streets. An education you can't get back east." Buck said sincerely.

"I understand," David replied. "I lost both my brothers in that damn war! Our family has never been the same. I couldn't practice law anymore, so I sold everything and decided to be an investor in the west. Here I am!" David said as he swept his open hand across the front of him, referring to Wichita.

Just then David spotted the toe-headed boy, Henry, running across the road again, dodging one obstacle after another. He seemed to be able to jog left or right on the run like a cat with that proverbial dog snapping at its tail. Springing away from that dog just before it bites down on the sensitive tail.

"Hi Buck, hi Mr. David. I have a delivery of finished laundry for Mr. Williams," Henry declared as he arrived almost sliding to a halt with the heavy load on his shoulders sliding off in front of him.

"Your mother finished that load fast," Buck acted sincerely surprised although a rhetorical question.

"No, this is last week's order," Henry said giggling almost like a young girl, and his prominent teeth not taking away from that infectious smile. "Oh, Buck, I won't be able to see you as often," Henry volunteered.

"Why is that, Henry? I enjoy your visits at the stage company. I've always found a way to get you the magazines you like...right?" Buck inquired in a sad tone. He paid out of his own pocket for the Police Gazette and Henry's favorite dime novels. The paper drummer that shipped the papers on his stage carried extra copies for bartering and taking care of friends.

Henry explained: "Mom says it is time for me to help Uncle Bill in building our cabin. My brother Josie will live in Uncle Bill's cabin. I will be staying there a few days a week. I hope the rest of the time I will work drumming up business. I enjoy meeting people. I tried to explain to my Mom that I am learning a lot on the streets, but she is having none of that. Especially, after that man killed Mr. Ledford not far down the street from the laundry. She really became fearful of the streets from that time on."

David spoke up: "Don't fault your mother from that, son. I've not met her, but I've heard she is a good person with good judgement. Heck, I'm still learning how many things my mother was right about...ha," David chuckled.

"Now, that I can believe, pilgrim," Buck added.

"Henry, we'll be seeing each other. The stage line has been giving me two days off almost every week. We agreed to seven days a week only to fill in for drivers that quit, which has happened too often lately. Mostly, from getting themselves killed."

"So, you check in at the stage office when you're in town and they will have my schedule for the next week

Henry volunteered: "Buck, I've always known half your tall tales can't be true, but I can't figure out which half!" David belly laughed out loud at that one.

"Well, that is good. Truth is, heck, I can't remember sometimes myself. I've told them so many times they just become a story, almost like they happened to someone else and I'm just telling their story. I know better, but that is what happens with time passing."

"Mostly, they are true. Some have been exaggerated a bit here or there...ha," Buck gave that deep bellowed laugh of his. Almost like Santa Clause.

"Say, don't you have a delivery to make?" Buck inquired.

"Oh, yes! Almost forgot," Henry replied and took off at a run into the building. David had turned his head for just a second and when he turned it back Henry was gone out of sight.

"Are you sure that kid isn't a ghost?" David asked Buck.

"He is fast! I can't recall ever seeing him at a walk. You saw him cross this street today. I've seen him run through a herd of cattle and few animals even moved, or stopped. Sometimes even they looked surprised," Buck informed.

Henry showed back up with a stool chair in his hand.

"Henry, is your mother going to get angry about you getting back late?" Buck firmly asked.

"No sir, I told her I'd be talking a bit with old Buck. She said it is ok, but not too long. Buck, how long is too long?" Henry smiled with the question.

"Most likely before she closes shop or sundown, whichever comes first, would be a good bet Henry," Buck said.

David was still curious about the gunfight that had happened on the street in front of him. He wasn't naïve, the west was dangerous, but a gunfight on a city street would affect real estate values. It would increase the risk of his investments in Wichita.

"Buck do you know why U.S Marshal Bridges and the Cavalry were after a Wichita Hotelier? I would think the authorities would be more cautious about shooting in broad daylight on a busy city street." said a concerned David Turner.

Henry perked up to this question. He had heard several versions on the streets, but Buck's answer would be accurate in a matter like this. If he knew.

Chapter Thirty-One

Buck Educates the Pilgrim

Buck contemplated David's question. He could understand his concern. He decided to tell him what he knew.

"David, their dispute went back a ways. Fact is, I kept a close eye on John Ledford myself. I could have filed charges on him also. I didn't because he seemed to be going straight in Wichita. Although, I knew where he got the money to buy the Harris House Hotel." Buck stated point blank and revealed he knew a lot more than even locals knew about John Ledford.

"The rest of the story?" David asked. Henry was all ears. This was a Police Gazette type story coming alive in front of him.

"I guess it means no difference now...he is dead. Most early settlers here knew John Ledford as a branded Chief of all kinds of desperadoes. He stole horses in Indian country and sold them all over the Kansas Territory."

"He also recruited some boarder ruffians together, holdings up stagecoaches. I confronted him, and he denied having anything to do with the banditos. I told him that is a shame, and he quickly inquired why."

"I said 'it's a shame because I will have killed you if they ever attempt to rob a stage I'm driving, and you haven't anything to do with it. He asked me: 'You would kill me for what someone else did?' I replied: 'Yes, I sure will.'"

"What happened?" asked Henry.

"Nothing...not one attempt of robbing my stagecoaches." Buck concluded.

Henry replied with his quick young mind:

"That proved he was the Chief. Didn't it?"

"Yes, Henry, it did."

Henry heard all the rumors on the street, he asked Buck:

"I heard our Justice of the Peace put a warrant out on Marshal Bridges. I heard Mr. Ledford shot first. Isn't that self-defense? Henry sincerely asked.

"Drummer, I've been giving you too many of those dime novels, huh?" Buck replied jokingly.

"Buck, sir, I know self-defense," Henry replied.

"Well, the law is a funny thing out west to the writers of those books. Most of those writers are from back east. The law is a bit different there," Buck explained to Henry.

David, being an attorney from back east had to interrupt:

"The law of the land is for all the land and its people, Buck," David declared with authority.

Buck nearly laughed out loud, and then replied:

"If you believe that, you're not going to live long enough to resale all those lots you're trying to buy,"

David started to argue his point and Buck hushed him up:

"Quiet, my young overeducated young friend, and learn a thing or two. The laws of the west are simple, taking no book learning. Look how many starving attorneys there are in Wichita. Some day that will change, and the west will be civilized, but it's not now!" Buck concluded.

"Can you give me an example, so that I might learn more?" David asked the old plainsman.

Henry's eleven-year-old ears were perked and his mind ready to absorb every word Buck had to say.

Buck thought a second:

"Alright, I'll give you a few simple ones:

1. Don't call a man a liar unless you're prepared for an immediate gun, knife, or fist fight.
2. Don't insult a woman in public.
3. Don't threaten a man. He then has the right to kill you even from ambush, even if you are unarmed."

David blurted out: "Wow! Wait a minute. Are you sure Buck? That is horrible!"

Buck calmly replied: "Yep, quite sure. Don't forget it either."

Also, ifin' you're beaten in a fair fight, fist or gun, don't retaliate in ambush, or in the open. You'll be found guilty even if the other man shoots first. That is why Marshal Bridges has a warrant out for his arrest.

Henry interrupted: "I remember now, Mr. Ledford beat up Marshal Bridges in a fist fight last month, didn't he?"

Buck replied without hesitation: "Yes, pretty badly too. Then he threw him out of his hotel," Buck then changed the subject: "Henry, you don't miss much on these streets, do you?"

"I guess not, sir. If I don't see it, I sure do hear about it," Henry replied like a cat with a feather in its mouth and a grin on its face, and the family pet bird missing.

Henry went on to explain: "Truth is Buck most people think I'm much younger than I am and won't understand what they are talking about anyway. I learned back in Indianapolis it is best to know when not to speak and as well as when to speak."

"What do you mean by that, for example?" Buck asked sincerely.

"You know about the ruffians at the corner that surrounded me last week?" Henry inquired.

"No, I don't," Buck quickly replied.

"Well, I was running around the corner and they suddenly had me surrounded. Just a bunch of Bullies that were going to beat up the next kid that came along. They set the trap and I fell into it," Henry confessed.

"One kid, about 12-years-old, pushed me in the chest. I had a chuck I stole from the saloon. I slammed him in the top of his stomach, so hard he lifted from the ground and landed on his back gasping for air. The other kids were staring at him on the ground when I asked loudly if there were any other brave guys in the group. I think they were in shock, because the biggest among them had been laid out so fast. The fact is had they all jumped me I would have not had a chance. I hate bullies, Buck," Henry finished his tale of bravery.

"I do too, Henry. Job well done! Usually they are really cowards. Someone stands up to them and they fold like a pheasant at 20 paces shot with a Springfield...ha ha!" All three belly-laughed at that short tale.

David observed: "There wouldn't be any meat on that pheasant!"

Being an attorney David had to also comment: "Henry, you just confessed to stealing that chuck. Doing that makes you a street Arab. Is that what you want to be?" David said in a consulting manner.

"Sir, I don't mind much what anyone calls me. I do know I need an equalizer on these streets, or I won't grow to be a good citizen like you." Henry tried to explain, but knew he was guilty as hell.

Buck changed the subject:

“Did you hear if the Justice of the Peace is going to Ft. Harken to serve that warrant?

“I heard the Doc telling old man Fletcher he was not going to do that, but hopes it keeps him out of Wichita.” Henry related what he had eaves dropped on. He like to sneak up behind groups of men talking and get the latest news. Rarely did they even know he was there. The few times he was busted they just sent him away to street game somewhere else.

Once Henry was caught behind a table at The Keno Corner! He thought for sure the saloon keeper was going to haul him to his mother. The City Laundry was only a few doors down. Whew! He was grateful when the big guy grabbed him by the back of the collar and threw him out in the back alley. His street gamin days would have been over had the former happened.

David Turner had a solemn look on his face and said:

“Buck, you are so right about things being different here in the west. Back east if there was a warrant out on a man, a lawman will hunt the person down wherever he is.” David concluded.

Buck replied quickly: “Well, we have that sort of thing here too. Just depends on the circumstances.” he said and then turned toward Henry.

“This happened not too long before your family arrived her,” he directed to Henry and then continued the story with David Turner.

“A very popular saloonkeeper named Jesse Vandervoort by George Murray over a land dispute.”[85] Henry interrupted:

“No sir, I mean yes sir...ah what I mean is we were here, sir. I’ll never forget that!” Henry said excitedly.

Buck thought on it and agreed he had his time line off:

“Your right Henry, in-fact that was about the time I first met you, which was after the killing...am I right about that my little genius?" Buck said sarcastically with a grin.

“Yes, sir you are. Go ahead and tell Mr. David the story. I’ll keep you straight if you mess up!” Henry said as he ducked Buck’s friendly slap toward his head.

---

[85] Reference Billy The Kid, The Endless Trail by Michael Wallis Pages 27 and28 and Wichita Vidette October 13, 1870.

"Anyway, that Murray fellow made a big mistake. Jesse was best friends with Allison J. Pliley. Allison Pliley is an experienced Indian fighter, and has been in Kansas since he was knee high to a grasshopper. He enlisted in the Union Army in the war and was so good they promoted him to a Commissioned Officer. He is a natural born leader, tracker and fighter."

"Once after the war, like now, the southern border tribes, from one end of Kansas to the other, were on the war path raiding every settler they ran into. Allison Pliley recruited a small white army and dealt a severe punishment to the offending tribes. That was a big help to me."

Henry interrupted: "Buck, tell him what happened!"

David interrupted too, "Yea Buck, what happened...did he get his friend's killer?" David said just as excitedly as had Henry.

"Ok, ok! Yes, he did and very quickly! He put him in jail under the guardianship of the Justice of the Peace. Awaiting his trial, he made a successful escape. Fact is, our jail is flimsy at best. One could kick out a wall without much effort. Anyway, Murray hightailed his horse out of this country (Wichita).

David interrupted again: "Did Pliley go after him again?"

"Both of you don't give a man a chance at finishing his story, do you?" Buck asked his rhetorical question and continued his story.

"Yes, Allison took off after him again. After a month we figured one of two things had happened. Allison got killed in ambush, no way could Murray win a straight fight with him, or they killed each other."

"Two months later we were sure Allison had met a bad end. He could track a rattlesnake across granite rock, he was the best man hunter in the country. He must be dead."

"Three months after Allison had taken after Murray, a horse was found tied up on Main Street. It had Murray's saddle and his holster and revolver hung over the pommel."

"Allison left it there long enough for every citizen in Wichita to see it. I asked him where he had found Murray. He said in Indian country, and he won't be leaving it to go anywhere soon." Buck finished his knowledge of the killings.

"Wow, did you ask him if he killed Murray?" David asked excitedly.

"There you go again pilgrim! If he wanted to tell me he would. He didn't and that doesn't surprise me." Buck explained to the naïve easterner. David was shaking his head in amazement.

Henry volunteered: "If he doesn't confess, no one can prove he killed him, right?" Henry inquired of Buck.

Chapter Thirty-Two

Looks Can Be Deceiving

Buck looked at David and said: "I told you he is smart, this ten-year-old..."

Henry interrupted Buck: "Eleven-and-a-half!"

Buck Chuckled: "Excuse me, eleven-and-a-half-year-old, toe-head got it!" he directed to David.

David responded by just shaking his head again, then changed the subject back to Henry's youthful appearance:

"No offense young man, but you look a few years younger than you are," David declared.

Buck had his right fist crossing under his chin in a thoughtful manner, then observed:

"Henry, I figure the way you've been gamin these streets, you have found a way to use your youthful looks to your advantage. Am I right?" Buck sincerely inquired.

Henry started with a grin which grew to a full smile with his two front teeth prominent, but not taking away from his good looks.

Buck answered his own rhetorical question: "That's what I figured. Nothing more dangerous on the street than a boy with an adult brain that looks nine-years-old!" He concluded with his contagious chuckle.

"I'm no Arab! Just gamin' for me!" Henry declared.

David volunteered:

"I see you understand what a street Arab is?"

"Yes, sir, and I'm no Arab!" Henry repeated with emphasis.

Hank, one of the leather shop's assistants came out from with an announcement:

"Buck, your double rig tack is ready for you, sir," then he disappeared as fast as he had appeared.

Buck hopped up as spring as a young chicken declaring:

"Nice spending a half day with you two, but I need to fetch that harness and see ifin' it fits my new Missouri mules. I figure if they can haul those big white oak trees off the Ozark hills in Arkansas, well, they can haul freight and stagecoaches for me in Kansas winters." Buck said proudly.

David was well educated and well read, when he spoke Henry listened to every word:

"Buck, in California a Stockton Company is manufacturing what they call a Mud Wagon Express. The wheels are virtually good in all weather conditions. Many of the stages companies using Concord Coaches like yours are switching to the Mud Wagons." David informed Buck.

"Thank you David for the information, but I have too much tied up in my coaches. I make more money driving for the other guy than with all these expenses. That leather work alone is $40. That's more than a month's wages for a cowpoke. Almost fightin' wages." Buck replied.

Henry had to ask: "Why do you call cowboys, cowpokes?" Buck answered:

Well, Henry, I knew them when they were cowpokes. Calling them cowboys started after the war of the rebellion."

"The Mexicans herded cattle with a long stick. They "poked" them to get them to move the direction they wanted. White men just naturally called them cowpokes and took the name for themselves when they took up the same job."

"It is hard to imagine now, but there were no "ranches" in Texas. They were all run by Mexican cowpokes. Most Texicans were farmers from Tennessee, Kentucky and other areas. They picked up ranching and cow poking from the Mexicans."

How did "cowboy" come about, Buck?" Henry inquired.

"After the war the south was hurting pretty badly. They still are, they haven't recovered yet. A lot of the men returned to Texas and all that was left were thousands of wild long horns roaming all of the plains and mountains."

"The cost of the war in the north left a high demand for meat. So, the Texicans rounded up the wild cattle by the thousands and started driving them north through Indian country, then through Missouri to the rail heads."

"The other thing they were short of in Texas were mature men. Many had died or been permanently disabled in the war. There was an ample number of boys too young to join the

Confederate cause. The cattle owners put those boys to work cow poking."

"I see your anxious face, Henry. I'm getting to it. When the first large heard arrived at the rail head in Missouri a buyer noted to the reporter standing next to him: "My gosh! Would you look at that? Those are boys driving those cattle... those are cowboys! Some of them can't be ten or twelve-years-old!" He was right! Well that reporter felt that was the story and it was printed in the newspapers all over the east coast." Buck informed Henry.

"You mean, Buck! I could be a cowboy now?" Henry said excitedly.

"No, I don't think so Henry. Those boys are now 15-to-17-years-old and seasoned cowboys, and there are a lot of them.

So, I don't think the drovers need to hire 10 and 12-year-olds any more. Even if they are a damn smart 1- year-old like you Henry." Buck chuckled and observed:

"See those boys hanging around the Keno Corner? They can't be more than 14-years-old. So ifin' you have a hankerin' to eat dust, sleep on the ground, and put up with some rough string horses, you have at it!"

"Say Henry, I've seen your Uncle Bill hauling a lot of lumber out of town. He must be building a big house on that homestead?" Buck was his curious self. He always wanted to know everything going on.

The Kid kept him informed on the street's happenings, and he fed The Kid his magazines and dime novels. It was a good arrangement for both of them.

"He built two cabins, one for himself and one for us. Josie has worked with him on both. Heck, not just the cabins, they built fences, wells, and gardens for each cabin."

"I have to admit my brother has gotten pretty good at that building thing. Of course, don't tell him I said so, his head is big enough now." Henry answered ending in a chuckle.

"That's why I haven't seen him around for a while. He used to be with your Uncle all the time around town. They were hauling and doing odd jobs. I guess he still is, just not in town." Henry why haven't you worked building the cabins?

"Mom said it was because she needed me to help her in the laundry." Henry said with his voice falling off at the end of his sentence.

"So, you don't believe that is the reason?" Buck asked bluntly.

"Well, I suppose it is, but I overheard Uncle Bill telling her he just didn't like working with me, cause' I couldn't do a man's job. I suppose that is true too," Henry answered honestly. That was what Buck really liked about The Kid, he told it like he saw it, even if it was self-deprecating.

"Oh, now Henry, your being too harsh on yourself. Doing physical work like building isn't the only work that is a man's job." Buck declared and continued with: "Look here at David, he buys and sells land. He is a man doing a man's job."

David perked up to that statement.

"Heck, Henry there is nothing more dangerous than putting a hammer and nail in my hand. I can injure myself and the guy next to me!" Buck chuckled.

Henry really was perking up. He thought to himself: "Buck was right with what he said. There is a lot of work that isn't manual labor that men do... ah... ah well, there must be more like... (then he spoke out loud) shop keepers, gamblers, sheriffs," ending with a little excitement in his voice. He had never thought of that, only moped about what Uncle Bill and Josie had said to his mother.

"Yes, Henry...you got it now. The world is full of important jobs for men to do. What makes you a man isn't the job. It's how you do the job," Buck concluded his lesson for today. "Well, I best be going. I have to fit that new harness on those mules by night fall." buck declared as he headed for his buckboard. He placed the fresh smelling new leather in the back of it.

David spoke up: "Something about the fresh smell of new leather that warms a man's heart." He tipped his derby hat and said: "Good trails, Buck. I earnestly enjoyed your company (turning to Henry), and yours young man."

"Same to you, young whippersnapper! Keep your powder dry and your tongue still," Buck chuckled at his own joking salutation. David gave another tipping of his derby acknowledging the good advice.

Henry addressed Buck: “So long Buck. Watch out for the Kiowa and Cheyenne. They are on the warpath and raiding settlers all along the Kansas boarder,” Henry was showing off his street smarts. If there was news, Henry found out about it. He had learned that listening into cowboys’ conversations in Keno Corner. He hid behind a fake wall built for a guard and just listened. The bar keep had never seen him. Sometimes cowboys caught him and kicked him out, but the bar keep was blind as a bat.

“Thanks Henry! I’ll do just that! Of course if they mess with me there will be some empty ponies and crying squaws.” Buck replied as he lifted his double barrel sawed off shot gun to show Henry.

Henry observed: “Buck that will kill the Indians, their horses, and a couple bystanders too!” Henry said jokingly.

“That is the idea, Henry. It could also put some buck shot in the rear end of a toe headed smart-alecky boy too.” Buck replied with a twinkle in his eye.

Henry laughed and waved his hand good-bye as he took off for the laundry. He was running late now.

Chapter Thirty-Three

Bad News!

Catherine found it difficult to inform Henry she was discontinuing here delivery service. She was far too busy for the additional work. Her ulterior motive was she wanted Henry off the streets.

Her customers kept her well informed of his whereabouts, and knew he was just gamin. An Irish mother's instinct was telling her he was heading for trouble.

Henry arrive at their laundry shop from a delivery. She asked him to sit down for a minute. Henry knew that always meant he was in trouble. Everything flashed through his mind i.e. his confession of stealing that chuck in his back pocket. Had David, do-gooder, squealed on him? "What a snitch!" Henry thought to himself. There wasn't anything else, at least that anyone knew of. All this ran through his mind as he pulled up a bench chair to listen to what his mother had to say.

Catherine had a solemn look on her face as she began her explanation.

"Henry!" He was relieved. It can't be very serious trouble, or she would have said: "William Henry McCarty!" That would mean a serious problem. "Henry" meant a small problem...hopefully.

"Henry, are you listening to me?" Catherine inquired as she saw his mannerisms reflecting someone not paying attention.

"Yes, mom, I am. I was just thinking of something I heard earlier. It's not important. I am sorry," Henry sincerely delivered.

"OK, I must tell you that I am eliminating the delivery service all together. I am closing the shop two days a week, so I can build a garden at our new home, and other things that needs to be done out there." She said matter-of-factly.

Catherine had been spending one day out there now, and enjoyed that time immensely. It was like a vacation from the laundry business.

"I know mom. You told me you want me out there two days a week, right," Henry wanted to confirm that had not changed.

"Yes, but now I want you to help out there Saturday through Wednesday, and work here helping me close out the weeks orders Thursday and Friday." Catherine explained.

"No deliveries at all?" Henry quickly responded.

"None at all. You have done a wonderful job with all our customers, but as I said this is what I want to do now. I do want you to go out tomorrow and visit all our customers and let them know of these changes, so it won't come as a surprise to them, OK son?"

"Yes, ma'am," Henry replied with obvious disappointment in his voice. He knew his days of street gamin were over, and knew his mother well enough not to argue anything. Once she made up her Irish mind, it was done!

Over the next few weeks Henry was able to get permission to see Buck a couple times, but that was it. The work schedule in the last two days of the week was hectic. Six days work was crammed into five days, and everyone wanted to pick up their clothes on Friday.

He helped the best he could on the homestead, but his slight frame at eleven-years-old was not suited for much heavy work. Most of the work was heavy work on the homestead.

Josie was sixteen, medium built and strong. He helped Bill Antrim build his cabin and their own next door. Now, he spent more time with other tasks on the homestead. He had learned a lot working with Uncle Bill. Not only carpentry, but also freighting.

It was Friday and Catherine fell behind. Henry was doing his best to help, but just too young to be affective. She sent Henry to fetch a bail of water. The water was for herself, as she felt dehydrated. The hard work under a ceiling that seemed to keep every bit of heated energy contained in the room. Even with the doors and windows opened on both sides of the building, her body would sweat fluids profusely. She needed water in the worst way possible at that moment.

She hoped Henry would hurry back and not get distracted. It seemed like he was gone an hour, although it was only about five minutes.

Catherine leaned over to pick up a tub full of dirty clothes to carry to her washing tub. She made only a couple steps and dropped the tub to the ground. Strength had completely left her arms. She was out of breath too, and driven to find a place to sit or suffer passing out on the floor. She was determined not to have Henry find her in that condition. A bench was only five feet from her, but it looked like a block away to her struggling mind. She made it!

Her first inclination was to hang her head between her knees, but that worsened her condition. Her stomach pushed against her diaphragm and lungs. That caused a violent cough.

It was at that moment she knew there was more going on that just being over tired from lack of sleep and hard work. More than the sauna effect of the heated work room. Something was going wrong inside her body.

She calmed herself down by saying to herself: "Whatever it is, worrying will not help it." Catherine always disciplined herself to be practical, pragmatic, and a problem solver. She could change her mind, or changes her priorities in a heartbeat if logic argued it best to do so. The first thing to do now was to talk to Dr. Allen.

Arriving back with a full bucket of water, Henry immediately knew something was wrong with his mother. His heart raced in panic. She was pale, shaking, and wheezing in breaths taken.

"Son, don't worry, I'm ok, but I would like you to go fetch Dr. Allen for me, ok? She asked in a calm and low tone.

"Yes, mother!" Henry replied and took off at lightning speed to Dr. Allen's office. He could not avoid the tears from falling as he did.

Arriving at the doctor's office Henry exclaimed:

"Doctor! Doctor! Come quick! My mother is sick... terribly sick!" Henry yelled loud enough for people in the next building could hear.

Dr. Edwin Allen was always busy being the only permanent doctor in Wichita. His partner Dr. Andrew Fabrique was a traveling doctor for all the southeaster Kansas territory. This day Dr. Fabrique happened to be in the office. Dr. Allen asked if he could take over his scheduled appointments for a couple hours. Of course he agreed, and Dr. Allen was off with Henry to the City Laundry.

Upon arrival he met Catherine feeling much better, but still concerned. Henry was elated just to see color back in his mother's face and she was standing on her own.

Dr. Allen spoke first:

"Henry, I must give your mother an examination and I need you to visit one of your friends without relating anything about your mother illness? Do you understand that?"

"Yes, Doc. I understand. That could affect our business... right?" Henry replied.

Doctor Allen turned to Catherine: "I never cease to be amazed at just how smart your boy is," grinning as he said it.

"Yes, he is," she replied and continued with directing to Henry: "Not your gamin friends. Find you friend Buck." Catherine said firmly.

"Yes, mother. I will," Henry said and took off feeling a lot better about his mother's condition. She was with the Doc.

Dr. Allen gave Catherine a full and through examination. He was always straight forward with his opinions without beating around the bush. He looked into the tired blue eyes of an over worked woman he respected greatly.

"Catherine, you have contracted the lung sickness of consumption. There are a few things you can do to lengthen your life, possible even see Henry reach maturity if you do those things quickly." He said this with his low monotone voice that instilled confidence in who ever received his advice.

Catherine had suspected what he would diagnose, but hearing the actual words still made her heart slump. She knew "Consumption" was a death sentence. A few words had upset her whole life! At that moment she had no idea just how much it would do the same.

"I'll do whatever you suggest, doc...whatever!" Catherine said matter-of-factly.

"First, you cannot spend one more day in this laundry...not one day! I can hardly breathe in here right now, and I have good lungs! Have the boys finish all your orders you have now, and then close this business. Let them work out the details while you rest for at least a week to gain strength for the rest of the things you need to do."

"And what are those, Doc?" Catherine replied.

"You need to move to a highland with clean cool air. Not too high where there is little air, but high enough to have clean cool air."

"I have read that Denver, Colorado Territory is just such a place. I can't say for sure as I have never been there myself, nor treated anyone that has been there. I am depending on newspaper articles, which could have questionable motivations, because the same papers have consumption sanatoriums and retreats advertised in them."

Catherine was confused:

"Are you recommending Denver, or not, Doc," Her pragmatic side came out clearly.

"I am, but with a caveat. If for any reason, after a couple weeks there, you are not feeling better, or your condition worsens, then leave and head to the southwest, like New Mexico or Arizona Territories." Dr. Allen was very specific.

"Why not go there in the first place, Doc?" Catherine inquired.

"Denver is a well-established society. That I do know. The southwest territories are not. They are suffering from every imaginable societal problem, Indians on the warpath all the time, Texas outlaws hiding out there, monopolistic corrupt governments. To name just a few problems. On the other hand, the Spanish-Mexican societies there are very old and well established. They have their outlaw problems too, but by-in-large they are a God-fearing people. I don't know if that explained my suggestion or not, to your satisfaction?" Dr. Allen sincerely inquired.

"Yes, it did Doc. Perfectly. Thank you so much for all your professionalism and your friendship. It means a lot to all the McCarty family." Catherine sincerely declared.

"Catherine, now it is up to you to use that brilliant Irish mind of yours to do the right thing for those boys. Oh, yes, don't listen to any doctors that recommend you take alcohol or Laudanum[86]. Those two can be worse than the lung disease." The doctor said as he left the shop.

---

[86] Laudanum was often prescribed by doctors for a number of ailments, included Tuberculosis aka "consumption", Lung Disease, etc. It contained 10% powdered

"I won't, Doc. I promise you that. You have always been a good friend and I treasure your advice," Catherine said and went on to volunteer: "I have never thought of my mortality. Silly huh? We all have to die of something. I just wonder what will happen to my boys when I'm gone. I'm all they really have."

"Their father just had to be a hero and get himself killed in that damned war. They never really knew him. We were separated while Michael looked for work in Indianapolis, and when we joined him there, he was working two jobs. Josie didn't see him much, and Henry was just a baby. Then he joined the damn Army!" Catherine looked up with tears in her eyes and ask Dr. Allen:

"What is going to happen to my boys, Doc?" she said as a tear left her blood shot blue eye and rolled down her cheek.

"I don't know Catherine, but what I do know is that they come from good stock. I know that, and that is the best anyone can give a child...good stock. You have already done that."

"How do you know that?" She asked, and Doc replied:

"Your only worried about your children, not just yourself, you're a good woman and a good person. Now you clear those tears before your youngster thinks I gave you a hard time." Dr. Allen instructed gently.

"You did!" Catherine replied with a chuckle.

"Now, now, I did not. Good night Catherine. I'll see you again in a few days," Dr. Allen informed.

"Next week, same time, same place?" Catherine requested. He agreed knowing she didn't want anyone seeing her go into the doctor's office. He also knew she would not close the business immediately. He would keep a close eye on her.

. . . .

Faithfully, Dr. Allen stopped by to check on Catherine's progress. He observed the disease was not progressing fast. On the fourth week, upon his arrival, Catherine was coughing pretty aggressively. He noticed she had a hot water cleaning tank steaming with the cooler air in the room.

---

opium and contained almost all of the opium alkaloids of morphine and codeine. It did not require a doctor's prescription until early 1900s. Advantage was pain suppression and disadvantage it is highly addictive. Today it is still in use for pain suppression and to help heroin addicted new born babies. It is a "Highly Addictive Schedule II Narcotic" in the USA.

He sat Catherine down and explained that she needed to warm the air to eliminate and least reduce the steam. She pointed to the wood stove.

Doc saw it was empty and there was no wood stacked in the shop. It was a late and cool spring.

Walking out back he saw a large pile of several cords of wood. That meant she was too weak to carry the wood. It also meant she didn't have any help in the shop. Doc knew this situation was grave. He would soon find her dead from exhaustion.

Returning inside with a large armful of wood he began filling the stove. Lighting it up, he made several more trips to the wood pile.

Catherine was curled up on her resting bench sound asleep. Doc knew that meant she had been up all night with that cough. The first time she stopped moving without the cough her brain went to sleep.

Doc looked at the clothes in the hot tub next to her wooden roller ringer. He looked back at Catherine and thought to himself: "You rest up. I'll finish that tub for you."

Dr. Allen rolled up his sleeves and went to work. Time slipped by so quickly. He had finished two more tubs full and ran out of room on the indoor drying lines.

Just then Henry came in from a day of gamin on the streets.

"Shhh, your mother is sleeping. Follow me," Doc said in a very light whisper. So light Henry's keen hearing barely heard him. He followed the Doc out to the back yard.

"You must keep secret what I have to tell you. I am telling you only because your mother needs you right now, and she is too proud to say so," Doc explained.

Henry was all ears.

"Your mother has a bad cough, as you know. The cough is keeping her from sleeping. You must help her to keep the shop warm all day and night. The same goes for your homestead. She is too tired from working so hard, she can't carry wood in for the stove. All the wood you see in there now, I brought in earlier. Can you do that?" Doc asked more like a command that a question.

"Yes sir, Doctor Allen," Henry replied.

"Ok, son, I must leave now. Let your mother sleep as long as she can, ok?" Doc requested.

"Yes, Doctor Allen, I will. I'll take care of her," Henry replied. Doctor Allen slipped out the back yard toward his own home. He was tired himself and couldn't imagine how Catherine was doing any of those tasks alone. Just wasn't right.

Henry returned inside the shop. He loaded some more wood in the stove, curled up near it with a brand-new Police Gazette Buck had given him earlier. He sat quietly reading it by the firelight. The sum had long gone down.

Catherine was sleeping soundly. Henry noticed her breathing was deep and noisy, and every once in a while, short with a cough. Then she began to wheeze. It left Henry feeling helpless to help her. The Doc said to let her sleep as long as she could. He wanted to awaken her to stop the terrible wheezing sound, but he heeded to the Doctor's instruction, and left her sleeping.

Catherine slept to early morning the next day. Henry had kept the fire going all night. Her wheezing came and went all night.

Even at Henry's young age he knew enough to be concerned, this was no ordinary cold as she had led it up to be. He had seen his mother work hard before while having a cold. This was different, and her sending for the doctor was very different.

Chapter Thirty-Four

Bill Antrim, Scared but Taking Care of Business

That morning "Uncle" Bill and Josie were up very early. They hadn't slept much worrying about Catherine and Henry. Both had stayed over before, but always had told them in advance they would be doing so.

Henry's sharp ears heard them pulling up out back. He saw his mother was still asleep, so he scurried out the back door.

"Mom is still sleeping. She is very sick with breathing hard. Doctor Allen was here last night. He said he would be back today. He also said Mom is not to lift anything for a while, and I am to keep the shop warm." Henry finished his report as quickly as possible.

Bill Antrim spoke up first:

"There remains little to do to have both homesteads completed. I'll finish the details and you two stay with your mother. Make sure she listens to Doc Allen." Bill said in an authoritative manner and voice.

Normally, Henry didn't listen when he said things in that manner. In-fact, most of the time he would do exactly the opposite. Which was the main problem had with Henry. This time would be the exception, he would do exactly what "Uncle" Bill wanted.

Bill added: "I'm going to Lily's Restaurant and prepaying breakfast, lunch and dinner for all three of you for three days. I'm then picking up supplies and returning to our homesteads to finish your mother's well. Tell her all this and that her fencing is done, garden is cultivated and planted," Bill then added: "I'll finish the well in three days, return and pick up all of you. Let her know all this," Bill concluded.

Josie replied first:

"Ok, don't worry...we'll handle everything here,"

Henry just stared at "Uncle" Bill. Ironically, he somehow wasn't surprised that he had not included on his list of things to do, coming in to see how his mother was doing right now, or before leaving town. "Uncle" Bill wouldn't be back to see her for three days.

Bill Antrim made direct eye contact with Henry, then reined his horse and with a kick to its sides, left the property.

To Henry, it seemed like "Uncle" Bill knew this was coming and his whole attitude had changed. Henry was too young to know Bill was fearing the worst: consumption, and he didn't want to face that possibility yet. Bill handled fear by escaping it. Almost like if he didn't see Catherine the disease would go away on its own. When he saw her next she would be fine!

Bill thought to himself: "This was happening just as both of them were realizing all their dreams coming true. 320 acres was enough to have a very successful cow-calf ranch." He had his eye on another 160 acres on the other side of Catherine's homestead.

They both had many lots in town that would bring long term security. He thought it was very close at hand to ask Catherine for her hand in marriage. He knew she had finally stopped mourning Michael's death six years earlier, and had achieved her goal of being financially independent before remarrying anyone.

Michaels's death had scared Catherine near to death herself. Two boys to feed, school and clothe with no husband. Many women she knew gave their children up to orphanages, and became prostitutes to survive. She was determined to succeed on her own, and she had so far. She loved Bill like a close brother, but she knew that he wanted to marry her in the worst way. She just wasn't ready for that yet.

So much went through Bill's mind that day. He was sure if Catherine had asked for Dr. Allen to come see her at the shop...well that alone said it all!

Henry watched "Uncle" Bill pull away and for the first time he felt a little contempt for him: "Why didn't he even check on Mom...why?" he asked himself.

"Henry, give me a hand," Josie asked as he held out an arm full of wood for Henry to carry inside. Henry grabbed the wood and delivered it very quietly inside. Josie tip-toed behind him.

They rounded the in-door clothes line and were startled to hear:

"Why are you two Indian' up on me?" Catherine said in a forceful and energetic voice.

Henry pointed to the bench she was sleeping on and said: "Ah...you...were asleep there," he said stumbling his words.

"Well, I'm not now, am I? Let us get to work!" Catherine bellowed out with a twinkle in her eye. "Doctor Allen said I will be much better if I keep a fire on in here. So, can you boys keep that heat a coming?" Catherine sincerely asked.

"Yes, mom, we will!" Henry replied.

Josie went out back to chop some more wood for the wood pile.

Somehow, Catherine felt normal...like all was well. It didn't last long. By noon she was so tired she had to lie down again and take a nap. She rested a full two hours before collecting enough energy to work only a couple more hours.

The boys were doing great! They took care of customers, took in new orders, and kept the fire going all day.

Henry arrived back at the shop after a delivery. He was full of all the latest news, which was of little interest to his mother at the moment, but he felt the impulse to tell her anyway.

Catherine politely listened to her son and then asked if he could ring out the last load in the tub and hang the clothes out to dry while she took a short walk.

Henry, of course agreed. He wanted so badly to ask her what Doctor Allen had said on his last visit, but he had been taught well by Buck, not to do such a thing. If she wanted him to know she would tell him.

Chapter Thirty-Five

Catherine Reflects on Everything

Catherine exited the front door of her business and walked down Main Street a couple blocks. So much ran through her mind, as to what to do first, second, etc. She knew her life was over as she had known it. One relatively short conversation with Doctor Allen and her entire life was turned upside down. She now knew she would have to close the business sooner than she wanted. She just didn't have the health to keep it up even with the help of the boys.

There was a resting bench ahead in front of a clothing store. She stared at it with every step that had grown harder and harder to make. Her mind was consumed with that bench, she must rest now.

This small walk had tired her whole body. She sat and thought how many times she had shopped in this store and had never noticed the bench out front. Now it was a beautiful sight to behold.

As she caught her breath and strength she looked up and down the street thinking how she always believed what Wichita would be someday. No cattle on Main Street, instead a trolley car transporting people all over the business section. Street lights lighting up the whole street, all night long. Policemen walking their beats all over Wichita making it a safe place for women and children around the clock.

Yes, someday this city (she refused to call it a town) would be the Queen of the Plains with a metropolitan opera, uptown New York plays and shops, schools of all levels of education, and churches of all faiths. Yes, the day would come that this city she helped found would be a great city. Now, she knew she would not see that day, but she remained confident it would happen, just not with the McCarty family.

Her thoughts went to Bill Antrim. For the first time she realized how important Bill was to her feeling of well-being. He had been there for her and the family for the past six years. The fact was he was more like a brother to her than a lover. She loved him as a brother, but had never lost her romantic love for Michael. Even though that was never said, Bill knew it to be the truth. He was caught in a love triangle with a dead man. He always believed in time he could win her over, and if not he enjoyed every minute they had together. He loved Catherine with all his heart, body and soul.

Catherine had an urge to set everything right with Bill. She knew how well he was doing in Wichita. His carpentry and freighting skills were in high demand. He could make more in one day than the average man made in a week.

She knew Bill loved his Wichita land. It was his first homestead, first cabin, first fencing, first well, first garden. He was proud of all his improvements. That was more important to him than the money he made. He had followed her lead and invested in town lots. She was there once when he scooped up a handful of dirt on his homestead and smiled as he let it sieve through his fingers. She noted the smile was of extreme gratification and love of every grain of dirt.

Bill had also built all the improvements on her section of homestead land. He worked so hard for her to realize her own dream. He had done all of that out of a sincere and deep love for her.

He was able to teach Josie carpentry and freighting skills. Although Josie looked at the work as chores, Bill and Catherine believed the skills he was picking up would serve him well in life.

Henry was another matter. He had always been nice to the boy for Catherine's sake, but Henry had a way of aggravating Bill to no end. He would read those darn dime novels and magazines and not get his work done.

Also, he had never met a boy so afraid of nothing, except hard work. Henry had a way of avoiding it at all costs. Possibly that was too harsh as he wouldn't turn it down, but never focused long enough on the task to complete it.

Always, something or somebody would distract him, and he was off in another direction in a heartbeat. Confronted later he would apologize saying he had "forgot about it." What bothered Bill the most was that he was probably telling the truth? Yet, possibly he was not. In Bill's mind, Henry could not be trusted with what he says he is going to do, or not do.

Catherine was aware of all that, yet, seemed to "protect" Henry a little more than Josie. She felt Henry was a chip off the Michael McCarty block, or a perfect example of, as the old English/Irish saying goes: "The apple does not fall far from the tree."

Her thoughts went to Michael. Henry was growing up very much like his father. If Michael stayed in one spot, one thought, or one moment very long it was a miracle. She was still angry at him. She joined him in Indianapolis, and he joined the Army, without any thought of its impact on his family. He decided he should defend the Union and freedom. That was it! And off he went to get himself killed.

She stilled loved Michael dearly. His smile and twinkling blue eyes that danced as he talked, and, oh my, the sweet talking he could do!

Often she acquired the foolish feelings of a jealous school girl when she observed other women hypnotized by his eyes. They could see nothing else of his face but those fun-loving dancing blue eyes.

No matter how disgusted she may be about something he had done, or declared he was going to do, in two minutes he could have her laughing. It was a wonderful quality and she saw the same in Henry. She knew now he was a little man in a kid's body, and someday he may be a kid in a man's body, just like his father!

Catherine clasped her hands over her face and said aloud:

"What will become of Josie and Henry? I must do everything Doc Allen said. I must stay alive long enough for Henry to grow to manhood."

Chapter Thirty-Six

Catherine Meets Mr. Roberts/ Henry Drives the Buggy Home

"Are you OK ma'am?" a stranger's soft and polite voice asked.

"Oh...yes sir. I'm sorry to have spoken aloud my woes. That is poor manners," Catherine replied collecting her wits about her: "I will be fine soon! Thank you."

"Please let me escort you to your destination," The gentleman volunteered and continued with the fact: "The sun has set, and you should not walk these streets alone at night, ma'am."

Catherine had not even noticed the sun had set.

"Alright, sir. Please, just to the City Laundry down a couple blocks. I would appreciate the escort." Catherine replied. The man was so polite and of such good manners.

Just before arriving at the laundry Henry joined them. He had gotten concerned and was about to launch a search for his mother.

"Mother, I was getting worried about you," Henry exclaimed immediately.

"Henry, where is your manners? This gentleman escorted me back and is a perfect gentleman." She was going to introduce him but realized she had not even asked his name. This was definitely not like her.

"Young man, my name is Mr. Bill Roberts. I am glad to meet your acquaintance," Mr. Roberts declared as he pushed his hand out to greet Henry. Henry gave a half salute and took his mother's hand.

"Thank you sir for the comforting escort," Catherine said sincerely.

"You're welcome ma'am, and I see you are in good hands now," He replied.

"Yes, she is sir," Henry replied quickly as he walked toward the shop with his mother in tow.

Entering the shop Henry asked his mother:

"Do you know Bill Roberts, mother?"

"No, not until tonight, son," she replied frankly.

"Mother he is a famous gambler who it is said has killed many men." Henry said point blank.

"Well, I am a woman!" she replied with a chuckle and continued with: "I judge people by what I see and hear, not by what other people say about them. They are usually quite wrong, son. Now, let me see here...oh! You have done a fine job of it! All the clothes are hung, and the buggy is pulled up out back, I suppose?" She asked the rhetorical question.

"Yes it is, mother...I must say..." Henry was interrupted by his mother. "Now that is enough about Mr. Roberts. All is well that ends well, my son. Will you drive the buggy home?" She asked to change the subject and allow him to feel important.

"Yes, of course I will...I would love to! Thanks mother, for trusting me." Henry said with honest surprise. She never let him drive through town, and only a few times when they got out of town.

Henry helped his mother up into the buggy. Hopping up on the other side, he felt very grown up. He was on the driver's side. When he was allowed to drive it was always on the passenger's side. The driver's side was important, the driver is in charge!

Off they went to their new cabin and homestead. Well almost off they went. Catherine asked Henry to stop and asked:

"Son, don't you think it would be wise to light the buggy's lanterns? It is getting pretty dark. She said it in a very low consulting tone, after-all he was the driver.

"Oh, yes mother, I forgot," Henry excitedly replied. He jumped from the buggy lighting each lantern, one on each side of the buggy, and hoped back in with a big smile on his face.

Catherine sat quietly as Henry drove the wagon out of town toward their homestead.

She thought long and hard over how she was going to tell Bill and the boys what Dr. Allen said. Even more so on what she is going to do about it.

A few words from the doctor and all her dreams went up in smoke. She would leave Wichita as soon as practical. She decided to sell all her assets acquired, and not to do so as a "fire-sale." She would get market price for every lot, land, and building she owned.

She would not blame Bill if he decided to stay in Wichita, in-fact she intended on recommending that to him. He may feel committed to taking care of her, especially with Dr. Allen's diagnosis.

She knew how hard it would be for her to give up her dreams and assets acquired, but she must. It would be just as hard for Bill to give up everything to follow her. Maybe even harder, as she knew among the two of them she was the stronger person. Bill was a good person and loyal friend, but she'd not ask him to leave with her. She made up her mind to that.

Suddenly the normally calm horse they had nick named Betsy locked both front legs and came to an abrupt stop. It almost thrust both driver and passenger out of the buggy.

Ironically, Henry instantly called out: "Whoa!" Catherine looked at him with the expression of that certainly wasn't needed. She decided to say nothing and see how he handled this minor emergency.

Henry began to talk to Betsy in a soft reassuring manner. He had watched Bill handle these things many times:

"Whoa, girl...you're ok. Settle down now. Nothing bad out there." Just as he said that a big old long horn bull came into view. That sight even scared Henry and his mother a little.

Henry knew if the horse picked up on his emotions they could be in trouble. Bill taught him that a long time ago and many times he had been stupid enough to forget it. Horses know your feelings, not your thoughts, but they do know your feelings.

"It's OK. That old boy is just telling us he owns that spot on the road, Betsy." Henry said as he lightly pulled back on the reins to signal a backing up of the buggy. Betsy was more than happy to adhere to those instructions. She backed up almost too fast.

The old long horn bull didn't come forward, but just stood there staring at them.

"Old Buck told me about some wild long horns that stopped his stage every once in a while. Mom, I think this is one of those long horns. He is looking at us like he hasn't seen a horse and buggy before." Henry concluded.

Catherine replied calmly: "I think your right. He isn't afraid at all though."

Henry agreed with a nod and then volunteered:

"He is trying to decide if he should kill us or let us be."

Catherine's head swung toward her son with surprise written all over it. Her little Henry read that animal pretty good.

Henry backed up the buggy another twenty feet and stopped. Betsy settling down. She had been twitching from nerves gone wild, and sweating a gallon of water from her body. She was very scared and now she felt much better being 50 feet away from that monster she felt for sure wanted to eat her.

Henry relaxed the reins and put on the buggy's brake, which he knew would do little good if Betsy freaked out.

"Let's wait a few minutes and see what that big boy wants to do" Henry declared.

Catherine just nodded in the affirmative.

It soon became clear the bull was not going to move.

Henry pulled on the right rein lightly and Betsy turn to the right and began to walk out in the grassy area south of the road. He then gave a left pull which Betsy did not want to obey. Henry slapped her rump with the free rein and she began to obey.

They circled the bull and just before they got on the road behind him he did a startling thing, he turned 180 degrees in a heartbeat. He had seemed to have lifted all four hooves off the ground and swung 3000 pounds of animal in midair.

Betsy needed no coaching to trot east away from that menacing killer bull. She wanted nothing to do with that animal.

"Mother, I've seen thousands of those long horns come through town, but I can't say I have ever seen one that looked like that one. That bull was really thinking about killing us." Henry said matter-of-factly.

Catherine thought for a moment and then remarked:

"Son, I was very proud of how you handled that situation. I don't think I could have done as well," she said just as matter-of-factly.

"Thank you, mother," Henry replied sincerely and beamed with pride.

That menace out of the way Catherine went back to thinking of their situation. All her investments and the homestead were kept to ensure a stable environment for her boys.

She hoped Joseph would take over the business someday and Henry would grow to love the land and raise live stock of his choosing.

Suddenly she admonished herself and thought:

"Stop thinking of what was and start thinking of what will be!" Catherine was a strong-willed woman and once she put her mind to something that was it! And she had just done that!

The homestead came in view, Bill and Josie were standing out front to greet them.

"How was your trip from town," Bill asked noticing Henry was in the driver's seat.

Catherine instantly replied:

"By gosh, that was the best ride home I have ever taken! It was a most interesting, revealing and safe ride. I was in good hands with Henry at the reins," She declared clearly.

"Good job Henry!" Bill exclaimed and in Henry's memory it was the first time he had ever said that. Bill was always finding something wrong with what he did...always! Josie had jealousy written all over his face.

"You were running late, so I cooked up a steak dinner for us. I know you must be very tired and hungry." Bill informed Catherine.

Chapter Thirty-Seven

Catherine Announces Her Decision

Henry started to say something but remembered, as his mother looked sternly at him, that she had told him not to say anything about what happened, or the doctor. She would tell them after dinner. Henry changed the subject and asked if Bill cooked those fresh big potatoes for dinner too. Josie replied for Bill in the affirmative.

Henry came around and helped his mother down from the buggy.

"Thank you son," she murmured. He grinned knowing the thank you was also for not saying anything yet.

As tired as Catherine was she knew she had to share everything that Doctor Allen had said to her. She could not work another day in the laundry. She decided to just be straight up and say what she had on her mind, she would sell everything and move to Denver. As the Doc had said, if that doesn't work well for her health, she will head south to a drier climate.

They all gathered around the large table that Bill had built for Catherine. It was a fine piece of woodwork. He had put a lot of love into making that dining table.

They enjoyed the wonderful meal that Bill and Josie had prepared. Henry was like an anxious cat and fidgeted with everything, fork, spoon, and knife. He would have done the same with the plate, but it had food on it.

Catherine asked everyone to say nothing until she was able to tell her whole story and then she would listen to all they had to say. They agreed, and she did so. She covered every detail of the doctor's diagnosis and recommendations.

All three were in a state of surprise, bordering on shock. They couldn't believe their ears. Consumption was something that happened to other families, not their family.

In the naivety of youth, Henry had dismissed the doctor's visit altogether because his mother seemed back to normal, just a bit tired. She would get home, rest up, and be herself the next day. Obviously, there wasn't anything seriously wrong with her. She wasn't in pain, just very tired.

Even Henry knew "consumption" was serious, a death sentence. Yet, in his naïve mind he felt that if they did as the doctor said, she will live on normally. All will be ok. His mother had stopped talking and everyone was quiet. Henry broke the icy air first:

"When do we leave? Tomorrow?" He seriously asked his mother.

Catherine smiled and replied: "No, son. It will be sometime before we go. I must sell all my holdings, and I want a fair price for them. I need to know if you boys can help finish up all the jobs in the laundry? Doc Allen said weeks ago I shouldn't do even one more day in the shop. I now know he is right."

Josie spoke up: "Of course, mother. Don't worry about any of that. We grew up watching you run your business. We know it almost as good as you do."

Bill volunteered: "Catherine, don't you worry about anything but getting rest and well enough to make that trip you're talking about. I'll take care of selling all the lots and last, but not least, your homestead.

There are plenty of buyers in town, you know that. You tell me what you want, and I'll get it done for you. You're a bonny of a lass, and as tough as they come. If anyone can beat this thing, you can." Bill Antrim concluded confidently.

Catherine smiled a welcoming smile to those complimentary words. Henry didn't know what "bonny of a lass" was, but that his mother liked it, whatever it was.

Bill then went on to say: "I'm going to keep my homestead. I'll lease it out to whoever buys yours. That could double the amount of cattle they could raise, and I'll make them a great deal."

Catherine thought when he started to talk that he was going to explain why he was staying in Wichita, but it was obvious he was not saying that at all. She decided to suggest differently.

"Bill, I will not blame you if you want to stay here. Your skills are in great demand now. You're making a lot of money, and you love this land..." she was interrupted.

Bill had a shocked look on his face. It was as though he had just lost a close relative. In his mind...he had! It took everything he had to keep himself together and not break down like a sniveling kid. Then anger sprang up in him, was she was dumping him? Right there on the spot...dumping him!

"What? Are you dumping me...throwing me out? Why? How can you say that after six years together? We are a family! You would throw a family member out just like that?" Bill's words flowed out one after another without any forethought, or consideration as to how they would be received.

"Uncle Bill, mother didn't mean that. She thought you wanted to stay!" Henry observed quickly, his mind was at work.

"Is that right, Catherine? You thought I wanted to stay here while you took off alone with kids across the plains to a land you have no knowledge of? Is that right? How long do you think I would stay sane? I would worry every minute you were gone, I would become the town drunk and lose everything..."

Catherine tried to interrupt.

"Heck, besides that, my dream has always been to find a gold or silver mine and retire rich! I'll bet Denver is full of successful miners. I'll find the newest strike and find my El Dorado!" Bill concluded

"Ok, ok, I got it. Don't get carried away. You sold me with the town drunk thing...ha," she chuckled. "I won't say another word of it, except to ask how many times did you kiss that Blarney Stone?" Catherine asked Bill.

"Not once my bonny lass, not once! I tell you true! I have always dreamed of finding gold in the side of a mountain, and living my life like a bonny-be-good." Bill Antrim concluded.

"Ok, we are all going. I'm very happy you're coming. Now we must all get some rest. Tomorrow will be a very busy day." Catherine declared.

"Not for you mother. You are staying right here and resting all day tomorrow," Josie said authoritatively.

"Well, I guess one days rest wouldn't hurt me," Catherine said as though it was her idea.

They all went to bed with much on their minds. All their worlds had just been turned upside down. Henry was getting more and more excited about it. He could hardly get to sleep. He loved adventure! He had read about Denver. It was a wild town. At least that is what the dime novels said. He read there were men there that would bet on anything. They loved to gamble.

Then his thoughts went to the trip its self. They would have to cross the Kansas plains, and according to the "street news," the Indians were on the warpath all over Kansas. That was exciting to him. He wanted to see as many Indians as he could. He gave no mind to the dangers.

Most travelers prayed they would not see any. Henry wanted to see them all. He had read so much about how they looked. His immortal, youthful naivety shrugged off any thoughts of danger. This would be a very exciting trip.

Just before falling asleep he thought to himself: "I wonder what a bonny-be-good is?"

Chapter Thirty-Eight

Bonny-Be-Good/ Catherine Does Her Homework

Henry was up early; his mother was cooking breakfast for everyone. She planned on going back to sleep after that chore was done.

Not giving a salutation, he asked what was last on his mind before going to sleep and did so in Gaelic. They all spoke Gaelic the first four years of his life. He picked up English quite fast as a five-year-old. Now he could speak both languages quite well.

"Ma'am, an meid a bhi Bill Uncalil ag caint faoi, ah laoch ar Lass Bonny?" (In English: "Mom, what was Uncle Bill talking about calling you a Bonny Lass?")

Catherine frowned: "Henry, please speak English from now on. This is our country and you were born here. Besides, people will think you have something to hide. What will they think of you then?" She admonished her son.

"Ok Mother, what is a bonny-be-good, or a bonny lass?"

"Good morning, Henry." Catherine informed him that he had not given a proper salutation before blurting out his question.

"Good morning Mother," Henry corrected his manners.

"To answer your question 'bonny' can be used to mean several things. Most often to mean 'happy' in English. If I say, 'it's a bonny good day', I'm saying 'it's a happy, good day.' So, a 'Bonny lass' or 'Bonny Ladd' is a happy, good Lass or Ladd. It's an old Gaelic word to describe a good person, a strong person, and a happy person."

"Oh, I guess it is a good word. It certainly does fit you, Mother. Uncle Bill was right."

Over the next couple months Catherine did her homework, collecting newspaper articles and advertisements targeting her condition. Many ads did promote Denver, Colorado Territory. Each ad taunting how clean the air was.

Reading all these ads in Wichita, which had horrible air quality, reinforced her decision to act as quick as possible. She would go to Denver, but also kept in mind Dr. Allen's advice to seek out Santa Fe, New Mexico Territory without hesitation should her condition not improve in Denver. Furthermore, she would know that in a couple weeks. He felt strongly that dry air was even more important to longevity, and he had no idea if the "clean air" of Denver was in fact dry air.

Bill came in after reading some of the newspapers and pointed out all the ads for freighters. Denver was a mining boom town and central distribution point for the entire mid-western territories.

The railroad was shipping tons of goods, and people into Denver every day. Bill pointed to an advertisement for an "Experienced Mule Skinner, Teamster, Stagecoach driver, and Express Agent".

"ok, Denver it is first. We must liquidate all our holdings here to give us the capital to do whatever we need to do in Denver, or Santa Fe if need be. I've decided it should be a boarding house. The boys could be a big help and it would free you up to find your El Dorado," she ended with a chuckle.

Bill explained again he wanted to keep his quarter section, and buy the quarter section on the other side of hers.

"Catherine, I'll help sell all the lots in town. Could you help me to sell a lease to whoever buys your homestead? It would be a natural for them and I'll make them a deal on it."

"Of, course I can't say for sure my buyer would want to lease your land, but I'll do my best to convince them," Catherine committed.

Her best was good enough for Bill. She put the word out all over Wichita and many offers came forth. Everyone knew the honest dealing Irish lady that owned the laundry.

A TRIP TO KANSAS CITY

Ironically, Uncle Bill Antrim had written his family on several occasions as to the wonderful opportunities he acquired in Wichita. His homestead, city lots purchased and the condition of more work than he could handle. Well, they all showed up in the spring of 1871 in Wichita. Yep, mother, father, sister, and brother.[87] They all arrived in Wichita just as Bill and Catherine are planning to leave. It was very awkward for Bill, as good as it was to see his whole family.

Catherine and Bill spent all summer selling off their acquired city lots. On June 16, 1871 she sold her quarter section with all improvements on it. She moved into town for the next two months until everything was sold and completed.

She had raised enough money to finance the trip to Denver (or beyond if need be) and purchase a place to live where ever they settled on. She had thought everything through. She would run a boarding house for a living from now on. No more taking in laundry. She had two strong boys to help with a boarding house while Bill sought his El Dorado. She owed it to Bill to allow him to seek his get rich quick dreams.

Besides, sick or not, she was determined to care for her family until they could care for themselves. She didn't worry about Josie, he could do that if he had to now. Henry should have as much schooling as she can give him.

Uncle Bill not only decided to lease out his homestead, he did end up filing on the other 160 acres on the eastern side of Catherine's homestead that summer, and paid for it from profits of his lot sales. That left little doubt he was hopeful that Catherine would find her health again and they could return to their dreams in Wichita.

Catherine sold all her properties by the end of August, 1871.

They were all loaded up and were on the trail to the rail head in Kansas City. As they pulled out of Wichita heading northeast on the same trail they had taken to reach Wichita, Catherine advised the boys as they stared back to Wichita in the distance:

"Boys, don't look back. Always look forward. That's life!" The latter of her statement caused both her sons to look at their mother confused. They were old enough to understand not looking back, but the "that's life" part was confusing.

---

[87] James Antrim, brother of Bill Antrim, became a popular lawman of Wichita. source: Billy The Kid The Endless Ride by Michael Wallis pg. 38, paragraph 2, ln 7 and Billy The Kid: The Trail of a Kansas Legend by Waldo E. Koop Pg. 13

Catherine kept staring straight ahead and never looked back herself. Wichita was behind her, she figured she would never return to it. It wouldn't be of her choosing, but she felt it would be her fate.

Bill Antrim was an excellent freighter. He convinced Catherine to sell as much personal items as they could. The cost of freighting on the railroad had escalated exponentially.

The west was opening up and everyone wanted to bring everything they had to settle in the new territories. Just as they had done when migrating to Wichita. The railroad owners wanted a good return on their enormous investments, and they were getting it.

Bill purchased four mules he knew he could sell for a large profit in Kansas City. There was a gluttony of horses at the stockyards there. It was the gathering place for roughly broken horses to ship back east, satisfying the high demand of carriage owners. Supply and demand would result in a low price for horses. Mules were in great demand and were plentiful in south Kansas.

The first two days was adventurous for Henry. He knew many land marks from their prior trip on this trail. White Oak and Cottonwood Trees prominently line the river to the east of them. To the left was the expansive grass prairie the wind that seemed to make dance for their enjoyment.

Chapter Thirty-Nine

A Lone Rider with A Dire Warning

A lone rider approached, and Bill reined up the mules.

The man stood tall in his saddle and had an air of authority about him:

"Good morning, my name is Sheriff Barrick of Linn County, Kansas," the big man said with a "gentle" giant's voice, low and firm.

"Where are you folks heading?" he asked politely.

Henry became very interested. This was another man coming alive out of his Police Gazette magazine. Just like its writers described of western sheriffs: tall in the saddle, brave to the bone, with a big iron on his hip, and words you wanted to hear him speak. Henry was glued to every word.

Uncle Bill replied directly: "Good morning sheriff, we intend on catching a train in Kansas City for Denver. Do you have information about the road ahead for us?"

"I do. There have been some Indian problems. Nothing serious on this road yet, but you should be aware for your family's sake. Also, until I return from this trip, La Cygnet (pronounced "Luh seen") will not have any law officers, and it can become unruly quick. I'm afraid that is also my fault. I just arrested the most popular saloon keeper in town for shooting the town marshal in the face."

"Oh my!" Catherine exclaimed.

"Marshal Sandell is very lucky to have survived the shooting, but I'm afraid he will be one ugly, mean person when facing trial himself. You see he started the affray. I had to lock up Lloyd[88] the saloon keeper, to prevent Marshal Sandell's friends having a lynch party and stringing him up.

"I'm on my way to obtain an impartial judge to try both of them. I'm telling you all this because I think it would be wise of

[88] Fort Scott Daily Monitor September 15, 1871 article titled "From La Cygne."

you to turn east toward Fort Scott." Sheriff Barrick delivered his warning matter-of-factly, forcing one to seriously consider it.

Bill Antrim replied in agreement and asked: "We will do that sir. Is that road the one we passed a few miles back?"

"Yes, that road leads to the Fort Scott road, and it's well worth that short back track to keep your family safe," the Sheriff suggested.

Uncle Bill immediately began turning the mules back toward the entrance to the road to Fort Scott.

Sheriff Barrick continued with more advice:

"You will be going around El Dorado Lake and when you reach the Fort Scott road, turn back west a couple miles to the town of El Dorado. I say that because the cavalry has escorts leaving there regularly for Fort Scott. About four days on that road east and you will reach Iola. Its 80 miles from El Dorado."

Bill Antrim interrupted: "I have not heard much of Iola."

The sheriff grinned: "You must not be from Kansas? Iola's fight with Humboldt for the county seat of Allen County is quite famous. During the war we all affectionately called it Fort Iola. It did get the county seat and has good solid citizens. Sir, I almost forgot why I'm suggesting you make it your destination.

I think you're not aware that the Leavenworth, Lawrence, and Galveston Railroad now have passenger and freight cars going from Lawrence to Coffeyville with a stop at Iola."

"Really!" both Bill and Catherine said at the same time.

Henry interrupted: "I could have told you that, but you never asked me."

Bill snapped: "How would you know that?"

Henry replied sarcastically: "I read the newspapers!"

Catherine got a good chuckle and a sense of pride her youngest was so well informed.

She volunteered: "Thank you very much Sheriff Barrick. You are a valuable asset to the people of your county. We certainly appreciate your time and advice."

"You're welcome ma'am. God speed your journey," the sheriff replied and spurred his horse down the road ahead of the mules.

Chapter Forty

Destination: Denver Colorado Territory

Bill and Catherine followed the Sheriff's advice to the letter, and everything he said was realized. They ended up with a cavalry escort to Iola, and were able to book passage to Lawrence, Kansas.

Bill was able to sell all the mules quickly in Lawrence because it was where the army bought mules from a local businessman.

Catherine sought out the Kansas Pacific Railroad office. She learned they had merged with the Denver Pacific Railroad and there was an express train that traveled northwest from Comanche Crossing directly to Denver Colorado Territory. She purchased train tickets for the four of them, and negotiated a great freight rate for the family goods. Who could turn down the beautiful, dancing blue eyes of a mourning, war widow? She usually got what she wanted using her power of persuasion.

Catherine asked how long it would take to reach Denver.

The Ticket Master said: "It depends on too many variables for me to give you an accurate time table. Ma'am, buffalo herds have stopped us dead in the track for hours. One herd can be a million strong and they take their sweet time crossing the tracks. We are scheduled to be in Denver day after tomorrow. Theoretically we have 19 hours rail time, ten stops of approximately a half hour, so the math says in 24 hours. Ma'am, railroad math does lie!" He had to laugh at his own inside joke.

"I understand, sir. It will still be a lot shorter than by covered wagon," Catherine declared.

"Yes, ma'am...it sure is that!" the ticket master handed her four paid-up tickets and smile to remember.

They all embarked and found their seats. There were two seats facing the other two seats, and toward the front of the passenger car. Catherine and Henry sat facing the passengers, while Bill and Josie faced them.

Finally, they were on their way to Denver, Colorado Territory. Josie was a bit bored with the long train trip. Henry was excited, and had introduced himself to half the people on the train before reaching Comanche Crossing, Kansas.

A kindly-looking gentleman sat across from Henry. They recognized each other from waiting for the train in Iola.

"You're the young man that likes to read newspapers...right?" the gentleman asked Henry.

"Yes, sir, and you're the kind gentleman that helped my mother loading in Iola...right?"

"That I am. Our second stop is Junction City, and I happen to know 'The Junction City Weekly Union' is one of the finest of its kind on the plains. I will be happy to purchase a copy for you, of course with your mother's permission?" He volunteered while seeking Catherine's permission.

"You do have it sir. I thank you again for your assistance in Iola." Catherine said as she glared at Bill. Turning back, she said to the gentleman: "May I know the name of my son's benefactor of a newspaper?"

"Charles Clark, ma'am, at your service," the gentleman replied in a soft tone. There remained something mysterious about the man that Catherine's Irish instincts found curious, but she would refrain from probing into something that is none of her business.

The first stop was Topeka, Kansas. A few passengers disembarked and a few embarked, and they were on their way again.

The trained slowed and the Junction City train station sign came in view. Henry was getting excited. Mr. Clark had promised a newspaper, it may even be a brand new one. Most of the ones he had read in Wichita were a month or two old.

The conductor came through the car announcing a half hour stay at Junction City.

"Can I go with Mr. Clark, Mom?" Henry asked in his best begging tone.

"He will be safe with me ma'am, as if he were my own," Mr. Clark stated.

"Alright, just don't be late coming aboard...be early!" Catherine instructed firmly.

"Yes, ma'am," Mr. Clark replied, and they were off as soon as the train came to a complete stop.

Bill just looked at Catherine with that expression, the one that said: "What are you thinking, why would you agree?"

Catherine said: "Because I trust both of them."

Bill and Josie just looked out the window at the small town. It was small, but very clean as western towns go. The first thing one saw was the tall, white peak of a beautiful church on the other side of the main road into town.

"If they have a church like that, it must be a good community," Catherine said aloud, half-justifying her decision.

Fifteen minutes later in came Mr. Clark and Henry with plenty of time left over. Catherine was relieved and gave the "I told you so," look to Bill.

"Look Mother! A brand-new newspaper! This is The Junction City Weekly Union, Saturday September 24, 1871! That is today! I have never seen such a newspaper," Henry said excitedly.

"Well, you might consider reading it," Josie said sarcastically, trying to shut his little brother up for a moment.

"I will! Right now, I will do just that!" Henry replied.

A few minutes later the train started up and began to move slowly. Several men were running to get back on board. Bill checked his pocket watch and they were leaving exactly on thirty minutes.

Henry delved into the newspaper. He even read all the advertisements. Suddenly he read an article that shocked him.

"Mother, it says here they have dug up old Abe Lincoln and moved him to another grave. Can they do that?" Henry asked sincerely.

"What? Read it to me," Catherine replied.

Henry read the article to her in a hushed tone as to not embarrass his mother in front of the other passengers. Catherine paused and considered his question: "Yes, I suppose they could. It sounds like they are putting all his family together, so they can all rest in peace together."

Sitting behind Bill and Josie were two easterners talking about how primitive the seats were on the train. All four of the McCarty family grinned at the same time.

Josie spoke up: "Those folks should try a wagon across those plains. You wouldn't hear them complaining now."

"Now now, Josie, don't be passing judgements, for fear you be judged," Catherine admonished her son.

One man sitting with the group behind them said: "Oh, no ma'am, the lad was quite right. I came across that plain in buckskins, and a broken down old wagon pulled by two broken down horses. God had his angels working overtime for the next four hundred miles. He must have because there was no logical way I could have made that trip."

He then spoke to the two across from him that had made the comment and said:

"This railroad and those seats you're in are a gift from above. You are not staring in every direction, looking constantly over your shoulder wondering if you're going to have your hair lifted. Then throwing away half of what you own so your animals don't die on you. If they die, you die!"

One of the men spoke up: "I'm sure you are correct. We were just expressing our own experience, sir. Had we experienced what you did, we would be far more grateful to have these clap boards we are sitting on."

Chapter Forty-One

McCarty's Meet William A. Pinkerton

The man sitting directly across from Mr. Clark changed the subject by asking Catherine:

"What is your destination ma'am?"

Bill Antrim decided he would answer the question: "Denver, sir. My name is Bill, this here is Josie McCarty. That is Henry McCarty and their mother Catherine McCarty. What is your destination, sir?" Bill inquired.

Normally Catherine would have interrupted Bill wanting to answer, as the question was directed to her. This time she allowed Bill to act as the head of household. This was the first time she had done that in six years.

"Oh, I see, you are all family. Thank you for setting me straight on that matter. To answer your question, I am investigating a possible crime against this railroad company. I work for the Pinkerton Detective Agency of Chicago, Illinois."

Although Henry was deep into an article of a man named Belden being murdered by Indians... "Pinkerton Detective Agency!" That brought him back to the present real quick. He had read many articles about them in the Police Gazette. He scrambled to find his latest copy, finding it in his pocket. He just blurted out:

"Oh, yes! Right here sir!" pointing to the front cover that said "Pinkertons on the trail of James Gang."

"You're after Jesse James, aren't you?" Henry asked point blank.

"Well no, not to my knowledge. Fact is I wish I was, I bet that would draw down some good pay," the detective chuckled and continued:

"Young man, do you read that magazine faithfully?" He inquired.

"Yes, sir I do. At least I tried to. I had a friend, a stagecoach driver in Wichita, he got me everyone he could," Henry declared.

"What did you give him?" the quick-thinking detective replied.

That got Catherine and Bill's attention. They had never thought of that.

"I kept him up to date on all the street news that happened while he was gone. He liked my reports. He said I earned every one of my magazines and newspapers," Henry honestly replied.

"Street news is valuable, so I agree you must have earned those magazines. So, did you read that the Pinkerton Agency had been hired to hunt down the James Gang?"

"No, sir I didn't. I did read that the editor thought the railroad should do that, so I figured maybe they had hired you. Then there was this headline," Henry explained.

"Do you think they should?" Mr. Clark asked sincerely.

Henry thought for a second and then replied:

"I suppose so, if they really want to catch those boys. I wouldn't want the Pinkerton agency after me."

William Pinkerton grinned and said: "Me neither."

Catherine and Bill looked at each other in amazement. They didn't have the slightest idea of what Henry or these strangers were talking about.

"Good morning, please do forgive me for not introducing myself. My name is William Allan Pinkerton. My father Allan Pinkerton stated our agency in 1852, and has run it himself since 1853. Your son here is very well read, a credit to you both," the detective concluded.

"It is all her doing," Bill said pointing to Catherine.

Catherine volunteered:

"I was just adamant Henry learn his A, B, C's and helped him with learning English."

"Lordy-be, speaking English? His English is near perfect, and it wasn't his birth language?" the detective was truly surprised.

"No, we spoke Gaelic in the family. His father learned English in an Irish school." Catherine informed.

Mr. Pinkerton turned to Henry and spoke a broken Scottish dialect of Gaelic.

Henry replied in fluent and perfect Irish dialect of Gaelic.

"Young man, you should become a detective. Being multi-lingual is a big help at times. When you grow a little more, look me up!" Mr. Pinkerton seemed quite serious with his offer.

Josie just sat there as his little brother was getting all the attention. Nothing new for him. Henry always got the attention, and loved it. He was alright with that, as he really didn't like attention.

Mr. Clark had purchased several papers to share with his fellow passengers, too. He had the Osage County Chronicle, The Junction City Weekly Union, and the Daily Kansas Tribune of Lawrence, Kansas.

The gentleman sitting next to him had introduced himself as a cattle buyer from Chicago. His name was Brian Murphy.

Mr. Clark handed him The Kansas City Tribune newspaper and said:

"Mr. Murphy, I understand they are pretty accurate on the cost of beeves," Mr. Clark declared as he handed him the paper.

"Thank you, I have heard the same," Mr. Murphy acknowledged.

"We are coming up to Abilene soon. Is that where you're heading?" Mr. Clark inquired politely.

"Yes, sir I am. Look here! On the second page is an article about Abilene. In one week they shipped 100 cars of cattle to Chicago! Hopefully McCoy has filled all his orders and there are some left for me to buy." He laughed at his own joke.

They all got a chuckle out of that. This was the final push of the year to drive cattle from Texas to Abilene. There would be plenty of cattle to buy.

"It says here that the total so far this season that have been pushed through Wichita is over 400,000 head," Mr. Murphy read.

"We can attest to that as factual, and every darn one of them passed in front of Catherine's City Laundry," Bill Antrim volunteered.

Wild Bill Hickok Source: Adams Museum

Chapter Forty-Two

Abilene and Wild Bill Hickok

The man sitting across from Mr. Murphy volunteered:

"Abilene has been tamed pretty well with Hickok the Town Marshall. It should be a bit safer for you to do business there. My name is William Shane," he declared and tipped his hat to all seated on both sides of the isle.

Henry had to ask: "Wild Bill Hickok?"

"Yes, the same. The Pistolero of the Plains," Mr. Shane added.

"We know Wild Bill!" Henry blurted out.

Catherine interrupted: "We have met him on the trail to Wichita a year-and-a-half or so ago. We don't **know** him," she said with emphasis on the "know."

Everyone was listening now. Just saying Hickok's name would draw immediate attention.

"Well, Mother is right, but I feel like I know him. I've read a lot about him in dime magazines," Henry explained.

Mr. Shane volunteered: "He took the Marshal's job last April in Abilene. Things settled down fast. Well, there was a close call with the James Gang," Mr. Shane noted.

Henry was almost falling out of his seat, glued to every word the stranger was saying. Mr. Shane went on to say:

"They were on the lamb and wanted to get rest and fresh animals in Abilene. Jesse sent a messenger to Hickok. My friend claimed the note said: 'If he tried to arrest them, Jesse had bought a grave plot for Hickok.'

My friend said he was there when Hickok received the message. He told me Hickok got a great laugh at it. Then he told the messenger to return to Jesse and tell him: 'He holds no warrant for his arrest, and if he doesn't break any laws in Abilene he won't be harassed, but if he does he would be obliged to donate the grave plot for Jesse's use.'"

Everyone laughed out loud. Then Mr. Shane said:

"My friend said Jesse did meet Hickok once while in town and the meeting was very amiable. You would think they were old friends."

Mr. Clark interrupted with an article he was reading:

"Here in the Osage County Chronicle they say hogs are dying of hog cholera in La Cygne, and cattle are dying of Spanish fever in Cottonwood near Emporia."

Mr. Shane replied: "That should be added to the 'Herd Law' of Kansas. The cattle owners are not going to like that one bit, but something has to be done."

"What is the 'Herd Law'?' Detective Pinkerton asked as he had never heard of such a law.

"Well, it is a new law in Kansas where the cattle owners can be held liable for any damage their cattle make on the drive north through Kansas. They are fighting mad over it, but something had to be done. Some herd bosses were driving thousands of head through farm crops. Now, there is the break out of Spanish Fever brought up with their herds, and infecting stock of local ranchers."

Catherine looked at Bill Antrim and asked: "La Cygne! Isn't that where that sheriff we met on the trail was from?"

"Yes, it was." Bill replied.

Henry volunteered to Mr. Clark:

"He said he had just arrested the town marshal and a popular saloon keeper, which had shot the town marshal in the face! But the town marshal had started the fray, so he arrested both of them." Henry said in a matter-of-factly.

"That is what the sheriff said," Catherine confirmed Henry's story.

"Young man, you have to become a detective. You recalled a lot of detail," Mr. Pinkerton suggested strongly.

"Thank you, sir," Henry acknowledged his compliment.

Mr. Clark again quoted from the Osage County Chronicle:

"Look at these prices! Best coffee is 4 3/4 lbs. for $1, 10 lbs. of choice dried apples for $1, 7 lbs. of sugar for $1. Brown sugar 7 3/4 lbs. for $1 all cash prices good for thirty days. Those are pretty good prices. The further we go west the higher the prices will get. At least we have bench mark," Mr. Clark then asked Mr. Shane:

"Are you a land or cattle buyer, sir?"

"I am a land speculator, sir. Why do you ask?" William Shane inquired politely.

"Right here in the same paper are quite the number of land sale offerings. Here is 40 acres with a creek for $200."

"That would have to have some other attributes to be worth that amount," Mr. Shane observed.

"Here is 160 acres for $5.25 per acre. Oh, another 160 acres a half mile from town for $7.00 per acre."

"Can I see that article?" Mr. Shane asked Mr. Clark.

"Sure," Mr. Clark replied and handed him the newspaper.

"Now, here is one of interest. 110 acres with improved farm, one-and-a-half miles from town. Splendid farm, well improved, timber, water and stone for $4000 half cash balance 1 and 2 years for 10 percent per interest. Now that could be a good buy if it truly has splendid improvements." Mr. Shane declared.[89]

"Interesting," Mr. Clark said and chuckled, "I'm glad I buy and sell cattle. I know what I'm doing there."

Henry turned to his mother and asked: "Mother, he said those are good prices. Could we settle in Abilene instead of Denver?"

Catherine gave Henry a curious look and replied: "You just want to see Wild Bill Hickok again...right?"

Henry looked like the cat with a feather in its mouth: "Of course, but if it's a good buy...why not?"

---

[89] All prices written herein are actual prices for goods and real estate listed in The Osage County Chronicle September 14, 1871.

"No, Henry, we are not changing our plans," Catherine said sternly.

Henry looked disappointed. Bill Antrim just shook his head. Josie just ignored the whole conversation.

The train pulled into Abilene. Henry about broke his neck trying to see as much as he could out the window. Suddenly his two feet began to dance in place:

"Look, look there at the station!" he almost yelled out.

"Calm down Henry, calm down!" Catherine ordered as she rose to see what he was looking at. As she did Bill Antrim nonchalantly said:

"He sees Wild Bill Hickok at the station. I'm sure he is checking who is arriving in his town."

That statement caused most of the passengers on the other side of the train to cross over the isle to get a peek. There wasn't a soul there that didn't know the name Wild Bill Hickok.

Mr. Pinkerton politely looked over Henry's head and said: "Yes, young man you are correct. That sure is Wild Bill Hickok. I wouldn't want to be in his shoes for all the tea in China. He is the most famous lawman in the country. That is for sure!" Mr. Pinkerton volunteered.

Henry looked up at Mr. Pinkerton and asked:

"Why wouldn't you want to be him? He is famous, people look up to him," Henry said as he looked back out the window. He would have been out the door already if it wasn't for Mr. Pinkerton standing close behind him.

Catherine interrupted: "Son, you stay right here. You're not going out there!"

Henry couldn't believe it. She must have read his mind.

The passengers from back east in the next section were so close to the window their noses were flattened on the glass. One spoke up:

"Is it true he had killed a hundred men with those pistols?" directing his question to William Pinkerton.

"Don't believe all you read. No one knows for sure, but he has killed some, and he won't hesitate if challenged," Mr. Pinkerton replied.

"Someone would have to be pretty stupid to challenge him," Henry stated.

"I agree with that young man. Pretty stupid is right," Mr. Pinkerton agreed.

"Mother, just let me say hello. That would be polite, and he will remember us. I'll bet he will!"

Henry was out on the balcony of the car in a heartbeat. He moved like a cat around Mr. Pinkerton and was out of Catherine's reach so fast she missed his arm by a foot.

She arose and excused herself as she stepped onto the balcony. The car exit was directly behind where they were seated. The train came to a complete stop and she and Henry grabbed the guard rail to keep up-right and balanced.

Just as she was going to order Henry back in:

"Hello Mr. Hickok...over here!" Henry yelled out waving his hand toward Mr. Hickok.

Wild Bill saw the boy and did remember him immediately. He was the boy that had a dime novel with him on the front cover. He was with his family in a wagon driven by mules. Hickok waved back and yelled back:

"Hello, young man!" Just then Catherine appeared to him behind Henry.

"And hello to you ma'am. Welcome to Abilene." Mr. Hickok stated professionally.

"Oh, no, we are heading for Denver. Henry wanted so badly to say hello to you. You are his hero," Catherine confessed.

"Not yours?" Mr. Hickok said as he removed his hat.

"No sir, I don't know you well enough to say that," Catherine politely made an honest reply.

"I accept your answer with no offense, ma'am," Wild Bill replied.

"Son, you take good care of your mother. She is a very special person, but of course you know that," Wild Bill stated matter-of-factly.

"Good day, Mr. Hickok. It has been our pleasure to have met you," Catherine said as she pulled Henry back toward the car entrance.

"The pleasure is all mine, ma'am," Wild Bill said as he placed his wide brimmed hat back on his head.[90]

Catherine gave Henry a slight push back into his seat with a stay there look all over her face.

Half the car had pulled their windows open to hear every word of the conversation Wild Bill Hickok was saying to their fellow passengers. It became apparent the McCarty family did know him.

The conversations around that brief meeting didn't settle down for a hundred miles of track. Just as it did the train pulled into Hayes, Kansas. Then William Allan Pinkerton noted that Wild Bill Hickok had been a U.S. Marshal and County Sheriff while he lived in Hayes. The easterners couldn't get enough of the Wild Bill stories.

Catherine sat quietly thinking how the man she met seemed so different than the one all these men were describing. First, he had soft, blue eyes that were almost like those of a woman. His hands could be that of a pianist, long fingers that seemed gentle and at ease.

As they said he was taller than the average man, wide shouldered, and gave the appearance of being well fit. But, if you picked ten men at random, he would be the last she would pick as a ferocious man killer. He just didn't fit that image.

With all that conversation the train ride did go by quickly. The conductor announced that they were only a few miles from Denver, Colorado Territory.

"Mr. Pinkerton, I want to thank you for making this such an interesting trip west. I also learned a lot about my son," Catherine said quite sincerely.

---

[90] Wild Bill Hickok was marshal of Abilene during the time the McCarty family and Bill Antrim passed through there in approximately mid-September, 1871. It would be only a few weeks from this time, October 5, 1871 that Hickok would kill Phil Coe and accidently kill his own Deputy Marshal Mike Williams. That event affected Wild Bill Hickok for the rest of his life. He never again became a law officer. Although this is a fictional meeting written above, just imagine an 11-year-old that read Police Gazette and dime novels faithfully, and the town marshal checked each train's arrival for known "bad guys". It sure could have happened. Factually, The Kid knew Wild Bill Hickok and Jesse James through those magazines.

Henry had curiosity all over his face, but withheld asking what she meant by that comment. He felt she knew him very well.

"Thank you and your wonderful family for such good company. I did enjoy this trip and your family's company was all my privilege." He leaned over to Henry and said:

"Henry I hope you do become a detective someday. You are very smart and that would serve you well."

"Or make a very smart criminal!" Bill said sarcastically.

"Oh Bill, don't talk like that!" Catherine snapped at him.

Mr. Pinkerton light-heartedly said: "I truly hope not," tapping Henry on the head.

Henry waved for Mr. Pinkerton to let him whisper in his ear. Mr. Pinkerton obliged Henry. Henry whispered:

"Most likely the criminal," he said with a half laugh and a giggle.

Josie spoke up for the first time: "I could have told you that," he grinned at Mr. Pinkerton.

Denver, Colorado Territory 1870 *looking down Lawrence Street toward Cherry Creek in background. How Denver looked upon arrival of the McCarty family in 1871.*
Source: Denver Public Library 90.82.5

Chapter Forty-Three

Denver at Last!

The train came to a full stop and Mr. Pinkerton said a final good-bye, and departed the train with a thought on his mind:

"I hope I never have to go after that boy. I hope he grows up straight." He observed a bright, eleven-year-old boy that enjoyed his Police Gazette too much, and after his comment to him about maybe growing up on the "other" side of the law, well, that said a lot about the boy's personality.

At their first meeting he thought the boy just a typical mischievous street gamer. The boy had all the signs, couldn't sit still very long, always looking all around to find a new interesting thing or person to look at, and quick to interject himself in an adult's conversation.

Now, he thought it also possible for him to become a teenage street Arab. That often leads to a life of crime. He shook the thoughts off as he held enormous confidence in the boy's mother. She would keep her son on the straight and narrow path to manhood.

The McCarty family departed, and Catherine immediately noticed a difference in her ability to breath, and it wasn't a good one. She could only take a few steps before losing her breath.

A fall rain had left the air very humid. Bill helped her to the train station where she sat on a bench to catch her breath. One of the station employees took the time to explain that most all "flat-landers" take a couple weeks to adjust to the high altitude of Denver.

Catherine noticed there were quite a few people sitting at the station and seemingly doing the same as she was. Possibly the employee was correct, and it would just take a few weeks to adjust to this altitude.

Bill was off making arrangements for their temporary accommodations. He must find a hotel with a room available on the ground floor. Catherine could not handle climbing staircases at this time.

F St. Denver, Colorado Territory Samuel Shell's Store. *This store is not far from Melvin House on Holladay. Source: Denver Public Library 89.451.854 1870*

Bill found a first story room at the first hotel he went to, The Melvin House on Holladay Street between F and G streets.

The clerk said that their timing was very good. One week earlier and there wouldn't have been a room available anywhere in Denver. [91]

The clerk, a well-dressed man of good manners, explained that Denver had just put on quite a fair. Thousands of people had come from all over the west to experience what Denver taunted as "the best fair west of the Mississippi." The people came by the train loads. Nearly all the miners attended within fifty miles, and surely expecting Denver to keep its promise.

Bill Antrim had to ask: "What made it so special to attract that many people?"

The clerk thought and then rattled off just a few of the events: "There were amusements of all kinds. A circus, an Indian horse race, several of the innocent little games cultivated by all good citizens of Colorado (side-shows and games of chance). Oh yes, a well patronized dancing party at the grand stand with music and drinking for all. The miners, ranchmen, gardeners all gave good credit of themselves at all the attractions of the fair. I must say all of us in Denver are quite proud of that fair.[92]

You know sir, I should say our good town had grown up quite a bit this year. Most of the beautiful buildings you see here now were built last spring and summer of this year. Yes, sir, Denver went from a rough and tumble western town to a sophisticated city in six months!"

Bill found all the information interesting, but still hadn't heard the prospects of the future of Denver for newcomers as himself.

"Are there jobs here still?" Bill asked point blank.

"Oh yes sir, excepting this one of course," he said with a chuckle.

---

[91] Daily Kansas Tribune September 29, 1871 republished Denver Tribune article of September 23, 1871 "The Fair was over!" The size of this fair was a great celebration for the huge construction projects taken place over the spring and summer in Denver, Colorado Territory. Denver had become a vibrant full blown city.

[92] Ibid. footnote 86, paraphrased for conversational literary purposes.

"We would like to stay here a few days, until we can find a permanent residence," Bill politely inquired.

"Cash in advance sir, and you may stay all the days you have paid for. Hotel policy not mine," the clerk finished with an accommodating smile.

He went on to ask: "How many in your party sir?"

"Four," Bill replied.

"Any children under ten-years-old?" The clerk inquired.

"No sir," Bill replied.

"That will be two dollars a day for three days...six dollars in advance sir," the clerk said again in an accommodating manner.

"Does that include evening meals?" Bill asked in surprise of the cost.

The clerk chuckled and replied: "No, sir it does not. We do have a top notch, first class restaurant. Dinner of your choice for two bits each."

Bill agreed and paid for the room only at that time. He left to retrieve the family at the train station.

Arriving back at the station Bill noticed Catherine was still struggling with her breathing. His first thought was they may not be in Denver too long after-all. That thought disappointed him, as he really wanted to try his luck in the mines, or at least prospecting for a mine of his own.

"Are you ok?" Bill sincerely asked Catherine upon his arrival.

"No, but I have been told this is quite normal for many new arrivals to Denver, and I should get used to the altitude in a couple weeks. Have you found accommodations for tonight?" Catherine inquired.

"Yes, I've prepaid three days a fine hotel. Now, don't say anything yet until you see it. And we were very lucky because just days ago one could not find a room in all of Denver, due to a huge fair put on by the city. Besides after our long journey, we deserve a little luxury for a few days," Bill tried hard to avoid her scolding for spending too much money when all they needed was a place to lay their heads tonight.

"And you will be warm all night!" Bill concluded his selling presentation.

The latter was sounding pretty good to Catherine at the moment, so she acquiesced.

Bill and the boys loaded their things into a half buckboard, half buggy waiting out front. Both boys helped their mother make it to the buckboard. That was the quietest both boys had been on the whole trip. They were very worried about their mother. She had to rest several times on the short journey to the buggy/buckboard.

Josie, being the stronger of the two, had to lift all his mother's weight into the buggy's seat. She could not contribute with any muscle power to assist her own lifting. Her legs felt like rubber.

She saw her boys concern and wanted to put their minds at ease: "While you two were exploring Denver a knowledgeable local said this is normal, and I'll recover my strength in a couple weeks." She said as she looked down the block heading north from the station and continued:

"Look how clean this city is. Very nice! And if the air is as clean as they say this will be very good for me."

The boys listened, but neither one was buying what she was selling.

The family arrived at the hotel and checked in. Catherine went right to bed for a long rest. The boys took off to explore more of the town. Bill went to the lobby looking for a local paper with advertisements for services needed for hire. Also, for available boarding houses that would be much cheaper than the hotel.

The clerk saw him asking another stranger that of course had no idea where to find one.

"Mr. Antrim," the clerk said as he held out a Denver Tribune newspaper in his hand toward him.

"Oh! Thank you, sir. How much is this?" Bill inquired.

"No charge to you sir," the clerk replied politely handing him the paper.

Bill ventured over to a table and chair, where he began going through the newspaper thoroughly.

He was not disappointed. There were plenty of part time jobs, and full-time labor jobs. All the miner's positions were looking for "mining experience", which he didn't have. He knew that wouldn't stop him if he wanted to become a miner. What he really wanted to do was strike to the mining districts and prospect for his own mine. That would have to wait until Catherine recovered her health.

He took the paper back to their room. Tomorrow Catherine could go over the many boarding houses advertising rooms for rent. He would let her organize a route to check out the boarding houses she chose.

Catherine slept right through the evening and night. By morning the boys were getting hungry, so Bill awakened Catherine, who thought it was still the day of arrival. He got a good chuckle on that comment. After explaining it was the day after their arrival, and the whole family was hungry, he asked if she thought she could come with them for breakfast, or would she rather he bring it to her.

Sitting on the side of the bed Catherine said: "I would like to try and make it. We must find a paper and look for a boarding house right away," in her authoritative voice.

"Already done that!" Bill replied while he held out his hand to help her up.

"Wash bowl is right over there, with fresh water in it," Bill informed Catherine as he exited the room.

He and the boys waited in the other room anxiously. Listening for any sound that she may need help. None came. Twenty minutes later Catherine came out with a smile on her face and said:

"Very nice accommodations boys!" She was hiding her still shortness of breath. It was chin up time, roll up her sleeves time, and get the job done time! And she was good at all that! She volunteered:

"I believe I just need to walk a lot slower for a while," she said as she walked to the opened door and down the hall. The boys all following right behind her. Josie was close enough to catch her if she fell.

Bill paid in advance for all their breakfasts. Catherine went through the paper as thoroughly as he had.

She saw his pencil mark next to several boarding houses.

"Ah! I see you have done this. Did you leave anything for me to do?" she quibbled sarcastically.

"Yes, the actual decision as to where we will live," Bill said just as sarcastically. The boys got a laugh at that.

"Oh! Of course. I suppose you have thought of the route?" Catherine inquired.

"No, that is your responsibility ma'am," Bill replied.

After breakfast they headed out in the rented buggy/buckboard on Catherine's devised route of boarding houses to check.

It took only a couple stops for Catherine to find the boarding house she wanted. She gave the proprietor a first month's deposit and the boys left to pick up their things at the hotel.

Arriving at the hotel bill requested a two-day refund. They had gone past noon, so Bill couldn't get a refund for that day. The clerk did give him a refund for the third day they would not stay there. He thanked the clerk for all his service and they were off to their new home.

Denver, Colorado Territory, Occidental Billiard Hall on Blake Street and 15th Street next to The City Bakery 1870. *Denver was a rough and tumble gambling town with all the people that follow gold and silver strikes. Its elevation was a disappointment to many that sought relief from lung problems. Source: Denver Public Library 89.451.277*

Chapter Forty-Four

Frustration in Denver

For Catherine, their arrival in Denver had been almost anticlimactic. She knew she was breathing much harder with each step she took. The early fall rain and then a warm spell had left the humidity high even for Denver. She was hoping with some time, as the person at the train station had said, she would acclimate to the altitude and be much better off than in Wichita. That did not happen.

Bill Antrim was very excited with all the news of gold strikes in the hills west of Denver. He was ready to explore them as soon as he could get Catherine and the boys settled in town.

Josie loved Denver! He loved the excitement of a large city. He hadn't lived in one since Indianapolis. There were plenty of jobs for a teenager willing to work.

He quickly got a job cleaning up a gambling hall and saloon on H Street. It was one of the busiest in Denver. He saw more money won and lost in one night, at one table, than he had seen in his entire life! It was very exciting for a teenager. He decided that someday he would have a "bank" and be one of those gamblers.[93]

The small boarding house was comfortable, and well kept up. A month had gone by and although Catherine felt a little better, she was still not comfortable enough to seek work. Just her every day chores for the family would tire her out completely. Every once and a while she could help around the boarding house, which did her psyche good.

Henry was bored to death! He was too young to seek work of any kind available in Denver. He was definitely too old to be sitting in one place very long. He was like a caged bobcat.

Catherine didn't want him "gamin'" in the streets of Denver. She had gone to a lot of trouble and expense to get him off the streets of Wichita. Denver was almost as wild as Wichita

[93] Joseph (Josie) McCarty Antrim fulfilled that promise to himself. Unfortunately, he was not a very successful gambler. His last known interview was with the Denver Post, April 1, 1928.

and three times larger! In fact, it was the same except Denverites wore nicer clothes, and their "saloons" were "gambling houses", and their "prostitutes" were "sporting ladies." Well, she had to admit Denver was a lot cleaner.

None-the-less, her boy, about ready to turn twelve-years-old, was not going to grow up on the streets! She was determined that would not happen.

Frustration with Denver was building for Catherine and Henry, for different reasons, but the result was the same. Something had to change.

Bill Antrim was preparing for a trip into the hills when he was told that would not be wise for him to do so right then. There had been an early snow in the mountains, and was told he should wait until spring to avoid dying of the elements. Only experienced mountain men could survive those mountains in winter. He was very disappointed with that news.

One-day Catherine was reading the Denver Tribune and the town name "Santa Fe" jumped off the page at her. She then recalled Dr. Allen's suggestion if she wasn't feeling better in Denver:

"Santa Fe was also high in elevation, clean air, but a dry climate. That combination is best for your condition, in my opinion," Dr. Allen had stated firmly.

Catherine informed her landlord they would be moving the first of the next month. That night at dinner she announced her decision to Bill, Josie, and Henry. Old Catherine was back. She left no room for discussion, the decision was made.

Josie still complained. He really liked his part time job and the new friends he had made.

"Mom! I've got a great job. I'm learning so much about the business world," Josie pleaded to the business side of his mother.

"I told you all that Denver may be just a temporary stop in our trip. You all knew that from the time we left Wichita. I must move to a drier climate, and I must do that as soon as possible," Catherine explained firmly.

"I'm old enough now, I want to stay here where my friends are," Josie pleaded again.

"No, you are not old enough, and you are needed by this family to do your part, which is to help us move to Santa Fe. No more discussion. My decision is final." Catherine put her foot down. Then she turned to Bill:

"Bill, I know your heart is set on prospecting, and I will understand if you don't want to go to Santa Fe," Catherine said in a soft and low tone.

"No, no, I'm going where you are going. We are partners, right?" he said in a matter-of-factly.

Catherine smiled and replied: "Yes, yes we are, and I was hoping you would say exactly that."

Bill did say: "We shouldn't travel in the heart of winter. I think we should stay here until the first snow melt."

Catherine thought for a moment and knew Bill was right. It could be very dangerous to travel in winter. Somehow she would have to make it for a few months. Besides a big town like Denver may be a good place for The Kids to have Christmas.

"Alright, it is settled. We head for Santa Fe in March," she declared.

Henry was ecstatic. He was so very ready to leave Denver right now, and was elated to hear Santa Fe was their destination. He had read it was the capital of the New Mexico Territory, and a mysterious ancient village.

"Mother, can we go by way of Taos on our way to Santa Fe?" Henry blurted out without explanation.

"I have no idea if that is on the trail to Santa Fe. Why are you so anxious to go to Taos?" Catherine inquired.

Henry's blue eyes began to dance. They were a bright, light blue that seemed to twinkle all the time. When excited, as he was now, they danced from one place to another. Almost, like his mind was busy thinking of what to say next, which it was. Henry excitedly replied:

"That is the home town of Kit Carson! He lives there right now! Mom, I could meet Kit Carson! He is the best scout ever, best mountain man ever. Mom, he fought ten Indians bare-handed and won!"

Catherine could always tell when Henry was authentically excited about convincing her about something, he started every sentence with "Mom".

"Calm down Henry. I said I don't have our trip plans yet. I'll let you know as soon as I know," Catherine responded firmly.

"But Mom..."

Catherine stopped and interrupted Henry with her dark blue eyes giving him that stare that said he really should not continue with this conversation. He dropped the subject.

The family had entered the dining room of their boarding house, which meant the boys were to put on their best manners immediately. Henry just had to get the last word in:

"Mom, just remember...Kit Carson!" Henry said in a low tone. Catherine did not reply.

All tenants paid room and board. The women took turns helping the proprietor with the cooking and serving. This was not Catherine's week.

As they approached their table they noticed everyone was staring at them. They had heard Henry say, "Kit Carson". That was a name everyone knew. He was America's greatest frontiersman, guide, Indian fighter, and United States Army Officer (Breveted Brigadier General) during the Indian and Civil Wars.

A gentleman spoke up: "Are you traveling to Taos, ma'am?" he asked politely.

"No sir, our destination is Santa Fe. My son was asking if Taos was on the way to Santa Fe."

"Please excuse me for not introducing myself. Thomas Atwood at your service, ma'am. I'm afraid your son will be disappointed to know that he would not be able to meet Mr. Carson in Taos, but would be able to visit his grave there. Mr. Carson passed away in the summer of '68," Mr. Atwood explained.

Henry was very disappointed. All the magazines made it seem he was still quite alive and well.

Mr. Atwood looked at Henry and said: "I am sorry to have brought you that news. Believe me when I say I would be just as excited to have a chance to meet that man. He opened the entire west up for America. He truly was a great man."

"Nice to meet you." Catherine said. "This is my dearest friend and business partner Bill Antrim, my sons Josie and Henry. I am Catherine McCarty, widow."

"I am sorry for your loss ma'am," Mr. Atwood politely replied.

"That was a long time ago. We lost him in that damned war. Excuse my language," Catherine explained.

"That it was ma'am, that it was. I can answer your son's question. Taos is much north of Santa Fe, but it is not a good trail from Pueblo. Most travel through Cimarron County via Las Vegas, New Mexico. The latter is the main Santa Fe Trail and has been traveled for hundreds of years. Although, it would be strongly advised to travel in large groups. It is not a trail to venture on alone." Mr. Atwood concluded.

"What is the problem with traveling alone...Indians?" Bill Antrim asked.

"Yes, sir. That is Comanche country, but it is also the northern territory of the Comancheros."

Bill interrupted, "I have heard of them, but know little about them."

"Well, I wouldn't want to frighten Mrs. McCarty..."

Catherine interrupted him, "I'm not frightened easily, sir. Go ahead and let us know what, or who these Comancheros are."

Mr. Atwood continued:

"They are Mexicans. Mestizo of Spanish and Indian blood, Comanches, Kiowas, and every other kind of mix of humans on the plains. They ride, raid, kill, steal, for only themselves."

Mr. Atwood then paused and looked Bill Antrim straight in the eye and said:

"Sir, they are a ruthless group of cutthroats, the likes of which has never been seen before. Their favorite preys are white women and children, which they sell into slavery in Mexico, and those are the fortunate ones."

Catherine interrupted again:

"Fortunate ones! What do you mean by that, that is horrible!?" she asked with emotion.

"Ma'am, the ones they don't think they can sell for much, they use as their own sick entertainment. The Comanche trade horses and captives to the Comancheros for knives, pots and pans, cloths, and food, which they get from raiding settlements and wagons. Even the Apaches do not mess with the Comancheros."

"That was a pretty good description, and actually did reach the point of frightening me little, but I know it was for our own good," Catherine volunteered.

Bill shook the man's hand and simply said: "Thank you Mr. Atwood."

"You're welcome and God's speed on your journey." Mr. Atwood concluded.

The family had dinner with very little further conversation. That was rare for them.

Catherine worried that she may have gotten her family into a very risky traveling venture. She knew she had no choice, to stay in Denver meant she would not live long. That meant she couldn't help Henry grow to manhood properly. What would become of him without her?

Chapter Forty-Five

On the Trail Again
March, 1872

Bill Antrim found a supply train that was planning on hauling their merchandise to Santa Fe. They had a contract for narrow gauge rail delivery on the Denver and Rio Grande Western Railroad to Pueblo, Colorado Territory.

There, they would load all the supplies on to mule drawn wagons, and drive to Trinidad, Colorado. From there, depending on the weather, they would take the Raton Pass on the road to Las Vegas, New Mexico Territory.

They would then lay over in Las Vegas to rest up animals and people to make the final drive to Santa Fe.

Bill inquired at the companies Denver office. He met a manager who pointed to a tall and large Scotch-Irishman with arms like tree trunks.

"Is that the foreman?" Bill asked the man.

"No, sir. He is Big John Henry and the owner of this wholesale mercantile store and the freight company! Don't cross him. We have a joke around here: he doesn't fire poor workers, he buries them ha!" the man laughed at his own joke.

Bill walked right up to the man, and without an introduction said: "Sir, do you need an experienced six team mule skinner?" matter-of-factly.

The big man looked at the man in front of him for a second and then commented: "You look more like a bookkeeper. Where did you mule skin?" Big John asked point blank.

"Indianapolis, Indiana with a private company before the war, United States Army during the war, Wichita, Kansas for the past two years. I also ran a short-haul freight business with my own outfit in Wichita. And I've carpentered on and off for six years."

Henry was standing next to Bill listening to the whole conversation. He just had to put his two cents worth in:

"Sir, Uncle Bill is the best darn mule skinner from here to Indianapolis east, and to Indian country south. He freighted for big outfits and messengered for Well Fargo," Henry said boldly.

"Enough! I'll hire you to shut that toe-head up. How much do you want?" Big John got down to business. He liked what he heard.

"I would like to exchange my time for freighting my family and all our goods on the railroad train to Pueblo, and your mule train to Santa Fe. Also, cover all the food they could eat on the trail, a six-man Sibley Tent, and four army cots. Oh, and Catherine wants two canvas walls for privacy," Bill ended with a grin.

"Well, would you like to have a private butler too?" Big John asked and thought to himself just how ridiculous this was. This guy would be freighting his own wagon, and he would be paying for the whole trip for him and his family. That's crazy!

"No, I'm not paying your way to drive your own freight wagon," Big John complained.

"Oh no, sir! I have a teenager that is very good at driving. My partner will trade off with him. I will skin one of your wagons! I wasn't trying to pull the wool over your eyes. I just want the family and all our goods to be safe on that road. I'm also good with a rifle and would expect to fight Comancheros or Indians to keep the family safe, and of course your train, too."

Big John thought for a moment. Now this was sounding pretty good to him. Guards, that were good with a gun, got $30. for the trip. He paid a $10 bonus for every gun fight they were in protecting the wagon train.

His mule skinners signed up at $25 each for the trip. That included loading and unloading merchandise from the railroad train and the mule train.

If this guy was good with a gun, willing to fight if needed, and would even be an average mule skinner, well, he had no problem feeding them all, and letting his own wagon join the wagon train.

"Well, mister... say, you never introduced yourself?" Big John complained.

"Bill Antrim sir," Bill replied quickly.

"Well, Mr. Antrim you have deal. I'm putting you in charge of wagon number three," he said as he pointed over to a warehouse. "You help load the merchandise onto the train. The wagons are waiting for us in Pueblo."

"Yes, sir. I do need to tell my family where I will be the rest of the day. Also, I must bring our things over to load. Is that alright Mr. John?"

"Sure, make it quick. We have a lot to do the rest of this day!" Big John replied over his shoulder as he walked away.

Henry smiled with a proud gleam on his face.

Bill gave Henry a stern look.

"What Uncle Bill? You heard him," Henry was referring to the man giving him the credit for hiring Bill.

"I can do my own talking Henry," Bill said with a voice that matched his serious expression, and he walked off too.

Henry turned to Josie: "What is with Uncle Bill?"

Totally out of character, Josie decided to tell Henry what he thought of Henry's actions: "Bill probably didn't want the ramrod having higher expectations. You delivered about as high an expectation as one could have done. I know you meant good for Bill, but he probably would have gotten the job without your speaking up when you shouldn't have. How many times have you heard Mom say, 'it is better to be seen, not heard'?"

Henry got it, but wanted to satisfy his own curiosity about something: "Josie, why do you call Uncle Bill just Bill? Mom has always called him Uncle Bill, but you do not. Why?" Henry asked sincerely.

"Because he is not my Uncle Bill. He is a friend and Mom's partner in business. He is not our uncle," Josie answered.

"Really! I always thought he was our uncle. Why would Mom call him Uncle Bill?" Henry asked simply.

"Well, because he is more family to us than just a business partner, I suppose. He is one of us even if not by blood," Josie did his best to explain.

"Thank you Josie. I think I understand now."

"You are welcome lil' brother," Josie replied.

Henry thought while he was doing so good he would ask another pressing question he had for a long time:

"Josie, why does Bill like you more than me?" Henry asked sincerely. That fact was quite obvious to everyone.

Josie chuckled before answering: "That is easy to answer! You are a know-it-all brat to him. Henry, you give more smart aleck remarks in one day than a kid your age does in a year! Heck, you drive me crazy too sometimes, and I know you. You just talk too much, Henry. You just talk too much! You have an opinion, or judgement about everyone and everything. That's why, believe me that is why! Bill is a man that measures another by his work, not his words." Josie explained the best he could and then walked off.

Henry was astonished! Surprised, and for the first time in his life... speechless! He always believed he was the "normal" one, Josie and Uncle Bill were the strangely quiet ones. People that were quiet were strange.

As Josie rolled off his list of perceived character flaws, Henry had a dozen incidents come to mind when kids his own age would just walk off from him. To him there was no rhyme or reason for that to have happened.

Now he realized, in all of them he had been the only one talking the whole time. He knew Josie had just given him a reality check. The shock was, he knew what Josie was saying was true. "Now what?" Henry said to himself and took off running toward their boarding house.

Bill had come home and told Catherine all the details of the deal he made with the owner of the freighting company.

Catherine was very pleased with the deal Bill had made. The only out of pocket expenses would be the tickets to Pueblo.

"I must get back right now to help load the merchandise on the train. Have the boys freight our things over as soon as you can... alright?" Bill asked Catherine.

"Don't you worry about us? We won't miss the train," Catherine chuckled.

Henry arrived looking rather frazzled. He wasn't himself. Catherine knew something was wrong. Henry spoke first:

"Mom, I don't want you to worry, but I need to be by myself a couple hours. I'll be right back," Henry wasn't asking as much as telling his mother, and that didn't get past Catherine.

"Are you asking or telling me?" She firmly asked.

"Oh... asking mother, asking," Henry corrected himself.

"Well then one hour... not two! We are loading the train right now," Catherine instructed firmly.

"Yes ma'am! One hour," Henry respectfully replied.

Henry walked a few city blocks from the boarding house, and then he climbed up a small knoll and sat atop a flat rock.

He cleared his mind and just thought of the sight in front of him. People and their animals going all which way in a hurry.

Looking across a road he saw some gentlemen standing, and some sitting, all in their Sunday best.

Henry turned his thoughts back to Josie's remarks, and he thought to himself: "He was right, but what can I do? This is who I am. I haven't only read the cops and robber stories. I've read about the new criminology records in San Francisco, California. I've read about the Missouri families supporting their hero's Frank and Jesse James. I love to read, but just as much I love to share what I've read, what I've learned. I love sharing as much as reading. What good is learning if you don't share what you've learned?"

His thoughts continued: "If someone says something about a subject I have read about, well, the impulse is too great to keep my mouth shut and just listen."

Henry then just searched the scenery in front of him again. Almost fifteen minutes passed when a rewarding thought came to his mind: "What if I tell myself to shut up at my first urge to talk? That might work! Just delaying my response doesn't mean I can't speak, it is just delaying it a while. Then I'll decide whether it is right to talk on it. If it is, I'll charge ahead as usual."

"I like that idea!" Henry said aloud. "That is what I'll do!"

Henry got up and ran all the way back to the boarding house. Arriving, Catherine could instantly see her affable, out-going, laughing son with his eyes sparkling with happiness was back!

Catherine did not inquire as to why he left, she figured he would blurt it all out at any second. "Huh?" she thought... "He didn't." That was a surprise, and kind of a pleasant one, but it did tickle her Irish curiosity.

"Apparently you feel better?" she asked Henry sincerely.

"Yes, mother I do," Henry replied without explaining himself.

Catherine looked at him just nodding her head slightly in the affirmative and said: "Good," in a low voice.

"Yes Mother, it is good," Henry nodded back.

"Alright son. Load all your things in the wagon," She directed. "I do have some news for you. Uncle Bill wants you, me and Josie to take turns driving our wagon from Pueblo to Santa Fe. Uncle Bill will be mule skinning one of the freighting company's wagon in trade for our passage. You two must be on your best behavior on this trip." Catherine concluded.

Henry wanted so bad to tell her he already knew all those things as he was there when they came to an agreement. The urge to say all he knew was busting out all over him, but he thought to himself: "Shut up! Why repeat what she knows already! Shut up!" Out loud he did ask excitedly:

"Really Mom! You will train me with our horses?"

"Yes, to a point," Catherine replied, wondering what caused her son's exuberance.

Henry thought to himself: "This went from the worst to the best day of my life, and all because I shut up! Ha!" the laugh was out loud.

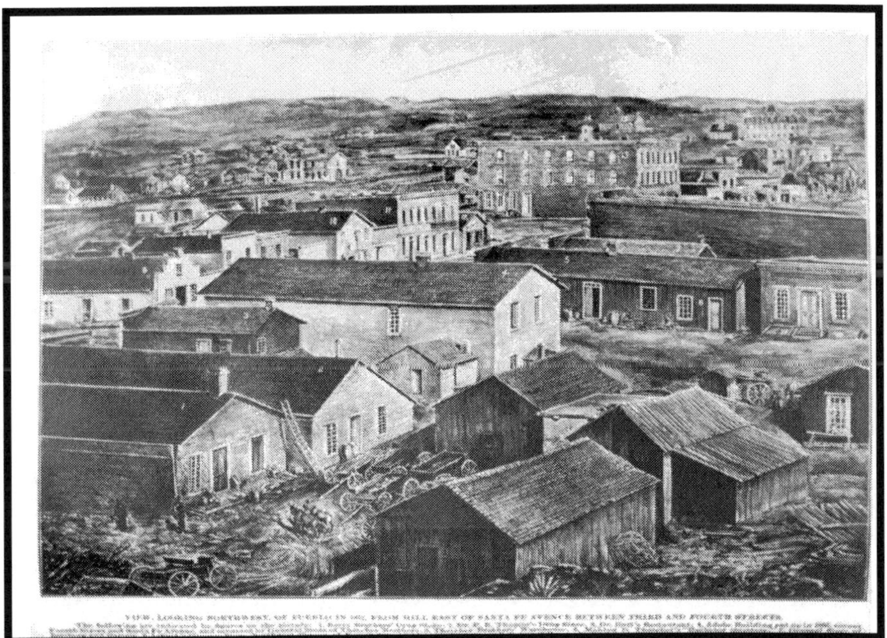

This is a drawing of Pueblo in 1872. This is the exact time the McCarty/Antrim party was coming through and would have been what they saw coming into town. *Source: Pueblo City-County Library District*

Chapter Forty-Six

On to Pueblo

It was late February 1872, when the small gauge railroad cars were all loaded and ready to roll. It took two days, with one delay after another. Big John gathered everyone together, including all the passengers.

He spoke loud enough to hear him a block away.

"Now is the time for anyone that wants to back out of this trip to do so. If you do not back out now, you will not be able to back out later! I will explain why just once. We have planned this trip to allow for everyone to be safe. This is a dangerous trail, and has been for at least a hundred years. There are Comanche renegades, Mexican banditos, and Comancheros. It will require every man to do his job to make sure we all arrive in Santa Fe safe and sound.

Anyone who drops out in Pueblo, or anywhere along the trail, and this train will be less safe. If you want to drop out, do it now. That will be fine because I can get a replacement in Denver easy. Once on the trail, it's not so easy." Big John ended his speech, and said not another word for a full minute.

Everyone was looking around at each other to see if anyone would drop out. No one did.

"Alright, train leaves in five minutes, so get to your seats," Big John bellowed out.

Catherine leaned over to Henry and whispered to him: "I think he is hard of hearing. Those people always yell thinking they are whispering," she chuckled.

"Yes, I am!" Big John said. "But I can hear a whisper a mile away...go figure that out?" He laughed at himself.

Henry found it very funny his mother got caught whispering about someone. She always corrected him for the same thing.

"Do as I say, not as I do," Catherine said staring at Henry's sarcastic grin.

The train finally pulled out. It seemed like it took forever to an anxious twelve-year-old.

Henry sat across from one of Big John's scouts. The man was very quiet, stood six feet tall, and appeared to be a mestizo of Indian and Mexican. His face was strong and reflected a hard life. Although in his early thirties he looked in his forties. Just sitting there, he perpetuated an air of confidence. One was glad he was on their side, you would not want him as an enemy.

Henry wanted to start asking him a hundred questions about the Indians on this trail, but refrained from doing so.

Catherine did ask one question of the gentle giant:

"Sir, do you know why Big John picked this time of the year for this trip?" she asked sincerely.

The big Indian didn't hesitate with an answer:

"Good moon. It is time for hunting not fighting. They must get enough meat for winter. Trains have goods, not meat."

"Thank you, sir," Catherine said gratefully.

"That is not to say that renegades may want these goods to trade with," the gentle giant volunteered.

"Oh, I understand. You speak English very well. Where did you learn the language?" Catherine asked politely.

"I grew up to manhood with some missionary people that bought me from Comancheros. I was their slave for many moons. They raided our camp and took all the women and children. I was a child then, or I would have been killed."

"My people spoke Español and Tanoan Kiowa. I had learned two languages before I was saved by the missionaries. They spoke English and Español, so it was very easy for me to learn English," the gentle giant replied.

"My name is Catherine, these are my two sons Henry and Josie. That is Uncle Bill Antrim in the first seat across the aisle," Catherine introduced her family.

"My real name is Bounji Tap (pronounced "Boni Tap"). In English it means: "I see deer." Big John calls me Eagle Eye. That is even better I think," Boni Tap explained with a smile.

"If you like Eagle Eye, that is what we will call you," Catherine declared.

Another scout, a vaquero, stopped by and spoke Spanish to Eagle Eye:

"Decidimos que no deberias ser el explorador principal de Las Vegas. (We decided you should be the lead scout to Las Vegas)" the vaquero said matter-of-factly. Eagle Eye replied:

"Si, como lo has dicho, asi sera. (Yes, as you have said so shall it be.). Hedge, no crees que deberias presentarte a esta familia?"(Hedge, don't you think you should introduce yourself to this family?)."

Hedge quickly turned to the others seated there:

"Oh si! Forgive me to interrupt so rudely. My name is Hedge. I am in charge of all scouts for Big John. Today, it is my honor to assign Eagle Eye as the lead scout on the trail to Las Vegas." Hedge continued, "Through his veins runs the blood of those we might run into on this trail. I trust him with my life, as you should too." Hedge spoke with perfect English. That was because he was an American vaquero. He lived and worked with Mexicans in old Mexico for many years.

Eagle Eye introduced the entire family. Catherine was impressed that he had memorized all their names from the first meeting.

Eagle Eye volunteered:

"Hedge wears your skin, but he thinks like us. He will also be in charge of all fighters should that be needed. It's good to know that he really knows how to fight Indians and Mescalero."

Bill Antrim perked up at that, as Hedge would be the one to report to in a fight, and he had committed to Big John to do just that if needed.

Henry was amazed at how easily Hedge and Eagle Eye had switched from Spanish to English. He spoke English since early childhood and now needed to stop and think about his birth language, Gaelic, when he wanted to speak it. Henry knew if he learned Spanish he would have to use it every day if he wanted to speak both as good as Hedge and Eagle Eye.

Hedge left, and Henry finally got a chance to ask a question, and wasted no time in doing so:

"Mr. Eagle Eye, where is your home?" Henry asked politely.

Eagle Eye smiled and said:

"Mostly we called the Rio Grande River Valley our home. It was where we looked forward to returning to. We were on the hunting trail all year. We followed the buffalo as far north as what you call Dakota Territory now, and as far south as the Sierra Madre Mountains in Mexico. In the winter we went south and in the summer we traveled north.

It is hard to explain, but our home is the sky, the earth, the water. I must say though we really looked forward to the Rio Grande Valley. We stayed there longer and as children we had far more fun there." He then pointed to his head and said:

"Memories, if you know what I mean?" Eagle Eye concluded his very long answer.

Catherine replied: "Yes, I do know what you mean."

Henry waited patiently to see if everyone had really concluded talking before asking another question. The question definitely demonstrated Henry's intelligence, and even took Catherine by surprise.

"Mr. Eagle Eye, do you consider yourself white or Indian?" Henry asked directly.

"Good question, little man. I think I have one foot in each family. I still think like an Indian, but I grew up in a white family. They were fine people who looked at me, and treated me as their own. Yet, as you saw, when asked my name I give my Indian name. I was about your age when the Comancheros stole me. Who you are has been completed in here," he said pointing to his head. "From now on you will learn from all your life, but that person in here," he said, again pointing to his head, "won't change. You are made already. I have seen few change unless something drastic happened to them."

Catherine was astounded by this half-breed's (common name for mestizo) answer. He was a very intelligent Indian. She believed his counsel was true. She had learned something from him that seemed to comfort her.

"I am glad you are our scout for this trip," Catherine declared. "I hope my curious son's questions are not bothering you?" Catherine asked sincerely.

"No, ma'am, not at all. No bother to me at all. Makes the time go by faster. Look, we are almost at our first stop."

"How long does it take to reach Pueblo?" Henry asked.

"We could make it in five hours, but we won't. Too many stops along the way. I expect we will be there late this afternoon. Just enough daylight left to unload all the cargo onto the wagons waiting for us there." Eagle Eye answered Henry's question.

Bill Antrim asked his most important question:

"Do you know if wagons are plentiful to purchase in Pueblo?"

"I may be mistaken, but I think Big John bought up every wagon in town for sale two weeks ago," Eagle Eye informed Bill.

Bill leaned toward Catherine and said: "Don't be concerned, I'm sure there will be one for us there somewhere."

As much as he tried to take the worried concern from his voice, he failed at it, because he was concerned. Just then Big John came walking down the aisle.

"Mr. John, do you know if there is a wagon for me to purchase in Pueblo?" Bill asked point blank.

"I bought one I'm not going to use. Would you like to buy it for what I paid for it?" Big John asked.

"Yes sir, we would," Bill Antrim did not hesitate to answer.

Catherine interrupted: "Don't you think you should ask how much that was?"

Again, without hesitation Bill replied: "No, I don't have to do that."

Big John chuckled: "Ma'am, he is a smart man. He knows no one pays less than me for anything, ha!" he bellowed out a laugh. Then said directly to Catherine:

"Forty dollars for the wagon, and forty dollars for four mules. Including a Sibley Tent, four cots, and two canvass room dividers. Is that a good price, ma'am?" Big John asked firmly.

"Yes sir, it is. Please do except my apology for questioning you," Catherine sincerely begged.

"No need for an apology. We just met. Your Uncle Bill did his homework and knew more about me than I did him at our first meeting. That is why I hired him, oh, and he said he was a good shot... Is that true ma'am?" Big John asked pointedly.

"Yes, actually he is a good shot," Catherine agreed.

"Good, then I made a good hire... I think," he said looking back at Bill Antrim. "Frankly, you look more like a bookkeeper than a mule skinning Indian fighter...ha!" Big John laughed out at his own joke again.

Bill grinned and said: "Looks can be deceiving. You look more like a mule skinner than a freight-line owner."

"Good answer... we will see on this trip. You will need all your skills. Nice meeting you ma'am," Big John tipped his broad banded hat and went on down the aisle.

"He had to wire ahead to buy and equip our wagon," Bill observed.

Henry continued his questions to Eagle Eye all the way to Pueblo. Eagle Eye seemed not to tire of answering the young man's inquiries. His answers were in the form a teacher would give. Explaining things as he responded.

Finally, the conductor announced they were pulling into Pueblo, Colorado. Everyone was ready to get off that train. That short trip from Denver seemed harder on them than the whole trip across Kansas. The difference was small gauge versus large gauge rails. The cars move around more on the former. Their bodies were constantly compensating for the jolts. One would think the car was going to jump the track at any minute. However, they made it safe and sound.

Eagle Eye had projected their arrival pretty spot on. They had enough day-light left to unload the train and load the awaiting wagons.

The McCarty's pitched their new tent not far from their new wagon and team of mules. The next day would be a supply purchasing and organizing day.

The following day they would leave for Trinidad, Colorado. It is 84 miles due south of Pueblo and near the border with the New Mexico Territory.

The 84 miles would take a lot longer than the last 114 miles from Denver. Instead of five hours without stops it would be five days if they had no problems.

It was a well-worn trail. They were going to be on the infamous Santa Fe Trail. First taken by the Spaniards hundreds of years earlier. The Indians had used it for probably at least a thousand years. In fact, Eagle Eye's tribe had oral histories and stories going back to 1200 A.D.

Big John ran his outfit like a military commander. The night guards started their watch while still in Pueblo. They didn't understand that. They wanted to party in town their last night. Big John had other ideas. His ideas always won out.

Chapter Forty-Seven

Trinidad or Bust!

Big John was leading his operations like a general, and a good one at that. This was not his first time on a hostile trail freighting everything every Indian and Comanchero wanted for themselves. They wanted it at the price of a few bullets and/or arrowheads.

Scouts were advanced at one day's ride (approximately 15 miles). Their orders were to not be detected by anyone, and record everything they saw. No matter how small the detail. Obviously, should they find enemy camps, they were to observe for as long as they could, and report back as soon as possible. The observation period was for movement of enemy combatants.

If the forward scout could not write, he was to cut drawings on a bark, place evidence found in a possibles bag, and memorize what he saw. Big John insisted that he report in his native tongue to an interpreter. That was to prevent mistakes in messaging. The chief interpreter was Big John's right hand man. On this trip he had two: Hedge and Eagle Eye.

Scouts were also sent out on a half days ride in advance (approximately 8 miles). One on the right flank and one on the left flank. He knew some of the Indian tribes like the Cauijoga (Kiowa) would attack from flanks, and then encircle the train. By encircling they shot at fixed targets and the whites shot at moving targets. These scouts would always remain in their flanking positions until called in or relieved.

Catherine McCarty's camp became a favorite stop for all the scouts. She always had delicious food and snacks for them when they were relieved on their posts.

At night those men not on guard would gather at the McCarty camp fire. Big John would stop by for a taste of her cooking. He really was happy with himself about making the deal with Bill Antrim. Antrim was a good mule skinner, but even more so because Catherine was such a good cook.

Young Henry was having the time of his life. He had never traveled with a large group. People fascinated him. Especially the Mexican vaqueros. They seem to be the embodiment of the western characters he read about in the magazines. Good guys and bad guys. They also represented a mystery to him. He wanted to understand them and their culture much better.

Every chance Henry got he drilled down with questions to the scouts who visited their camp. He had learned to ask a question and then shut up, no matter how long it took for the answer to come to him. One question was not answered for three days, but he got an answer. He was learning so much on this trip.

They were on the trail several days when Henry finally gave his mother a gentle reminder that she had promised him he could drive the wagon.

Catherine knew as soon as that promise, and those words rolled off her tongue, it was a mistake! Josie was old enough, and skilled enough to drive the wagon. Horse and buggy was one thing, a freight wagon was much more difficult. She believed Henry was not, but she gave her word. She immediately gave the reins to Henry. She observed he held the reins perfectly in his hands, which made her feel a little better. Henry had been studying all the drivers he could.

Henry secretly knew he was holding the reins even better than his mother, but this was a moment to keep quiet and not share that information.

One mule began to lunge on a small knoll. Catherine started to take the reins back, but Henry had pulled that mule's line gently to signal a slowdown. The mule responded, to Catherine's surprise.

"That was very good, son. You have learned quickly." Catherine immediately remarked.

Henry had an almost uncontrollable urge to tell her all that he had learned, but instead he just smiled and nodded in acknowledgement.

"I'm very proud of you, son. You do drive very well," Catherine remarked.

Henry was so glad he had constrained himself from self-promotion. To hear those words from his mother, well, he would keep them the rest of his life. It was what the first "job well done" on a man's job at hand. His mother had complemented his work before, but it was work any child could do. This was a man's job!

At their camp that night several vaqueros and scouts had gathered around the family's fire. The scout Hedge had helped set up that night's camp site. Bill Antrim had the duty of picketing the mules.

Catherine always had food to share, and she was a very good cook. Her cooking was the real reason the vaqueros and scouts rarely missed an evening at their camp. This night the vaqueros had arrived with freshly baked bread to contribute to the meal.

One vaquero spoke quickly to his friend and in his native language. It was a matter of habit, not to be rude to the English-speaking people there.

"Creo que su hijo tiene diez anos. (I think her son is ten-years-old). Y lo vi conduciendo su carro hoy. (And I saw him driving their wagon today)."

Hedge interrupted them: "No señor, tiene doce anos. (No sir, he is twelve-years-old)."

Henry was intently listening to every word, although he understood little of the language. He was enthralled how easily Hedge switched from English to Spanish, and spoke so fluently. Then he realized he too could do that with Gaelic and English. It still was mysterious to hear that in a language he did not know.

Henry's quick mind saw a real value in speaking in a language people around you didn't understand. It was intriguing and seemed a bit mischief to him.

Hedge spoke up: "Please forgive my good Mexican friends here. They meant not to offend by speaking in their native language." He directed his apology to Catherine and then nodded, acknowledging the same to Henry.

"No offense taken. Thank them for the bread," Catherine asked of him assuming the vaqueros knew no English.

Hedge said to the vaqueros: "La dama le da las gracias por el pan. (The lady gives thanks for the bread). Wait a minute! You guys speak English. You know what she said!"

The vaqueros had to give a good laugh at their boss's lapse of memory.

José Gonzales said: "Thank you ma'am and de nada for the pan...oh...bread." He laughed at his mixture of languages and his friend Geraldo San Martin Vegas joined in the laugh.

"I laugh at myself for my poor broken English, Señora. Not at you!" José clarified.

"Your English, even broken, is a lot better than my Spanish." Catherine confessed. "What counts is that I could still understand what you meant."

Henry was mesmerized by the whole conversation. He couldn't explain why. It was just a beautiful language that they spoke. He had heard Spanish spoken by some Indians in Wichita, but it didn't impress him the way these two Mexican vaqueros had.

It seemed like their language rolled off their tongue almost like music. Henry liked it very much. He promised himself right there and then, he was going to learn Spanish and speak it as well as any Mexican.

José asked Henry in his broken English: "Is it true you are twelve years of age?"

Henry replied: "Yes, sir."

José turned to Hedge and asked what "sir" meant.

Hedge replied in Spanish then English:

"Es el repeto o el jefe." "It is respect, or boss."

José replied: "Oh no! Mi no boss. Mi vaquero worker with horses." Then in Spanish: "Trabajador con caballos."

Hedge started to speak when Henry interrupted:

"He said to call him a vaquero who works with horses...right?"

Wow! You figured this out just now?" Hedge asked Henry.

"No sir. I knew caballos was horses, and you translated the rest, Mr. Hedge."

Hedge turned to Catherine and commented:

"You have a smart boy to remember all that. I didn't even remember what I said...ha," Hedge chuckled.

Catherine looked at Henry and said:

"Yes Mr. Hedge, I have a very smart young man," she said in a sincere tone of voice.

Henry gleamed with pride. Josie sulked with disdain. She could have said both of her young men, but didn't. He felt slighted.

Henry asked José and Geraldo: "I love your language. How long did it take you to learn English?"

"Not a long time, if you live with people that speak it. We worked – lived with Gringo drovers for many years. I say lived with them maybe two years... I speak well enough." José concluded in his broken English.

"You speak English very well. Someday I hope to learn your language." Henry said sincerely.

José replied: "Ah first teaching: algun espero aprender su idioma."

Henry believed he knew what José was doing, repeating what he just said to him. He asked: "Please say that one more time."

José obliged: "Algun dia espero aprender su idioma. Which is: 'One day I hope to learn your language.' Once more: Algun dia espero aprender su idioma."

Henry concentrated and then attempted to repeat the sentence for himself: "Algun dia spero prender to dioma."

José knew not to laugh at his slaughter of the words. He remembered how it was when the drovers laughed at him.

José declared instead: "Muy bien. You do well! It was pretty close. Will take a lot of teaching (meaning practice)."

Henry said: "Muchas gracias," (demonstrating something he did know). He continued: "You are kind José. I know I didn't sound anything like you...ha," laughing at himself. José laughed with him. Much better than laughing at him.

Geraldo San Martin Vegas didn't talk much, and trusted people even less. Yet, he sensed this young, toe-headed gringo was serious about learning their language. When he did talk it would be wise to listen.

"Señor Henry, to learn any language you must master the small words: a, is, here, go, the, that, into, or out. Learn not how the professors speak, learn like the people speak."

Geraldo went on: "Professors know too much! La gente comun, vaqueros like us have no school. If you talk like a professor, we get a good laugh." He said with a grin on his face.

Henry asked what "la gente comun" meant.

"Common, ordinary people like us," Geraldo replied.

"Muchas gracias, señor," Henry thanked him sincerely.

"De nada, (your welcome)," Geraldo acknowledged.

Henry observed: "That is why it is better to live together, right?"

José volunteered: "Si, eso es correcto mi pequeno hombre inteligente."

Geraldo translated: "He said: right my smart little man."

"I like that, José!" Henry said tongue-in-cheek.

Everyone laughed except Henry's brother Josie.

Catherine took notice and declared it was time to sleep.

The wagon being full they all slept in a five-man tent.

Geraldo volunteered:

"I help you keep the snakes and ground crawlers out of your camp, ok señora?"

"Of course," Catherine replied.

Geraldo scooped a hand full of ash from the fire. He did that several times laying a line of ash all around the tent.

"The smell, they don't like it and stay away." Then he placed a rope completely around the tent. "They don't like the lariat too," Geraldo said with a smile. "Now you are safe," he said as he tipped his sombrero and left.

"Muchas gracias!" Catherine declared as he walked off.

"De nada, señora," Geraldo replied.

"Buenas noches...Good night," Geraldo said in Spanish and English.

"Buenas noches...Good night," Henry then repeated it to himself ten times. He made a pact to himself to do the same on every word he learned in Spanish.

Although very young at the time he had a clear memory of doing that to learn English. Also, his mother insisted that everyone speak English in the house.

Anytime Gaelic slipped out she would remind them: "We are Americans now. I will not reply to Gaelic." Before that declaration by his mother everyone spoke Gaelic in the house frequently.

He knew José and Geraldo were right. Someday he would live with people speaking Spanish. Until then he would study hard, determined to be fluent in Spanish.

Henry awoke in the morning just before dawn. A noise had stirred him awake. The noise source was Geraldo recovering his long rope. Just as Henry recognized him, Geraldo locked eyes with him. A chill went up Henry's spine because he had not moved a muscle. Geraldo had sensed someone was looking at him, as was the case.

"Buenos dias, hombrecito. Es mi cuerda larga." In English: "Good day little man. This is my rope," Geraldo explained.

"Si, gracias...no muchas gracias," Henry replied.

Geraldo corrected Henry: "Mucho gracias," with emphasis on "Mucho".

"Si, mucho gracias señor," Henry answered.

Geraldo replied excitedly: "Si, si, muy Bueno!"

Henry hopped up and began his morning chores. He was allowed to prepare everything for cooking except the eggs. Only his mother was allowed to retrieve them from their "safe place."

Catherine prepared a wonderful breakfast.

Bill Antrim had to comment: "Your cooking is always very good, but it is so tasty when we are traveling and camping out," he said sincerely.

"Thank you Uncle Bill, but mother nature has something to do with that," she replied with a big smile.

TRININDAD TRAIL

The wagon train approached a small mountain range with a pass on their trail. The green horns thought that was Raton Pass. The experienced travelers had a good chuckle at that.

Big John explained to Catherine and Bill: "Raton Pass is through a much larger mountain range ahead. We will be in Trinidad in a few days. Soon we will have the Spanish Mountains to the west of us. We will keep them to our right all the way to Trinidad."

"From there we will begin the long travel through what we call Raton Pass. At Trinidad we will check all our supplies. That is our last chance to buy anything we have forgotten, or we are low on. The pass its self is only twenty-five miles, but it will feel like a hundred, and take us two days. When we reach the village of Raton we will be in New Mexico," Big John concluded.

Trinidad founded in 1862 with the discovery of coal. *A large mounted statue of Kit Carson was erected in recognition of Trinidad's importance on the Santa Fe Trail. Another notable resident was Bat Masterson who served as town marshal in 1882. When McCarty's came through in 1872: pop. 1300. Elevation 6025 ft. would have been hard on Catherine. Source: 1907 Trinidad, Colorado Library of Congress*

Chapter Forty-Eight

The Wagon Train Faces A Dangerous Spring Run-off and Dangerous Renegades

They knew this journey would be a long and arduous one. Winter had stretched into spring, with some late snow flurries. The flakes didn't stick, but melted as fast as they landed on the ground. This created mud several inches thick.

The McCarty/Antrim wagon had a wider than normal wheel, with a strip of thin iron around the entire circumference of the wheel.

It made for a little rougher ride on dry ground, but rarely got stuck in mud. Also, it would be much better for crossing soft bottom rivers like the up-coming Cimarron River.

They knew for most of this trip they would have to contend with deep mud from spring rains and melting snow flakes.

The large rivers like the Cimarron, Canadian, and Arkansas would have to be crossed by attaching floating logs on both sides of the wagons. The heavier wagons would need two logs on each side.

Another trick Big John had was to send a ferryman's rope across by horseback. Then anchoring it on a large tree on the far bank. This did backfire once when the tree was pulled out of the bank due to weak roots from erosion. That was the last time a tree was selected on the actual bank. From then on a strong Cottonwood or Oak back from the bank was utilized.

Big John had departed in late winter to avoid the strong currents of late spring. He had been a drover with Charlie Goodnight and learned much about driving cattle and wagons across these furious rivers.

Although he knew his vaqueros were very experienced with river crossings, he still had a one-hour meeting with them going over all the details. He opened the meeting with the story when Goodnight's lead bull did a switchback in the middle of the Arkansas during a spring run-off current.

The 600-pound steers were being swept down-stream like corks. They became exhausted and drown. The two drovers had tried to turn the lead bull back around. One actually threw a rope around the bull's head. Big mistake! That 2500-pound bull thrashed one horse and then the other. They lost fifty head of cattle and two drovers before the switch back could be halted. Charlie Goodnight sent two drovers down both side of the river for 20 miles. They never saw the lost drovers again.

That night they held a drover's funeral. All hands held their hats in their lowered hands, head bowed. Hats only came off in the presence of a lady, in a church, and at a funeral.

Big John swore if he ever ramrodded he would never cross any rivers in late spring. Even if that meant leaving in snow storms.

He had no intention of losing any cattle, wagons, or people on his crossings. He made that quite clear to all his men at the meeting.

Henry McCarty listened intently from his usual hiding place, out of sight of all attendees. This was so different from traveling with just his family. That was exciting and kind of a camping trip, but this was going to school about being a drover and driving wagons. He also knew he was learning from the best!

This was one of the reasons his Mexican vaqueros had stayed with him so long. They knew he really cared about his men, not just the goods. They were also able and willing to fight for him if necessary.

UTE RENEGADES!

On this trip to Las Vegas, twice desperados tried to take the wagon train. One by the Southern Ute Indian renegades who thought they had a soft target. Were they so very wrong!

Big John had practice drills on several occasions. He held a war counsel, and laid out his defensive and offensive plans.

Big John's scouts discovered the renegades set up for an ambush about five miles ahead of the wagon train. After the scouts reported to him. He decided to lead out front with only two men. Then his twenty-five fighters would be split into two groups and circle on the right and left flanks of the renegades.

Just before reaching the ambush point his fighters would attack from both flanks and rear of the renegades. They had no escape.

Henry snuck out the back of their wagon enough to look around the back flap toward the front of the wagon train. He saw the whole attack. Big John did not leave one renegade alive. He killed them all.

The wagon train drove right past the dead bodies. It was a morbid sight. Big John himself rode his Buck over to their wagon. He knew this was most likely the McCarty/Antrim family's first experienced of such a fight.

He reined up and turned his horse in the same direction of the McCarty wagon. Looking straight ahead he declared:

"That is what they intended to do to us, ma'am. Their moto is 'dead men tell no tales'. Had I left one alive, they one would raise another group and attack us in revenge. In another attack they would be much smarter, and we would lose men. We lost no men!" Big John spurred his big buck and headed back to the front of the train.

Catherine didn't change her expression. She understood his logic, but as a Christian she could not condone the slaughter. She saw several renegades were trying to surrender, but were shot down by the vaqueros on Big John's orders.

Her toe-headed boy was listening from right behind her in the wagon. When Big John concluded his comment to her, Henry thought to himself: "Smart." Then he noticed Geraldo was at the back of their wagon.

"Si, Señor Geraldo, muy bueno," Henry rolled off his tongue like a native.

Geraldo smiled and tipped his sombrero as he reined his horse away from the back of their wagon. He was checking to make sure no one in the wagon had been hit by a stray bullet.

Big John's plan had been executed like a Swiss watch. Not one of his men hurt and not one Ute Indian left alive. He also knew that would save many lives on the trains following his wagon train.

Big John gave a sigh of relief as his train passed into the New Mexican Territory. The rest of the trail to Las Vegas and Santa Fe should be free of renegades of any kind.

Fort Union was guarding the Santa Fe Trail. They were responsible from the border to Santa Fe itself. This used to be the Comancheros raiding territory. They were known now to be raiding on the old mail route from Santa Rosa to Punta Del Agua, far south of Las Vegas.

The weather was bad still in the high country around Cimarron. The Santa Fe Trail branch through Taos would be shorter, but much tougher to transverse in the mountainous region. He remained confident in his choice of the main trail through Las Vegas. Longer but safer.

His plan was to lay over in Las Vegas to rest the animals and allow them to graze a few days. Then he would have only one pass to traverse to Santa Fe.

Chapter Forty-Nine

Big John Was So Wrong

The Comancheros had tired of their slim pickings on the old Texas mail route. They were not afraid of the U.S. Cavalry and had beaten them more than once since the end of the war of rebellion.

Most of Fort Union's soldiers were new recruits with no fighting experience. Their leaders were veterans of many fights, but not the pony soldiers they led. Combine that with a low morale having been posted in what they thought was the middle of nowhere, desolate, and a long way from civilization.

To the Comancheros leader the Santa Fe Trail was well worth the risk. All his men were hardened desperados with much fighting experience.

The large wagon trains had not only goods, foods, guns and ammunition. They sometimes had white women. They could sell them in Arizona and Mexico as slaves. The going price was $100 for an average woman. $150 for a strong young woman, and up to $200 for a beautiful, young, healthy woman.

One good raid on the Santa Fe Trail could yield thousands of dollars for the Comanchero's leader. It was certainly worth the risk to them.

Big John's intelligence had been received in Pueblo from a Comanchero spy. It was José who'd heard it in a saloon.

Scout leader Hedge had confirmed the information through another vaquero that was present. It seemed to be good and important information to give Big John, and therefore he did just that.

Big John had asked if he trusted the source. Hedge told him he did not know the man personally, but had no reason to not believe what he said.

BACK ON THE TRAIL

It was a beautiful day. The only annoyance was the wagon driver in front of the McCarty's wagon. He was having a hard time controlling his mules. Catherine's mules kept zigging and zagging with the wagon ahead. She was about ready to send Henry to relieve the man. Of course, she would not do that, but the thought ran through her mind. She turned to Henry and said:

"Son, I believe you could control those mules better than that man. Oh! Please, don't tell anyone I said that!"

Henry grinned and replied: "Don't worry mother, I won't." He grinned with that mischievous twinkle in his eye.

"No, I mean it. That was terrible for me to say. I know nothing about him or what trouble he may be having with those mules," She explained her remorseful statement.

"I know, mother. Seriously, I won't say a word," Henry said this time very seriously.

"Thank you son," She replied sincerely.

Henry declared:

"Look mother! Hedge and a scout are coming at a full run! They must have important news!"

Hedge and his loyal Pawnee scout Eagle Eyes brought both their horses to a sliding stop in front of Big John. Big John had already halted the train.

Hedge's report was not a good one. Big John called a general meeting of all men on the train.

Big John gave his opening statement while looking directly at Bill Antrim:

"This is exactly why I normally do not allow women and children on my freight trains." He said it in a self-damnation tone of voice. He clearly was blaming himself. Then he turned to the business at hand.

Using a stick to draw in the dirt he explained the scouts report:

"Here is where we are. This is the Cimarron River." He said as he scratched a line in the dirt.

"My scouts said there are thirty-to-forty Comancheros here, about five miles down the trail and in good cover."

To the man one could see the surprise and fear in their faces. Everyone knew who and what the Comancheros were, blood thirsty killers. They made the Apache look like Sunday school teachers. They were known to skin people or set them on fire alive, just for entertainment. Sometimes burning just a limb until all the flesh is burned off, then cutting the limb off and cauterizing the wound. Then waiting until the victim came to, and repeating it on another limb of his body. The screaming until the victim passed out, or died, was the entertainment. They were truly gruesome, evil animals.

Henry McCarty had moved like a cat. He stalked up behind a wagon wheel to listen to Big John's speech.

One of his drivers asked: "Can we get help from Fort Union?"

Big John replied: "These killers aren't young renegade Utes on their first raid. They'll have scouts posted and will know every move we make."

Hedge volunteered: "They already have."

Big John continued: "One man may get through to Fort Union, although it is near impossible. But we would be giving up another fighter to defend the train. Furthermore, it will be all over one way or another by the time the soldiers got here.

No, the only choices are to turn tail and run back to the Colorado Territory, or cross the Cimarron and have a straight up fight with the best fighters in the plains. I called you together because I believe it is your choice, not just mine. You will be the ones that will do most of the fighting." Big John explained.

Bill Antrim asked: "Why wouldn't they just follow us back and attack from our rear?"

"I don't think they would as this is as far north as I've ever seen them operate. It becomes dangerous for them to get too far from their base camp. They wouldn't be able to resupply food and ammunition quickly."

Big John thought of another reason: "Their enemies are also the Navajo, Ute, and Comanche. All of those are stronger in the north."

"Hedge, what are your thoughts?" He really needed his counsel.

Hedge was deep in thought when Eagle Eyes spoke to him in Pawnee, so no one could understand. He was attempting to not alarm all the others.

Eagle Eyes said in Pawnee:

"I counted thirty pack animals. They can go anywhere they need to. They will know when we turn around. Their animals faster than ours. They will cross the river and catch up to us in a half day...no more than one day. We would still have to fight."

Hedge translated what he said to the whole group. Their reaction was as Big John expected... disappointed. No question the majority until then like the idea of running for the Colorado Territory.

Hedge then gave his conclusion: "I don't think we should cross the river now. They want us to tire our animals and our fighters forging the river."

Bill Antrim interrupted: "Remember the train leaving behind us? It shouldn't be too long before they reach here. Then we would have more guns...right?"

Big John agreed: "Yes, we would. Hedge please have Eagle Eye keep track of the Comancheros while you ride back to talk to their wagon master." He said with excitement in his voice. It was the first real flicker of hope.

"When I find them, I shouldn't tell them all we know. They wouldn't come. I wouldn't if I was that wagon master," Hedge admitted.

"You may be right. He may just watch out for his goods and people. Just report back to me so I can do the same for my people."

Henry had heard all of this conversation. He feared for his mother and brother. He even found it strange that he had no fear for himself, or his Uncle Bill. He was proud that Uncle Bill was contributing to the conversation, and seemed to be one of the bravest men there.

He was only twelve-years-old and swore he would die before a Comanchero would touch his mother. She was the only woman on the train. She was strong and beautiful, but not one would touch her.

Deep in his thoughts, Henry was startled by a poke in his side. It was Eagle Eyes' stone-cold stare, and his face said it all. He was one not to argue with. He was pointing back toward the McCarty wagon and Henry took off like a cat.

Of course, Bill Antrim never knew he was gone, but his mother did. Henry wanted to tell her all that he heard, but decided this was a time to be quiet.

Catherine spoke in a low monotone voice: “Son, Josie and I were the only ones not at the big meeting. I can be a founder of a city, but not be able to attend that meeting.”

Usually at such a time Henry would blurt out all he knew. Once they moved out to the homestead she discovered just how much Henry contributed to her knowledge of the happenings in Wichita.

This time Henry sat quietly staring out to the prairie. Catherine was patient feeling he would explain at his own time, she would not pressure him.

Catherine looked ahead at the rushing river, which she thought was the subject matter of the meeting and calmly asked:

“Did they decide to cross the river tomorrow?” she calmly asked.

“No, I think we will be here for a while. They said there was another freight outfit coming. Big John said it would be safer from here to Santa Fe to travel together,” Henry calmly said without elaborating why it would be safer.

“Are you frightened about something?” Catherine asked point blank. She knew her son very well and he was acting far too calm. He was hiding something.

Henry turned his head quickly toward his mother and replied: “Yes mother, I am,” he said holding back the tears that were welling up his eyes.

Catherine put her arm around him, pulling his head gently toward her side. Intuitively she knew not to probe any further.

“It will be alright son. We have God’s angels with us. He will care for us and see that we get to Santa Fe safely.” Catherine assured Henry.

“I don’t care about myself. I am afraid for you. I will tell you. They said there are Comancheros five miles on the other side of the river. They are there waiting to attack us.”

Henry’s voice changed to an authoritative one: “No matter what happens I will not let them get you, mother,” he said as a tear let loose from his eye.

“I know I am safe with you, Josie and Uncle Bill. I promise all will work out, son. I promise you that!” Catherine assured Henry. She said in a calm, collected, and intelligent manner. Her bravery calmed Henry and the tears stopped.

Chapter Fifty

William Atkins, Wagon Master Meets Big John, Wagon Master

The next two days were the longest in the McCarty family's lives. Hedge and Eagle Eyes came and went three times in one day. Each time everyone waited with anxious thoughts of an attack being imminent.

On the late afternoon of the second day they could see the dust before the heard the wagons of an approaching wagon train.

The wagon master and his scout arrived at Big John's camp. After dismounting and introducing themselves. It was clear that the wagon master was not too happy about not receiving an earlier warning.

William Atkins, wagon master of the approaching train spoke plainly:

"Why were we not given an earlier warning of the Comancheros? Your scout decided to tell us as we came in sight of your train," Mr. Atkins said in a monotone voice. He showed no emotion, but seeming more disappointed than angry.

"I take full responsibility for that," Big John admitted and went on to explain: "I told my scout to make sure you didn't know we were waiting for you."

"And why is that?" Mr. Atkins asked this time with a tinge of anger in his voice.

Big John calmly explained: "No doubt I was watching out for my train. None-the-less, if they were successful in attacking my train, you could possibly be attacked as well. They have spies in Pueblo. We know that because we were given misinformation to make us believe they were raiding further south."

Mr. Atkins interrupted: "We heard the same."

Big John went on: "I noticed you have a lot of families, women, and children. They also know that now. I have only one family and only one woman. There is little doubt in my mind they want both trains."

"You still haven't answered my question why you didn't warn us," Mr. Atkins asked plainly. "Of course, I know. You thought we would not come to your aid. I get that. You don't know me or the people on my train. Had your scout explained everything, I would have held a vote. And I would bet a month's pay they would have voted 100% to come join you. That is the kind of people they are." Mr. Atkins concluded his mild reprimand.

"You're right, I don't know you or your people. Had I known that I would have acted differently," Big John replied matter-of-factly, with no apology for his actions.

"I will still conduct a vote," Mr. Atkins said as he sent his scout back to do the same.

His scout arrived back with the results: "30-to-0 to fight if necessary," the scout reported.

Mr. Atkins shrugged saying: "I told you so."

"You do know your people well," Big John acknowledged.

"I will let them know, as you're the lead train, you will oversee planning our defense and offensive strategies. Of course, with my having veto power. Does that meet your expectations?" The intelligent Mr. Atkins asked sincerely.

"That is close. I believe in a military structure for any military actions. I suggest that we are both captains, but with you reporting to me. No exceptions. Too much is at risk for both our trains." Big John concluded.

Mr. Atkins contemplated for a moment: "I agree assuming you have experience fighting Comancheros?"

"I do." Big John replied point blank.

"I agree then, captain," Mr. Atkins agreed to Big John's overall command.

Captain Atkins also agreed to have his scouts report to Hedge. The organization was complete, they agreed to meet for a war counsel the next morning at Big John's camp.

Chapter Fifty-One

Planning the Fight that Needed to be Won! Or Lose Life and Liberty

The morning air was chilly. Dew was clinging to the grass leaves. Like Catherine, the women in the other wagon train were preparing breakfast. They would wait for the war counsel to end before serving anything other than coffee.

The war counsel began as the sun peeked over the eastern horizon. All the men were present except for two scouts: Eagle Eye and one of Mr. Atkins' scouts, a Navajo named "Ahiga" or "He Fights." They stood watch south of the river.

Big John towered over Mr. Atkins physically. In short order, after discussing tactics and strategies, it became clear Mr. Atkins was the smartest man in both wagon trains.

Big John asked Mr. Atkins point blank: "What was your rank in the rebellion Captain Atkins?"

"Brigadier General, United States Army sir, and yours?" Mr. Atkins replied and asked.

"Captain, United States Army, 11th Infantry, Iowa Volunteer Regiment. Under Commanding Officer Colonel Abraham Hare and later Colonel William Hall sir," Big John replied.

Captain Atkins turned and declared to the entire group of men assembled: "I am proud to serve under Captain John. Gentlemen, the 11th Iowa was under General Sherman from the beginning to the end of the war. Their bravery at Shiloh will never be forgotten," he said with sincere pride in his voice.

"What happened?" Bill Antrim asked.

"General Grant was caught asleep in the wheel house, as the old saying goes. He believed the Confederates were fifty miles south of his camp at Pittsburg Landing. He was wrong! They attacked on the morning of the 6th of April, 1862 completely surprising General Grant. He was literally still asleep. The entire Union army collapsed except the center. You got it, it was the 11th Iowa. they held, suffering one of the worse casualties of any regiment in the war, but they held!"

He continued, "General Grant was given the time to expedite his own reinforcements, and the arrival of Major General Don Buell Army of the Ohio for more reinforcements. That was enough to turn the battle to a victory for the Union. Keep in mind that General Grant had in the end defeated the best two generals the Confederate States had in General Albert Sidney Johnston and General P. G. Beauregard.

General Atkins concluded, "The battle of Pittsburg Landing (Shiloh) was the first major victory for the Union Army. That drew President Lincoln's attention to General Ulysses S. Grant as a winner, which led to him eventually leading the entire Union Army. All that because the 11th Regiment held the center line at Pittsburg Landing."

Most of the men listening clapped. The ones that did not were most likely former Confederate soldiers.

Big John allowed all this war discussion to go on because he saw how all the men were hanging on every word General Atkins was saying. It was obvious Atkins was a great orator. Also, his talk was a good "pep-talk" for the coming battle.

"Thank you General Atkins. Now, General, I would like to hear your proposed strategy to defeat the forty-to-fifty creatures from hell we are about to fight tomorrow?" Big John asked professionally and respectfully.

"Yes sir, I have thought about this in anticipation for our meeting this morning." General Atkins said and went on to explain:

"They will be concerned about resupplying their efforts. I have a wagon load of dynamite for the Maxwell Mining District. Tonight a small squad of our best scouts could blow the hell out of their supply wagons, scatter their animals, and escape back."

Hedge and Eagle Eyes raised their hands to volunteer. Another man in Big John's outfit stepped up and said:

"I scouted out of Springfield for two years, and I'm still here."

"Your name sir?" General Atkins asked.

"Joking around I call myself Dave Tutt," he said with a chuckle.

Henry got so excited because he knew that name very well. Wild Bill Hickok had killed Tutt in fair street fight. Every magazine he read covered it a couple times a year. He was so excited he almost gave his hiding place away.

"What is your real name, sir?" the general asked again.

"Pawnee Smith, sir. My father named me after Jedidiah Smith, my mother was Pawnee" Pawnee answered.

Big John spoke up: "We need one more volunteer. How about you Mr. Tucker? Do you have experience?"

The tall, black-skinned man replied: "My name is Cleef. Yes, I do. I will go."

Big John nor General Atkins asked anything more about Cleef's qualifications. The answer was written all over the man's face.

Big John got quite serious:

"Hedge, Eagle Eyes, Pawnee, Cleef, this could be a suicide mission. It is highly likely you may not get back. If they discover you, the odds are forty-to-four." Big John stated straight-up how dangerous the mission would be.

"You trying to cheer us up?" Cleef joked. Eagle Eyes laughed out loud.

"Just trying to tell you the truth, but you just might save all the lives on both these wagon trains. If it is your last day, you will never be forgotten." Big John concluded with a sincere emotion in his voice. Very unusual for him.

"What's your plan?" Cleef asked directly.

Hedge stepped forward extending his arm to Cleef. Cleef clasped his arm half way to the elbow in a show of a warrior's brotherhood.

Big John answered Cleef's question:

"Cleef, you just met the head of scouts, Mr. Hedge. That man there is Eagle Eyes, my Pawnee scout who lives up to his name."

He then turned to the General Atkins: "I know you enough to know you have been further thinking about our situation. Share your thoughts?"

"You are correct, I have been thinking a lot more on our situation, and I think you are more experienced fighting Comancheros," the general replied.

Big John quickly replied: “If that was a rebel general over there, what would you do beyond blowing up their supplies?”

“First I would realize they are a fierce fighting force that will attempt to scare the hell out of us enough to throw us off our game. Probably attack from several directions to confuse our retaliation attempts, or at least to cause us to make a fateful mistake,” General Atkins answered.

”Perfect! I agree General. What do you think of a wagon with five of our best shooters armed with repeaters? Then when they attack it breaks rank and draws raiders to them.”

“Suddenly, the canvas would be thrown back and all the men will open fire on their horses first, then on the riders as they fall to the ground.”

Big John went on to say: “Also, we will tie all the remaining wagons together to free up their drivers for fighting. Each lead animal will be roped to the back of the wagon in front of it. I figure between both our trains we would then have fifty fighting men.”

Big John gave his plan to even the odds and then gave his fighting plan: “After crossing the river, we’ll send twenty men upstream and twenty men downstream. They will cover the left and right flanks of the Comancheros. Our war wagon, with ten sharpshooters in it, will not be tied down. Then we do what they don’t expect, attack them! That wagon chases raiders wherever they go.” Big John concluded his war plan.

“I like it all except the ‘wherever’ part. Keep the war wagon close to the other wagons,” General Atkins suggested and explained: “That lessens the possibility of them dividing and conquering us. Also, have each man in the war wagon possess two sticks of dynamite. That gives each man the ability to blow up four or five raiders. They would have rained hell upon themselves.” General Atkins recommended and then added: “We will need the best skilled driver on the war wagon.”

Big John turned to Bill Antrim: “You got it. Bill, you are our best mule skinner.”

Henry was proud to hear that. Then Uncle Bill replied:

“I must tell you I was just a prison guard in Indianapolis during the war. I didn’t do any fighting, but I can drive. I’ll drive that wagon!”

"You will be so close to them your Colt will be effective," Big John informed, he knew Bill had a Colt pistol.

"I do have a repeater too," Bill replied.

"You won't have time for that, Bill. I need you zig-zagging all over the place. You will be our decoy. They will think you're trying to find an escape and charge at you. Then our boys will give them hell... right boys?" Big John shouted the latter.

All the men cheered and felt they were part of something bigger than their selves... which they were.

Hedge admonished: "Shhhhh! They could hear you men five miles away!"

The men just laughed. One man said: "I hope they did, they should prepare to meet their maker."

Big John and General Atkins were pleased with the men's positive attitude. That was a long way from where they were when the meeting first began. They sounded like fighting men now.

Henry knew they would break up the meeting soon, he needed to escape without being noticed. He crawled backwards to the other side of the wagon he was hiding under. He did so without making the slightest noise.

As he came out on the other side, there was Eagle Eyes again. He just stood there with his hands folded across his chest. Henry just tipped his bowl hat and took off to his wagon.

Henry reported all he heard to his mother. Josie listened, but had an obvious attitude of frustration. His mother had sent his younger brother to spy for her.

Catherine knew what he was thinking without asking. She addressed it immediately:

"Josie, you know Henry is a lot smaller than you. If I sent you, well, they would have probably discovered you. I know you are as brave and would have done your best. Do you understand?" She sincerely wanted to know.

"I know why," Josie replied as he jumped down off the wagon.

Catherine shook her head. She knew no matter what she said Josie would always believe she favored his little brother.

"Tomorrow, I drive this wagon, and you and Henry will lie down in the back." Josie said with authority. His message was clear. He was now a man and not a child. He then began to leave to check on the animals.

"Yes, sir!" Catherine said in a low voice she thought he couldn't hear.

Josie stopped and turned around and said: "Good!"

Catherine grinned ear-to-ear.

Everyone was busy preparing for the next day. Men were cleaning their guns. Doubling up the grain supplement for their animals. The animals would need the extra energy. Crossing the river was hard enough on them. Then they will be frightened by the fight. They needed all the energy they could store.

Women prepared the day's evening meals. Of course, fearing it may be their family's last supper.

Bill Antrim greased two wagons. The bedding camp wagon, the one that was going to be used as the war wagon and his own. That chore took several hours. Then he cleaned his pistol and rifle. All the while thinking about Big John's instructions of zig zagging the war wagon. Such a pattern was more difficult than the average man may think.

The scouts showed up to have dinner with the McCarty family. If it would be their last meal they wanted it to be Catherine's supper.

Chapter Fifty-Two

The Crossing

It was 3:30 am and the temperature was below freezing. The normal temperature this time of the year would be a low of 25 degrees, and this morning was all of that.

The thin air was full of the sounds of leather cracking and slapping as the scouts saddled their mounts. They kept their voices low as the Comancheros would have their own scouts watching the camp. The sound of leather would not travel far, but even a whisper would be heard on the other side of the river. Helping them was the rapid moving spring water of the Cimarron River.

Hedge had ordered the two groups of scouts and their fighting men to leave side by side north and south. That way an enemy scout would only see a profile of one to three men. That would be expected, several scouts looking for the best crossing, and would not raise any alarm.

It was a new moon of less than a quarter, but above a Crescent. There was just enough light to safely travel very slowly. That was the plan for the first few miles up and down the river. Then the unknown terrain would dictate their speed.

The one thing they could not control was their breath freezing in the air at these temperatures. Therefore, all men had their faces covered with a scarf. The horse's and mule's noses were also covered. That was Pawnee's idea, it was a good one.

The two groups left in synchrony. They were very quiet.

In the McCarty camp Josie and Henry had not slept a wink. They were sitting on the driver's bench watching all the preparation by the scouts and their men.

Although they knew not to talk Josie said in Henry's ear:

"You keep mother's head down when the fighting starts. She will try to join me, but that can't happen," Josie explained.

Catherine squeezed in between her two boys and said very lowly: "I promise to stay down boys, but right now I want to join you. We must not talk anymore. Just observe," she said as she wrapped her two arms around her boys.

They sat quietly and watched all the men leave. Although Catherine knew the plan, she felt less safe with all those men gone.

All the animals were acting as though they sensed something was happening. They were not their quiet selves. All the men leaving had them anxious.

The remaining people waited to sunrise to begin their crossing of the Cimarron River. Bill Antrim was in the lead war wagon with ten sharpshooters in it.

They had selected a crossing point at a small area above the big bend in the river. Up and down the river for miles were large embankments on the south side of the river.

After crossing they would head south/southwest along an easy low pass between ridges of mountains that stretched north-east to south-west of the river. About five miles from the river there was another narrow pass that would be a perfect place for an ambush.

Catherine became very busy keeping the animals in line during the crossing. Small talk stopped. Water was slapping the side of the wagon so hard Catherine thought it might collapse, but all went well.

After the entire two trains had crossed, Geraldo went to work.

Geraldo dismounted and tied his horse off with a long rope. Then taking another long rope, he tied their rear axle to the wagon behind them. Then tied a long rope from their lead mule to a hitch on the wagon in front of them. It took a half hour to complete all the wagons.

Many of the other wagons were being tied off by their drivers. Geraldo did all the wagons being driven by women.

Geraldo arrived back to the McCarty wagon. They thought he was going to untie his horse, he did not. He instead said:

"Buenas dias, señora. I drive your wagon now. Then your old son drive wagon and I shoot long gun," he said in rough, broken English. He did do well enough to get his message across.

Catherine replied: "Si señor, tu el jefe (Yes sir, you're the boss)." She remembered their previous conversation.

Geraldo smiled which showed all his perfectly aligned and white teeth. His dark tanned skin made his smile stand out. He was sincerely pleased she understood what he had said.

"Only for fight señora, only then," Geraldo gently informed her.

"I am happy you are with us, and so are my boys," Catherine was certainly telling the truth. She felt far more secure with Geraldo in their wagon.

Josie at first felt a bit slighted, but then thought to himself: "What man would turn down help to defend his family? None!" He felt better after that thought.

Geraldo informed Catherine: "I saw your young, cat-boy at the war counsel. He come back and tell you everything."

Then they heard a voice from the back of the wagon:

"I knew you saw me Geraldo. If I wanted, you wouldn't have seen me," Henry declared.

"I think not young cat," Geraldo replied.

"I think so," Henry had to get the last word.

Catherine enjoyed her son standing up for himself.

Henry was now right behind Geraldo studying how he handled the reins. He noticed Geraldo had each mule in individual control. The reins passed through his figures so that a twist of his wrist and/or a finger resulted in a specific direction for a mule.

He had seen a lot of mule skinners in his twelve years, but Geraldo was a master mule skinner. He heard that term used on Buck in Wichita, but it didn't mean anything at the time. He thought all mule skinners were the same. Now, he knew differently, he was watching a master at work and knew it. Geraldo was really good!

The driver ahead was having problems, specifically pulling the rope so taught it might snap. Geraldo was constantly trying to get slack without doing the same to the wagon behind him. Henry's quick mind saw the problem. He called back to his brother to have the wagon behind them pull forward more, giving slack in that rope. Josie did and added to relay the message to the wagons behind them. They all must keep slack in the rope.

Chapter Fifty-Three

Preparing to Ambush the Ambushers

The scout leading the men south soon realized the bank on the other side of the river was too high for several miles. Finally, they found a good place to forge the river and cross through a passage cut by an ancient river through the bank.

The trail ran all along the eastern side of the mountain range. It would position them perfectly to cross over the ridge and attack the east flank of the Comancheros.

Hedge was leading the men west. He found the Cimarron bending north-west. He found a good crossing just before the river took another bend west.

The problem was that they were now too far northwest of their assigned position on the west flank of the Comancheros. Fortunately, there was a line of trees along a tributary to the Cimarron. It ran south-east.

Hedge told the men in order to arrive in time to be effective, they must ride hard along the tree line to arrive in time. He had sent Eagle Eyes ahead to scout the path all the way to the Comancheros.

They took off at a full gallop for a mile. Then Hedge reduced them to a trot to rest the horses. A horse can trot thirty miles, but can't run full out but for a few miles.

Two miles from their destination Eagle Eye arrived with a good report. He had found a small pass in the mountain ridge that would position them on the Comancheros west flank. Furthermore, he saw no guards posted anywhere near it. That was great news.

Arriving at the west flank above the Comanchero camp, they could see the morning camp fires. There was very little smoke, and what was dissipated quickly in the morning air.

There was hustle bustle all over the camp. They noticed each man had at least a hundred rounds on a cross bandolier, two pistols, and one rifle. The rifles were a mix of single shot

Springfield, and Winchester repeaters. In-other-words, each man was armed to the teeth!

General Atkins had said they must hold absolutely still until the Comanchero leader orders the attack on the wagon train. Then they were to scream as loud as they could as they attack each flank!

They were to fight fire with fire. Frightening their fighters, and disillusioning their leader. Also, their screaming is the signal for the volunteer scouts to blow up the Comancheros supply wagons. All hell will break loose on them!

Hedge found it amazing just how well the plan was going, besides a few logistical problems, all was now well. They didn't have a clue they were completely surrounded. The strangest part was that guards were not posted where he would have strategically posted them.

Hedge then noticed jugs scattered all over the camp site. That was it! The Comancheros had drank all night long. A foolish thing to do the night before a fight.

The wagon train was two miles out when the wide pass came into full view. The sun had tipped the eastern low mountain range. The air was still cold enough to see your breath.

No one had to tell anyone on the train what was about to happen. They still felt very alone and scared. They knew the plan, but would it work? They knew they were calmly driving these wagons into hell.

Henry had a strange mixture of fear and excitement interacting with his mind going so fast. Thoughts seemed to race from one thing to another: "Protect mother, be ready to take the reins, hide in the wagon bottom, watch how the men fought these devils, and be ready to join the fight." Each seemed to contradict the other.

He remembered the same feeling when he witnessed the street fight in Wichita's Douglas Street. An Indian had gotten drunk and was shooting at anything that moved on Douglas Street near the bridge.

Henry was the thing moving at the time. Fortunately for him the Indian couldn't see accurately past the end of his arm. None-the-less, bullets flew near him as he zigged and zagged across the street and ran toward Main Street.

That Indian had emptied his gun trying to hit him. It was the last thing he did. Buck shot him dead with one shot a block away. Henry had turned to wee why the firing stopped. Just as he did he saw Buck's bullet slam into the Indian lifting off the ground and falling on his back. He didn't move a muscle.

Looking back up the block he saw smoke coming out of Buck's new 44-70 Sharps rifle. He waved a thank you to him and thought to himself: "I now know why only a foolish man would try to rob Buck's stage."

That same mixture of fear and excitement was with him now, and was increasing as they got closer to the pass.

Suddenly, Henry saw out of the corner of his eye an Indian pulling his horse back out of sight. He was a Comanchero scout and on his way to report to their leader.

Geraldo asked Catherine to lie down in the back of the wagon. She tried to pull Henry with her, but he refused and stayed directly behind his brother who was now driving.

Geraldo chambered a round into his Winchester rifle and moved to a better aiming position and said:

"Josie, the animals are yours now."

"Si señor," Josie politely replied.

They had reached the pass!

Chapter Fifty-Four

All Hell Breaks Loose!

Henry's keen ears picked up the Comanchero leader yelling: "Ataque, ataque, ataque! (Attack, attack, attack!)"

Suddenly, there were guns firing, and horses screeching cries of pain and agony. There were so many guns firing from so many directions it sounded like Gatling guns going off.

The war wagon Bill Antrim was driving pulled to the left. The first wagon after his followed and began to form a defensive circle. Some horse driven wagons tried to bolt away on their own, but could not. Tying them together paid off immediately.

The wagon behind the McCarty wagon had a mule let out an ear-piercing scream, bucking, and yanking all its tack with tremendous force. It had been hit several times, none with fatal shots. Several Comancheros had focused on killing that mule to stop the formation, or at least slow it down.

Comancheros were yelling at each other in Spanish. They fired volley after volley into the wagons, and from several directions. Their leader and ten men circled the wagons firing into them in rapid fire.

Bill Antrim pulled his war wagon out perpendicular to the circling wagons. He put himself in a side-on collision with about twenty Comancheros.

"Now!" Bill yelled out and the canvas cover was pulled back. He had pulled his wagon to the left just as the Comancheros approached.

Ten sharp shooters opened up on the attackers, and emptied twenty saddles! Amazingly, few of their horses were hit. Comancheros were flying out of their saddles bullet riddled as they hit the ground. Several were hit twice. All that violence in less than a couple minutes.

The Comancheros leader was wounded. Hanging over his saddle and gripping his horse's neck, he spurred his mount away from the fight.

Geraldo was focused directly on the outward side of the McCarty wagon. He levered his Winchester ten times and four Comancheros would not be seeing another sunrise.

It was total chaos from then on. Of the forty Comancheros half were dead, and ten were seriously wounded. Although the latter got away, they would not live long.

The remaining ten were scattering in all directions, high tailing their mounts away from the fight. It did not take them long to realize they were the ones being ambushed in a trap.

A couple men began to chase those escaping when Big John fired his shotgun into the air to get their attention. He ordered everyone to stop fighting and gather around him.

Women were crying, men and animals screaming in pain. Some men began celebrating their victory. Big John issued another order: "No celebrating. We have had to take men's lives. It had to be done, but no celebrating it."

"General, what are the casualties?" Big John asked calmly.

The General had anticipated the question and was prepared: "Two of our men killed, Thomas O'Reilly from my train and the very big man from your train, two of mine are not seriously wounded. Twenty renegades killed. I estimate ten mortally wounded and ten missing, assumed escaped." He said in a professionally.

Big John replied:

"The big man was Martin Hansen, the Swede. A good man. Very good report, sir."

"Now, put the animals and the mortally wounded out of their misery. Then..."

A woman from General Atkins train interrupted:

"Aren't you going to try and save them? Aren't going to bury all those poor souls?" she yelled at Big John through her hysterical crying.

"Poor souls? They just tried to kill you. No, ma'am, I am not. They chose to live like coyotes, they will die like coyotes."

"Fact is: by providing food for the vultures, it will be the only good thing they have done lately" Big John declared. He then turned back to General Atkins and said:

"General, please take a squad of sharp shooters and all our scouts to the renegade campsite."

"Determine, in your judgement, what women are gentle and bring them back. Those that you decide are being, or will be dangerous, kill them. Look for captives and bring them and all the children back. Assign them to wagons with women for care. I'll provide the food and comfort for all of them." He said militarily.

The same woman that had criticized him before blared out at him again:

"That is murder! You would kill a helpless woman?"

Big John was getting frustrated with her interruptions:

"A woman can kill you as fast as a man, and there is no fury as a woman scorned, ma'am. The good women in that camp will protect their children and cause no trouble. The others will most likely fight." Big John then turned to General Atkins:

"Are you still here, sir?"

"I am gone, sir!" General Atkins replied.

Big John addressed the remaining men: "Wrap up our dead and put them in the war wagon. We will bury them when we reach Salado Creek, which is where we will camp tonight."

Salado Creek wasn't far, but everyone had been through a lot that morning.

The burial party was sent ahead. By the time the trains reached the creek the two dead men had been buried and some branches used to form crosses.

Big John saw the crude crosses and ordered new ones to be erected with the lumber from his lumber supply wagon.

Also, George Slater, the man best with a knife, was to carve their names into the cross board and today's date.

He knew Martin Hansen was from Michigan, so that was added too. Catherine McCarty suggested Ireland to be on Thomas O'Reilly's cross. It was done.

General Atkins provided the eulogy service, and everyone was in attendance. He concluded the service with:

"Thank you God for these two men that gave their lives so that so many of us could live. Forgive all their sins and hold them tight in your arms for their great service to your children."

All the men and women present said:

"Amen!" in unison. It was a wonderful service, and all could tell it wasn't the General's first.

That night there were several camp fires with people talking about the fight, and they went on late into the evening. Although very tired, it gave them all comfort to talk to their fellow survivors. That is exactly how they felt, like survivors from hell itself.

Several families joined the McCarty camp fire. Also, José, Geraldo, and another older Mexican they did not know.

At first everyone was a bit uneasy. They thought the lone stranger amongst them may be a Comanchero. He had returned with General Atkins from the Comancheros camp.

Then José introduced him as: "José Montoya de Don Fernando de Taos who was a captive of the Comancheros."

Everyone could tell that name meant something to the vaqueros. Geraldo almost knocked his hat off looking up at the man.

Geraldo excitedly asked: "Es su relacion con Pablo Montoya la Santa Ana Del Norte?"

"Si, su hijo," the stranger replied in Spanish.

José translated as Geraldo always spoke Spanish when excited. "This man's father is Pablo Montoya La Santa Ana Del Norte. Who is very, how you say... famous in New Mexico."

Catherine welcomed him to join their camp and share their food.

José Montoya accepted Catherine's invitation in very good English. Even José and Geraldo were surprised at the perfect English diction and accent.

Henry was also amazed. As always, he was listening carefully, but this time he didn't have to hide. He always seemed mesmerized by those that could speak those two languages so very well. One day he was determined to do the same.

REST AND RECUPERATION

Big John walked from one camp fire to the next making sure everyone was alright and announcing they would be resting animals and people for another day. He knew both had been through a lot that day. For some, it was their first violent confrontation of any kind.

The Atkins party had come from St. Louis on the Santa Fe Trail. They were told to take the new Raton Pass Trail as it would be "safer." All they could think at this moment was they could not imagine any place more unsafe.

Coming across the plains the only trouble they had were the large herds of Buffalo. If stampeded they could wipe out a train like theirs in minutes.

At the time they were looking for savage Indians. Their scout said: "Don't worry about Indians, worry about a lightning strike on a herd of a million buffalo." Fortunately, neither happened.

They did meet a train whose wagons were filled to the top with Buffalo hides. Who could miss the stench of rotting buffalo meat west of Fort Dodge? No one! They prayed the next day they would get out of the smell range, or at least the wind would shift.

The fight they experienced this day would never be forgotten. It happened quickly but was so very violent.

General Atkins' trip to the Comanchero camp had resulted in collecting ten women, five children, and one hostage being held for ransom. The latter was José Montoya.

Geraldo asked him how he learned English so well.

He replied: "My father sent me to St Louis to learn the language, customs, and culture of the Americans. He wasn't a friend of the Americans, but wanted one in his family to learn their ways. The Comancheros kept me alive because they thought they could get a big ransom for me. Of course, I was the one that convinced them of that." He said with a big smile.

The whole group gathered shared in the humor, and had their first laughter since the fight.

Geraldo spoke frankly: "His father was a traitor, both to Mexico and to the Americans. No good man," he said in his broken English.

José started to admonish his friend for insulting a guest.

José Montoya interrupted:

"No...he is right! My father was not an honorable man. He paid the price for that when Colonel Price hung him and fourteen others in the Taos Square in 1847. He paid the price and I am not my father!" Then he looked into Geraldo's eyes and said:

"If you are calling me dishonorable, we will have trouble together," Mr. Montoya said firmly.

Geraldo replied just as firmly: "I don't call you dishonorable. I don't know you" Clearly reflecting he was not intimidated by anyone.

Catherine interrupted, breaking the icy atmosphere: "Well, I think we have some experts here that could tell us something about Santa Fe. That is all of our destination and few of us know much about it. Please, anyone that would like to inform us, join in.

Chapter Fifty-Five

A History Lesson from the Stranger

The others yielded to José Montoya. His family lived many generations in northern New Mexico.

In a much calmer, friendlier tone Mr. Montoya began to answer Catherine's curiosity, but first he had a question:

"How far back would you like to go, ma'am?"

"As far as you know sir," Catherine answered sincerely.

"Santa Fe was named by the second Spanish Governor: Don Pedro de Peralta. Its true name is La Villa Real de La Santa Fe de Dan Francisco de Assis. In English: The Royal City of the Holy Faith of Saint Francis of Assisi. More commonly known as Santa Fe."

"You said second Spanish Governor. Who was the first Governor?" Catherine inquired. Her son Henry was intently hanging on every word. He repeated the names several times to memorize what he thought was important. Josie was bored to death, and left to check on the animals.

"Don Juan de Onate in 1598, but his villa was north of what is Santa Fe today and they called it Ogapoge in the Tewa language. The first people were the Tanoan, who had settlements all along the Santa Fe and Rio Grande Rivers. Some say they have been there a thousand years," Mr. Montoya explained.

"Did you learn all that back east?" a curious Henry asked.

Mr. Montoya smiled as he replied.

"No, I did not. They knew little of our history here. They had the Taos Rebellion and the destruction of Taos by Colonel Price. Oh, yes, also the search for the seven cities of gold called Cibola by Francisco Vazquez de Coronado."

Henry lit up with gold fever: "Are they real...the cities of gold?" Henry asked excitedly.

"Not that I know of. Coronado went home to Spain a broken man in great debt," Mr. Montoya replied.

Henry followed up: "Maybe he just didn't look hard enough," that statement brought a chuckle from Mr. Montoya.

"Young man, in 1554 Coronado had 300 Spaniards and 800 Indians in his expedition. They covered all of what we call Texas, Indian Country, Kansas, Colorado, Arizona, and New Mexico. He did find Cibola, but it was a simple Zuni Indian village. No, someone led him down the wrong path from the beginning." Mr. Montoya concluded.

Catherine interrupted: "Henry, that is enough about gold, we want to know more about where we are going to call home."

"Yes, ma'am" Henry acknowledged.

Mr. Montoya picked up where he left off, at least he thought he left off:

"For a long time Santa Fe was a military post and Taos was the New Mexico Territorial government center. When Colonel Price destroyed Taos, he moved the territorial government to Santa Fe. It has been there ever since. Today it remains the government, financial, and cultural center for New Mexico Territory. Well, kind of that."

Catherine interrupted again: "Why, kind of that?" she inquired.

"Southern and Northern New Mexico has always been two different worlds. Texans call southern New Mexico: The Badlands. They are accurate in that description too," Mr. Montoya declared.

Steve Adams, the older son in the Adams family that had joined the McCarty's' for dinner, asked pointedly: "Exactly what do you mean by Badlands?"

José Montoya replied with a question: "Is that where your family is headed?"

"Yes, we heard the Mesilla Valley has very good land," the young man replied.

"It is a beautiful valley fed by the Rio Grande River."

José went on to explain:

"To answer your question, why I agree with the Texans that call all southern New Mexico 'the badlands'? That is simple, there is no real law there... Well, there are sheriffs in Don Ana and Lincoln Counties, but they all work for the Santa Fe Ring."

Catherine interrupted: "Who are they? This Santa Fe Ring?"

José thought for a moment on how exactly to answer

that question. It was more complex than what meets the eye. He did have a unique position in understanding the Santa Fe Ring.

"They are a group of businessmen and attorneys that control everything in the territory. They own the judges, lawmen, merchants, politicians...everyone!" José answered honestly. It was not a good picture for these newcomers to the New Mexico Territory.

"Do these leaders of the Santa Fe Ring have names?" Catherine asked point blank.

Mr. Montoya knew he was now on dangerous ground. The Santa Fe Ring enforced their will on the people in steps of pressure. First, they use financial pressure, next they inserted legal pressure, lastly they simple hired killers to eliminate the problem.

What he was about to tell the group gathered around the McCarty fire would bring him immediately to their ultimate control technique, have him killed. No question about it. He decided these good people needed to know the political environment they were moving into, and he would tell them the truth.

"Stephen Elkins and Thomas Catron are the leaders of the Santa Fe Ring. There are many smaller leaders, but they all yield to the decisions of Elkins and Catron," José Montoya explained.

He went on to give an example he was very familiar with:

"We are now camped in Colfax County. There has been a war going on here since Elkins became President of the Maxwell Land Company..."

One of Big John's experienced mule skinners, Pat Wagner, interrupted: "I know Lucien Maxwell. I have met him, many years ago. Mexicans were saying he stole their land. He did not seem like one that would do such a thing," Pat declared.

"Your observation is correct. My family knew his family very well. He was an honest man. In 1858 a man named Carlos Miranda sold one million acres to Lucien Maxwell for a total of $2,745."

The whole group gasped at such a low amount for so many acres.

Bill Antrim was first to ask what was on everyone's mind:

"Why so low an amount?" Bill was always on top of the numbers.

"People said Miranda had escaped to Mexico in fear that the Americans would hang him as they did my father. He was probably right about that. Like my father Miranda had supported the Taos Revolt. To Miranda the land was worthless. He was never returning to New Mexico. He liked Maxwell, who had married his partner's daughter. His partner Carlos Beaubien passed away leaving his half of the grant to Maxwell."

"What was his total acreage then?" Bill Antrim quickly asked.

"Maxwell then owned one million, seven hundred thousand acres." [94]

"How do you know so much about these people?" Big John asked point blank.

José replied: "I am representing three parties: Department of Indian Affairs, United States Treasury, and a large British investment company interested in buying his land. The problem is that many of the early settlers in this county are challenging his legal right to several portions of the original Mexican Grant. I must sort the mess out before we can continue with the purchase." Mr. Montoya explained.

"What are the early settlers claiming?" Big John followed up.

"The Cimarron area ranchers say that Miranda abandoned his grant after the Mexican-American War. All abandoned grants become public land, which they then could file homesteads on, and they did just that." José went on to explain his interest:

"My job is to investigate all the documents, evidence, and testimony. Then report my opinion to the Justice Department in Washington D.C. who will make the final decision. It could take years to settle," José concluded.

Big John asked: "Are you a lawyer?"

"I am, sir. I am also an accountant, and since I am fluent in both languages involved, I was selected for this terrible task." José added with a smile.

---

[94] This was one of the largest contiguous land ownership in the history of the United States of America.

Big John added: "I have heard of the two men you mentioned as the leaders of the Ring. I have been told to stay clear of them, it would be best not to do business with them. What is your opinion?"

Without hesitation José Montoya replied: "My job is to collect the evidence and then make a recommendation. I have not completed my investigation, and therefore it would not be proper to come to any conclusions yet. I can tell you that Stephen Elkins and Thomas Catron have applied for ownership recognition on over thirty Spanish and Mexican land grants, which total almost two million acres." José informed Big John.

"Is the Maxwell Grant in that total?" Big John inquired.

"No sir, it is not. As I said, Stephen Elkins is the President of the Maxwell Land Company, and therefore will control over three million acres should all their applications be approved." Mr. Montoya informed them.

"Wow! That is an incredible story. It certainly explains how and why they control everything in the territory," Catherine observed.

"Yes ma'am, it most likely does. Unfortunately, my focus remains only with the legal title of the grants. Someone else will have to address the political and corruption issues of the territory." Mr. Montoya replied.

Big John had a follow-up question: "What about the Territorial Governor?"

"I can give you my opinion on that subject. I like Territorial Governor Marsh Giddings. He is an honest man and a hard worker."

"President Grant had first asked his former Brigadier General Willard Warner, who was then Senator from Alabama to be the governor. He flatly turned down the opportunity. President Grant then asked Marsh Giddings, and Giddings accepted the offer. In my investigation I found he had an excellent political record. He was well liked and took care of business. Grant appointed him Counselor to India. He could not go to India due to health issues. Then Grant appointed him as Territorial Governor for New Mexico Territory. Having said all that, the Santa Fe Ring still rules with everything that matters in the Territory. They call the shots."

Big John declared: "It sounds like the advice I got was good advice."

"Probably so, sir, probably so!" José haphazardly agreed.

Steve Adams thought out loud: "What have I gotten my family into?"

José volunteered: "I have talked too much! I don't mean that New Mexico is a helpless cause. We need good people like you folks for the future of New Mexico. The Mesilla Valley is beautiful! It should be a wonderful place to live and grow your family. Sir, anywhere in the frontier is rough now... anywhere! You are the settlers, you will bring the good civilization to this land. Be patient with our lady New Mexico. She is a bit wild now, but working together we'll tame her." José declared.

Steve Adams spoke next: "I hope you are right. I just want to start a mercantile store."

José replied and suggested: "You should do fine in Mesilla Valley. I would suggest the new fort town of Los Cruces. They need a good merchant."

"Don't let anyone talk you into anywhere in Lincoln County." José said authoritatively.

"Why is that, sir?" Mr. Adams inquired.

"Laurence G. Murphy, that is why." José answered point blank and continued: "He owns Lincoln County, lock, stock and barrel. Catron is his financier. This means he has the full force of the Santa Fe Ring behind him. Competing with him is a death warrant ready to be issued" José said matter-of-factly.

"Los Cruces is your best bet," José declared.

Catherine and her family were listening intently. She did speak up now: "Big John Henry, thank you and the General for saving this man. Mr. Montoya may have saved Mr. Adams and his family with this advice," Catherine volunteered.

That brought a small applause from those gathered.

"Thank you, ma'am, but your men, both trains, broke up the most vicious Comanchero outfit I've ever seen, or heard of."

Big John replied and continued:

"Everyone did their part and there was not one coward in the group! I was blessed to have all of them during our hour of need." Big John then turned to all the men gathered:

"You all deserve to give yourself a round of applause."

They did exactly that and began leaving the McCarty camp fire to return to their own wagons.

"Mr. Montoya, please stay for a minute," Catherine requested.

During all this Henry had taken all that was said in like a sponge. On the trail he had learned so much staying hidden while adults talked. At night there was always a crowd around his mother's cooking camp. There he didn't have to hide, but he knew not to speak before being spoken to.

Henry wasn't just learning facts and opinions, but also how people reacted to certain information.

José Montoya agreed to stay as long as Catherine needed him too.

"Thank you, sir" Catherine sincerely said.

"Ma'am, please just call me José. It would be my honor for you to do so," José requested.

"José, you mentioned that Ring in Santa Fe owns everything in Lincoln County, is it the same in Santa Fe?"

Catherine intended to open a roadhouse.

"Ma'am, it could be rough anywhere on the frontier. I think Santa Fe is a good town. Sure, it is being run by some ambitious and greedy men. But, again where will you not find that now-a-days?" José asked rhetorically.

"I understand that. I had a business in Wichita and it certainly had many of those kinds of men." Catherine admitted.

"Wichita!" José smiled and continued:

"Santa Fe will be a Sunday-go-to-meeting town for you."

Catherine grinned and replied: "I hope you are right Mr. Montoya...ah...José."

"You will do fine ma'am, and buenas noches, señora," he said as he rose to join Big John Henry and return to his wagon.

Catherine turned her attention to her two boys:

"It is time to clean dishes and feed the animals before tucking in," she informed her two boys.

Josie took off to feed the animals and check on their picket line. Henry poured water into a large bucket and placed in on the fire to heat up. He then went to work washing the dishes. Josie returned just as Henry finished up.

Henry declared on his arrival:

"Someday, mother will exchange our duties and you can do the dishes and I can feed the animals."

Catherine looked up and realized her youngest son was right. There was no reason for the boys to always do the same work.

"Maybe, I will think that over" Catherine said to the chagrin of Josie. He really didn't like that idea one bit.

Henry grinned that cat-with-a-feather-in-his-mouth smile. Both the boys knew what it meant when mother said "Maybe." It meant she liked the idea or at least it was a fair suggestion.

"Good night, Mother." Henry said as he hopped up into the wagon.

The next morning both wagon trains crossed the small Salado Creek. Both animals and people were well rested.

Big John assigned José Gonzales and José Montoya to the McCarty wagon for the remainder of the trip. They would trade off driving and guarding.

Big John was far more cautious with all that he did after the Comanchero attack. He knew their prime target was the women and children they could sell. He felt responsible for their safety. He had not asked Catherine or Bill Antrim their permission, which he didn't need to do. He just did it.

Catherine thanked him later for it. Only Josie and Henry complained. They thought they could take care of the wagon and their mother themselves.

Las Vegas, New Mexico Territory

Above: Las Vegas Hanging Windmill. Located in the town plaza. Quite possibly these people are awaiting the hanging of "law-breaker". They also hung an Indian from the mill just to send a message to other local Indians to not think of attacking their township. Las Vegas, New Mexico was a very rough town during the time the McCarty family passed through there. They believed in having lawmen that were worse than the other bad guys. Source: City of Las Vegas Museum

Left: Old Las Vegas Freighter, Source: Palace of the Governors Photo Archives

Right: The structure in the center of Plaza Park is where the old Hanging Windmill was located. Seems peaceful enough now. Historical note: The building directly in the background is where Doc Holliday last practiced as a Dentist. Building to the right and in the background, is the Plaza Hotel. Doc and Big Nose Kate resided there. He operates a card game in its saloon, and there was an attempted assassination while he descended their staircase. The assassin missed, and Doc did not, although his second shot went wild and that bullet supposedly is still in a wall there.

Chapter Fifty-Six

Las Vegas, New Mexico Territory

Both wagon trains made very good time. It took only five days to reach the outskirts of Las Vegas. Each night Gerald San Martin Vegas, José Gonzales, and José Montoya ate with the McCarty family. Beyond the obvious, Catherine's great cooking and the two José's assignments, the two vaqueros enjoyed Henry's sincere interest in learning their language.

As per Big John Henry's instructions the two José's had their bedrolls just outside the McCarty campfire. They took shifts and kept the fire going all night.

Mr. Montoya continued to give history lessons at the campfire to all that wanted him to share his knowledge. He light-heatedly commented to Catherine: "Ma'am, I think I missed my calling. I should have been a teacher."

"We do appreciate your sharing your knowledge, it is invaluable information for us. If you asked me, I think you are doing now what the Good Lord has called you to do."

"Of course, ma'am, I believe you are correct in that observation."

Catherine asked: "What can you tell us about Las Vegas, Mr. Montoya?"

All ears perked up when Mr. Montoya spoke: "Las Vegas has been a very old frontier camp on the Santa Fe Trail. Good water from the Gallinas River and tall green grass. The Indians have camped here for hundreds of years just as we are doing. It became Las Vegas in 1835 when The Plaza was built to act as a fortification protecting the travelers on the Santa Fe Trail."

Mr. Montoya continued, "Currently it is most famous as the place where Stephen Kearny gave his speech at the end of the Mexican-American War, declaring all of New Mexico Territory for the United States of America. That speech sent terror over the whole territory. That was the first my people had learned Mexico had given the territory to the U.S...

Just imagine you were granted land from the King of Spain, or the President of Mexico. The land was measured by how far you can ride a horse for one day to each of the four corners of your land. That is about forty thousand acres as your people measure such things. You have protected your land grant with your life. Some had to do so for generations. Then you are told your land is not part of Mexico any more. Have you just lost everything? Were the Americans going to confiscate what you spent a life time building?

No one knew the details of the Hidalgo Guadalupe Agreement signed by Mexico and the United States. For example, all the local population instantly became United States citizens. Had they not, I think the Santa Fe Ring would not be so powerful. It was here in Las Vegas, that important speech was given."

Geraldo, usually very quiet, interrupted: "I was born here. You forgot to mention the Hot Springs, Señor Montoya," he declared.

"Si, si, señor. You are right! How could I forget that?" Mr. Montoya replied and continued:

"Mr. Vegas is correct. I must include the Montezuma Hot Springs! People travel from all over the frontier to the healing hot springs. If you go there you may be sitting next to a Governor, Mayor, or a famous outlaw," he chuckled aloud.

"What he says is true. I know because that happened to me! No, I will not say who I met there. It is said to be very bad luck to ever name anyone you met there," Geraldo said with a smile.

Geraldo's friend José said: "Si, it was the other man who met you, a bandito famoso." Everyone broke in laughter, it needed no translation.

"Many believe sometime the iron horse will come through here. Raton Pass is the best for a railroad. It makes good sense. I know Mr. Chisum is betting on it. He is building the largest herd in all of Texas and New Mexico" José Montoya speculated.

José Gonzales volunteered: "Si, señor, I worked for John Chisum for over a year. He is a tough man. A hard man to work for. No siesta with him. Siesta is when the sun goes down. I told him we work better and harder with a siesta after the high sun meal. No señor! He catches you and you're down the hoot owl trail."

"Is that why you left him?" Catherine asked.

"Oh no señora, I go away because my friend here told how great this job is." José pointed to Geraldo and continued: "Señora, he forgot to mention the Comancheros," every got a chuckle from that.

"I never saw them before I talked to you...maybe you bring them with you, my bandito friend," Geraldo quickly replied in jest.

Those two were always jabbing each other, and everyone knew they were like brothers. It was entertaining for the travelers.

Big John Henry interrupted and asked: "I have heard some big things about John Chisum. How many cattle does the man have in the Pecos Valley?"

José replied the best he could: "Not sure, even when I rode for him I did not see all the herd. I worked Basque Rotunda. I was told by his, how you say brother's son?"

"Nephew." Catherine answered.

"His nephew told me when I worked there he had 50,000 head" José estimated.

"That is a lot and that is what I heard too," Big John acknowledged.

Catherine, as a business person, was very interested in when the railroad would come to Las Vegas, because soon after it would go to Santa Fe. She asked José Montoya his opinion and he replied:

"Ma'am, the land speculators say one-to-two years, but more realistically it will be five-to-six years. There are too many disputed land titles all along the route, no matter what direction they take. Nearly all of the Mexican and Spanish land grants in the northern New Mexico Territory are in dispute. It will be years before any railroad company will know who they can buy from," José explained.

Big John Henry walked from wagon to wagon making sure everyone knew he had decided to stay a full three days in Las Vegas. The General's wagon train would do the same.

It was time to get a good night's rest. The boys started their chores. Catherine said good night to everyone. It was her good Irish manners that left no one out. They all had a good time and enjoyed José Montoya's exceptional knowledge of the area. They knew they were very fortunate to have saved him from his captors.

The next morning after their morning chores Josie and Henry got permission to explore the small town of Las Vegas.

Catherine agreed, but that they were to be on their best behavior and return in the afternoon in time to do their chores before supper. The boys agreed.

Chapter Fifty-Seven

The McCarty Boys Visit Las Vegas

It was a very exciting trip for the McCarty boys. Even for Josie. They scampered up the creek to town. Then they took Bridge Street toward the old Plaza.

Most of the buildings were a mixture of adobe and wooden structures. It was completely different to Wichita. That had been built by easterners, and there was some unity in construction design. Las Vegas was hodge-podge of designs. Even though they seemed to build in somewhat of a line toward the Plaza. Some buildings were set back, and some were not.

Adobe buildings seemed to all be connected. Most were two-story adobes, but practically none were aligned together. One would be set back, one would have a small yard, almost all a small balcony on the second story. From a distance it looked like an irregular mud cliff with holes scattered in it.

Large wooden ladders leaned against the small walls on the second story rooms. It was the only access to the second story. Dogs and a few naked children were running all over the place. It definitely gave the appearance of an ancient township. The closer the McCarty boys got to the plaza the better the buildings became, more well-built wooden structures.

The boys entered the Plaza area, and both froze in their tracks. Before them in the center of The Plaza was a tall wooden tower over a water well. Hanging from one cross board was an Indian, a quite dead Indian!

Both boys were startled by a by a commanding voice from behind them: “That is what happens to law breakers around here.” The voice was low, monotone, and authoritative.

Henry’s quick mind asked: “What law did he break?”

“He was an Indian with bad intentions. We will leave him up there awhile to let other Indians know not to get such bad intentions. We hung two street Arab kids last week, who broke into Walker’s Store,” the man informed.

Josie wasn't buying that one: "No, you didn't. You're just trying to scare us."

Henry interrupted: Well, he is doing a good job of it!"

The man laughed out-loud and replied to Henry: "Is he your big brother?"

"Yes, sir he is," Henry said politely.

The man liked these two Irish lads.

"Well, he is right, I was joshing you youngin's... But it is true that we take street Arabs real seriously in Las Vegas. So you two behave...got that?"

The boys answered in unison: "Yes, sir!" Henry added: "We sure will!"

"That is good." The man suggested: "Let your folks know at the wagon train, the weather here has extreme changes. Like today it can be beautiful during the day, downright hot in the afternoon and be freezing at night. Their water barrels can freeze. You boys use extra blankets on you at night." Although he was still authoritative his voice was much kinder.

"Are you camped at Gallinas Creek?" the man asked pointedly.

"We don't know. We hiked down a creek to the bridge and came up this street," Josie replied pointing down Bridge Street toward the bridge.

"OK, that is Gallinas Creek. North of the bridge has great grass and a good place to rest your animals. I assume you boys are heading for Santa Fe?"

Josie replied: "Yes, sir. We're just resting animals and people."

The big man rubbed his chin in a contemplative manner and asked: "Did you boys hear about a big fight up north two weeks ago, where dozens of men were killed?"

Josie started to reply, but Henry interrupted: "Two weeks ago? No sir. Our wagon trains fought off Comancheros that tried to rob us." Henry's intelligence told him this man was more than just a Las Vegas curious citizen.

"Oh, I see. Maybe the same story. Comancheros huh?"

Josie replied: "Yes sir, Comancheros."

"Ok boys, skedaddle back to your train before you earn a hanging like that Indian," he said with a chuckle.

"Yes, sir!" Henry said as he turned and took off at a run

down the street like an escaping convict. Josie was several strides behind.

The man thought to himself: "That older brother will never catch the little guy. He is fast as lightning and runs like a cat with buck shot in his rear." Then he chuckled out-loud.

Upon returning to their wagon they excitedly related to their mother and Uncle Bill their experience in The Plaza, and with the man in Las Vegas.

Bill Antrim called Big John Henry over who happened to be walking by. He had the boys repeat the story to him.

Big John said: "I smell trouble. We'll take a wide trail around Las Vegas day after tomorrow (leaving a day earlier than planned). We will travel a few days and rest again at the Pecos River." Big John decided on the spot.

After briefing General Atkins and obtaining his agreement, Big John called a meeting of both wagon trains:

"Based on information I have received, I do not trust the law in Las Vegas. We will leave one day early and make a large swing around the town. We do not want any men to go into town. If you do, you do so at your own risk and if buffaloed, we will not rescue you. We will not risk the lives of other people for one fool who doesn't obey orders." Big John Henry made himself clear knowing some really wanted to hurrah in town.

"You will find nothing but buffalos in town," Big John concluded his announcement.

Josie asked his mother: "What does he mean they will only find buffalos in town? We were just there and there were no buffalo in town."

Street smart and well-read Henry answered before Catherine had a chance to say anything:

"Buffaloing is a hit over the head with a black-jack or pistol barrel," Henry informed Josie.

Catherine looked at Henry and said:

"Maybe I should be checking those magazines closer that you read so much?" Obviously, a rhetorical question.

"Too late Mother," Henry smiled.

Catherine immediately replied: "You better keep the Good Lord on your side, or you'll pay a God-awful price young man."

"Yes, Mother, I understand." Henry assured his mother.

Chapter Fifty-Eight

Back on the Trail to Santa Fe

Both wagon trains left making a wide berth around Las Vegas. The animals were well rested, even though they left one day early. They were making good time and arrived as planned at the Pecos River in three days.

Also arriving at the Pecos River was a hard core looking group of men. They were mounted on good horses, excellent saddles, and fancy tack.

Big John Henry, General Atkins and José Montoya approached the men. Their scouts Hedge and Pawnee took both flanks, which sent a clear message to the strangers.

Those two scouts had the appearance of man killers whom would not hesitate to take on the entire gang by themselves.

The man that appeared to be their leader spoke first:

"No trouble for ya'll here, boys. We are on our way to sign up with John Chisum. He put the word out he will now pay fifty dollars a month for drovers that can shoot straight. Mescalero Apache Indians are raiding his remuda. He is said to not mind them taking some beeves for food in the winter, but when they turned to his remuda, all hell broke loose. Now he wants them punished."

Big John Henry replied: "I know the cost of animals now-a-days. I can understand that. Not only is he out the horse, but it leaves him one drover short too."

"You are welcome in our camp if you leave the hardware behind on your horses. That way you show us you have no bad intentions." Big John said firmly.

A man in the rear of the group of strangers spurred his black stallion with a fifty-dollar pair of spurs. He stopped directly in front of Big John, nudging the other man over. Although a smaller framed man, he spoke in a deep authoritative voice:

"It is a free country, and we'll do what we damn well please," he said as he arrived in front of Big John.

Big John Henry did not flinch when he replied: "Yes sir, you are right about that, and you have the right to die too!"

The foolish young man started for his side arm on his hip. Big John had a cross draw holster and had his colt out cocked and aimed at the man's head before he cleared leather.

A man that had been quiet the whole time, and was directly behind the first man that spoke to them, moved forward and spoke at the same time:

"Whoa there boys! You two hot heads get to the rear and out of my sight. If you clear leather I will kill you first!" The man talking was the real leader of this group of strangers.

Both the hot headed young men swung their mounts around immediately, doing exactly as they were instructed.

Big John holstered his gun. He also knew the leader had given him a message too. That message was that he was extremely fast and accurate. He had said that if they drew their guns "he would kill them first." Big John got the idea that man could do exactly that.

In the time he pulled his trigger the man would have placed a bullet in someone's heart, and it may, or may not be, one of his men.

The man introduced himself to Big John Henry:

"I'm John Kinney of Mesilla Valley. Don't listen to those two hot heads, their still wet behind the ears. You won't have any trouble from my boys, as long as you don't start any."

"And your name, sir?" he asked friendlily.

"John Henry, most people just call me Big John," he too answered friendly enough.

"Well Big John Henry, please take no offense, but we will not disarm. We will camp up river, and the boys will stay clear of your camps and your animals," John Kinney offered as a peace agreement.

John Kinney knew those two scouts were ready to kill every man he had, and just may pull that off with some back up they obviously had on the wagon trains.

He knew they weren't facing sod-busters with no experience in fighting. Experience was written all over many faces in front of him. That didn't mean he was afraid. John Kinney was never afraid of any situations or any man.

A newspaperman in Mesilla had called him the worst and meanest scoundrel in the Territory. He wore that title with pride, and worked hard to live up to it.

Big John tipped his hat in as a gesture of agreement and good-bye. Turn his mount around and with his entire party, except his scouts, returned to, and dismounted at the McCarty wagon. He was invited to partake in Catherine's good cooking.

Hedge and Pawnee sat as still as statues, as did their well-trained mounts, until the strangers were out of site to the north.

They would follow-up later to confirm exactly where they camped and how many men remained in their camp.

Both men were so good that even seasoned men like that group would never know they were watching, even if they posted their own guards.

José Montoya and Big John sat next to each other on a convenient log in front of the camp fire. Catherine poured both men a cup of her coffee.

"Ma'am, with this coffee you should open a restaurant. People would come for miles around just to get a cup of this coffee," José declared.

"It is ironic you said that Mr. Montoya. I have seriously thought about having a small comfortable restaurant with my roadhouse. All roadhouses serve food, but I'm thinking of having a pinky finger food restaurant to serve all the local folks too."

There were some strange looks around the camp. It was quickly obvious Big John and José Montoya were the only two people that knew what Catherine meant by "pinky finger restaurant".

"I think that would work very well in Santa Fe. You would be surprised how many well-off people there are in Santa Fe. They will travel a long way for good food and atmosphere," José gave his opinion.

Now, most of the people gathered learned what Catherine meant. None confessed not knowing before José explained it. "Pinky finger" meant aristocrats who spend large amounts for simple well-prepared food.

José turned to Big John and asked in a low tone, but not a whisper, that would be rude: "Do you know who that man" José was referring to John Kinney.

"No, I don't, but I know the type," Big John replied.

José volunteered: "He has a ranch near Los Cruces in the Mesilla Valley. It makes no sense for him to be joining John Chisum to do anything."

"I think he is going to maybe rustle Chisum cattle. That I would believe. Right now, his gang is this far north to find good horse flesh. He could have saved a hundred miles on the old mail road to Ft. Sumner. No, he is now looking for good horse flesh. Then he would be prepared to rustle large quantities of cattle," José Montoya concluded.

Hedge reined up just as José finished his conclusions of the Kinney gang.

Hedge reported: "They have a twenty horse remuda north of their camp."

Big John turned to José and said: "Looks like your assessment is correct. My job is to get this wagon train to Santa Fe safely. Double the guards tonight and shorten their shifts. I don't want a mouse to get through without the sound of an alarm. Not a mouse!" Big John directed to Hedge, Pawnee, and Eagle Eye.

General Atkins gave his wagon train the same instructions.

The following two nights were quiet. Finally, on the third day those rascals left. As Hedge had said they were driving a small herd of very fine horses.

It was also obvious that they stayed to see if they could find a weakness in the two trains' security, and found there was not any.

The morning of the third day Big John gave the order to pull. Destination was Glorieta Pass.

GLORIETA PASS

They camped just below the pass near a year-round creek. The small hill had good, tall grass for all the animals for both trains.

José Montoya accepted Catherine's invitation for dinner again. At dinner he informed everyone:

"Glorieta Pass is the sight of our most famous battle during the recent war," he paused as though to get permission to continue with his story about the Battle of Glorieta Pass.

"Yes, why so famous?" Bill Antrim asked.

"Well, it was there that Confederate General Sibley's grand plans were thwarted."

"He had been very successful invading the northern section of New Mexico. The Confederates own the southern New Mexico territory. They renamed it the Arizona Territory. I should explain better. Sibley did not do any of that. That was done by Lt. Colonel John Baylor. General Sibley went to Confederate President Jefferson Davis with a grand plan. He would not only take northern New Mexico, but march into and take the mineral-rich Colorado Territory from the Union."

Mr. Montoya paused to take a bite of Catherine's delicious dinner then continued:

"His plan was to use those resources to march further north and take Ft. Laramie. That would stop all shipments heading west-to-east along that trail. After that he was to march west and conquer the mineral-rich Nevada Territory for the Confederate States. Up there on Glorieta Pass," he said pointing to the mountain pass just ahead of them, "all his grand plans ended."

José Montoya was interrupted by young Henry McCarty.

"What happened Mr. Montoya, what happened?" he asked excitedly.

"Well, young man, it truly is a history lesson. I think one for the entire War Between the States. What happened was happening all over the south. Confederate generals were just as good as their northern counterparts. The problem was they couldn't get resupplied in time to hold any geographical gains attained through hard earned victories. General Sibley had marched north, up the Rio Grande taking care of all the resistance he met. He had made one tactical error, but it did not have to be the disaster it turned out to be for him."

"His goal was to reach the gold field in Colorado quickly. After winning the fierce Battle of Valverde, he chose not to spend more men and supplies taking Fort Craig. He did take

Albuquerque, and Santa Fe. Then he marched on to take Fort Union. That completed it would be a straight march to the gold fields."

José saw he had the attention of everyone around the campfire. They were hanging on every word he said. He started to go on with his story when Henry interrupted:

"What happened sir?"

Catherine admonished her younger son: "Henry, let the gentleman take a breath! Stop interrupting him!"

"I'm sorry sir," Henry said in a much lower tone.

"That is alright young man. I am glad to know young people are interested in these things," José replied, and he continued with his story:

"Where was I?" he thought out-loud.

Big John asked: "What was his tactical error?" Big John liked strategy and tactics.

"Oh, yes, he left Colonel Edward Canby[95] at Fort Craig. The Colonel was able to regroup and march to his rear. The Colonel's troops wanted revenge for their loss at Valverde. The Colorado Volunteers marched here to stop General Sibley. They came to join the troops at Fort Union and its command. Colonel Canby arrived at Sibley's rear. At the start of the Battle of Glorieta there were about 5000 total divided Union forces, and General Sibley had about 2500 troops."

"Yet poor Sibley couldn't win for loosing, as the old saying goes. Technically, he initially won that battle: pushing the Union forces back to Fort Union. Yet, Colonel Canby and some Colorado Volunteers destroyed all his supply wagons from the rear. They even shot all their mules. It was over! He knew he had no choice but to retreat from his victory and skedaddle back to Southern New Mexico Territory[96]. General Sibley couldn't resupply there either. Therefore, he had to retreat all the way back to Texas. Neither he, nor any Confederate Commander

---

[95] Colonel Edward Richard Sprigg Canby rose to the rank of Major General (3 Stars) and was the only general killed in the Indian Wars. He was assassinated by a Modoc Indian leader at a "peace" meeting April 11th, 1873 at age 55-years-old. He was Commander of the Pacific Northwest at the time of his death. The Modoc Indians of Northern California refused to move to a reservation in Oregon where they would be forced to live with their traditional enemy the Klamath Indians.

[96]The Confederate States named the area part of the Arizona Territory.

ever returned to our New Mexico Territory. So folks, now you know why that pass is so important to natives, Americans, and all of New Mexico's citizens."

Big John Henry always seemed to understand the big picture of anything. He suggested: "Sounds to me like everyone west of the Mississippi should be thankful for what happened in that pass. I have brought many trains through there. I've heard of the battle, but I never knew its importance. Mr. Montoya, thank you for enlightening me. I guess it was worth saving your hide back there!"

The whole group broke out into laughter. No less than José Montoya and he replied: "You don't talk much Big John, but when you do you sure say a lot." All enjoyed another chuckle.

For the first time General Atkins spoke on the subject: "In my humble opinion General James Henry Carleton was another good reason for General Sibley to get out of New Mexico and not to return," he declared.

"Why was that?" asked José Montoya.

"He knew General Carleton personally and professionally. General Carleton is a brilliant logistics man and fierce fighter. I believe Sibley felt there was no possible way he could beat the 1st California Infantry led by his old friend. He must have had good intelligence reports and knew General Carleton was about to enter the New Mexico Territory. It is true that lack of supplies ended the war for General Sibley, and most of the south. But we should not forget the impact of General Carleton."

"You seemed to like the man?" Big John asked a rhetorical question.

"You seem not to?" General Atkins replied.

"No, I don't pass any judgements on someone I don't know."

General Atkins responded: "Actually, I know you like General Sibley a lot!"

"How do you know that? Big John said with emphasis on "know."

"You bought all those Sibley Tents didn't you?" General Atkins asked with a grin.

"Well, I guess you got me there. I know it is the same man. He invented that tent before the war. Yes, I do like the tent a lot" Big John admitted.

Catherine spoke: "That is interesting. Even as you told the story, and the fact we own one, I didn't even think it may be the same Sibley. I know he knew how to make a tent. Ours has stood through some pretty rough weather."

José Montoya turned to Big John Henry and said: "I learned a lot too. I think you are correct in your assumption Mr. Big John."

"Sibley was an excellent general. Who knows what he could have accomplished had Jefferson Davis kept him supplied, and with reserve troops at his call. He may have taken the entire western section of our country. He would have cut off all the financial resources used to fund the whole war effort. Therefore, it may have been the north that ran out of supplies. You see I just learned something more about how important the victory at Glorieta Pass was to the Union. Thank you Mr. Montoya. Now we better get some rest, so we can make that pass in the morning." Big John Henry informed the group.

"How far is it to Santa Fe over the pass?" Bill Antrim asked.

"About twenty miles," Big John replied.

"Wow, we are almost there, huh?" Catherine said as she signaled to the boys to do their evening chores.

"One more night of camping and the following day we will pull in Santa Fe. I know you're thinking we could make twenty miles in one day." Big John said looking at Bill Antrim, absolutely reading his mind.

"Tomorrow we will take the grade down the other side of the pass very slow. I've seen more than one wagon lost on that grade just before their destination was made. It is well worth one more night to arrive safely," Big John ordered.

Chapter Fifty-Nine

Over Glorieta Pass, Down the Last Mountain, and Their Last Night on the Trail

The next morning they cleared Glorieta Pass, and began their slow decent to Santa Fe.

All the stories José Montoya had told them had everyone much more excited to see that ancient town. It was all becoming very real to them. Santa Fe was a special place. Holy to the Indians, Mexicans, and exciting for the Americans. The latter was going to see the town that long trail was named after.

The trail down the west side of the mountain was really a very well-worn road descending southwest through a valley with mountains on both sides.

At the bottom the valley it took turned northwest along the bottom of the mountain on the right.

There they stopped at a good spring. The grass was green and tall for the animals. The downhill road had been tough on the animals, and they smelled the water a couple miles back.

Many people were anxious to hear more history from José Montoya. None more anxious than young Henry McCarty.

Henry and Josie scampered off to fill water buckets to in-turn fill their water barrel. It was low and their responsibility to keep it full.

"We must get back to hear José speak," Henry declared to Josie.

"I'm not much on that history stuff. I am for right now, and it will take us several trips to fill the water barrel. We have no idea if there is any water on this last leg of the trip," Josie insisted.

"History helps with that, Josie. This road has been used for hundreds of years. It has to have water, or it wouldn't be here," Henry replied.

"We will fill the water barrel!" Josie said firmly.

Henry was good with math and he did some calculations in his head.

"Big brother, It's a fifty-gallon barrel. Our buckets are five gallons each. That's ten trips to fill that barrel. Five trips for you and five trips for me. I will do my five trips and you do yours," Henry said as he took off running full blast toward the creek.

Henry passed Josie on his way back, long before Josie even reached the creek with his empty bucket.

Josie complained: "You are spilling half the water!"

Henry slowed down, putting two hands on the handle and just walking very fast. He still beat Josie by a long shot.

Completing his five runs he sat down next to the fire catching his breath. He was just in time for Mr. Montoya to join them.

Hedge had earned his supper starting the fire for Catherine. Normally that was Uncle Bill's chore. Hedge asked to do it this morning. He did make a good fire.

Uncle Bill hustled the animals to the best grass, there he picketed and fed them. He had some ground up Cottonwood bark they absolutely loved. He once said that was his secret to why animals were so loyal to him. Big John Henry observed that and asked him to feed his animals the same. So much for keeping it secret.

It took too long for one man. He decided that Josie would help from now on. No more did the thought get out when he realized this was their last night on the trail. That thought was a relief in itself.

The truth was that Catherine was getting awful tired of feeding so many people. Her health was much better than in Denver, but feeding all the people interested in Mr. Montoya's stories was a bit much for anyone.

She said nothing about that, but did enlist the boys to deliver the food. She was glad this was the last night on the road. It also gave her second thoughts about opening a restaurant.

Henry arrived back from his chores. He sat on a rock back from the fire, and where almost everyone would be seated closer to the fire than he would be.

He had learned it was better for him to be out of sight out of mind. Although he was twelve-years-old he looked ten-years-old. When he sat close to the others he noticed the adults changed the content their conversations. He felt he was a "man" already, but they didn't see it that way.

Bill Antrim returned walked directly over to Henry: "Why aren't you helping your brother fetch water?" He asked curtly enough to even get Catherine's attention, but she decided to allow it to play out.

"I did Uncle Bill. I had five trips and he had five trips. I finished mine faster," Henry said in his jovial manner, almost comedic. After answering he looked to his mother, but didn't get a clue whether she was buying that answer. She hadn't counted the number of trips.

Josie heard the question and answer just as he arrived and commented:

"That is true, but he probably lost a half bucket running so fast."

Henry looked to the ground and mumbled: "What a tattletale!"

"Henry, one more bucket and walk back." Uncle Bill demanded.

Henry got up, picked up a bucket and took off like a deer. He would never trust his brother again, with anything! Their relationship was strained from that moment on.

Returning at a walk Henry saw and could hear José Montoya starting to answer a question from one of the people gathered at the fireside.

He listened carefully as he poured the water into the barrel. Putting a lid on the barrel he slithered over to his regular spot behind everyone.

Mr. Adams asked José Montoya: "I think you mentioned once that Santa Fe is the oldest town in America. Is that a fact?" He sincerely wanted to know.

"Kind of, I'll explain. You see, it is a matter of town names. Don Juan de Onate arrived at the river he called Santa Fe in 1598, but he then called the new village San Gabriel. It didn't last long. He decided to move a few miles down-stream to a better location. He and his priest were proud to now name their town La Villa Real de La Santa Fe de Francisco de Assis."

José caught all the strange looks quickly and translated the Spanish name to English: "In English: The Royal Town of the Holy Faith of Saint Francis of Assis," he explained.

"That is still a mouth full." Mr. Adams grinned.

"Yes, yes it is!" José admitted. "It has ever since been referred to as Santa Fe, which means 'Holy Faith'" José explained. "One of the pioneers from General Atkins train was a history teacher from Boston, Massachusetts named Tommy McLaughlin. Englishmen landed at Jamestown in 1607. Of course, they didn't last long. It is believed they starved to death, and killed off by hostiles.

"A couple decades later the pilgrims landed at Plymouth Rock, and shortly after that more came and landed where Salem is now. They established the Massachusetts Bay Colony[97], which was formed by the Massachusetts Bay Company. They were strong Puritans, some Quaker, and some Baptists. My point is that your claim of Santa Fe being the oldest American town is a strong one."

"We did acquire the New Mexico Territory as the rewards of defeating Mexico in war, but we also inherited its history too" Mr. McLaughlin declared.

Josie was bored with all this history. He left for his bed roll.

Catherine was interested in the people in Santa Fe now: "What are the people of Santa Fe like now?" she asked pointedly.

"Very good people. It remains ninety-percent Mexican and Indian. Of course, the Americans don't like being the minority," José Montoya had to chuckle a little and then asked the group:

"Anyone here familiar with St. Francis of Assis?"

"Yes, I am," one man admitted and explained: "I was reared in a convent of Franciscan Nuns."

"Ah, then you do know how special St Francis of Assis is to all Christians, Catholics, and Protestants. To have your town named for such a great Saint. Well, the people of Santa Fe feel a responsibility to live up to that," José explained.

[97] The author's decedents, the Rumsey brothers, were with the first Englishmen to form the Massachusetts Bay Company, subsequently the Massachusetts Bay Colony.

Catherine asked: "St. Francis is the Saint of Poverty, and St. Joseph the Saint for Travel, correct?"

Henry was shocked. His mother only spoke in general terms about religion, like be good or God will punish you. He had no idea his mother knew anything about Saints.

José Montoya responded to her question: "Yes, ma'am, you are correct. Are you Catholic?" He asked very politely hoping not to offend her.

"No, sir. I come from a Protestant sector of Cork, Ireland. It is on the southwest corner of Ireland. For a long time Cork had been about half Catholic and half Protestant. My husband and I left because of the potato famine. Thousands in the country rushed to Cork. We had to leave to survive at all. We were the lucky ones. We first lived in New York City. That was dangerous, too much fighting on the streets there. We got out as quickly as we could."

Henry had never heard his mother talk about New York City. He was too young to remember anything about it.

He also didn't have a single memory of his father. Just some flashing glances of him, but nothing solid. He wished he did, anything would do. Josie said he remembered him and said he was just like him, whatever that meant.

José Montoya spoke to the whole group and volunteered: "When you arrive you may be greeted by the Franciscan Sisters of Loretto. They have the building on the right side of the road a short distance after entering Santa Fe. Bishop Lamy recruited them in 1852, and they have done a bang-up job. The first building of four they have is the Nuns school. They want to build a chapel, so expect them to solicit donations for the new chapel."

He then addressed Catherine again: "Catherine, across town is the First Presbyterian Church. They have the first, and the only English speaking school in Santa Fe. All their teachers are bilingual," José informed politely.

Catherine smiled, and her eyes went directly to Henry. He knew what that meant. His mother's teaching was coming to an end. He harbored silent thoughts that it might be a lot more fun than his mother's strict teaching schedules.

Also, there would be a lot more people his own age. Between his chores, helping his mother, and working for Uncle Bill, there was little time to spend much time with friends.

Most of Henry's friends were much older than him. He enjoyed learning from them, and they seem to be sincerely interested in him.

They constantly complimented him to others on, "how smart he is", or "he is quick as a cat". That was good for his ego and challenged him to live up to the accolades.

Now all that changed with one look from his mother. A look that said it all. He was going to a real school!

José noticed the cringe on Henry's face and said: "Many Spanish speaking children are in that school. They send their children to learn English. It will be a great place for you to really learn our language. Remember, I said the teachers are bilingual."

"That is great! Wow, sign me up mother!" Henry said with a chuckle. His blues eyes were sparkling and dancing all over the place.

Henry's personality was so strong no one noticed his prominent two front teeth. His baby face was one everyone instantly liked. You had no reason to base your opinion on...you just liked him.

Mr. Adams interrupted: "Mr. Montoya, how many people are there in Santa Fe?"

José Montoya replied: "I'm not sure, but it is less than ever before" he replied and continued:

"If it wasn't for the American invasion, and the gold in California, I don't know if it would even exist today."

"If I were to guess, I would say 7000 Mexicans and 1500 Americans." José estimated the population.

Catherine volunteered: "Sir, you have been back east too long. That is a large town on the frontier."

"You are right, ma'am. I stand corrected. It does remain a very poor town," José added.

Henry was thinking: "7000 Mexicans! I'll bet I can learn Spanish quickly there."

He had picked up as much as he could from the vaqueros on this trip, and was thankful for their help. Even they said: "It would be better to live with Spanish speaking people to learn the language."

Big John Henry didn't talk much, but when he did everyone listened: "Those of you planning on Santa Fe as your new home, learn Spanish. This country was Mexico until recently. If you want to sell your products or services you need to know the language, or hire all Mexicans."

"Creo que es un consejo, Señor Henry," José said and repeated in English: "I think it good advice, Mr. Henry."

Mr. Adams intended on opening a general merchandise business. His focus was on selling to American travelers on the Santa Fe Trail. He had not even thought of such a large population of Mexicans.

This was the first time since his decision to move to Santa Fe that it struck him he was investing everything in a culture he really didn't know. He asked a question that was on everyone's mind:

"Mr. Montoya, is Santa Fe a safe place to bring up our children?" His sincere question caught everyone's immediate attention.

José knew the image Americans had of Mexicans. They thought them as of the bandito class, knife wielding, small men with facial hair that would just as soon cut your throat as look at you. He enjoyed changing Americans minds and putting them at ease. He responded:

"It is most likely safer than New York City, or any other large eastern city. It is most likely safer than any frontier town you can think of. Please let me explain. Santa Fe is a very old town and from its very beginning founded by religious leaders. A large part of the population is devout Catholics who live their day to day lives as Christians. I think you will find the Mexicans of Santa Fe a gentle, loving, and God-fearing people. I'm sure you'll think me biased when I say it has always been outsiders that brought violence to Santa Fe. Yet, they are still not a violent people today. The Santa Fe area Indians are also not violent people. They are cliff dwellers and agricultural workers. The exception is the Apache further south. They were raiding often in the north because we were easy targets."

Mr. Adams politely interrupted: "You say 'were' easy targets. Do they still raid in Santa Fe?" He asked concernedly Mr. Montoya was not only speaking of the past.

"You are correct Mr. Adams, I have blended past with present. I apologize for that. No, not in Santa Fe. The Apache do raid a lot in the south. Like Lincoln County along the El Paso trail, and on the border between Arizona and New Mexico territories. No longer do they raid even near the larger towns anywhere in the territory."

Mr. Adams had to ask: "What changed that? People, Indian or others, are creatures of habit."

"The Americans changed all that. General Carleton's policies have been to severely punish any raiding Indians. He will send troops with orders not to return to their fort without punishing the offenders. Fort Craig is one of the largest forts in the west and located on the main trail traveling north and south just off the Rio Grande River. The pony soldiers there protect us very well from Apaches. Fort Stanton in Lincoln County keeps the Mescalero Apaches under control. At least from venturing north. It is located too far from the southern trail from El Paso, Texas to Messila, New Mexico. Hence the problems there. John Chisum protects his cattle interest in the Pecos Valley. He has a small army of two-gun cowboys that wield punishment on the Apaches. It is said that he didn't mind them taking beef to eat, but when they started raiding his remuda, he went crazy. The man has a temper, and the Mescalero's paid a severe price."

Mr. Adams asked: "Did they stop?"

José turned to Hedge and asked: "You worked for Chisum, right?"

"Yes, I did. No, they have not stopped raiding Chisum. That old Mescalero Chief is as stubborn as he is. He increased his raids on the remuda."

Big John Henry volunteered: "God help those Indians!"

José agreed: "Yes, you are right Mr. Henry. I don't know what Chisum will do next, but it won't be good on those Indians."

"Thank you Mr. Montoya. I hope I did not offend you?" Mr. Adams sincerely apologized.

"De nada (of nothing or your welcome). I would ask the same questions if I had a family coming to a new area."

“Thank you again, we are all in debt to you. If you ever need help, just ask,” Mr. Adams volunteered.

“Someday I may do just that. Right now, I must call it a night. Buenas noches my friends,” then he looked at Henry and said:

“Buenas noches Señor Henry.”

Henry replied: “Buenas noches mi amigo” In English: “Good night, my friend” and it rolled off his tongue like a native.

“Muy bueno Español, hombrecito,” José replied to Henry (In English: “Very good Spanish, little man”).

Henry knew hombre was ‘man’, but didn’t know “hombrecito”. He just smiled and tipped his hat rim.

Catherine instructed Henry: “Off you go to your bedroll. You’re helping me with breakfast, and I need you up before sunrise. Please wake your brother early too.”

Henry was off in a blink.

Josie was laying in his bed roll seriously thinking about striking out on his own in Santa Fe. He felt himself plenty old enough to do so. He had good skills, mule skinning, freighting, and carpentry. At least good enough skills to be a paid hand.

He had left early because he could care less about history. Josie was about Josie right now, and everything else right now!

Josie had little childhood, having been the man of the house since he was nine-years-old. His best time was in Indianapolis where he had a lot of friends. That was the closest he had to a childhood. There he was young enough to play and have fun, and not old enough to do a man’s work. That all changed when they moved to Wichita.

Each time the thought of striking out came to his mind, the next thought was his mother’s health. He just couldn’t do it now. “Someday!” he thought to himself “Someday!”

When Henry arrived under the wagon Josie had fallen asleep. Henry was so keyed up about all he had heard he just could not sleep. He lay with his hands folded behind his head day dreaming, although it was nighttime.

It was a quiet night until Bob Ashworth ran from wagon to wagon with an alarm: “Check your animals...Indians got two of mine!”

Bill, Josie, and Henry ran to the pasture so fast Catherine couldn't stop her boys. She immediately imagined Indians stealing them!

Sure enough, Uncle Bill's saddle horse was gone!

"Damn them! That was the best horse I ever had!" Bill declared. The boys knew he was really upset because he never cussed in front of them, only when he was powerfully angry.

There was a half-moon out, giving enough light to see clearly a hundred feet. Henry has great night vision. Not only could he see much further, but his excellent hearing could hear the slightest movement a hundred yards away.

"You see or hear anything Henry?" Bill asked knowing his talents.

Henry turned to Bill and stepped very close. Talking at a whisper, even Josie could not hear, and said:

"Don't tell mother. I'll be fine. If I yell, come running." Henry instructed as though he was the adult.

In a split-second he had scurried off into the darkness. About ten minutes later, which seemed like an hour to Bill Antrim, Henry came walking out of the darkness leading Bill's gelding saddle horse. He had its picket line in hand.

Henry said on arrival: "I was going to tell you I stole him back from the Indians, but that would be a lie. I saw his head over the other-side of the creek embankment. I was careful Uncle Bill, I know there could have been Indians out of sight. I figured he probably pulled his picket frightened by the Indians." he said as he handed Uncle Bill the picket line.

Bill was so very happy at that moment. He loved that old saddle horse: "Thank you Henry! Those are great eyes you have" Bill declared.

"I did see some Indian sign, but I think they got scared off. Buck, my friend in Wichita, taught me about reading sign," Henry explained.

"I knew Buck. That was the right man to learn from," Uncle Bill declared.

"He did, and I have been practicing on our trip." Henry said smiling, and was telling the truth.

"I thought you were always looking for gold,"[98] he said grinning and continued: "Fetch me the rope under the seat. I'm going to hobble that boy every night now. I was too attached to him, and trusted him not to pull his picket."

Henry ran off and returned quickly with the rope Uncle Bill wanted. Josie had left to go back to sleep.

Uncle Bill showed Henry how to hobble a horse:

"Form a slip knot, place one loop around one front hoof. Then tie a loop with a knot on the other front hoof, only with a double half hitch. He will have enough rope to make small steps for grazing." Bill instructed.

Henry liked Bill teaching him something new, and he studied it.[99]

The next two days were uneventful. They cleared the summit of Glorieta Pass and descended the long valley. Reaching a high knoll above Santa Fe where they rested their animals. People from both wagon trains stood gazing at the magnificent sight before them.

To the north were snowcapped mountains. Across the valley below were high foot hills and a plateau. The first surprise was how few trees there were, and no grass anywhere in the city area. In-fact, they couldn't see grass anywhere near the city.

It looked like a huge sandy basin with adobe building by the hundreds. They saw many ranches on the out skirts of town. A few within the town. All had animals: goats, horses, sheep, and mules.

Mr. Adams asked what was on all their minds: "Where is the grass to feed their animals?"

Mr. Montoya replied: "There are grass suppliers all over town. That is all they do for a living."

"You can't see it from here, but further south is Albuquerque with very good grass land. It was founded by ranchers suppling grass to Santa Fe. Many of their families have been doing that for many generation," José informed them.

---

[98] Bill Antrim always dreamt of striking it rich finding gold. Here he is being sarcastic inferring Henry was following in his footsteps. He knew better.

[99] Henry McCarty was an excellent horseman, but like Bill Antrim would be over confident, and lose several horses in his life when he didn't hobble them. Sometimes costing him a very long walk.

"I should have known a town that size had long ago solved that problem. It just seemed strange to me, not to see grass for the animals."

"I don't see any trees either. I assume there are also lumber suppliers?" Mr. Adams asked.

"Si señor, there are many lumber suppliers," José replied and point toward the towns north end. "See over there is a very large lumber company."

"Yes, I do!" Mr. Adams acknowledged.

Catherine looked for churches and two-story buildings. There were several church steeples. Also, group of two story buildings, and one three-story where downtown must be.

She took a deep breath. The air was clean and dry. That was very nice! Definitely better than Denver.

Catherine's attitude was always positive. Her glass always half full. At this moment she was happy, not just trying to be positive. She could feel the difference with every breath. This was a good decision to come to New Mexico Territory. She thought to herself:

"If that town has been around so long, I will find a way to make a living and take care of my family," She committed to herself. She decided to ask José Montoya about her intentions:

"José do you think a small boardinghouse could survive in Santa Fe?" she sincerely wanted his opinion.

"Yes, of course it could. I've eaten your cooking. You'll have a lot of repeat business, too. You already have half the people on both these trains sold on your cooking," he finished with a chuckle and added: "Is that your intention?"

"Yes it is! Yes, as long as you will see us every once in a while, to perk us up with your wonderful words," Catherine said heartfelt.

Santa Fe Wood Supplier
Source: Santo Fe History Museum

1883 Birds Eye View, Santa Fe, New Mexico Territory
Library of Congress Control #75694742 Loc. G4324.S3A3.W4

*The Exchange Hotel was the unofficial, **"End of The Santa Fe Trail"***
Source: Santa Fe History Museum

Chapter Sixty

Santa Fe

It was mid-spring of 1872 when the McCarty family passed in front of the Sisters of Loretto's school. The school took up an entire block. There were four buildings. They were all surprised at how large it was.

Sure enough, there were the Sisters with an upside-down sombrero extended out. Every wagon, with only a few exceptions, placed coins in the hat.

Catherine was so impressed she committed to herself that if she couldn't get Henry into the Protestant school she would put him with the Sisters of Loretto. She was not so religiously biased as to deprive her son of an education.

She was determined Henry would get a good education. She knew he had "the brains for it" as she said many times to herself.

Of course, her favorite saying to him was: "You're too smart for your own britches." She picked that up from a customer in Wichita, who was referring to her son at the time. It seemed to fit Henry well, so she found no reason to argue with the lady.

Catherine greeted what seemed to be the Mother Superior of the Sisters of Loretto: "Hello Mother. Here is my humble donation to your chapel," Catherine said dropping a five-dollar gold piece in her sombrero.

"Your name, ma'am?" the Mother Superior asked.

"Catherine...Catherine McCarty ma'am," she replied.

"Well, Catherine McCarty, if that is a humble donation, I do want to see you when you're not so humble." The Mother Superior laughed out loud and continued: "Believe me it is rare I see a five-dollar gold piece! Thank you so very much, señora," her Spanish slipping out automatically.

"You're welcome, Mother. On top of that I am Protestant," Catherine smiled as she replied.

"Oh God forbid! A Protestant!" Mother Superior replied, and again laughed out loud at her own joke. She then continued more seriously:

"The First Presbyterian Church has a good school! The wagons usually go by the Plaza. If you turn left on the far side, pass Lincoln, Sheridan streets, and then turn right on Grant Avenue. It is a couple blocks up on the left. Corner of Grant and Griffin Streets."

"Thank you, Mother!" Catherine acknowledged.

Catherine smiled and whipped her mules on down the road to catch up to the train.

Catherine would follow Mother Superior's instructions later. Their first stop would be The Exchange Hotel. Bill Antrim had heard it was a good hotel and restaurant. They would stay there a few days while looking for a permanent place to live.

Josie drove their wagon while Bill settled up with Big John Henry. He delivered the freight wagon he drove to the designated merchant's store.

Josie pulled their wagon up in front of The Exchange Hotel. Catherine, Josie, and Henry entered the lobby of The Exchange Hotel.

There was much excitement going on in the hotel. They had to wait some time for the hotel clerk. Finally arriving he introduced himself as proprietor Mr. Thomas McDonald.

Catherine introduced herself, the boys, and the soon to arrive Bill Antrim. She then informed him she needed two rooms, as she was a widow and Mr. Antrim was a single man.

Mr. McDonald begged: "Please do forgive me for the delay. I just announced to my staff, that I have asked Laura Crothers to be my wife, and she has accepted!" He explained in his deep Irish accent.

"Congratulations Mr. McDonald! And here I was hoping you were not asked for," Catherine said with her wonderful chuckle and Irish accent.

"Oh! Me Lassie, had I only known sooner," Mr. McDonald said in a most flirtatious manner.

It was obvious Josie didn't know what was going on. The look on his face said it all. He thought he may have to defend his mother's honor any moment now.

Mr. McDonald addressed Josie:

"Come on lady, you know you have a beautiful mother. It is the highest honor to send such flirtation her way." Mr. McDonald informed the confused young man. Josie just stared at him with no expression at all.

Henry broke out in laughter. He had never heard any such language directed to his mother. He also got the jolly nature of the comment. He got it!

Mr. McDonald and Catherine had to laugh out loud with Henry.

Catherine then got down to business she thought he could be very helpful with: "We of the Gaelic persuasion must stick together," she said with a sly grin.

"Ah..." Mr. McDonald said glancing down at Catherine signing in as "Catherine McCarty".

"I am of the Scottish McDonald clan, you know the sons of the world rulers. Therefore, although you are setting me up so well, I would be honored to assist you in any way that I can ma'am," Thomas volunteered so eloquently.

"Is there an English-speaking school here now," Catherine asked what was on her mind.

"Yes, ma'am, and a very good one, The First Presbyterian Church on Grant St. The pastor is Dr. McFarland. Also, you are lucky..."

Catherine interrupted: "Why is that?"

"Because his wonderful wife Amanda has arrived to join her husband. She is also a healer. A very good physician I have been told, although, she has not graduated from a medical school. She obviously learned the profession somehow. I understand she has assisted her husband in his teaching during the war."

Catherine felt an urge to ask: "Is he a 'lan' or 'land' McFarland?"

Mr. McFarland had to chuckle: "It is 'land', so yes he is Irish. No offence taken" he said smiling and went on:

"He was sent here on a missionary assignment for the Pueblo Indians. I think he said around 1866, after the war ended. The first thing he did when he arrived was set up a school for the Pueblo Indians. Then the Americans arrived so he expanded to serve their needs. Then there were many Mexicans that wanted to learn English and the Sisters of Loretto's school was full. So, he hired a bilingual teacher and expanded again. Now, his wife is here to assist him, and she is needed. Dr. McFarland is getting worn out with too many pans in the fire. He is a man that when he sees a problem, he will do what he can to solve it for people. A very god person" Mr. McDonald concluded.

Catherine asked politely: "May I ask one more favor?" flashing her twinkling blue eyes at him with a warm grin and her soft Irish accent.

"I pity the man that lands you ma'am," McDonald declared.

Catherine frowned not expecting such a response. Henry, even at 12-years-old knew more was coming from him.

"Why is that sir?" Catherine asked curtly.

"Why the poor man could never say no to those beautiful eyes of yours," Thomas said sincerely and then noticed Henry's eyes.

"Lordy be...you have those eyes too! Well, you came by them honestly. I'll bet you use them to your advantage, young man," Thomas surmised.

Catherine declared: "Could have been his father too. He is the spitting image of his father. He was killed in that damned war! You can probably tell I'm still mad at him for leaving his family, just to get himself killed. He didn't have to join."

Catherine said and changed the subject: "Anyway, I see you have a restaurant here."

"Yes, I do, ma'am. Are you thinking of opening one?" Thomas McDonald asked point-blank.

"Yes, Mr. McDonald, but not like yours. Maybe a boarding house and a space large enough to have a small restaurant. What do you think of that?" Catherine asked sincerely.

Mr. McDonald thought as he pinched the end of his chin in contemplation. He was thirty-years-old of average build, but wiry strong.

"Hmmm... let me see. A boarding house competes with my hotel... a restaurant that competes with my restaurant...hmmm. Heck yes! You should do exactly that! Santa Fe could use a dozen or more boarding houses. I'm too expensive for many travelers, as is my restaurant. I kept increasing my prices and business never slowed down. Finally, I ended up with a couple rooms available for nice people like you. I was full all the time and have to turn down travelers in need." Thomas said with enthusiasm.

Catherine was so relieved, and much more relaxed. She wanted to learn from somebody in the business, but didn't want to create and enemy her first day in town.

"Is it too late to be invited to your wedding?" Catherine asked.

Thomas pinched that chin again: "Could you prepare some Irish muffins?" he asked with a twinkle in his eye and then added: "At my expense of course."

"Of course!" Catherine replied

"Then I must invite you. It will be at the first Presbyterian Church April 9. Dr. McFarland will be conducting the ceremony," Thomas informed her.

"What did you say the lucky bride's name is?" Catherine inquired.

"She is Indian Agent William Crothers' daughter, Laura Crothers," Thomas replied.

"I wish you two a long and happy marriage, and may both of you get to heaven an hour before the devil knows you are gone," Catherine smiled.

"Thank you Mrs. McCarty. You know, I may know just the place for you. As the old Irish saying goes it is 'spitting distance' from Dr. McFarland's school," Thomas recommended.

"It's not on the main trail through town, but I can assure you I'll be giving you plenty of referrals. I'm now referring people to The Bed Bug Inn," Thomas said with disdain in his tone of voice.

"Bed Bug Inn! Are you serious?" Catherine blurted out.

Henry couldn't help himself from letting out a chuckle. He understood what Thomas was doing. His mother always took people at their exact word.

"No, ma'am, but I can't give the real name of the Inn. You'll know soon enough," he chuckled, and Catherine joined him.

"My goodness! The owner of the building I'm referring you to is eating dinner here right now. Please wait over there," Thomas said while pointing to a nice Victorian couch with a tea table in front of it.

Catherine was going to ask him not to disturb his dinner, but didn't have a chance. Thomas was off like a bolt of lightning.

Arriving back, he sat Mr. Tucker down next to Catherine and made the introductions.

Mr. Tucker was a man born a cynic. He was a bit off his game because now he was dealing with a woman. He decided to inform her of his personality flaw:

"Ma'am, you must forgive me but I'm a man who does not even trust myself, besides anyone else," he volunteered and proceeded to inquire about her experience in business:

"Do you have experience in business?" he asked point blank.

"I do, sir. I'm one of the founders of Wichita, Kansas. It was founded by 123 men and one woman...me! I owned a business, quarter section homestead and several town lots. Before that I ran a business in Indianapolis, Indiana for ten years. I have supported my two boys and myself since 1861," Catherine stated like a professional.

"I am sorry for your loss," Mr. Tucker said assuming she must have lost her husband in the war.

"Thank you sir, my husband was so excited to fight for his new adopted country. Frankly, I tried to talk him out of it, but he insisted." Catherine explained.

Henry was most surprised by what she said about Wichita. He never knew his mother was one of the founders.

Mr. Tucker volunteered: "He wasn't alone ma'am. I was also in the 1st Brigade Indiana Volunteers. Old Abe declared war on April 12, 1861, Governor Morton offered Abe 10,000 volunteers April 15, 1861. Abe had only asked for 5000. The Governor's Adjutant General Lew Wallace[100] formed Camp Morton in Indianapolis immediately. He had 500 recruits on April 16, 1861. I was one of them. One week later we had 12,000 volunteers from all over Indiana. We were the first state to not only meet, but beat Abe's quota. We were all very proud of that. I can tell you ma'am, to the man, none of us had any idea what we were getting into. The word was that the war wouldn't last for three months. Heck, we were afraid it would be over before we got to fight. Wallace insisted on us having training and uniforms. We said: 'Just give us ammunition and guns to fire it with and let us get there before it is over.'"

Catherine respectfully listened to Mr. Tucker, and for the first time realized that contagious march to glory was not only her husbands. She replied:

"That was almost exactly what he told me, and I thought he was kissing the Blarney Stone again."

"No ma'am he was not. We were all young and naïve. May I ask what kind of business did you operate?"

In both towns it was a laundry service. In Wichita I named it 'The City Laundry'," Catherine answered.

"Is that what you're going to run here?" Mr. Tucker asked knowing what McDonald had told him.

"No sir. I'm going to have a boarding house and small restaurant. I will be the cook," Catherine replied.

---

[100] The same Lew Wallace that would become Territorial Governor of New Mexico. If he only knew how much one of those soldiers he recruited would affect his own life. Had Michael McCarty survived the Civil war, much may have been different.

Henry interrupted: "My mother cooked for half our wagon train workers every night. There were no complaints, she is the best cook you have ever seen!" Henry said with those dancing eyes fluttering all over the place, as they always did when excited.

Catherine just smiled.

"I believe you young man...I would never argue with you on that!" Mr. Tucker said to Henry and then returned to Catherine.

"I hope he is in charge of your publicity," Mr. Tucker said with a chuckle.

Now it was Catherine's turn for questions: "How many square feet do you have? How many rooms for boarders after two rooms for the boys and me?" Catherine asked.

"Five rooms plus a large living room, and fireplace at each end of the building. Total square feet is 1,500." Mr. Tucker informed Catherine.

"I'm sorry, but I don't think that is large enough for what I need, but thank you Mr. Tucker for interrupting your dinner to talk to me."

Mr. McDonald and Henry were just listening in amazement how these two business people were negotiating. They both thought it was over...not so!

Mr. Tucker replied: "Wait again, ma'am. My rooms are 10 x 10, 100 square feet each. That leaves plenty of room for a wash basin, clothes closet, and a good size bed. Heck, you could have a small couch reading area left over. Single boarders don't need more than that. Oh yes, I forgot, I also have two out-houses. One for men and one women. How often have you seen that?" Mr. Tucker asked.

"No, I haven't seen that," Catherine replied as she ran the math in her head, while rubbing her chin in thought. Everyone was quiet.

"How much?" Catherine asked point blank.

Mr. Tucker answered quickly: "$100 a month for all of it." He declared as though it was a great deal.

"No, thank you Mr. Tucker. You are too far off the main road, and I'm not Mr. McDonald. I can't get that much for the rooms no matter what they have. My patrons will be those that cannot afford The Exchange Hotel rates. I will have to charge

$12 a month per room. Two rooms will be for the family. That leaves three rooms bringing in $36 a month in income. If the restaurant brought in another $36 a month that is an income of $72 a month... Where do I get the other $28 a month to pay your rent? That is at break-even! Now, Mr. Tucker, do I look like a business person that wants to break-even?" Catherine asked matter-of-factly.

"No, ma'am, you don't. You made a good argument. Give me a one-year guarantee, and I'll cut it in half to $50 a month. That is it...no less. That is my bottom line. Also, you take care of anything that needs fixing now, or during that year. I don't want to hear about the property for one year," Mr. Tucker concluded and sat silent while Catherine contemplated. So did everyone else.

Catherine stuck her hand out and said: "Will you fix anything broken when we move in? If so we have an agreement." Catherine made a counter-offer contingency.

"I will, but don't you want to see the property first?" Mr. Tucker asked politely and clasped Catherine's hand with a firm shake. He was surprised at Catherine's firm and strong grip and said: "I can see why you were one of the founders of Wichita. You are a good businessman...ah businesswoman."

"Thank you sir, as you are...businessman that is. That is why I need not see the property first." Catherine replied.

Chapter Sixty-One

Santa Fe
Business as Usual

Catherine's business took off like a prairie fire. Every single month she increased the business from the previous month, and business did not slow down even for a few days.

Mr. McDonald kept his word and was sending more and more business her way.

Boarders paid a flat fee of $4 a day, per person. It also included up to three meals a day. The rate did not change for only one meal a day.

Catherine's business was making good money. Henry was doing very well in school, at least academically. She was a happy person. Although, she noticed she was getting more tired sooner in the day. Josie was cooking the evening meal, which helped a lot.

One of several of Henry's teacher informed her she did have to correct Henry often about cross-talking in the classroom. All his teachers, including her, liked Henry very much. That same teacher declared:

"Your son could charm the devil himself out of sinning. I believe he could do just that.

An assistant teacher, who also had her own Spanish speaking class, assisted his teacher with the bilingual needs of her students.

Unbeknownst to Catherine, Henry got himself transferred to her class which she taught in Spanish. Most of her full time students were sent by their parents to learn English. Henry was the only Anglo-American in the class.

Catherine found out and requested a meeting with Dr. McFarland. She wanted to know why her son could make such a change without her knowledge.

Dr. McFarland agreed if she would please bring Henry to the meeting, as he "is all about God's children".

Arriving at the meeting with Henry she saw that Dr. McFarland had also invited Henry's Mexican teacher.

Dr. McFarland said: "Please do come in Mrs. McCarty"

Ironically, she had seen Dr. McFarland at several social parties, but had never met him or his wife. She was too engrossed in her business and weaker health. It was getting harder and harder to get everything done.

Dr. McFarland greeted Catherine: "Good Morning, I would like to introduce you to Henry's teacher Mrs. Francis Hernandez Gomez, our teaching assistant and Spanish speaking class teacher.

"How do you do ma'am?" Catherine asked politely.

"Thank you for asking, I am quite fine. I enjoy teaching your wonderful and talented son. He has learned Spanish. He now speaks the language in the most elegant and conversational manner," she replied.

Catherine was taken aback by her perfect English response. The woman's language just didn't match her simple pion appearance. She decided to get right to the point: "Dr. McFarland, I didn't enroll Henry to just learn Spanish. I enrolled him to leave the three R's, sir."

"I do understand, Mrs. McCarty, and that is exactly what Mrs. Gomez is doing. She has taught Henry, and all his class mates, the three R's. She and his fellow students have also taught him an important language in your new home. His tests will be on the three R's. That way you and I can evaluate his progress. To date I have not been dissatisfied with Mrs. Gomez's ability to teach," Dr. McFarland concluded.

"Please demonstrate." Catherine asked Mrs. Gomez

Mrs. Gomez and Henry began a conversation in Spanish. Catherine was surprised at how smooth Henry had become in the language. Of course, she knew little of what they were saying, but none-the-less, she could tell he knew a lot more than he had learned from the vaqueros.

"Alright, enough! I believe you! As long as he is learning his three R's too..." Catherine declared.

Henry interrupted: "Mother, I have. Mrs. Gomez teaches the basics very well. She said I am now a full year ahead of students my age. Also, Mother, all my class mates are Mexicans and Spaniards. I help them with their English. They are some of the best kids I have ever known. I know you would love them. Please don't take me out of her class!" Henry begged.

"Alright, you can stay…" Catherine agreed and was interrupted by Henry's celebration.

"If you agree to mind Mrs. Gomez!" Catherine finished her sentence. They all got a chuckle on that one. Discipline was still an issue for Henry.

Mrs. Gomez volunteered: "Henry tends to do what he wants, when he wants to. We are working on that," she said with great emphasis on "we."

"Good!" Catherine replied as both women stared at Henry, who had a cattish grin on his face.

"I'm glad you're not speaking what that grin is saying young man," Catherine informed Henry.

They said their good-byes. Catherine and Henry headed for home.

Over the next few months Catherine's business continued to grow. Catherine's restaurant became the place for business-people to meet.

Its proximity to the Palace of the Governor, legislators, and even the court house made it very convenient for territorial government and private business people to meet outside of their offices.

Chapter Sixty-Two

The Visitors

José Montoya kept his promise to Catherine and stopped by to rent a room for a week. After their salutations and expressed mutual admiration he got down to his mission:

"Mrs. McCarty, I pray you have a room I can rent for a week?" José asked in the most conciliatory manner.

"I do. It is yours sir," Catherine declared.

"Thank you! I have business with our territorial government. Also, a good friend of mine, Juan Bautista Patrón, wanted to have a meeting with me. I recommended your place as it should be better for a confidential meeting. He will be staying with prominent friends of his in Santa Fe, so he won't need a room," José informed and concluded.

"Mr. Montoya, you can have anything you want. I will make it happen! I will close the entire restaurant for your meeting, if that is what you want," Catherine committed and explained: "The knowledge you gave me at our camp fires on the trail has been very valuable to me. I am in your debt Mr. Montoya."

"Gracias señora, it was my pleasure. I enjoyed every minute and certainly your great food. Your people saved my life...it is I who is in debt to you and the others on that train" He kept talking and changed the subject:

"How is your wonderful family, ma'am?" José asked sincerely.

"I think very well" Catherine replied and continued:

"Henry has done a very good job in school, which makes me very happy. You will like that he has learned Spanish very well, according to Dr. McFarland... You have my permission to test him when he arrives." She said with her Irish eyes dancing with happiness.

"Si señora, I will do just that. I would like that week to be the third week of this month (February 1873)." José requested.

"I will make that happen, señor," Catherine agreed.

“Thank you, señora, thank you very much, and buenas tardes,” José politely said.

“Good afternoon to you too, señor.”

After leaving the restaurant José gave it all good thought. For one thing, he wanted to meet his friend there because almost all the patrons were English speaking.

He knew there would be some very sensitive information his friend would be telling him. Information that might get them both killed if it reached the wrong people.

He had totally forgotten about Henry McCarty. In fact, he had encouraged him to learn Spanish. Now, that could be back-firing on him. The young man could understand enough to make it dangerous.

Giving it a second thought to the matter he concluded that it possibly would not matter. Henry was still very young. If he did understand the information it may help him understand his new home.

He would still ask him to keep any information he over hears confidential. José remembered well how he was always hiding in the back ground listening to all the conversations around the camp fire.

Juan Patrón
One of the most influential Mexican-Americans in the Territory of New Mexico ca 1870-80's

Chapter Sixty-Three

Santa Fe
Beginning of Spring 1873

The last of winter was finally giving way to signs of spring 1873. José Montoya arrived at The Adobe. Josie McCarty helped José with his carpet bags and showed him to his room.

José tried to tip Josie:

"No sir! My mother said none of us are allowed to accept any tips from you. She said it is because it is we that are in debt to you, or something like that. Anyway, you'll get me in trouble." Josie informed him.

José slipped the money into his shirt and said: "I'm not going to tell her if you don't."

"Thank you, sir."

"De nada, hombre."

Josie smiled as he knew "hombre" was "man".

Later that day Juan Patrón arrived for dinner with his friend José Montoya. José was waiting in the restaurant for his friend. Josie guided him to his seat. Catherine arrived just as they were all seating. Immediately, both men rose to greet her.

"Sit down gentlemen. You keep that up and I'll have you very tired of rising up in a short time. I am running this restaurant you know?" she comically informed them. Both men had to chuckle out-loud at that.

"Yes, ma'am," José said and then did his introductions.

Just as they sat to order dinner, Henry came in and recognized José immediately. He ran over to their table. He intended to show off his Spanish, and of course didn't think of José's guest.

José was taken aback thinking he may not be able to stop his forward motion and crash into their table. Henry did stop short of that and blurted out:

"Hola Señor Montoya. Te quedas con nosotros?" (Are you staying with us?).

"Si lo soy. He oido que has aprendido me idioma." (Yes, I am. I heard you have learned my language) José answered.

Henry replied with a wide grin: "Si, un poco!" ("Yes, a little").

José introduced Juan Patrón: "Esto es Juan Patrón del condado de Lincoln." (This is Juan Patrón of Lincoln County).

Henry turned to his guest: "Tengo el placer de conocerlo, señor." (I have the pleasure of meeting you, sir).

There was no one else in the restaurant. Only Catherine, Josie, and Henry. She was patiently waiting to take their order.

Juan Patrón surprised his friend by saying: "We are in an English-speaking restaurant, let us speak English in respect."

José replied: "You are right my friend. As you were most of the time of our youth with Sisters of Loretta." He chuckled. "Can you bring me up to date on you and your father?"

Juan replied: "We have partnered in a store at Lincoln."

"Juan that is a very dangerous thing to do. The Ring owns Laurence Murphy and company." José replied solemnly.

Juan responded with a grin: "Yes, yes but I have stocked it with Mexican merchandise and food only. They don't want that business. My biggest concern is how they treat our people."

"Jimmy Dolan talked Murphy into making John Riley a full partner. Of course, you may know Dolan is also a full partner now. Dolan is a man that enjoys violence" Juan said, concerned.

José paused and then asked a question that directly relates to his mission in The New Mexico Territory:

"Juan...what have you learned about our peoples land grants and the Santa Fe Ring?" he asked pointedly.

In replying Juan disclosed he knew what his friend's mission was:

"What I know is that Catron is a brilliant lawyer and Stephen Elkins is a master strategist. I know they hold a strangle hold on the territory. If they can't beat you one way, they will turn John Kinney's boys loose on you, and you're dead." Juan gave his perspective of the dire situation in New Mexico, and then asked his own question:

"José, how do they get away with all this?" asking his own pointed question.

"The President, Congress, Interior Department, Secretary of War, and Justice Department are all strong Republicans. Catron and Elkins are respected Republicans and took turns as the Territorial U. S. Attorney who approves land grant transfers. The U.S. Surveyor lives here and I believe is on the Ring payroll, but I cannot prove that. Everywhere I smelled fraud I found perfectly legal transactions stopping me in my tracks." José was obviously upset and discouraged.

"Aren't you a Republican?" José asked to the point.

Juan replied: "Yes I am. Isn't it ironic that I'm a Republican and Murphy and company are Democrats? I live in a county with a strong Democratic party. The Ring doesn't mind as Murphy always does their bidding. The House is financed by Catron. He personally holds the first deed on The House."

Juan continued and calmly requested: "Please do not give up! You are the hope of our people right now! You do know that, don't you?"

"I won't give up, but I could be called off this mission at any time, and would have to stop my official inquires." José honestly replied.

"I understand, but you haven't even scratched the surface yet. Somewhere they must have made a mistake that even their friends in Washington won't stand for."

"A lot has changed since you left here, my friend."

José wanted specifics: "What do you mean by that?"

Juan replied: "Our people have lost all power of governance. When you were here our people at least had a strong voice in the legislature. We might as well be talking to the walls. Every bill we pass gets challenged and over turned, or just not enforced. What is worse if we challenge their power in any way, a drunken Texas cowboy shoots you dead. He gladly goes to jail and is released with all charges dropped if he agrees to take care of another killing they need done. If a good judge does anything they don't approve of he is relieved of his duties as a judge. That simple!" Juan explained and summed up: "The Santa Fe Ring controls everything my friend...everything!"

"You make it sound like my investigation is of little matter. I have no chance at getting to the truth or finding any evidence?" José was discouraged.

"No, not at all! It is very important! It gives notice to the Ring that their days are numbered, and that they are being watched. Just watch your back my friend. Give no clue to anyone what you have found, present company excluded." Juan ended with a chuckle.

"Of course, Juan. How are your father and mother doing? I'll bet Encarnacion is quite the young lady now?" José sincerely inquired.

"I forgot it has been awhile since you left. My mother is with Christ. She was so sick for so long, it was a blessing when she left us to stop her suffering. Juana, my oldest sister, has taken over the household, and she is doing very well at it. And yes my baby sister has blossomed into an attractive young woman. Half the county wants to marry her," Juan grinned.

"And your father?" José asked.

"He is doing well, much better than here in Santa Fe. In this town he was one of many small farmers scratching the earth to feed and clothe his family. In Lincoln everyone knows him, barters, and buys from him. When he sold his farm here he had enough to buy a farm there and open a store, which I run for him. I ran for Probate Court Clerk and won!" Juan said with pride written all over his face.

"Wow! When did you do that?" José asked.

"I was elected November '71[101], and I was just re-elected this past November," Juan replied.

---

[101] For more information on Juan Patron, a true forgotten important person in the Lincoln County War, I recommend "Juan Patron" by Paul L. Tsompanas, forward by Frederick Nolan, Copyright 2013 Belle Isle Books, available at Amazon Books.

"I know your father is the proudest man in the territory! I am too, amigo... Wait a minute, you said 1871? You were 19-years-old! Right?" José was astonished!

Juan laughed: "Yes, amigo, and I'm only 20 now."

"Well, amigo, you will still be a few years younger than me, and you must respect the old ones." José laughed out loud and a serious thought came to his mind:

"Amigo, who is the Probate Judge for Lincoln County?"

Catherine interrupted: "Excuse me gentlemen," she said as she grabbed Henry by the back of the collar and guided him out of the room. Looking down at him as she did and she said:

"Henry, these men are having a private conversation, and you have no business listening in," she directed to him.

"But Mother, that is José Montoya... we always listen to his stories," Henry tried to explain.

"That was on the trail and he was talking to all of us about our new home. He was a teacher. Now this is private. Do you understand?" Catherine asked firmly.

"Yes Mother, I do now." Henry replied.

Both men appreciated her efforts to keep their conversation private.

"Thank you, ma'am," José acknowledged her effort.

He then continued his conversation with his friend Juan:

"Who is...?"

Juan interrupted answering his question: "That is my problem. It is Laurence Murphy, owner of The House. He is a Democrat, I'm a Republican. He absolutely rules Lincoln County like a monarch. Ninety-percent of the farmers barter most of their crops for in-store credit. If that isn't bad enough because of high prices, each transaction is treated as a bank loan with steep interest added on. When he built the two-story store we now all call The House, he called in notes from the farmers and insisted they provide the labor to build it. That was the reason my father and I opened the store. We too give credit, but not as a loan. They pay us when they can. So far it has worked out well." Juan concluded.

José confessed: "I knew Lincoln County was in trouble, but I had no idea it was that bad."

Juan explained: "When I arrived in Lincoln it had no school, no church, and no feeling of community. I was only 17, but I opened a school out of my house. I was the first teacher in Lincoln. The community was illiterate. I saw that as my first task at hand. I only had four or five students in the beginning, but they were determined to learn English. That is what I taught first, then the three "R's." Oh, I had two Anglo students too. Next I joined the Tularosa priest in raising money to build our first church. I knew that Probate Clerk is not a powerful position, but felt our people needed some representative in the local government."

José Montoya's professional hat was put on quickly. Juan may help him more than he thinks: "Juan, in that position you must have a good handle on how the county is being managed?" he asked pointedly.

"I do, I see the length and depth of Murphy's corruption. John Riley's sole job is to buy stolen cattle. He pays $5 a head. Then Murphy cheats the weight on resale," Juan declared.

"Doesn't the Fort buyer inspect the purchased beef?" José asked.

Juan had to laugh and said: "Murphy has the same fatten cattle brought in as a sample of the cattle being sold. The buyer, who is debt to The House, signs off on the whole herd sold to him. Next, the Indian agent, who is in debt to The House, exaggerates the number of Mescalero Apaches he must feed. That keeps the order quantity high. Murphy makes huge profits. I talked with a long-time employee of his, who thought I was his employee too. He said Murphy was the quartermaster in charge of all purchases for Colonel Kit Carson at Fort Sumner. The Colonel was illiterate and trusted the Irishman with every document placed in front of him to sign."

Juan continued to inform a shocked José: "He also said that when the government closed the Fort selling it to Lucerne Maxwell he transferred to Fort Stanton. At the end of the war Colonel Fritz was the base Commander and helped Murphy set up the Fort's sutler store on Fort Stanton. He was secretly a full partner in the store. I'm not saying I know that as a fact, but I wouldn't put it past them. I know when Colonel Fritz was discharged he became a full partner. When Jimmy Dolan was discharged he became their clerk. That is a fact.

José Montoya had a very concerned look on his face. He explained why: "Muy bueno amigo, you know too much! Please don't let The House know how much you know about their fraud!"

"They know, as Probate Clerk all the county's business passes across my desk. They hire our people to handle their cattle. They have told me every detail, and they know that too." Juan concluded.

"You are the one that told me how they handle oppositions to their ways of doing business. Be careful my friend. This is not one of our bandito games we played as kids," José warned Juan.

"Ah! But I used to win most of those (which was not true)," he said chuckling.

"Sure you did!" José said sarcastically.

Catherine approached their table. She had a question of her own: "Mr. Patrón, do you know anything about the gold and silver strike called Silver City?"

"Yes, I have. Many jobs available in Silver City itself, too." Juan informed her, and José agreed.

"I lived in Wichita when it boomed. My partner Bill Antrim said Silver City is different than any other boom town. I know he wants to go there, but I'm not sure about another boom town..." she explained her predicament.

José volunteered: "I must side with your partner, ma'am. Silver City is quite different from Wichita. It is a clean town."

Juan had information, too: "Ma'am, I have been to Silver City. Lucerne Maxwell of Cimarron is one of the founding fathers and investors in Silver City. He and the other founders and investors didn't want another Wichita. They were determined to make Silver City a sophisticated community with an opera house, restaurants, and up-scale gambling houses. Recently they began a money drive for a school house, and full time school teacher."

"Are you planning on moving there? We would hate to lose this wonderful restaurant." José asked.

Catherine explained: "My partner is also my fiancé. Bill has the prospector's itch to strike it rich. He has for some time now. He has tried hard to convince me to settle in Silver City."

Juan and José smiled, and Juan replied:

"I know that itch you're talking about. If I indulge in one drink, I'm hunting down a Monte table." He said with a laugh.

José commented: "We would miss you very much, but to tell the truth, you would do very well in Silver City. It is a boom town! Your fiancé is right about that."

Catherine left for the kitchen. She grabbed Henry just as he was about to return to the eating area:

"Whoa young man! You are to not bother those two again. They are discussing important private information." Catherine demanded.

"I know mother, I just want to learn more about our new home," attempting to appeal to her softer side, which did not come forth. She just gave him that look he better not take another step.

"Ah shucks, alright I'll stay ignorant!" Henry said as he ran off.

Juan and José continued their conversation. These two men were almost like brothers that had not seen each other in a long time.

José Montoya hoped his friend could help him with his investigation, he asked Juan:

"I am going to try and see the Governor Giddings. What do you know about him?"

"Grant appointed him September 1, 1871. One of his first acts was to veto a Ring sponsored bill to reassign the Chief Justice of the Territory Joseph G. Palen to a remote lower court. The Ring was furious and men showed up with guns in the legislature. Governor Giddings ordered the U.S. Military in and all sides calmed down. The Governor met with his opposition and brokered a compromise. He got his pet project to raise taxes for a public-school system," Juan concluded.

José asked directly to his point: "Is he an honest man?"

Juan did not hesitate answering: "Yes, he is honest. His health isn't good. I heard his friends in Michigan convinced him to take this job to help his health."

"Can you imagine the stress an honest governor must have against the Ring?" Juan asked rhetorically.

"It certainly would not be an easy job, and most likely a dangerous one." José volunteered.

Chapter Sixty-Four

Gold Discovered Near Silver City

Just then Bill Antrim came running in as excited as a child on Christmas. He said hello to José who introduced Juan Patrón. Bill could hardly contain himself through the introductions.

Catherine, Henry, and Josie all rushed into the room expecting some terrible news. Bill turned to Catherine and declared: "Pack for a trip. We are leaving for Silver City after our wedding! Gold has been discovered near Silver City!"

Juan Patrón informed: "Yes, sir. I believe they named the gold rush town Georgetown. Some say it is a big strike, and others say not so much."

"We will check it out on the way to Silver City. José, do you want to come to our wedding?" Bill changed the subject.

"I would love to, when is it?" José asked.

"March 1 at Dr. McFarland's church," Bill replied.

"Oh I'm sorry, I won't be here then. Thank you so much for the invitation."

Catherine interrupted: "No offense gentlemen, but Bill gets carried away." Then she turn to Bill and said "Remember, small wedding with only our family?" she said firmly.

Bill was quiet.

José replied "No offense taken, ma'am. We understand."

One person, not so happy, was a toe headed thirteen-year-old boy sitting at the corner table. It did not go unnoticed by Catherine and their guests.

Bill Antrim was too focused on his exciting news to notice Henry at all.

Later that evening Catherine asked Henry if he would take a short night walk with her. He agreed but thought it unusual. There was still a late winter chill with a wind blowing from the high western bluff.

His mother usually stayed inside during the evening. She rarely went out in fear of catching a cold. She had a terrible time recovering from it. Henry figured she was stunting all that fear to walk with him.

Catherine stuck her head through the opening of her new poncho. A Mexican woman friend of hers insisted she use it if she went out at night, or anytime in a cold wind.

"All you need now is a sombrero Mother." Henry chuckled.

"Well, I don't have one or I would use it, young man. Remember the Mexicans and Indians have been dealing with New Mexican weather a long time. I figure they know something about staying warm out here," Catherine defended herself.

"Yes, ma'am, I figure you are right." Henry replied as they stepped out into the chilly air.

They walked only a short distance to an uncompleted adobe wall she used as a resting bench. Catherine was out of breath.

Henry knew her breathing was getting worse, but just didn't want to believe it. He believed God would save his Mother. She was a devout person who obeyed the Ten Commandments.

His mother deserved God's special handling. She worked so hard for her family, never allowed her boys to cuss or be mischief in public. She loved God and He would eventually heal her.

He was old enough to know what she had does kill people. It just would not happen to his mother. God would save her.

They sat for a while not saying anything, but just looking at the late winter moon peeking through the cloudy dark sky.

Catherine broke the silence: "Son, I wanted to talk to you about our move to Silver City. I know you're not happy about it," she said in a low sympathetic voice.

"No, Mother, I am not happy about it. I have just made some of the best friends I've had in my whole life. I mean real friends!" Henry said as though he was fifty-years-old, not thirteen, and continued: "I have the best teacher ever! I'm learning the three R's as you wanted."

Catherine replied: "Yes, I know. Your teacher is bilingual, and has taught you Spanish very well. I know you like her a lot, too. I've never seen you so excited to learn, and that does my heart good. I really do understand that, son."

Henry uncharacteristically sat silent. He thought to himself: "She does know, so why would she move again. All we do is move, why again?" He decided to ask her:

"Why do we have to move again? Just because Uncle Bill has gold fever?" Henry asked sincerely.

"So, you know about gold fever?" Catherine asked surprised. "Did you read about that in those magazines?"

"Yes Mother, I did. It drives grown men near crazy." He replied.

"You're right, but a man sometimes has to figure that out for themselves. You are old enough to have seen grown men do a lot of foolish things. Some will drink themselves to death. Most men can have a couple drinks and go home. Others cannot stop drinking, they just can't put the bottle down. Gold fever is the same. Some see it as a business opportunity to mine the miners. Large capital companies back east let the prospectors do the hard work and they come in buy them out after a strike."

"Very few prospectors make it rich. Even when they find color, all their hard work just makes expenses. Most end up working for the capitalist." Catherine concluded.

"Mother, you don't have to worry about me. I won't do anything like that. No gold fever or drinking for me. I've seen what it does to Uncle Bill." Henry informed and then got to his point:

"If you know Uncle Bill has gold fever, why up-root all of us to satisfy him?"

"I'm not doing that. You haven't thought of your brother, have you?" She replied quickly.

Henry looked at her strangely. He hadn't, but Josie always seemed to not care where they were living.

Catherine then explained: "You should know that Josie felt the same way you do now about Wichita. He had good work, good friends, and was making good money. Also, had learned two trades! The future looked very good for him in Wichita. I had no choice. I must live in dry, clean air country to stay alive. Had I stayed there I would be dead now." Catherine stated bluntly and for the first time talked openly about her health to Henry.

"No ma'am, God won't let you die! I know it!" Henry blurted out almost angrily.

Catherine sat quietly for a few minutes. She knew instinctively what she said next would be important to Henry.

"We all die, my son. What matters is how we live. We should all live as long as we can, but never fear death," Catherine changed the subject.

"I agreed to move to Silver City because a boom-town can provide more opportunities to all of our family. Your Uncle Bill can prospect which is his dream in life. Also, there will be mining, freighting, and carpentry work to make his living. Josie will have no problem finding work in carpentry and freighting, which he likes. Before I pulled you out: you were in the restaurant listening to José and Mr. Patrón. You heard Mr. Patrón say his father sold their farm in Santa Fe and bought one in Lincoln. His family had many generation in Santa Fe. Why would he do that?"

"I don't know, Mother. He had a farm here." Henry could not see the reason.

"Yes, but how about his growing family? He wanted a growing community for his growing family. When he did move his family, he made enough money to have a farm and a store." Catherine stated and then paused in thought for a second.

There was something Henry had not asked about or figured on: "It would make me very happy! That makes three of the four of us happy to move." Catherine informed him of that fact. Inferring he was just thinking of himself...which he was. Henry was always for Henry!

"Why would it make you happy? You have everything here," Henry sincerely wanted to know.

"First, doing what I think is best for my family always makes me happy. It also could be better for my health. I've been told Silver City is a little lower in elevation, but has clean mountain air blowing constantly. The woman that told me that has been there, she said the seasons are not harsh, and there are mountain trees in sight of town! I love trees! You know that." Catherine delivered her answer very emotionally.

Henry's quick mind replied: "Then why did that woman move back to Santa Fe?" he said somewhat sarcastically.

"She is a military officer's wife, and they were posted at the fort near here. He was ordered back to Albuquerque. You might remember her. She stayed with us and dressed every day in her Sunday best?" Catherine inquired.

"I do remember her. She shopped every day and we all talked about where she got so much money." Henry chuckled.

"That is her. She buys Pueblo Indian goods and sells then from her store in Albuquerque. She talked about Silver City fondly, hoping someday her husband would be assigned there again. I'm sure I will like Silver City more than here. If we don't like it, we could always move back here." Catherine concluded.

"Mother, I can't tell you a lie. I'm still not happy about moving away from my friends and my teacher. I really thought Santa Fe was going to be a real home!" Henry confessed.

Without hesitating Catherine said: "You will make new friends in Silver City and I promise you we won't move again, unless we return here. How does that sound to you, son?" Catherine promised.

"It is an offer I cannot turn down," Henry replied and chuckled knowing he really didn't have any choice.

"You are too smart for your own britches. Where do you think you got your brains from? Seriously, I hope you understand better, now?" Catherine asked.

"Yes Mother, I do." Henry replied more seriously.

Mother and son walked the short distance back to their boarding house. Henry remained uncharacteristically quiet the whole way back. Catherine had done her best to convince Henry he would enjoy Silver City too. She knew that he didn't buy it, but was respectful enough to go along with whatever his mother wanted.

Chapter Sixty-Five

The Big Day Arrived

Bill Antrim and Catherine McCarty had been together as close friends for nearly eight years. He desired her hand in marriage from the time he met her after taking the boys camping all those years ago. He knew he could never display any romantic affection until she took off her mourning arm band, and had been so happy when she had taken it off at that first family dinner.

He was ready then...he thought. Catherine had "designated" his title Uncle Bill. She was fond of Bill but she never harbored any romantic feelings toward him. He was her best friend, and any other relationship never came to her mind.

Bill had lost his nerve to tell her he was in love with her, and wanted her to marry him. He was obviously afraid of her rejecting him, and what he might do after that.

In Wichita Bill finally get the nerve up to telling her he was in love with her and then she simply said: "I know, Bill. This is not the time for me. I want to make sure I can independently support myself and the boys. I never again want to be in the position Michael left me. Maybe later." Catherine had rejected his proposal, but left the door open in the future. Bill accepted that.

Time heals all wounds. After her health gave way in Wichita, she began to truly appreciate all that "Uncle Bill" had done for her and the boys. He had supported her independence, but was always there when she needed help with anything.

She knew it was now time to formalize what had already formed, a family unit. She agreed to marry Bill and change all their names to Antrim. She told the boys as of their marriage on March 1, 1873, their last name will be Antrim.

Catherine and Bill decided to spend a little money and take the whole family out to dinner at the Exchange Hotel's restaurant after the wedding.

Bill Antrim was busy doing as he always did before a move: buying a freight wagon and team. He sought out a wagon train heading south along the Rio Grande River trail. He wanted to take that trail to the Messila Valley around the end of March. That giving them enough time to liquidate what they wouldn't be freighting.

Finding the wagon master of one such train he again agreed to drive one of the wagons for the owner in exchange for travel expenses for a family of four.

Josie would be responsible to drive the family wagon, and Henry would relieve him periodically. Catherine would not be working on this trip. She was not up to it, and made sure Bill didn't include her cooking for half the wagon train's employees.

1st Presbyterian Church & School of Santa Fe, N.M.
Museum of New Mexico 1868 Negative No. 37895
Photographed by Nicolas Brown

March 1, 1873 arrived with all preparations complete.

The family arrived at the First Presbyterian Church just after noon.[102]

[102] The First Presbyterian Church was first built by Baptist missionaries in 1854. Its adobe walls fit into the Santa Fe landscape very well. Santa Fe was 95% Mexican American at that time. There was only a small Anglo population, and even smaller Protestant population. In-fact not enough to support the church, so it was closed and sat empty until 1867 when the Presbyterian Church purchased it. Immediately they built a tower, added beautiful windows, and expanded the building to accommodate a church school. Reverend McFarland, his wife Amanda, and their daughter Katie made a success of the church and school.

Bill, Catherine, Josie, and Henry entered the church and saw Rev. McFarland standing at the alter waiting their arrival.

Catherine quietly whispered to Bill:

"Isn't that a beautiful alter?"

"Yes, it is." Bill and Henry both replied.

Mrs. Amanda R, McFarland ***Dr. David Fulton McFarland***
Source: Department of History and Records Management Service, Presbyterian Church, Philadelphia, Pennsylvania

As they approached they noticed in the first pew stood Amanda and Katie McFarland, and Harvey Edmonds. The latter was Rev. McFarland's volunteer to be present at all weddings, funerals, and baptism ceremonies as an official witness.

Catherine was the calmest of their family members. She was confident in her decision to marry Bill. Her illness was progressing, and she hoped he would care for the boys once she was gone.

Bill had waited eight years for this moment, and frankly had given little thought of his future "fatherly" responsibilities.

The ceremony went without a hitch. Rev. McFarland added Josie and Henry as witnesses in his church ledger.[103]

---

[103]No one in that wedding party, or anyone else who knew the family in Santa Fe, would in their wildest guess think Henry McCarty, in a few short years, would start a career in criminal activities. The result of which, in him becoming one of the most famous criminals in United States history. That bright, blue-eyed, toe-headed boy, who always had a smile on his face, would go so very wrong in life. The purpose of this book is to enlighten the reader on what caused that transition.

It was only a week after the wedding the Antrim family was back on the road. Their good planning allowed for a quick liquidation of what they were not taking with them. They had much experience in what they needed on the trail, and who had what responsibility.

The wagon train they joined was much smaller than the last one they took to Santa Fe. Most of the families had the same destination as the Antrim family. Only one was heading through the Mesilla Valley to its name sake Mesilla in the southern end of the valley.

They were traveling the El Camino Real along the Rio Grande River. It was one of the oldest roads in the United States, and used to be one of the most dangerous. Fort Craig was the largest fort in the western section of the country. Its presence had made it a safe trail. Many settlers were now farming and ranching in the good soil of the Messila Valley.

Every once in a while there would be a renegade Apache raid, but it was few and far between.

It took their wagon train four days to reach Albuquerque and another week to reach Fort Craig. They headed south to a trail that branched off the main road and headed due west toward Silver City.[104] The Wagon Master said it was only about a hundred miles from where they were.

That turned out to be the worst 100 miles the Antrim family had experienced since leaving Wichita. It was not an easy trail.

They enjoyed their stay in the Mimbres Valley. The local Indians were "friendlies." They soon found out not many pioneers would have made it through those mountains without their assistance.

The trail followed through valleys that would take switch-backs along rivers. If not careful they would face high cliffs that

---

Also, of course to disclose many discovered facts of his early life after four years of research.

[104] Near todays Caballo, New Mexico. Today it is 76 miles from Silver City using Hwy 152 which is roughly the old trail established by the indigenous Indian tribes. Large freight trains would travel further south and around the mountain range and back up to Silver City.

were insurmountable, gorges that were impassable, and being lost for weeks.

The Indian's trail would become the main road from the Rio Grande River to Silver City. The only exception would be for large freighted items that used a southern route.

They crossed over the summit and on the downhill side of the mountain range. The Mimbres had warned them that there they would enter Apache territory.

Chapter Sixty-Six

Apache Scout Seen

The Wagon Master Mr. William O'Brien was an Irish prankster if there ever was one. He rode alongside the Antrim family wagon.

He concluded he could put a good scare into what he thought was a ten-year-old toe-headed boy holding the reins (Henry Antrim was actually thirteen-years-old and had just relieved his brother from the reins).

Mr. Obrien asked Henry: "Did you see those heathen apaches back there?" Not giving a chance for Henry to reply he continued with his heavy Irish drawl: "Keep a keen eye out laddy, they like stealing ten-year-old boys like yourself."

Henry had read in his magazines all about the apaches. Ironically, he had already seen Apaches on several occasions. They lurked behind boulders, or laid prone on top a mesa to scout their train.

This train was well guarded and their sight did not worry Henry one bit. After the attack by the Comancheros a few Apache scouts didn't bother him at all.

Looking straight ahead Henry replied to the prankster: "It is the ones you cannot see you must worry about." He then turned his head toward Mr. Obrien. Ironically, just as he did he saw the Apache scout that had dogged them for days behind Mr. Obrien. The Apache was high on the hill.

"Yes, sir. I have seen the Apaches. There is one behind you on that hill. He has been dogging us for four days now." Henry said in a matter-of-factly.

Mr. Obrien swung his big bay mare around and sure enough the Apache scout rose quickly, and swung up on his pony picketed behind the hill. Then he disappeared.

Henry had to retaliate a bit: "I read they love bay mares at breeding time. Is your horse a filly or a mare, sir? Oh, that Apache couldn't tell anyway. I think that Indian is after your horse sir," he said with a full grin that showed his prominent front teeth.

Mr. Obrien was embarrassed and snapped at Henry: "If you saw that Indian four days ago why didn't you say something then?"

Before Henry could answer Catherine stuck her head out from the canvas: "Mr. O'Brien, he informed me of his siting each time. I assumed if my thirteen-year-old son could see the Indian scout, you would certainly know it was there," Catherine said in a condescending manner.

"Good day, ma'am!" Mr. Obrien spurred his horse on ahead. He thought to himself: "Damn, that kid doesn't look thirteen. Although he did act almost like an adult. He does have some kind of sharp eyes. Not once did I see that Indian. Had he not moved I wouldn't have seen him this time. Amazing kid!"

He rode ahead to report what he saw to the train's owner riding in the first wagon.

"I know Mr. O'Brien I saw that scout too. Put some extra guards on tonight. I don't think he is going to mess with us, but cross hobble our animals just in case," the owner instructed.

"Yes sir, will do." He replied and swung his big bay mare around. As he rode off he thought to himself: "Damn! I'm the only person that didn't see that Indian. I'm slipping up. I'm glad I didn't tell him it was that boy that told me...ha!"

He heard the owner calling to him and rode right back.

"I changed my mind. We'll camp here tonight and start down the ridge tomorrow. Have half the men on guard from here to Silver City. I don't want to take any chances. I got a bad feeling all of a sudden."

The Apaches go after easy prey. They don't like empty teepees with widowed squaws and orphaned bonitos. Mr. O'Brien, put on a strong showing.

"You have ten fighting men. Remind them if they have to fight I'll bonus them $5. Also, remind them if I catch one asleep on guard, I'll fine him $5 and kick him off the train. Do you have any questions, Mr. O'Brien?"

"No, sir, I'll let them know right now," Mr. O'Brien replied earnestly.

"Hobble that bay mare real good tonight. They like those bay mares you know," the owner warned him.

"Yes, sir, I'll certainly do that!" Mr. O'Brien replied with a little surprise in his voice. His boss was saying exactly what that toe-headed kid said. "Heck, maybe it's true," he thought to himself.

The owner thought his response was a strange one, but shrugged it off.

That night when all was quiet, and most everyone not on duty was asleep, Henry awoke startled.

He crawled out of his blanket, and peered into the darkness. There it was again! No question in his mind, Indians were moving around about a hundred yards out.

Josie appeared next to Henry. Immediately Henry placed his fingers across his lips. Then pointed his index finger toward the darkness ahead.

Josie listened and put up three fingers. Henry acknowledged his count with a nod. Then all went quiet. Not a sound of movement.

Henry pointed to his temple in a gesture that the Indians were contemplating and thinking out their next move. Most likely they had discovered the eight guards around the animals in that area. Also, the animals were hobbled, picketed and tied off on a long line rope.

Those Indians figured correctly that they would most likely lose their lives for that horse flesh. Suddenly there was a noise, but it was of the Indians scampering away from their wagon train.

"They are gone," Henry whispered to Josie.

"Yep, let's get some rest before morning chores," Josie declared. The two boys crawled back under the wagon and curled up in their blankets.

The next day the wagon train headed west down the back side of the mountain range. Every wagon owner had said they wanted to check out Georgetown before going to Silver City. Everyone had heard of the "big strike" in Georgetown.

It took the train only three days to reach Georgetown. The Wagon Master Mr. Obrien told everyone they would rest the animals there night, a full day tomorrow, and leave for Silver City the next morning.

Not as many guards were needed as there was a lot of activity near their campsite. All the animals were picketed and Bill told Catherine he was going to check out the town and would be back late for dinner.

Josie and Henry immediately asked to go with him, which he agreed to, providing that their mother agreed.

"Might as well cook later if all three of you will be late. I'll rest up," she said almost relieved she would not have to start cooking.

Bill and the boys explored Georgetown from one end to the other. Bill was excited by what several prospectors had told him.

One said: "Men have found a pretty good quantity of silver. One small group found placer gold, but it played out quickly." The man seemed honest, and telling it like it was, matter-of-factly.

In Bill's mind, and his mind only at that time, if there was placer gold then there had to be large gold veins still to be discovered.

This thinking proved how little Bill Antrim knew about mining. One old prospector had told him: "Gold is where you find it. That is the only certainty of prospecting for it!"

That went in one ear and out the other so fast all Bill could hear was the whistling of the air. What was worse, he misinterpreted what the man had said. Henry couldn't believe his ears when Bill said:

"Did you hear that boys, gold is here to be found!"

The boys had a blast exploring the town. They couldn't help but notice the strange looks some people were giving them.

Josie addressed it first: "What is with the strange looks?" he directed to Henry.

"I think they are try to determine if we are street Arabs, or street gamin'," Henry explained to his older brother.

"That makes sense little brother," Josie replied.

"They think we are scouting them to rob later, is my guess." Henry presumed.

One old timer saw them contemplating the dilemma and approached the boys: "Don't you never mind those folks. By in large they are good folks. We have no law here in Georgetown except the vigilantes. Those are the people checking you out so closely,"
the man explained.

"Thank you, sir. We understand now. If this was my town I would do the same." Josie replied.

The boys headed back for their campsite. It was getting late and they were hungry.

Bill brought up the subject of staying in Georgetown instead of going on to Silver City. He was the only one that thought that way. Not even Josie and Henry agreed.

Catherine put her firm, Irish foot down saying: "Bill, we all agreed to Silver City. It is civilized, and this town is not. We will leave with the train tomorrow."

Bill began to try and convince Catherine otherwise, and she gave the look.

Josie interrupted: "We better go in the morning," looking directly at Bill.

Henry added: "Very smart thing to do," in a jovial manner.

Catherine had her back to all three and could not help grin at what her boys were saying. Bill was seriously outnumbered on this issue.

Bill replied: "Alright, but I think we are making a big mistake."

The boys replied in unison: "I don't think so," then grinned at each other.

The family had the quietest dinner they had ever experienced. They were very hungry, and little conversation took place.

Henry helped with the dishes and packing them for the last leg of their journey. Josie and Bill picketed and hobbled the animals. That should be their last night having to do that. Silver City was only fourteen miles down the trail.

Catherine inhaled the crisp clean mountain air and remembered what the woman had told her about this country. It may be just her imagination but she felt like she was getting better already.

"How could the air make such a difference so quickly," she thought to herself. She took several deep breaths and smiled. Henry tapped Josie and pointed toward their mother. Josie gave a thumbs up and rolled over.

The Antrim family all fell asleep. Bill was last, still pouting over not staying in Georgetown. He thought he should be the one making the family decision now.

Then he realized he would never change Catherine's independent nature. She would not yield to anyone, husband or not.

Bill Antrim felt for the first time he wasn't the head of this household. He had been fooling himself. Since the marriage he really had thought he would be the head of the household. Tonight proved that was not going to be the case.

The next morning Catherine had breakfast cooking before sunrise. The smell awoke the rest of the family. Bill had a midnight guard watch so he had broken sleep. The rest of the family was wide eyed and bushy tailed.

Catherine believed with all her heart the mountain air was doing wonders for her.

After breakfast, the sun was just peeking over the mountain to the east. Josie and Bill hooked up the animals, Henry did dishes, and Catherine put all the bedding away, and packed the wagon for their last day on the trail!

The sun seemed brighter even though it was still early. The smell of pine and oak trees was in the air.

Josie jumped up on the wagon seat as Catherine declared: "Wagon's ho! When that sun sets we will be in Silver City!"

Silver City, New Mexico, Looking North on Bullard Street Late 1870's Silver City Museum. Taken from Chihuahua Hill. *Source: John Harlan Collection, Frederick Nolan's "West of Billy the Kid" page 24.*

Chapter Sixty-Seven

Hello Silver City!

The Antrim's wagon train descended into the Cienega Valley and Silver City came into view.

Catherine liked the city immediately! She saw many two story buildings, and a few three story buildings. The latter was unheard of in frontier towns. What's more, the city looked new! They had lived in the ancient city of Santa Fe. Silver City had grown fast over the previous two years.

She noticed there were actually scattered trees in town. Most frontier towns had no trees as they were used to build the townships. This city was different in so many ways.

Josie pulled their wagon in front of the Star Hotel. They would stay there until permanent housing could be obtained. Bill settled matters with the wagon master and made arrangements for their animals.

The Star Hotel was a two story long building on the west side of Main Street. Catherine went in to register for a couple days stay.

The very affable proprietor greeted Catherine:

"Good afternoon, ma'am. Will you be staying long term?" Mr. Phillips asked politely.

"No sir, we will look for a place to purchase or rent if nothing is available to purchase," Catherine informed him confidently.

The proprietor noted she had not asked how much the rooms were, and opened by saying she would be looking to purchase, this meant her family had some money.

"Ma'am, most greeners[105] are now living in tents. I know old John Swesshelm cabin right across the street is going up for rent. If I were you ma'am I would grab it quickly!" He sincerely suggested.

"Thank you very much, sir. You are an honest businessman," Catherine replied.

"If you would like I will introduce you to the current owner?" Mr. Phillips asked.

"Of course, I would sir." Catherine replied.

Mr. Phillips walked into his saloon area with Catherine following close behind. Introductions were made. The two came to an agreement of rent with a minimum of six month tenancy, and with an option to purchase the cabin at current market price during the same time period. If they moved out sooner, Catherine agreed to pay a prorated rent amount due to the owner at vacating the cabin. The deal was done.

While this conversation was going on Henry drifted over to the Monte table and observed the players. Catherine was so engrossed in her negotiations she did not notice his disappearance.

Henry had learned the basics of the game from his friends in Santa Fe, but had not seen it played in a gaming house.

---

[105] The term "greeners'" was applied to newcomers to the city. Also, "greenhorns" was another term.

His quick mind figured there was more players losing than winning on each deal, deal after deal. That meant the profit was always in the Monte Banker's favor.

"Come on Henry! Help me with the bags. We are staying here a couple days," she called out to him.

"Oh ma'am, I will help you with those" a young man came out of nowhere to say and explained: "I work for the hotel...it is my job, ma'am," he said in a manner that he would appreciate her letting him do his job.

Catherine replied: "Fine young man, but let my son help you."

"Sure, that is fine ma'am," the young man agreed.

Henry followed the young man into the lobby area. He took the two smaller bags and the bellboy took the two larger bags, at his insistence.

Bill Antrim arrived looking somewhat depressed and with bad news: "Catherine, there isn't one place to rent and no place to buy. All the owners are renting out their properties. I checked with the hostler, a saloon owner, and a dry goods store. Nothing available. I'll have to buy a large tent tomorrow, and find some space somewhere," Bill concluded.

Catherine let him finish his entire story before she handed him a rent receipt for $15.

"What...how?!" Bill exclaimed.

She told him the whole story and reminded him of her Irish luck.

"But you haven't seen it, again! Right?" Bill asked.

"Well, actually I did. It's right across the street. It's a 30-foot by 30-foot log cabin. I got it for so little because I told the owner that there was nothing my husband can't fix that needs it," she said as she flashed those sparkling, blue eyes on her submissive face.

"Great! Let's move in now!" Bill declared.

"I paid for two days here. We could use the rest and you can check out the cabin," she replied and turned toward the two boys and continued:

"And our boys can check out our new hometown tomorrow, and report back to us before dinner tomorrow. Before sundown in any event, understand?" she was firm.

"Can't we go tonight?" Henry asked,

“No, you are both going to rest tonight. No sneaking out in the night!” she demanded and then asked Bill:

“Can we have dinner in their restaurant here tonight?”

“Of, course. Our ‘welcome to Silver City dinner’,” Bill replied.

The boys had disappeared. The bellboy volunteered:

“I saw them go to the room you rented for them,” he said pointing to a room down the hallway.

“Whew! Thanks. I can’t believe how fast they disappeared.” Bill admitted.

Josie and Henry walked out on the balcony of the second floor. Across the street was their new home, at least until they could build one of their own.

Josie spoke first: “Little brother, we have a hometown” he said in satisfied, solemn tone.

Henry didn’t respond at first, then he said: “It looks very exciting, people moving all over the place. There must be a lot of kids our age here,” he said in a wishful manner.

“I’m sure there is little brother, I’m sure there is.” Josie went on to say: “I’ll tell you what I do like about this town. It looks like a real town, like a small Denver. Look how many brick buildings. I can’t see one adobe building.” Josie concluded.

Henry pointed: “There is one...over there.”

“Ah shucks...one! I can handle one!” Josie exclaimed.

Henry was surprised because Josie had never told him he didn’t like adobe buildings. He liked them a lot. They seemed warm, comfortable, and cozy. The heat stayed in in winter and cool air in the summer. Many of his friends in Santa Fe lived in adobes.

The Antrim Cabin Located at the corner of Main & Broadway, Silver City, New Mexico. *Source: Museum of New Mexico Neg. 99054. Photographed by Alfred S. Addis in 1882.*

Chapter Sixty-Eight

Silver City Cabin Settling In

The next morning Bill put the boys to work helping him get the cabin ready to move in.

Catherine said she was going to rest a couple days, and that is exactly what she did. Traveling had been very hard on her.

Bill met with the owner and obtained permission to add another large room off the end of the cabin. He agreed after Bill informed him he was an experienced carpenter.

The third day Catherine was ready to move in to her new cabin. New to her. She still had not seen the inside of the cabin.

She didn't have great expectations considering it was built by and used by a prospector.

Entering the front door she was pleasantly surprised how comfortable it was.

The extra room Bill created by dividing one room into two rooms would be completed in a few more days.

Catherine declared to Bill: "Bill you are a good carpenter." she said with sincerity and emphasis on "good".

"Thank you Catherine. I've had some practice." he replied with a chuckle.

One room was theirs and the other would be the boys. The original bedroom, which was the size of a large closet, would be for a boarder.

Both her boys knew they were going to school. Josie had demurred saying he was too old to learn and didn't need schooling to be a carpenter or freighter.

"Mr. Carpenter, I want a building 30-feet by 20-feet, 8 feet tall with a gabled roof, a false front 10-feet tall and 20-feet wide. How much lumber will I need?" she asked sarcastically, knowing he wouldn't have the slightest idea.

"Enough to build it." Josie sarcastically answered.

"Not the right answer, son, not the right answer. If you learned basic mathematics you will know, not guess. You are going to school. Have I made myself clear?" Catherine demanded.

"Yes, ma'am," Josie reluctantly agreed.

Catherine had both boys at their new dinner table. They sat directly across from her. She informed them: "I have inquired and a Mr. Peter J. Ott[106] has opened a school in his house. I enrolled both of you to start Monday." she said in her most authoritative tone.

Catherine had her small cabin well organized and was settling in pretty good. It was a must as all four of them would have to be sleeping, dressing, and eating in what was one large miner cabin's room.

---

[106] Mr. Ott was well trained and passionate about teaching, but with lack of support from the community as a whole he was forced to close his private school in August, 1873: "Silver City Mining Life" Aug. 9, 1873 Michael Wallis Pg. 66, Pg. 262.

It was nice that Bill was able to complete the separating walls quickly. He could work on the addition in his spare time.

It was a warm summer. There were no wild fires, and the mountain air swept down on the La Cienega Valley keeping the temperature very comfortable.

Catherine was feeling much better. Better than she had in a year. Of course, she knew a lot of how she felt that year had to do with all the traveling. In any event, she loved Silver City.

There was a knock on her cabin door. Catherine got a bit excited. She may be meeting her first neighbor. The thought fleeted by as she rationalized it is most likely for Bill or her boys, but she could hope!

She opened her door and grinned ear-to-ear. Her sparkling blue eyes glittered.

The lady at the door introduced herself: "My name is Mrs. Gerald Truesdell, but please call me Clara."

"Please come in Clara. Thank you for stopping by. My name is Mrs. William Antrim, but please call me Catherine," she replied inviting the polite lady into her humble cabin.

The two women had instantly taken a liking for each other. Of course, anyone that had ever met the jolly Irish Catherine instantly liked her, but not always did she like them. She really liked Clara Truesdell. She seemed so unassuming and honest in words and manners.

Clara explained her visit: "Of course, Catherine, I was being nosey, wanting to know who the new arrivals were..." both ladies laughed, and Clara went on: "I noticed, by being nosey, you have a couple boys who look school age?"

Catherine acknowledged she wanted both boys in school.

Clara continued: "Good, many of us have worked hard to raise funds for a new school house. Until that happens our teacher, Mr. Ott, will being holding class out of his house."

Catherine asked: "How many students are there now?"

Her two boys were listening intently on the other side of the wall. She knew when they were listening because they would go very quiet.

Clara thought a moment and answered: "We only have a couple dozen that could go to school. We don't get half that number to actually show for class. I may have just exaggerated a bit. Let me add them up. These are the kids that attend:

"I have two boys: Chauncey and Gideon. Our town brewery owner John Mays has two boys: John Jr. and Vincent. Then Cortie Bennett, the nephew of Judge Cornelius Bennett. Also, Wayne and Harry Whitehill, the two boys of our County coroner Harvey Whitehill and his wife Harriet Whitehill. Mr. Whitehill is also one of our founding fathers. He was the one to actually lay out our city here. Oh, yes, Harriet has a brother living here, and he has two boys: Albert and Charley Stevens. Oh, my! I can't forget David and Amelia Abraham's boys: Hyman, Louis, and Sam Abraham." Clara ended her list with a long sigh of relief.

Catherine was not only listening closely, but was taking notes too, and Clara knew it. Henry and Josie left without being noticed by Clara and Catherine.

"How many is that?" Clara asked

"Twelve," Catherine replied.

"Well, I'm probably missing a couple, but not much more than that." Clara declared.

Catherine volunteered: "I would like to contribute to the public-school building. We don't have much income right now, but I could give $25 now without hurting my family. Later I can give more."

"That would be great. I've arranged for the funds to go to the County treasury. Sheriff McIntosh was designated to hold it, but I trust him as far as I can throw a bay mare," Clara declared.

Catherine chuckled and said: "I know the kind."

She counted out $25 and gave it to Clara.

"All the kids thank you!" Clara replied.

The two women talked for over an hour like long lost friends. Henry came running in and slid to a stop before Clara at the table.

"I'm sorry, ma'am!" Henry declared, noticing he had startled Clara.

"I didn't know if you were going to stop in time," Clara confessed to Henry.

"This is my over active boy Henry. He is 13 going on 25." Catherine introduced Henry to Clara. She continued to Henry: "We just donated to the school building fund, and I told Clara you will not miss one day of school. Was I correct in telling her that?" Catherine looked for his commitment.

"Yes, Mother...what if I'm sick?" Henry asked sarcastically.

"You have not had a sick day in your life, Henry McCart...oops! Sorry, Henry Antrim," Catherine corrected her slip and then explained to Clara:

"Bill and I were married in March. I was a widow. I still slip with the boys. Just too many years calling them by their father's name McCarty."

"I understand. Sometimes I try to forget their first names too," both women laughed a loud at that comment.

Henry interrupted: "Sounds like I want to get to know your boys, ma'am."

He no more said those words and Chauncey Truesdell walked in the open front door Henry forgot to close.

"Mom, Gideon said you were here." Chauncey explained.

Clara introduced him and then asked why he was in such a hurry to find her.

Catherine gave Henry "the look." He ran over and closed the door.

Chauncey continued with his exciting news: "There is going to be a big dance at McGary's Hall tomorrow night. Everybody will be there. Can we go, can we?" Chauncey anxiously asked.

"Mother, can we go too? I've done all my chores!" Henry asked even before Clara could answer her son's question.

"Even tomorrow's chores?" Catherine inquired sarcastically.

"No, you know what I mean...all chores will be done today and tomorrow." Henry replied.

"If the Truesdell's are going we will go too," Catherine answered Henry and passed the buck back to Clara.

"Yes, we will go with the Antrim's," Clara agreed. The two boys locked arms and did a highland jig right there and on the spot.

Chauncey stopped and asked Catherine if he could show the town to Henry.

"Alright, but make sure you two are back for supper," she directed to Henry.

"Yes, ma'am" Henry agreed, and the two boys ran out the door.

Chapter Sixty-Nine

Henry's First Real Look at Silver City

The first question Henry had was:

"Where is this McGary's Hall?"

"I'll show you...not far from here," Chauncey replied and continued:

"McGary's Hall is used for everything important. Our first court house, church on Sunday, and some of the best socials..." Chauncey explained as they walked along.

"Look, over there is Ward's Hall. My mother doesn't like that one," Chauncey volunteered.

"Why is that?" Henry inquired.

"They won't allow women through the front doors." He answered with a chuckle and added: "Women have to go down dark alley out back, and open two large barn doors to get in."

"It sounds like you do like it?" Henry asked point blank.

"Yes, it is the biggest dance floor in town. My father said it is 200-feet long and 50-feet wide. He said it can hold every American in town," Chauncey replied with enthusiasm.

"Where are the Mexican bailes held?" Henry asked.

Just as he asked that of Chauncey two Mexican boys their age passed them, and overheard him asking Chauncey. One of them spoke up in Spanish. Showing off that he knew English:

"En la colina de Chihuahua una vez por semana." (Up on Chihuahua Hill once a week).

Henry shocked the two boys and Chauncey when he answered with a question in near perfect Spanish:

"Una vez semana. Que dia ya que hora?"

(Once a week. What day and what time?)

The two Mexican boys had stopped dead in their tracks. They had never heard an American speak in near perfect Spanish. One replied:

"Sabado a las ocho. A veces el Viernes a la misma hora."

(Saturday eight o'clock. Sometimes Friday same time.)

Henry asked: "Los Americanos son bienvenidos?" (Americans welcome?)

The older boy replied: "Si, varios vienen ahora." (Yes, several come now.)

Henry replied: "Muchas gracias. Cuales son tus nombres?" (Thank you very much. What are your names?)

The older boy answered: "Martin Martinez y mi hermano aqui José." (Martin Martinez and my brother here Joseph.)

Henry replied: "Encantade de conocerte a los dos." (Nice to meet you both.)

He replied: "Lo mismo." (The same.)

The two boys went their ways. Chauncey had to ask:

"Where did you learn Spanish so good?"

Henry thought and replied: "Some vaqueros that scouted for the wagon train we took from Denver to Santa Fe helped a lot. But, I really learned it when I got very lucky having a Spanish speaking teacher in Santa Fe. She also had mostly Mexican students. So she would speak Spanish to them and then English to me. I listened to that six hours a day. English isn't my first language. We spoke Gaelic in our house until I was four-years-old. Then my mother taught us English. She said she didn't want to teach us until she knew it as well as an American," Henry concluded.

Chauncey then qualified what he just heard: "You speak three languages right now?" he asked excitedly.

"Yes, I do. Languages seem to come easy to me. I learn them quickly. You have to feel the meaning in another language's word, instead of relating to words in your language. I learned that from the vaqueros." Henry explained.

"Makes sense to me," Chauncey acknowledged and then asked Henry: "See that fellow across the street?"

Henry looked and asked: "The one in his Sunday suit?"

"Yep, that's Mr. Owen Scott. He runs the newspaper in town. You see him, be on your best behavior or you'll find your name in his paper as a street Arab." Chauncey explained.

"Thanks, that's some good advice." Henry replied.

"Over there...the Orleans Club! Mr. Dyer owns that. Don't get caught in there. A friend of mine got hog-tied there, and Mr. Dyer told him if he caught him again he would hog-tie him to Charlie Sun's sows." Chauncey informed Henry.

Henry laughed out loud and replied: "I doubt that! What do you think would happen to a celestial that fed an American to his sows, no matter who tied him up there?"

Chauncey thought and replied: "I'm sure you are right, but the threat is enough to keep me out. I know that is why he said it, but it is enough for me!"

Chauncey explained and continued to tell Henry a true story: "Charlie Sun did throw his wife's black baby to his sow, and they ate every bit of that baby. That sow left no evidence. They say he told his wife if she cheated on him again, he would throw her to his sows too." Chauncey finished his story.

"Now, that is a man to stay away from!" Henry said.

The two boys decided to race each other around the block. Chauncey and Henry were neck and neck all the way.

Both boys pulled up at their predetermined finish line completely out of breath. They both had gone all out to best the other, and it ended in a tie.

Panting and almost still out of breath Henry said between gasps for air: "You are the first I've met to keep up with me."

Chauncey smiled and said: "Watch out for Harry Whitehill."

"Why is that?" Henry asked.

"He likes to pick on newcomers by betting them on a race with him. He is the fastest racer in Silver City. I know it happened to me. He will try you too." Chauncey warned Henry.

Henry thought a minute then suggested: "Maybe we could fix a race, and get him back for taking you. I love taking bullies down." Henry said with a grin ear-to-ear, and his blue eyes dancing a jig of their own.

Chauncey didn't even hesitate in replying: "Do you know how great that would be? By the way, it's not that I don't like the guy, but he is such a braggart. He says he is the fastest, smartest, and best fighter in our gang. I don't know how you plan to do it, but count me in!" Chauncey volunteered.

Henry chuckled and thought out loud: "I'll figure it out...maybe get my two New Mexican friends to help out on the trick." Henry laughed again.

"Good idea! He would never suspect them in with us," Chauncey surmised.

Chapter Seventy

Good Friends at First Sight

Catherine and Clara Truesdell truly became good friends at their first meeting. They talked none stop the whole time their boys were investigation the town.

Clara volunteered: "Harriet Whitehill is having a meeting, day after tomorrow, concerning our fund drive for the new school building. Mr. Ott will be there too."

"If you could attend I will introduce you to the 'society' of Silver City." Clara said with a grin and a touch of sarcasm.

"I will attend. Where is the meeting?" Catherine asked.

"Oh, I'll stop by and walk with you to Harriet's house. It's not too far from here," Clara volunteered.

Catherine first thought was: 'not far' for Clara may be 'too far' for her, but she decided not to say anything at that time. She would wait to see how far it was, and deal with the problem then.

Although she did feel much better, she counted her steps, and organized herself to minimize taking too many steps to do anything.

The boys arrived back from their exploring Silver City. They looked worn out.

Clara asked her son Chauncey: "Racing again, huh?"

"Yes, Mother. Henry is very fast!"

The Clara and Chauncey said their good-byes.

After they had left Catherine told Henry: "They seem to be very good people."

"Yes, ma'am, I think so too."

Catherine got back to her chores with Henry's help. Josie returned to help too.

Chapter Seventy-One

Everything Changes: Bill Antrim Takes a Stand

The next two days were beautiful summer days in Silver City. Blue sky, white, puffy clouds with a slight breeze keeping everyone comfortable.

Bill was up early. Catherine wanted him to go to the meeting at the Whitehill's house that night. He was washing up. After, he intended on putting a log in the fireplace when she approached him with the subject. He was still throwing water on his face.

"Bill, I expect you to be at the parents meeting tonight concerning the new school house," she said authoritatively. Even as she said it she thought it may be the wrong approach, no matter how well it worked in the past.

She went on after hearing no response from Bill: "Clara Truesdell is coming by at 6pm to walk with us to the meeting," Catherine informed him.

Bill still didn't say anything. He continued getting washed up, dressed, and pulling his old cavalry boots on. He always told his friends the best things he got standing guard at the Indiana State Fairgrounds, turned into Camp Morton, Prisoner of War Camp, was those boots, and two more just like them. He had already worn through two pair. Every time they moved they were the first thing Bill packed.

Catherine noticed the usual agreeable response was not forth coming from Bill. That was strange. He was acting oddly.

The fact was Bill had already decided he would not go to that meeting when he heard about it the preceding day.

"Are you coming, Bill?" Catherine asked point blank.

"No, I am not. Schooling is a woman's business, and I have no interest in meeting the town's socialites," Bill replied manner-of-factly.

Catherine continued preparing breakfast, but said not another word of it, which in her world said volumes.

She knew Bill had changed in the past two weeks, but couldn't put her finger on what it was, or why it was.

She decided to get right to the point: "What has come over you Bill? These two boys are yours too. Your responsibility, not just mine."

Bill was a mild-mannered man. Although he had Irish blood too, but he was raised to control his emotions. His father was a very successful businessman. He worked in his father's store before going on his own. He taught him to trust good logic over emotion.

Bill decided to let Catherine know exactly what he thought. He replied in a low, controlled, and matter-of-fact manner: "Josie is a hard worker. He has learned two trades, and is a man now. Yes, Catherine, Josie is a man now. You treat him like he is ten-years-old. He is eighteen-years-old. I grant you he looks fifteen, but he isn't. He should be on his own, earning his living as a man."

He didn't need to tell her she was holding on to him with her apron strings. Bill understood her two boys were everything to her, her entire world! She just couldn't let go, and accept Josie is full grown. He was still her first born little boy.

Catherine continued with breakfast, uncharacteristically not responding to Bill's comments. There seemed to be a long pause and then she simply asked: "What about Henry?" she asked in a low, monotone. They both knew the boys would be listening on the other side of the wall, it was far too quiet in there.

Bill thought a moment and then replied: "You know I never told you, because you never asked, I went to a very good country school. Most of the kids attending came from wealthy families in the area. It was a private school."

Catherine interrupted: "What does that have to do with Henry?"

Bill responded: "I'll get to it, be patient please. I was an above average student, but there were three or four very smart students in my class. A future doctor, attorney, and a congressman. Henry is smarter than any one of them. He is the smartest kid I have ever known. Although, he is too smart for his own britches. I know you know that, yet you give him a free rein when he should be hobbled. Catherine, there is nothing I could do with Henry that you wouldn't get in the way of. I have no control over him, because you have never let me. Years ago I would correct him and you would counter the efforts instantly."

Henry had heard that phrase: "too smart for his own britches", and he never could understand that. He thought smart should be good, not bad.

Bill concluded: "You go to your meeting. I have to find some work to do, and get a grub-stake together." Bill explained his priorities.

Catherine wasn't upset. She had asked for it, and realized she got it. At least she knew where he stood. After all, she knew prospecting was the reason he came to Silver City. He was chasing his dream of striking it rich, and she went along with that, albeit her focus was improving her health.

Her health was better now, much better. She decided right then and there she would again take in laundry, and have one boarder to support herself and the boys.

In the joining room the two Antrim boys were grinning with pleasure for what Bill had said about them. They liked every word of it.

Josie whispered to Henry: "You sure got him fooled. I don't think you're so smart."

Henry whispered to Josie: "He thinks you are a man, now that is funny!"

Josie smacked the back of Henry's head...a good swat. The kind that said: "I dare you to reply in kind".

Henry just grinned at his brother's attempt to rile him. It didn't work.

Catherine called out to the boys that breakfast was ready. They came to the new table that Bill had made the day before. That was the quietest breakfast they had ever had. The boys were processing all that was said and how it may affect them.

Bill felt like a load was taken off his shoulders. Catherine knew he was not going to be getting a labor job and give up his prospecting dreams, which she had hoped.

Bill had decided he would work part time to support a grub-stake for prospecting and help support the family.

Catherine was thinking of how long her health could hold out. Maybe she was beating the consumption. She had heard of such cases, albeit very few. In any event, she could no longer depend on Bill thinking of family first. The war had gotten Michael, and gold fever had gotten Bill. The result was the same.

Ironically, what attracted her to a friendship with Bill, many years earlier, he was a hard worker, and hated the war as much as she did. He was honest and forth coming with what he wanted, including her, and how much he hated the war. He had legally fought, with his father's help, not to be drafted. He compromised with the prosecutor and accepted a three-month enlistment.[107]

Shortly after Bill's enlistment the enlistment period went to three years. Bill had done what she wanted Michael to do. She had begged Michael to get a deferment, or pay the three hundred dollars for an exemption. She believed his boss at the time would have helped him with an advancement in pay. He never asked his boss because he wanted to enlist.

Catherine blamed herself for waiting so long to agree to marry Bill. "Maybe," she thought, "had she done so in '66 or '67 he would have felt the boys were his too. Maybe he would have cared more about their education. Now they were married, but he was still 'Uncle Bill' to both the boys, and worse, they were not his responsibility in his mind."

"Yes, I waited too long...my doing! No one else's." Catherine said to herself as she served a wonderful breakfast to her family. She decided to change the subject:

"Bill, will you come to the dance with me on Saturday at McGary's Hall?" she asked politely.

"Of course, I would love to!"

Catherine turned to the boys: "Yes, you two can come too." she declared.

The boys were excited. The whole atmosphere changed in the room instantly. Like a switch it was back to normal.

---

107 At the time the authorities thought the war would only last a few months. Six months at the most. Camp Morton was converted to a prisoner of war camp. Bill Antrim spent his three month enlistment guarding the Confederate soldiers incarcerated there.

Chapter Seventy-Two

The School Fund Meeting

Clara showed up at the Antrim cabin an hour early, and helped Catherine with the supper dishes.

Catherine had had a long day and was very tired. Yet, Clara's arrival gave her a second wind. She was determined to attend the meeting.

"Catherine, you sit down and rest up a bit. I had a good nap. I'm fresh as a daisy. I'll finish these dishes, and you can help me with mine one day," Clara volunteered.

Clara was a well-educated nurse. She knew Catherine had some signs of consumption. She would let her new friend tell her at her own time, and possibly she was wrong about her diagnosis.

Catherine almost fell asleep. She didn't, but the rest really helped her. Dishes done the two women slipped out into the early evening fresh air.

Catherine was surprised to see Clara had arrived in a buggy. A buggy never looked so good.

Clara volunteered: "I hope you don't mind. I didn't want to walk tonight."

"Mind? Definitely not. I'm loving your buggy right now." Catherine replied with a chuckle.

They arrived early at the Whitehill's house. Harriet was jolly on the spot greeting them.

Clara introduced Catherine as her "close" friend.

"A friend of Clara's is a friend of mine," Harriet declared.

The only men that attended the meeting were the teacher Mr. Peter Ott, and Harvey Whitehill, the county coroner. He was civic minded, and also curious as to who the "greener" was.

Catherine could read people very well. She picked up on his real intention. She privately commented to Clara:

"He sure has a large nose."

Clara chuckled and replied: “He sure does. Matches his personality perfectly.”

Clara saw Amelia Abraham, David Abraham’s wife. She commented to Catherine: “Catherine that is Amelia Abraham. She has the toughest job of all of us,” she said with emphasis on “toughest”.

“Why is that?” Catherine asked sincerely. She could tell Clara really meant that, it was a joke.

“She is the stepmother to six of David Abraham’s children. She has Hyman and Louis signed up with Mr. Ott’s class,” Clara explained.

“I don’t know how she does that. I have a hard time keeping up with two boys,” Catherine confessed.

Clara introduced several more of the town’s ladies. They all seemed to be good pioneer stock. Catherine couldn’t help but think how fortunate Silver City was to have so many good women. Women were scarce in Wichita when they arrived there. The ones that were there one didn’t socialize with, and civic duties were far from their minds.

Mr. Ott announced that classes will not be in his house after all. The county agreed to rent McGary’s Hall. That drew an applause.

“I assume that applause is because the county let loose some money for education, and not because my house was unsuitable accommodations,” that caused general laughter to erupt in the room.

Clara Truesdell raised her hand as she would in school. Mr. Ott acknowledged her and said she had the floor. She stood and began to talk: “I know everyone has met our new comer Catherine Antrim. Ironically, she is living in old Joh Swesshelm Cabin until she buys, or builds one of her own. The irony being Catherine is one of the founders of Wichita, Kansas, and now lives in the cabin of one of the founders of Silver City,” she concluded.

Mr. Ott spoke first: “So, Mrs. Antrim you are living in a lucky cabin,” he said humorously.

“Well, thank you for that information. Of course, I brought a bit of the luck of the Irish with me too,” she said with a big grin on her face.

Mr. Ott then got down to business: "Much still will be coming out of my own pocket. I will need to charge $2 per student for the summer session. The regular session next fall will most likely be $4 per student. Of course, these figures depend on a class size of at least 25 students."

Mrs. Whitehill had a serious question to ask: "Sir, as you know we have had two dedicated teachers before you. Will you stick it out longer than they did?"

Mr. Ott did not hesitate with his answer: "If I have the support of the community I will. If not, I'll have to do the same as they did. Teachers must eat and pay bills too. I would not be here now if there weren't enough qualified students to attend. There is, but it will be up to all of you in this room to participate and recruit more students. That will allow me to do what I love best, teaching young minds the three R's."

He then added: "Please inform those not here tonight that the friends these children make in school, during this formation year, will be remembered their entire life. Some will even stay here in Silver City and be an important part of building the future of our city," he concluded.

Mr. Whitehill spoke next: "If you can teach as well as you can talk, our children are in good hands," which brought another sound round of applause. The meeting adjourned.

Chapter Seventy-Three

Clara Proves Her Friendship

Clara drove Catherine home in the cool night air. They pulled in front of the cabin.

Catherine said: "Thank you so very much for all you have done for this newcomer. Introducing me tonight to all those fine people was extra special. I know the importance of that in the days and months ahead. You are a good friend I will always cherish."

Clara could tell it was coming from Catherine's heart. She felt she knew her well enough now to ask her a personal question:

"You are welcome, my dear. As a friend I would like to ask you. There is something that is bothering you. It is written all over your face. I know it's none of my business, but if I can help I will," Clara declared.

Catherine almost had tears in her eyes as she replied: "I do know that...thank you, again," she said without leaving the buggy. Then a single tear did fall down her cheek.

"What is it, my dear?" Clara whispered.

Catherine took a deep breath, sighed a long sigh, and then answered: "Well, it is all my own doing. I should have married Bill a long time ago, and let him be a real father to my boys. Clara, he is a good man that has caught the worst case of gold fever you have ever seen."

Clara just listened without interrupting, as though she knew it was more than that.

Catherine paused and then continued: "That's not the worst of it. He has been a platonic friend for eight years. The boys called him Uncle Bill. He wanted to get married seven years ago. I wasn't comfortable with that. He was good friend, but that was all. I left Wichita because I was diagnosed with consumption. The doctor suggested Santa Fe."

"And that is still not the worst of it!" Catherine declared.

Clara still sat quietly being a good listener.

"I married Bill for all the wrong reasons, and my boys are going to pay the price for my bad decision. That is the worst of it! That is what is bothering me. I brought it all on myself. It is not Bill's fault, he was always very honest with me. It's not the boys fault. It is all my doing," Catherine concluded.

Clara's reply shocked Catherine, she said: "Catherine, I couldn't disagree with you more. I think you can't see the forest for the trees."

"How is that?" Catherine inquired with real curiosity.

Clara explained: "It seems to me every decision you just told me about were all in the best interest of your boys. Catherine, you can't control how Bill accepts the decisions. That is up to him. First, you turned down his marriage proposal seven years ago. In doing so you clearly told him he was just a friend. Second, when you did decide to marry him, you and I know it was because you hoped he would care for the boys after you're gone."

Catherine interrupted: "Exactly!"

Clara went on to say: "Well, it is up to him to do that, or not. He seems to have somehow told you he is interested in prospecting and not 'boy sitting'...right?" Clara asked firmly.

"Yes, he did so quite clearly!" Catherine quickly replied.

"Well, there you go! It would not have made one iota difference had you married him seven years ago or last month, Bill would want to prospect now, and not care for the boys."

Catherine replied: "My boys carry his name now, Henry Antrim and Josie Antrim..."

Clara interrupted: "That does not mean anything. In his heart, yours, and mine now, they are still your boys, not his. Although, I think when you pass on he will do the right thing and care for them, in his way," Clara concluded.

"How can you be sure?" Catherine begged.

"You said to me he is a good man. If you are correct, he will do what he thinks is right. If not, you have no control over such matters then. You did all you could do for them," Clara reassured Catherine.

"You have helped me enormously. I have a much better understanding now. Thank you so much for listening and being my friend," Catherine said placing both her hand on Clara's free hand.

Clara grinned and said: "I told you I'm educated in nursing. I'll take care of you and keep an eye on your boys when you join the Lord in heaven. I think He is working in your life pretty well."

Catherine gave her a big hug and kiss on the cheek. Clara then placed her two large hands on both side of Catherine's head and said: "You are doing much better here. Enjoy every minute you have with your boys, and stop worrying about anything else!"

"It is time for you to do some Irish jigs and you'll be to heaven an hour before the devil knows your gone," Clara paraphrased an old Irish saying.

Catherine chuckled and replied: "The Good Lord has gifted me with a very good friend, and I appreciate you more than you can know."

"Now, you're going to get me crying," Clara said and whistled her horse to get going.

Chapter Seventy-Four

Silver City
Fall/Winter
1873 - 1874

Catherine took Clara's good advice. She attended every dance and baile on Chihuahua Hill. Henry attended all of them and Josie once a month. Catherine was feeling good the fall of 1873 and the winter of 1874. She began to believe that she was the one in a thousand that whipped consumption.

Mr. Ott only lasted until August of 1873, and had to quit to make a living. The Antrim boys and most of their friends attended faithfully, but it just wasn't enough to support him.

Mr. Jessie Anderson took up the teaching job from Mr. Ott, but conducted classes from his friend's house. He asked a fee of $5 per student. The Abraham's, Truesdell's, Antrim's, Bennett's, and Whitehill's all signed up, but that was all. He had to close the private school in October.

All the parents, including Catherine, were very concerned. The boys were all running together in what could only be described as street gamers. They pulled pranks on store owners and on each other.

Silver City saw a spike in violence among the adults of the town. The county sheriff, Charles McIntosh, had high tailed it out of town with $3000 of county funds in his pocket.

He had been wounded in a gun fight, recovering from his wounds he reassessed his low pay vs. high risk. His deputy had also been accidently wounded trying to apprehend a drunk. The drunk also shot a bystander.

McIntosh was then left with all the violence to be handled by himself. It was believed he was in Mexico.

His deputy made it clear he was not interested in the sheriff's job. Silver City and the county would go almost a year without a sheriff, or any other law enforcement. Many were forced to take the law into their own hands.

In August, one William Wilson cut up the face of Joe Dyer, Owner of the Orleans Club. He was caught, but claimed self-defense. There wasn't enough evidence to charge him, so they had to let him go. Joe Dyer would be scared for life. As a friend said, he was lucky to be alive.

David Abraham killed a man breaking into his house. Saloons were now open 24/7 with three shifts of employees. That matched the miner's shifts of three a day. There were too many desperate miners, drifters, and unemployed. Silver City was not safe after dark.

Fall turned into winter. The Antrim boys joined the other American kids "gamin'" the streets.

There was: Wayne and Harry Whitehill, John and Vincent Mays, Albert and Charlie Stevens, Louis and Hyman Abraham, Gideon and Chauncey Truesdell, and Henry Antrim. Josie Antrim was working full time.

Owen L. Scott, editor of Silver City's "Mining Life Newspaper" turned his pen loose on the street gamers, which he preferred to call street Arabs. He blamed every petty crime committed in town to them. The fact was most petty crimes were being committed by desperate men who had lost everything they had in the gaming tables of The Blue Goose, Red Onion, or Orleans Club.

The boys in the street gaming gang did commit some petty crimes, but by-in-large nothing serious.

The parents had another big meeting, and all agreed they needed to support a full time teacher. They needed to put pressure on the county to make funds available to do so. This is in a time that the county didn't offer enough for the sheriff's position to attract any candidates.

The Whitehill family spearheaded the effort and obtained funds to compensate a full-time teacher. They invited Dr. J. Webster to teach at the fifth-grade level all children five-to-fifteen- years-old, all would attend free of charge.

Dr. Webster announced that the next school semester would start January 5, 1874 and the semester and class year would end March 28, 1874.

Every member of the street "Arabs" attended school. They also all headed for the Antrim cabin after school to partake in Catherine Antrim's delicious homemade cookies. She was never without them for all the boys.

Louis and Hyman Abraham also had dinner often at the Antrim cabin. They had lost their mother and their father lacking those skills, hired a cook. Catherine heard this and invited them to dinner one night. The Abraham boys loved her cooking and said their "hired-cook" was not very good. Catherine invited them as often as practical.

That winter was a cold one that Catherine struggled with. A simple cold was devastating to her. It would not go away, and lingered for weeks at a time. That winter convinced her she had not whipped the consumption. Clara had said she may feel very good at times and worse at other times. She was right. The worse times were getting even worse! No matter how bad she felt the cookie jar stayed full!

Bill had taken a steady job as a butcher for Richard Knight. Richard had a ranch fifteen miles south of Silver City. It was nestled in a valley at the base of the lower Burro Mountains along the main trail south to Mesilla. He also had the butcher shop in Silver City. Prospecting in the winter was not practical, and he needed the steady income for a while.

Bill brought Henry to the butcher shop and Mr. Knight had him cleaning while there. Henry was always interested in becoming a cowboy and asked if he could see his ranch. Mr. Knight said he should ask his father as he was breaking animals for him at the ranch part time.

Bill agreed and took Henry out to the ranch on Saturday. Henry met the whole family and was instantly liked by Mrs. Knight. Her brother's son, Anthony Conner, was living with them and he and Henry hit it off immediately. Anthony liked the wild side of Henry, and Henry like the down to earth solid side of Anthony. Opposites attract.

Bill took Henry to the ranch several times, as much to keep him off the streets as anything else.

Henry really developed an interest in horses. Something attracted him like a magnet to those animals. Ironically, he had been around them all his young life, but this was different. Watching Bill and the other cowboys training them he saw just how amazing the animal was. He could watch them training them all day.

Richard Knight also trained the horses. One day Henry watched intently at how he handled the animals. He knew he was watching a great wrangler at work. Mr. Knight let one of the cowboys take over and join Henry at the fence line.

"You know your father is a good wrangler?" he said in his baritone low voice.

"My stepfather, you mean?" Henry replied with a rhetorical question. Mr. Knight chose not to respond. A few moments went by, and then Henry continued to answer his question:

"Yes, I know he is, and also a good mule skinner," Henry said in his normal, soft voice.

"I didn't know that," Mr. Knight said as he leaned on the corral fencing. Then he asked Henry: "How do you think this Arizona cowboy is doing with that grey?"

Henry turned his head back to facing Mr. Knight. He had the strangest look on his face.

Mr. Knight said: "Your first, huh?"

Henry replied: "Yes, sir, first time a grown man ever asked my opinion on anything."

"Well, are you going to answer?" Mr. Knight asked directly.

"Yes, I will. He is doing very well, in my opinion. As good as my stepfather, maybe even better. I like what he is doing right now," Henry explained.

The cowboy was changing directions with the colt very quickly. The colt only got a couple steps in one direction and he switched him to the other. A few more steps and he repeated it. Each time pointing the direction he wanted the colt to go and snapping his whip.

Mr. Knight replied: "I do too! He is controlling that greys head, body and mind." He explained his reasoning.

"Yes, sir, you are right. That is good!" Henry exclaimed.

Arriving home Bill and Henry found Josie trying to help his mother to a table seat. She had finished supper for them, but had nearly collapsed at the completion. She didn't have the strength to seat herself, besides delivering the cooked food to the table.

Henry ran to his mother who was coughing so hard it scared him to death. Bill left to find help.

Bill returned with Marty Hudson, wife of his friend Richard Hudson. He had worked for Richard who once commented that his wife was a "healer". Bill introduced her to Catherine.

Mary found Catherine fully recovered: "I'm sorry to have bothered you, Mary. I am fine now. I had a bad cold and it near killed me." Catherine did not want to disclose her real condition to this stranger.

Mary turned to Bill and the boys and said: "You boys leave the cabin for one hour" Mary said authoritatively. They all left.

Mary sat directly across the table from Catherine. She looked her right in the eye and softly asked: "Mrs. Catherine Antrim, how long have you had the consumption?"

Catherine looked down at the table like a little girl caught in a lie and replied: "Two years, but it seemed to have gone away in the summer and fall of last year. I did catch a cold and it was horrible, but I thought I was over that when I got the cough today."

"Have you tried the Mimbres Hot Springs? The natives call it 'Ojo Caliente'?" Mary asked politely.

"No, I haven't. Do you think it will help?" Catherine asked sincerely.

"I don't know for sure. I know it helped my husband a lot. It wouldn't hurt to try though," Mary suggested.

When the boys returned, without Bill, Mary informed them she would be taking their mother to the Hot Springs next week and asked: "Where is your father?"

Henry replied: "Our stepfather, he said he had to see his employer."

Mary thought that was strange this late in the afternoon.

"You boys take care of your mother. She is not to lift anything for the rest of tonight. No matter what she says...lifts nothing...got it young men?" Mary said firmly.

"Yes, ma'am!" Henry and Josie said in unison.

Catherine was listening and recalled every time she had a coughing fit she was lifting something. She thought to herself: "She knows what she is talking about."

Originally called the Mimbres Hot Springs. This photograph was taken when it was Hudson Hot Springs. People from left-to-right: Rilla Cooper, Mrs. Isaac James Stevens, Mary Stevens Hudson, Richard Hudson, & Mamie Hudson. Source: Silver City Museum, Silver City New Mexico

Chapter Seventy-Five

A Rough Trip and An Enlightened Henry

Mary kept her promise and drove Catherine the fifty miles round trip to the Mimbres Hot Springs. It took one full day to get there, starting very early in the morning and arriving at dusk. Catherine spent several hours in the hot springs water, but couldn't take any more of it. Then they spent the following full day returning home.

When they arrived back, Catherine was never so glad to see her cabin. Henry helped Mary unload the buggy of his mother's things. Then he took one arm and Mary the other and just about carried Catherine to her bed.

"Henry, I'm sorry to say, but I believe the Hot Springs did not help your mother. The trip was very hard on her. You watch out for her closely the next few days. I need to recover from the trip myself," Mary explained.

"Yes, ma'am, I will do just that. Thank you for trying to help her." Henry said sincerely.

Mary was taken aback by the very adult answer coming from this young lad in front of her. She continued: "If your mother gets a temperature, place a cool, lightly dampened cloth on her forehead. Remove it if she complains of a headache."

"Yes, ma'am, I will" Henry replied as he helped her into her bed.

Mary rose and then asked Henry: "Do you know Clara Truesdell?"

"Yes, she is Chauncey's mother," Henry replied

"She is a trained nurse. Ask her to stop by and check on your mother tomorrow, alright?" Mary asked politely.

"I will...maybe now!" a scared Henry exclaimed.

Mary quickly replied: "No, tomorrow. We know what she needs right now is plenty of rest, understand?"

"I do. Good rest now, and Mrs. Truesdell tomorrow," Henry acknowledged.

"That is fine, and don't worry, Clara will know what to do then. Tell her I will be over in two days to look in on her," Mary concluded.

Henry became enlightened and realized the severity and weight of what just happened. His stepfather was out of town prospecting. Josie was working full time at the Orleans Club. He was the only one to take care of his mother. He was growing up fast.

She was obviously worse off than before going to the Hot Springs. The thought came to him: "What would happen if I have to cook?" He thought reminding himself that his mother said he was the only one she knew that could mess up boiling water. Cooking was not one of his talents. Just the thought of doing it scared him.

After tucking his mother in he went into the living area and sat at the table. Henry then started a good fire to warm the house. At least he could do that.

He stared across the room at the fire and thought:

"How did all this happen? Why is this happening? It was only a few months ago Mother was dancing with me on my birthday. We went to every baile, every town dance hall. Mother was feeling great, better than ever!"

His thoughts continued: "Mother said I was a 'Bonny' good dancer," he almost said so aloud. "That is mother's favorite Irish saying to describe anything she really likes, or thinks is very good. What happened?"

"It doesn't seem to be the cold" Henry thought trying to think things through logically. "No, it is the consumption...it is back with a fury!"

Henry bowed his head with his hands folded in front of him on the table, and prayed: "God, please heal my mother. She has been one of Your angels on earth...for You! I know she has always said that about other good people, but now I say it about her, because it is true. Of course, you know that! Lord, she has always done your bidding...always! I have not, but of course you know that too, but she has...always! Mother always said you are a loving, healing God. I have always believed that! Please heal my mother. She does not deserve this terrible sickness. It is not fair...please heal her. We need her badly, we love her so much. God, heal your angel on earth, my Mother...Amen!"

Henry sighed and felt much better himself. God would heal her. His mother did say He does things in his own time, but that he does answer prayers. This would be no different.

His thoughts went back to imagining what it might be like if he had to do everything, earn enough to help support the three of them. At least until Uncle Bill came back. Just the thought was overwhelming! He wouldn't know where to start.

Henry was realizing just how much his Mother meant to all of them. Without her, there was nothing, no family at all. His mother was the glue that held the family together.

Then he remembered what Mary had said: "Clara will know what to do."

"Whew! She will!" he thought with a sigh of relief.

Then he admonished himself: "Stop thinking like this! God will answer my prayer! Mother always said He will answer sincere prayers. None was more sincere than mine. She will live!" he declared the latter aloud, albeit in a low voice as to not disturb his mother.

He thought to himself giving himself more reassurance: "I will fetch Mrs. Truesdell tomorrow, and she will know what to do."

After putting some more fire wood on the fire Henry checked on his mother, and then crawled into bed himself. This was very early for him to go to bed, but he wanted tomorrow to come quickly. He didn't even read by the candle light.

It was 3am when Josie came in from his first night working at the Orleans Club. Henry awoke and informed him of all that had happened.

Josie listed politely, as tired as he was, but did not respond to any of the information. It seemed to Henry he wasn't one bit emotional about his mother being very sick.

Henry had to ask: "I don't get it. Aren't you concerned at all?" he snapped.

"Of course I am, Henry. I'm just tired...very tired! We'll talk in the morning" Josie said and went off to his bed.

Henry did not sleep all night. He just laid there staring into the darkness. As soon as the sun light peeked over the mountains with light rays blanketing Silver City, Henry was dressed and on a full run to the Truesdell house.

Clara left the finishing of breakfast to her husband and hurried back with Henry in her curry. He explained all that had happened.

Arriving at the Antrim cabin she found Catherine still quite asleep. She pulled up a chair and sat there for four hours until Catherine awoke.

Catherine's first sight was Clara's gentle big brown eyes smiling at her.

"Good morning Catherine. You are staying down today, dear. I heard from Henry about your long trip to the Hot Springs. If you would have consulted with me, I could have told you, not only is hot steam not good for consumption but the trip could set you back a few days." Clara scolded Catherine in a most affectionate manner.

"I should have sent for you. Mary meant well," Catherine explained.

"Absolutely, she did. There isn't a person in town that hasn't heard of the hot spring curing her husband's gout."

Clara chuckled and Catherine joined her, but with a painful cough at the end.

Clara got serious: “Bill is gone for now. So, I’m feeding your boys at my house, and then I’ll have them bring food back here for you. Don’t argue, won’t do you any good. I’ll check in with you every day. Your job young lady is to rest...no house work period. You can make it to the privy that is it! You are strong enough for that, right?” Clara asked.

“Yes, I am. I think I could...”

Clara interrupted: “If you want my help, you must listen to my advice. No, you rest in bed...only the privy! Understand?” Clara was being firm.

“Yes, ma’am. I will do as you say, I promise. It will be difficult for me to do nothing for a whole day!” Catherine confessed.

“You are not doing anything. You are allowing your body to recover from being beaten up for three days.” Clara replied and turned to Henry and said:

“You, young man, are my spy. She breaks her promise you will tell me won’t you?” Clara demanded.

Henry instantly replied: “Yes, ma’am.”

“Good.” Clara said as she left the room and returned with some chicken broth she had heated when she first arrived.

“ok, Clara, thank you! I am so hungry,” Catherine’s blue eyes danced with joy at the sight. Henry felt guilty. He had not even thought that she probably didn’t have anything to eat on the long trip back.

Clara said good night and instructed Henry to fetch her any time he thought it needed to be done. Henry felt a lot better! Now, only God had His healing to do in His own time, and all would be right again.

Clara Truesdell faithfully checked on her friend and patient every day. Henry and Josie were never late for dinner at the Truesdell’s house. Henry developed a close friendship with Chauncey. He liked him, but more important to Henry, he trusted him.

Catherine took a full week to be able to function with the basics. Everything she lifted, anything at all and she paid a price for it.

Clara explained to her that her muscles demanded air to operate and when she lifted she made a severe demand on her lungs to provide the air needed to make the lifting possible.

Catherine asked point blank one day: "Clara, will I get back to where I was last fall?"

"I'm afraid you won't like my answer. I don't think so my friend...without a miracle. We will both know more over the next month. Miracles do happen too!" Clara told her the truth, as usual. Catherine wouldn't want it any other way.

Catherine asked at almost a whisper: "Clara, when I'm gone will you please watch out for my boys? They will need someone."

"Yes, my dear, you know I would. Don't you worry about those boys now, worry about taking care of yourself so you can watch out for them as long as you can."

Chapter Seventy-Six

School was Letting Out
Oh, My!

Clara was able to keep Catherine comfortable. She was with her every day. Bill Antrim helped with some of the housekeeping and maintenance when he was in town. He was spending more and more time away.

Clara kept it to herself, but thought Bill was acting awfully strange for a man who was losing his newly wedded wife to consumption. She didn't understand him at all.

Henry helped the best he could. He and Josie kept their promise to their mother to attend school regularly. Josie had to take a night shift at work to do so, but do so he did.

On March 28, 1874 Dr. Webster closed the regular school year as he said he would. Owen Scott, editor of the "Mining Life Newspaper" pushed for a summer theatrical production to keep the boys busy and out of trouble. The socialites agreed and were willing to fund the project.

Harriet Whitehill organized a minstrel troupe, which included most of the cities "street Arabs", including her own son Harry.

Henry Antrim loved the idea and became an enthusiastic participant. Not only did he participate, but the town quickly learned how talented he was. Henry landed the lead role. He also got all the solo singing parts. He could sing, dance, and act very well.

Catherine was proud of him. Clara helped to attend a couple plays. She was bursting with pride. Henry was the star of the shows. Of course that was to the chagrin of some of the other boys.

Harry Whitehill seemed to think because his mother was producing the plays, he should at least be given the lead sometime.

Harry and Henry did not see eye to eye on much. Harry thought himself "better" than Henry, and should get the next leading role. When Harry finally did get a lead role, Henry stole

"Well, if you don't, I'll tear this show up," Harry threatened.

Again, Henry had landed the lead in this play, and Harry couldn't stand it. Privately, he hoped Henry wouldn't pay up, or apologize for nearly drowning him, because he had a plan.

Henry stood behind the curtain awaiting the start, the opening of which was the cue for his opening lines.

Just as they were ready to open the curtain Harry ran through the curtain tearing it down, and of course disrupting the whole play.

Henry lunged for Harry, his face blood red. His eyes now looked like they belonged to the devil himself. Harriet Whitehill screamed to the top of her voice.

Charley Stevens was older and larger than both boys. He jumped between them and wrapped his arms around Henry holding him back. Harry took advantage of this to run like hell out of the building and down the street.

Later Harry told Chauncey: "You were right about Henry, he would have beaten me to a pulp. Charley said he could hardly hold him, and he is very strong."

Chauncey replied: "I warned you. He is my friend, and he is a good person, but just don't cross him. If you say you're sorry for starting all that, which you did. He will forget all about it and be fine with you. That's the way he is."

Harry answered without hesitation: "I'm not going to say I'm sorry. He started the pushing around, not me. He pushed me into that river after he knocked the breath out of me. I think he knew exactly what he was doing. Those men saved my life!"

Chauncey responded: "Harry, you are being over dramatic. He wasn't trying to drown you, and you did start it calling him names in front of all his friends. Well, anyway, it's your hide. Do what you want."

Harry thought about it for a second and calmly asked Chauncey: "You two are good friends. Tell me why he hates me?"

"Harry, sometimes you get on everyone's nerves."

Harry nervously followed up: "Why, I don't do wrong to anyone."

"It's the way you act sometimes. Harry, you act like you think you're better than the rest of us," Chauncey honestly replied.

"I don't mean to be that way. That is exactly how I think Henry acts. He always assumes he will get the lead roles. The best parts in every play," Harry confessed.

"There is one big difference!" Chauncey exclaimed.

"What is that?" Harry asked smartly.

"Henry has talent. No offense, he has more talent than I do, or Louis, or Charley, or Vincent Mays. The difference is, Harry, we all know that, and you don't. You blame him because he can sing, dance, act, and speak three languages. The rest of us really care about the play and its story, and message to the audiences."

Harry interrupted: "I do care about the plays...I do!" he sincerely informed Chauncey.

Chauncey replied: "Harry, if you really cared about the play, you would want Henry in the lead part. You would be arguing for that."

Harry was stunned. He had never even looked at the plays that way. He just loved the attention, and wanted to be able to boast he had the lead roles. He simply could not agree with Chauncey. His ego would not allow him to do so, therefore he simply replied:

"I thought everyone should have a chance for a lead role."

"Harry, plays don't work that way. Anyway, you now know why you have rubbed some people the wrong way. I think you could do so much better getting along with everyone," Chauncey concluded.

"I do. Thank you!" Harry said sincerely.

"You're welcome," Chauncey replied.

Henry and Harry never became friends, but they did not have any further trouble with each other from that time on. At least none that anyone knew of. What was not known was exactly what Harry told his parents about all that happened and why.[108]

---

[108] His parents are very influential, and Harry's father would finally accept the position of County Sheriff a year later. The County agreed to his terms, and agreed to build a brand new jail.

Mr. Owen Scott had backed off his stories of Street Arabs going wild. After-all, the community had listened to him and followed his advice to the letter. They had organized the minstrels, plays, and dances every week, sometimes twice a week. Now, all the town shenanigans and petty theft was the works of Mexicans.

The fact was the boys had not even slowed down what they considered their mischievous duties.

Chapter Seventy-Seven

Death Comes Slow and Violently

It was late May 1874 when Catherine became bedridden. Mary Hudson and Clara Truesdell took turns caring for all her needs. Bill Antrim was rarely around, just drifting in and out almost as though to see if she was still alive.

Henry and Josie suffered immensely. They watched their mother deteriorate to someone they didn't even recognize.[109] Her chest was bloated up, yet her arms and legs were skeletal. Her face had shriveled making her look one-hundred-years-old, and fear and pain was written all over it. She was suffering so badly and there was nothing they could do. It broke the boy's hearts. It ripped Henry's heart in two.

Henry was taking the situation worse than anyone. Many times he would come in and out of the cabin not even looking in on his mother. He couldn't say for sure why he did that. Clara noticed but said nothing.

Clara did not admonish him as she knew he was a child losing his mother. She had seen in her career as a nurse, every child seems to handle it in different ways.

Henry admonished himself. He felt guilty every time he left the house. He asked himself a dozen times:

"Why...Why can't I go in the bedroom and sit with her, and give her comfort?" He did when she asked for him, but if she didn't, he stayed away as though she had the black plague.

---

[109] Quote from public domain concerning death by TB: "When TB wakes up and gets into the lungs, it eats them from the inside out, slowly diminishing their capacity, causing the chest to fill up with blood and the liquid remains of the lungs. A wet hacking cough is evocative of TB. The lungs now in liquid form are sloshing around in the chest. Eventually, liquid replaces the lungs, the suffering patient cannot get enough oxygen, and respiratory failure occurs, they can no longer breath and they drown." TB is a slow long torturous death that can take months to kill. Before that happens even close relatives can hardly recognize the person they know and love. It is a horrible devilish disease. There are a million and a half people in 2017 dying each year from TB.

Three months Catherine suffered this horrible condition, gasping for every breath, coughing more and more blood than mucus. She could no longer hold anything down in her stomach. Towards the end, not even water.

Clara Truesdell came in to be with her and saw Henry at the table crying furiously. It was as though all the fear, anger, frustration and hate was exploding from him in tears.

She started to talk with him when he realized she was there, he sprang up from the table. It startled her at first. His eyes looked like the devil himself was looking at her. She dismissed that thought, and told herself to take control.

"I want to talk to you young man, right now, outside." Clara demanded and headed for the front door. Henry followed her giving her the respect she deserved. No one, not even Mary Hudson, had helped his mother more, not to mention also Josie and himself.

Outside the cabin Clara turned and came right to the point: "Young man, you know your mother is dying of that horrible disease. She is the same person inside, she loves you boys enormously," Clara said in a scolding manner. She had had enough of Henry coming and going without spending time with his mother.

Henry spoke honestly to her: "I don't know why, Mrs. Truesdell, I can't see her that way," Henry confessed his true feelings.

Clara continued: "Henry, I'm not here to talk about you and your feelings. I don't give a damn about your feelings right now!"

Henry was startled...and taken aback by what she said.

Clara went on to say: "I'm here to talk about your mother's last moments on earth before she goes to heaven. This is about her! Not you! Do you understand me Henry?" she asked firmly.

Henry gave a hissing sound clearly stating he didn't believe something she had just said.

"Henry, explain yourself," Clara asked point blank.

Henry replied just as frankly: "I don't believe there is a heaven. I don't believe there is a God!"

Clara interrupted: "Henry, there are both. Why do you say such a horrible thing at this time?" Clara asked.

"I will explain to you what I did. Not just because she is my mother, but also because she is the best person I have ever known in my life. She has believed in God, and lived by his rules. Well, where did it get her?"

Clara knew there was more coming so she was patient and listened.

Henry continued: "A loving, caring God would never let a person suffer like she is doing right now...never! What did I do? Do you know how many times I have prayed at that table in there for Him to cure her? Remember...God is a healer! Would you believe every night for the past three months? The more I prayed the worse my mother got. No ma'am, I don't believe He exists, and if I did I would damn him for what he has done to my mother!"

Clara wanted to slap some sense into Henry, but the more she heard him the more she knew Catherine wasn't the only victim of that disease. She let him finish, and then just said:

"Henry, nothing I could say will change your mind, but I want you to know that is NOT God's doing in there. I'll pray that you find Him again. Whatever you do, don't let your mother know how you feel. That would hurt her more than the disease."

Henry simply replied: "I won't." Then he ran off.

Chapter Seventy-Eight

Prankster Ends and Criminal Begins

Henry's pranks and general mischievous behavior intensified. All the boys were becoming more aggressive in their now truly "street Arab" tactics.

An adult, believed by some to be Charlie Sun's competitor in the laundry business, asked the boys to harass Charlie Sun until he left town. They accepted the challenge.

One boy threw a rock at a visitor of Charlie Sun. It hit him in the back of the head and neck area. The missile was thrown hard enough that the celestial was flopping around on the ground like a chicken with its head cut off. Henry had not thrown the rock, but was there at the time.

They didn't stay long enough to see if the man was killed or not. They surely did think so at the time. There was no complaint filed, and the matter just went away.

Henry then masterminded a robbery of old man Matt Derbyshire's store. There was costume jewelry hanging in the window. His partner in this caper was his friend, and fellow member of the street Arabs, Charlie Stevens.

There are several versions of what the plan was, but for sure it included breaking into his store, and stealing the jewelry. Most likely to sell to the traveling Mexican circus in town.

Charley got cold feet. He didn't want to confront Henry, so he told his father, Isaac Stevens. His father drug him directly to Mr. Derbyshire's store, and made him confess the whole plan to Mr. Derbyshire.

Matt Derbyshire and Isaac Stevens hunted down Henry and said the "town drunk" had told them of his plan. That he had overheard Henry telling Charlie the details. They chastised Henry in the most direct manner. Henry feigned remorse. The only real remorse was that he got caught.

Someone told his mother! That devastated Henry. She

demanded he talk to her about it. Now, his remorse was very real! He felt horrible!

Catherine simply told her son: "If you choose a life of crime, you'll hang before your 21."[110]

Catherine McCarty Antrim died September 16, 1874. Clara Truesdell prepared her body for burial. Bill Antrim was nowhere to be seen.

Henry and Josie, with the assistance of Louis Abraham, dug their mother's grave.

David Abraham's surrey was used as a hearse. The funeral was attended by the Abraham, Whitehill, Stevens, and Truesdell families.

Clara Louisa Truesdell kept her promise to Catherine and watched out for her boys. Clara made sure they enrolled in the new teacher's class. A few days after they buried their mother they were in class.

Mary Phillipa Richards
Edited Head shot from photograph taken by:
Daniel Fruwirth, London, England ca. 1868
Frederick Nolan's "West of Billy the Kid" pg. 30

[110] Michael Wallace, Billy The Kid, The Endless Ride 2007 pg. 77
Jerry Weddle "Antrim is My Step Father's Name" Phoenix: Arizona Historical Society, 1993 pg. 22
Catherine McCarty Antrim's prophecy was very close. Instead of "hanged before 21", "Henry was shot dead at 21." "Close enough for Government work" , as the old saying goes, and it was government work.

Henry fell in love with his new teacher Miss Mary Phillips. Like himself she was multi-lingual, ambidextrous, and very intelligent. He had never met anyone in his life that was all three. She could write left-handed and right-handed.

On top of all that she was born in England and had an aristocratic, English accent. He was enamored with her, the only trouble was he was 14-years-old (soon to be 15), and she was 28-years-old. Henry didn't miss a day of school!

Bill Antrim returned to quickly sell the cabin and farm out from under the boys before leaving to prospect in Arizona.

Henry and Josie first stayed with the Hudson family, then with the Knight family. He worked in the butcher shop after school each day.

Josie was able to get full time work in the Orleans Club for room and board with the Dyer family. Josie learned the gambling trade there, which stayed with him the rest of his life.

Gerald and Clara Truesdell took Henry into their family early in 1875. They had purchased the Star Hotel, and changed the name to The Exchange Hotel. Henry earned his room and board waiting tables and cleaning dishes in the hotel restaurant.

He was able to keep out of trouble for almost a year. In October of 1875 Miss Mary Phillips became Mrs. Daniel Charles Casey, and moved with her carpenter husband to Georgetown.

Gerald and Clara Truesdell began to have marital problems. Henry was not happy as he was not making enough hard cash to meet his needs and desires. He did his work very well, and Gerald later said he was the only one that worked for him that did not steal something. None-the-less, it was decided to send him to Sarah Brown's boarding house.

Henry met another boarder named George Schaefer, who insisted to be called with the alias of "Sombrero Jack." He did wear a small sombrero all the time.

George Schaefer *- Maxine Simons Collection*
Source: Silver City Museum - Access No. 2003.11

Sombrero Jack had one small personality flaw, he passionately loved to steal. It really didn't matter the object, it was the act of stealing he loved. He would literally shiver with excitement when he successfully stole something.

Henry slipped into a career of petty theft to put cash in his pocket. He wasn't motivated by the "thrill" of the act, but for the financial success of the same. Although he did like the planning and scheming.

He devised a plan to steal butter from a farmer, Abel Webb, and sell it for cash to a Silver City merchant. The merchant contacted the new County Sheriff, Mr. Harvey Whitehill. The father of Wayne Whitehill, the fellow street Arab that he had trouble with.

Sheriff Whitehill scolded Henry well, but released him on the promise of future "good behavior." Again he would try to go straight. This time he had actually executed the plan with no partner, and still got caught.

Josie was able to convince Joe Dyer to give Henry a job in the Orleans Club. Henry was given odd jobs around the club at first. In doing so he learned the Faro and Monte games. He approached Mr. Dyer with a business plan.

"You know I look a lot younger than I am. Those miners will surely believe they can beat a kid. Let me be the banker and I'll make you and me a lot more money. Don't forget I can speak Spanish as good as a Mexican." Henry pleaded.

Mr. Dyer had no idea if it would work, but was willing to try it, on the caveat if he was losing he would pull him in a heartbeat. "Kid Antrim" was born and he was successful on the Monte table.

Henry liked the brazen, young man Sombrero Jack he was boarded with. He hung out with him in his off hours at the Orleans Club. The guy was likable with one small fault...petty theft. Henry couldn't hold that against him as he had done the same, but for the money not the thrill.

One day George got drunk as a skunk and broke into Charlie Sun's laundry. He stole two revolvers, blankets, and clothing.

George brought the loot back to the boarding house. He begged Henry to hide some of it for him. He was skinning out to

Georgetown until it cools down for him. Henry agreed and that was a big mistake.

Hearing of the robbery Sarah Brown suspected her two young boarders. She searched the boy's rooms when they were out, and found the blanket and clothing in Henry's room. She turned him into Sheriff Whitehill.

Henry was arrested September 23, 1875. He was brought before the Justice of the Peace Isaac Givens.

Sheriff Whitehill made it clear that he believed Sombrero Jack actually committed the crime, but also made it clear about Henry's involvement. The Sheriff and Mr. Given decided to "teach the delinquent Henry a lesson".

Mr. Given charged Henry with larceny, and ordered him locked up until the next session of the Grand Jury.

Henry got a cell in the brand new Jailhouse. Sheriff Whitehill later admitted his wife Harriet was furious with him. She was a close friend of Catherine Antrim, and demanded he bring Henry to their house. He could be under "house arrest" and she would care for him. As she said: "At least he will eat properly"

Sheriff Whitehill thought he and Mr. Given's plan would be best for Henry. After all this was not his first theft, and the last time he promised good behavior. Being a cohort of Sombrero Jack was certainly not good behavior.[111]

He did promise Harriet not to keep him too long, just enough to scare him out of making a life of crime.

Well, two days was too long for Henry. He talked the jailer into letting him exercise outside the cell. The jailer agreed as he sat outside the only door out of the cell area.

Henry quickly shimmied up the flue of the fire place, and on September 25, 1875 he escaped. He was covered from head to foot in soot, but he was free! That flue was the size of the average man's leg. No one would have thought that possible. Henry proved them wrong.[112]

---

[111] Author finds it almost amusing that George Schaefer would go straight and become the Justice of the Peace for Georgetown, New Mexico Territory. Talking about "hiring a thief to catch a thief".

[112]This was the first of many escapes Henry would have in his criminal career. He had sloping shoulders that were near double jointed, he could collapse them over his chest. His hands were small compared to his wrists, hence handcuffs

Henry went to his surrogate mother Clara Truesdell. She cleaned his soot laden clothes. He spent the night with the Truesdell family.

The next morning Clara sent him to Ed Moulton's saw mill on Bear Mountain. She then proactively met with Sheriff Whitehill to get Henry's release to her custody. He refused and made a bee line to Moulton's.

Henry was tipped off and ironically returned to the Truesdell house. Clara had already prepared a "plan B".

She paid the stage coach driver to take Henry to Clifton, Arizona. It was the next stop in Arizona and she knew his step father was working as a miner there.

Clara gave Henry traveling money, a blanket, lunch, and some of Chauncey's clothes. Henry "Kid" Antrim left New Mexico Territory, not to return for two years.

The End

---

could not stay on him long. Last, but not least, he had an excellent brain. Henry truly became an escape artist.

15342800R00251

Printed in Great Britain
by Amazon